RICHES, CLASS, AND POWER

RICHES, CLASS, AND POWER

America Before the Civil War

Edward Pessen

With a New Introduction by the Author

Transaction Publishers
New Brunswick (U.S.A.) and London (U.K.)

Originally published in 1973 by D.C. Heath and Company

Library of Congress Catalog Number: 88–30494
ISBN: 0-88738-806-X
Printed in the United States of America

Library of Congress Cataloging-in-Publication Data

Pessen, Edward, 1920–
[Riches, class, and power before the Civil War]
Riches, class and power: America before the Civil War/Edward Pessen.
p. cm.
Reprint. Originally published: Riches, class, and power before the Civil War. Lexington, Mass.: Heath, 1973.
Bibliography: p.
Includes index.
ISBN 0–88738–806–X
1. Wealth—United States—History—19th century. 2. Social mobility—United States—History—19th century. 3. Social classes—United States—History—19th century. I. Title.
[HC110.W4P47 1989]
305.5′23′09730903—dc20 89-30494
CIP

To Adele

Contents

PART IV
Influence and Power

Appendixes

Illustrations

Maps

Introduction to the Transaction Edition

When the original version of this book was published sixteen years ago, Alexis de Tocqueville's image of an egalitarian America was taken as gospel by most American historians in their treatments of the United States during the second quarter of the nineteenth century. No book compared with Tocqueville's *Democracy in America* (part I published in 1835, part II in 1840) in its influence on the thinking of American scholars and public alike as to the nature of early nineteenth century American society.

In Tocqueville's social portrait, a general equality of condition was the central feature of American life. According to the brilliant young French aristocrat, there were no great fortunes in this youthful and vigorous nation because wealth was distributed almost equally among Americans. Blacks and some recently arrived Irish immigrants were the only ones not partaking of the cornucopia.

The rich in America were rich only in a manner of speaking, their fortunes supposedly not comparing in magnitude to those that had been accumulated by great wealthholders in Europe. Nor did wealthy Americans long hold on to their riches. Flux reigned in this kaleidoscopic milieu where men swiftly made, lost, and regained their fortunes in amazingly brief time. In Henry Clay's catchy phrase, the rich in America were "self-made men." In Tocqueville's memorable words, the American rich had "felt the sting of want." Social classes or clusters of families whose wealth, standing, and influence set them apart from others did exist in America as elsewhere. But in the United States pictured by Tocqueville, class barriers were not firmly in place, class lines were easily and regularly breached, a democractic social mingling was the norm. Instead of the domination of society by the wealthy elites that ruled the Old World, commoners lorded over the New World. A tyranny of the majority prevailed in the United States, said Tocqueville. The people ruled over America, he observed, as does the Deity over the universe. And these were the words of a staunch Catholic.

American historians who might quarrel among themselves over the relative merits of Andrew Jackson and Daniel Webster or about the validity of Turner's frontier thesis, which explained American democracy and values as a byproduct of the nation's moving western border, were in agreement that the United States before the Civil War was indeed an egalitarian society. Their chapters on social history (in their books of a generation ago and earlier, focusing as they typically did on national politics) were entitled, "The Era of the Common Man," "The Rise of Tom, Dick, and Harry," "The Age of Equality," or other rubrics of similar character.

Not that acceptance of the egalitarian model was unanimous. A few studies pointed to pockets of poverty amidst the alleged plenty. Students of the antebellum South had to know that not only enslaved blacks but many free, poor whites were denied power, prestige, and the good things of life. My 1969 book, *Jacksonian America: Society, Personality, and Politics,* observed that the egalitarian version of American society rested on very little evidence. The sight of one prisoner shaking hands with a warden was enough to convince Tocqueville that his informants were right in telling him that in the United States, one man's son was as good as any other's. The absence of beggars on the streets convinced other visitors that poverty was absent here. That the wealthiest man in America, John Jacob Astor, was the child of German parents of humble rank and modest circumstances was taken as proof that the race in America was won not by the well born, but by the hardworking and able, whatever their beginnings. In other words, the egalitarian version of pre-Civil War America was based not on substantial evidence but, rather, on snippets of evidence that were treated by Tocqueville and by most of his contemporaries, whether Americans or European visitors, as though they illuminated the society as a whole.

Tocqueville, whose best friends conceded that he had little interest in 'mere facts,' simply concluded that a political democracy such as the United States had necessarily to be a social and economic democracy. His powers of deduction led him inevitably to the conclusion that the scattered examples of equality that he chanced to glimpse replicated the equality that ostensibly permeated the entire society. Boastful Americans, certain that their youthful society was superior to decadent Europe's, were delighted to have their prideful feelings confirmed by a learned and prestigious source. Scholars, disinclined to challenge a theory so long in place and so consoling to believers in American exceptionalism, had convinced themselves that further research or additional evidence was hardly necessary to confirm what seemed to them the obvious—that the dynamic, democratic, pre-industrial United States was the closest approximation to a land of equality that the Western world had yet produced.

As a congenital skeptic, I remained unconvinced. Goaded by a colleague who, while applauding my observations in *Jacksonian America* on the thin evidentiary basis for the egalitarian thesis, nevertheless reminded me that I had not unearthed substantial evidence of my own, I decided to dig up that evidence and once and for all find out whether the facts of American life sustained Tocqueville's conclusions. *Riches, Class, and Power Before the Civil War* was the result of my labors.

The book represented more than five years intensive research on the wealth, family backgrounds, careers, marriages, residential patterns, uses of leisure, lifestyles, social standing, and the influence and power of the wealthiest persons in four of the five largest cities in the United States—New York City, Philadelphia, Boston, and the then separate city of Brooklyn. In attempting to determine precisely who were the rich, I had had to ascertain the wealth of everyone else; I thus wound up with a data bank that enabled me to fix the distribution of wealth and to do so with some precision. Since I learned what everyone was worth, I could determine the extent to which wealth was represented in political office and positions of social influence and the extent as well to which wealthy individuals chose friends, spouses, dinner partners, and neighbors according to an ideal of social exclusiveness. Private papers, correspondence, and diaries were an indispensable supplement to the raw tax assessment records I unearthed. And since I gathered evidence both for the 1820s and the 1840s, it was possible to discern the changes that occurred in social patterns over the course of time. I trust it is not giving away too much to note that the evidence I had gathered sharply refuted every one of the egalitarian axioms.

The response to *Riches* was soul-satisfying. Thorough research, like virtue, may be its own reward. It was nevertheless comforting to find that critics were appreciative of the patient labor I had performed to reach my conclusions. Which is not to say that there were no fault finders. At a scholarly conference in Denver just after the book came out, an admirer of Tocqueville, told that the book was a National Book Award finalist in history, responded publicly, "But it didn't win, did it?" (Alas, John Clive's *Macaulay* took the honors that year.)

An avant-garde quantifier complained that I preferred easy-to-understand statistics to the more esoteric sort he favored. Another critic bemoaned my preference for prose over scattergrams. A third, while favorably impressed with my research, accused me of being at heart "a card-carrying narrative historian." The pain of this terrible judgment was assuaged by the pleasant stranger who wrote in *The American Historical Review* that he detected the influence of William Makepeace Thackeray on the literary style of *Riches*.

A radical critic found disconcerting my sympathetic treatment of some of the swells I wrote about. What can I say in defense? I plead guilty to adhering to the Shavian belief, expressed in *Major Barbara,* that the beneficiary of an admittedly inequitable social institution may yet be a not altogether unworthy person. The point about the social and economic elite of Tocquevillean American is not that they were unattractive individuals, but that they had inordinate wealth, status, and power that doomed others no less worthy than they to rather grim lives. Growing up in a society in which few people were inclined to challenge its fundamental social and economic arrangements, the elite simply accepted what they thought was coming to them. They demonstrated social conscience by participating actively in a variety of humanitarian voluntary associations, guided, unsurprisingly, not by an ideal of radical change or revolution, but by the ancient principle of *noblesse oblige*.

Riches appears to have had some effect in changing historians' minds. The survey history texts that are used by undergraduate students taking what is usually their only course in American history are no longer describing the second quarter of the nineteenth century in egalitarian terms. Thus James MacGregor Burns notes that, "looking for democracy and equality, Tocqueville plunged into a nation that was sharply unequal in its distribution of wealth" and that "economic and social equality were, on balance, still largely unrealized in the Jacksonian 'Age of Equality.' " To George Tindall, "a supreme irony of the times was that 'the age of the common man,' 'the age of Jacksonian Democracy,' seems actually to have been an age of increasing social rigidity," a viewpoint that he credits largely to this author's "researches... in major eastern cities." Thomas A. Bailey's and David M. Kennedy's 1987 text observes that while "many myths about social mobility grew up," in fact "rags-to-riches success stories were relatively few" in an era marked by a widening of the "gulf between the rich and the poor." And John Garraty and Robert A. McCaughey in the same year, after noting that I have shown "that in the 1830s and 1840s a wide and growing gap existed between the rich and poor in the larger eastern cities," conclude that "few modern students of Jacksonian America" would now accept Tocqueville's sweeping generalizations.

Although I did glance at social patterns in earlier and later America as well as in Europe in order to throw my findings into clearer historical perspective, my focus was of course on the four communities that I researched intensively. Ascertaining the wealth owned by roughly 185,000 New Yorkers in 1828 and the 371,223 New Yorkers of 1845, to take but one city, and digging up in additional material on their family origins, economic activities, uses of leisure, memberships, courtships, and political roles, among other things, sufficed, I felt, for a single volume.

At the time I wrote *Riches,* there was not much evidence on smaller locales of the sort I gathered on the great cities of the northeast. Things have changed during the past sixteen years as scholars have proceeded to examine the distribution of wealth, status, opportunity, and power for small towns and fishing ports in New England and the northeast, cotton counties in the southeast and southwest, the rural and urban midwest. These recent studies fill out our portrait of the United States in the age of Alexis de Tocqueville.

Inevitably, the social structure of small or frontier towns differed from the social structure of the great metropolitan centers. The rule appears to have prevailed, for example: the greater the total wealth of a community, the more unequal or skewed its distribution of wealth. And yet the most striking feature of the evidence on rural and small-town America is that it too points to an inegalitarian society markedly unlike the one envisioned by Tocqueville. For not only was wealth everywhere distributed unequally, amazingly large proportions of the populations lived bleak material lives, possessing nothing that had any market value—however marginally serviceable it might be. Exclusive town, village, and rural elites dominated the society and usually the politics of their communities. For all the era's reputation for social fluidity, movements up the social ladder or from low to high prestige occupations was anything but commonplace. It turns out that an inegalitarian social, economic, and political order prevailed throughout the United States in the so called Era of the Common Man.

Of course not everyone reads the evidence the same way. Unreconstructed Tocquevilleans have expressed outrage at my insistence on subjecting the Great Man's undocumented generalizations to an empirical test utilizing mundane data, as though his lofty *aperçus* are to be treated as the observations of a mere mortal. At a meeting of the Southern Historical Association, one eminence remarked that I intend to bury the marvelous French theorist under a "mountain of tax lists from Brooklyn!" (He could have strengthened his indictment by noting that my Brooklyn evidence was not even drawn entirely from hightoned Brooklyn Heights. Talk about *lèse-majesté!* While a number of historians have praised what they call the "Pessen thesis," a noted cliometrician suggests that, for all the value and originality of my research, it has not quite dealt a death blow to the "egalitarian hypothesis." His critique rested largely on the thesis that he and a number of conservative economic historians have presented, that age accounts for most of the inequality that I and others have found glaring.

According to their argument, since most men become richer as they become older, the essential cause of whatever inequality obtained at any given moment was not the result of private property and inheritance or an inequitable social system. Rather, it was because forty year olds as a group do better than thirty year olds, who in turn, make more money than twenty year olds. They mount impressive equations designed to show, therefore, that when the influence of aging on earnings is taken into consideration, the United States of Tocqueville's time was a relatively egalitarian society. Alas, this critique has a fatal statistical as well as historical flaw.

The increasingly unequal distribution of wealth in America appears to have owed far more to changes in the historical circumstances than to a shift in the demographic or age structure. It was the dissimilar origins, circumstances, and careers of men, not differences in their ages, that primarily accounted for what some scholars call the shockingly unequal distribution of wealth in the antebellum United States. Working people of whatever age had little and earned little; merchants, financiers, and large planters of whatever age had much. That an older age cohort was on average richer than a younger group was due mainly to the fact that the very small number of very rich men who owned most of the wealth of every age group tended to have greater fortunes as they grew older. Thus an older group did have more wealth than a younger, but most men of all age groups were poor or had little wealth. As Samuel B. Richmond, one of the nation's leading statisticians, has observed, "We don't care about the infinite number of models, based on unrealistic assumptions, that can be created or plucked out of thin air to yield distributions of wealth purporting to show that age accounts for inequality. Our interest is in how the distributions we have discovered got to be what they were." Abundant historical evidence indicates that the great majority of the population were working people or small farmers who held little of the nation's wealth, for all the slight increases in income they might experience during an age of inflation.

I do not mean to suggest that *Riches* answers all questions. I do not share the conviction of some historians that the social patterns revealed for select communities necessarily disclose the patterns of all communities. The historian's work, like Sisyphus's, is never done. For all our heroic efforts, we have to date illuminated only a small corner of the darkness. The appropriate mood in undertaking research on hitherto ignored communities is to be alert not only to confirmation of trends we have uncovered in our earlier work but to be alert, too, to the inevitable distinctions in nuance that will be disclosed for every community that we view afresh. *Riches* says little about the mindset or social ideology of the urban elites. It touches only lightly on the implications of its evidence. There are doubtless other omissions. Yet I am content.

No book can tell it all. *Riches* is what it is: a substantially researched essay that sought to test the accuracy and validity of the important egalitarian version of American nineteenth century society. I patiently gathered a massive quantity of germane evidence, on the assumption that he who purports by reference to factual evidence to test the accuracy of a theory so durable and prestigious as Tocqueville's is well advised to gather a great deal of such evidence. I intended not to close the discussion but to open it. I am delighted that many American scholars think the book did so "admirably." I am no less delighted that the book has been applauded for its readability and for its interest in the rich as individuals.

Data and evidence are indispensable in answering questions of: How much? To what extent? How often? Yet facts are only the beginning of wisdom. I have always believed that history is an art form; certainly I was guided by that principle in writing *Riches, Class, and Power.* There is no conflict between answering questions on the basis of much evidence but doing so, too, in a manner accessible, even pleasing, to the sensible reader. And since the subjects of history are flesh and blood human beings, I have tried to write about them as though they are something other than faceless statistical data.

Preface

A friend unwittingly bears much of the responsibility for the form this book has taken. Some years ago I showed him an essay in which I expressed skepticism about Alexis de Tocqueville's assertion that in the United States of the 1830s most rich men had been poor. My paper noted that this widely accepted viewpoint rested on a "frail factual foundation." My friend's reaction, as I recall it, was polite, something to the effect: "Mmm. Yes. Nice paper. Too bad you don't produce any evidence of your own." What could a proud man do but find that evidence and find out once and for all whether successful men in the "era of the common man" were characteristically self-made?

When I was able to turn my attention to the project, I believed that the job would consist essentially of digging up material on the families and backgrounds of rich men whose names could easily be plucked from "the record." The belief was a delusion; the record was not so cooperative. Contemporary published listings, which I had originally thought I could fall back on, turned out to be unreliable, their itemizations of rich men erratic and incomplete, and many of their estimates of wealth mere guesswork. Something better was needed for a serious investigation, and I found it in the form of manuscript tax-assessment rolls located in the Municipal Archives and Records Center of New York City. Creating reliable lists of the rich of New York City from this full but chaotic data took the better part of a year, even with the assistance of student researchers and clerical assistants. In view of the cryptic nature of some of the entries made by the assessors and the need to make decisions or interpretations about hundreds of notations, it became apparent that reliable research would have to be research in which every item recorded by an assistant was personally double-checked by the author.

As the table of contents makes clear, the book I have written goes far beyond the scope of the book originally intended. Detailed information on the assessed worth of all taxpayers at different points in time suggested the possibility of estimating both the distribution of wealth at these times and the extent to which fortunes rose and fell over the course of time. Abundant material on the backgrounds and families of the rich threw a great deal of light on their lifestyles, their actions and influence, as well as their fortunes and situations at birth. And in a decision that added several years of work—but I trust made the results more representative and significant—I early decided to make the study a tale of four great cities instead of one: Brooklyn, Philadelphia, and Boston were added to New York City.

There are many paths to scholarly fulfillment. The one I chose was to take the most influential contemporary and later generalizations about the nature of pre–Civil War or antebellum American society, transpose them into questions, and try to answer them by gathering as much data as possible. Evidence was gathered on total populations rather than on samples. "Representative individuals," even when selected through the most sophisticated statistical techniques, sometimes turn out to be less than representative. Counting the wealth owned by every taxpayer in a city of 371,223—New York City in 1845—or accumulating biographical information on the intercity rich, who numbered more than two thousand, is a time-consuming process. It is a rewarding one too, not least for the occasional unanticipated nuggets of information secured in the performance of these menial tasks of scholarship. When questions arose concerning the use of statistics, I was fortunate to be able to repair for advice to a cooperative friend who is also a master statistician—Samuel Richmond, Dean of the Graduate School of Business of Columbia University. I have tried in all cases to make my points in clear English or, where mathematics was unavoidable, in simple expressions likely to be understandable to a nonspecialist reader, rather than in technical language and equations.

Whatever merits this book may possess are due largely to the assistance and cooperation given me by many people and institutions. Awards of faculty research fellowships by the Research Foundation of the State University of New York in 1967, 1969, and 1970 enabled me to do much of the necessary research. The staffs of many libraries were splendidly cooperative, particularly those of the New-York Historical Society, the Long Island Historical Society, the New York City Municipal Archives and Records Center, the Massachusetts Historical Society, the Historical Society of Pennsylvania, the Department of Rare Books and Manuscripts of the Boston Public Library, and the Local History and Genealogical Division of the New York Public Library.

Assistance far beyond the call of professional courtesy was rendered by John H. Lindenbusch, Director of the Long Island Historical Society, and Sandra Shoiock, the society's former librarian; Kathleen A. Luhrs, Arthur J. Breton of the New-York Historical Society; and John Daly, Archival Examiner of the City of Philadelphia. In selecting pictures I am indebted to Wilson G. Duprey, Curator of the Map and Print Room, New-York Historical Society, Nicholas B. Wainwright, Director of the Historical Society of Pennsylvania, Charlotte LaRue of the Museum of the City of New York, my daughter Mrs. Beth Shub, and Miss Luhrs, for their valuable advice. Students who assisted in the research were June Cressy, Dinah Pessen, Kenneth Jacobson, Diana Thompson, Lorraine Henderson, Elizabeth Ann O'Brien, and above all, Rina Okonkwo. Andrew Pessen performed many computations.

Colleagues and scholars who offered useful advice and information include Dagoberto Molerio, Stuart Blumin, Henry Steele Commager, Alice Hanson Jones, David Spring, Peter N. Stearns, David Landes, Gordon W. Kirk, Jr., Ira Leonard, Brian Danforth, Stanley Buder, Margaret C. Jacob, Henry L. Feingold, Myrna C. Engelmeyer, William W. Cutler, III, Donald E. Emerson, Edwin J. Perkins, John V. Mering, Frederic C. Jaher, Alexander W. Williams, and Robert Doherty. Several of these gentlemen and women, strangers to me personally, unsolicitedly sent me material that helps fill a folder that I am very fond of, entitled "scholarly cooperation." Carl N. Degler, who chaired a panel at the 1970 meeting of the American Historical Association, at which I presented a paper on several of the themes in this book, and Stephan Thernstrom and Rowland Berthoff, commentators on that panel, made helpful criticisms. Louis Auchincloss offered his uniquely knowledgable observations on elite families. Milton Cantor in a sense provoked me into doing the job. Arthur

Schlesinger called a factual error to my attention. It goes without saying that all remaining errors and faults in this book are mine alone.

My chief debt is to my family. I have mentioned several of my children who performed scholarly chores. I wish also to mention Abigail and Jonathan, whose love and encouragement, like that of their sisters and brother and my son-in-law Michael Shub, were better than meat and drink to me during the years I worked on the book. As for meat and drink, they were supplied by my wife, to whom this book is dedicated. Although I find her a matchless creator of such creature comforts, I value most her cheerfulness, patience, tolerance, and warmth, which made my study so pleasant a workroom.

Edward Pessen
Brooklyn, New York

Acknowledgments

I have discussed several of the themes of this volume in different form in the following publications: "The Wealthiest New Yorkers of the Jacksonian Era: A New List," *The New-York Historical Society Quarterly* (*hereinafter N-Y HSQ*), *LIV* (April 1970), pp. 145–72; "Did Fortunes Rise and Fall Mercurially in Antebellum America? The Tale of Two Cities: Boston and New York," *Journal of Social History, 4* (Summer 1971), pp. 339–57; "The Egalitarian Myth and the American Social Reality: Wealth, Mobility, and Equality in the 'Era of the Common Man,'" *American Historical Review, 76* (Oct. 1971), pp. 989–1034; "A Social and Economic Portrait of Jacksonian Brooklyn: Inequality, Social Immobility, and Class Distinction in the Nation's Seventh City," *N-Y HSQ, LV* (Oct. 1971), pp. 318–53; "The Occupations of the Ante-Bellum Rich: A Misleading Clue to the Sources and Extent of Their Wealth," *Historical Methods Newsletter, V* (March 1972), pp. 49–52; "The Marital Theory and Practice of the Antebellum Elite," *New York History, LIII* (Oct. 1972), pp. 388–410; "Philip Hone's Set: The Social World of the New York City Elite in the 'Age of Egalitarianism,'" *N-Y HSQ, LVI* (Oct. 1972), pp. 285–308; and "Who Governed the Nation's Cities in the 'Era of the Common Man'?" *Political Science Quarterly, LXXXVII* (Dec. 1972), pp. 591–614. Appendix B of this volume appeared originally as "Moses Beach Revisited: A Critical Examination of His *Wealthy Citizens* Pamphlets," *Journal of American History, LVIII* (Sept. 1971), pp. 415–26. The publishers of each of these journals graciously granted permission for reprinting portions of the above articles.

The information here given, we have persuaded ourselves, will be duly appreciated by those who regard facts as necessary to the illustration of the history and condition of a people, and of their means of progress and prosperity.

Lemuel C. Shattuck, *The Census of Boston for the Year 1845*, p. 179.

1
Introduction

This book is about the American rich during a time in which, supposedly, their numbers were few, their wealth unimpressive, their ranks accessible, their status faltering, and their influence meager. It has been widely believed that if the second quarter of the nineteenth century was marked by the rise and increasing prominence of the masses, it also witnessed the decline and growing political impotence of the classes. The concept that the period was an "era of the common man" has rested on a surprisingly frail foundation of fact. My purpose therefore was to determine the extent to which these beliefs about antebellum America are borne out by the evidence. What follows is not a narrative, designed either to celebrate or denigrate the rich, but a discussion of their actual situation and the light it throws on long-accepted views of the era.

The chief architect of the traditional interpretation of American society was Alexis de Tocqueville. The young French aristocrat visited this country for nine months in 1831 and 1832, ostensibly to report on its prison system for his government. He and his colleague, Gustave de Beaumont, did in fact publish an illuminating and still readable treatise on the American penitentiary system.[1] Tocqueville observed much more than American prisons, however. In 1835 he published the first part, and five years later the second part of *Democracy in America*, a work recognized almost immediately as a classic.[2] Justly acclaimed as the most penetrating single book ever written about the United States, Tocqueville's *Democracy* ranges over a wide array of topics, offering insights and judgments dazzling in their originality and boldness, almost frightening in their prescience. The volumes also contain the most influential as well as the most durable evaluation yet written of Jacksonian America. For while sectional and class interpretations of the era's great political issues have been largely forsaken by scholars in our own time,[3] Tocqueville's egalitarian rendering of Jacksonian society continues to command their wide support. The controversy that has enlivened the discussion of party battles in the age of Henry Clay and John Caldwell Calhoun has been strangely missing from the consideration of the era's social developments. Jacksonians and anti-Jacksonians, now as earlier, continue to subscribe to the Tocquevillean version of antebellum society.[4]

In the case of Tocqueville's *Democracy*, as with Tacitus' *Germania*, it is not always clear whether the generalizations are based on facts drawn from the society ostensibly under observation or from the author's fertile imagination. Both these great theorists were more concerned with conveying wholesome historical truths—one to his Roman audience, the other to his French—than in offering factual descriptions. Particularly in the second part of *Democracy*, Tocqueville does not always make clear whether it is the *American* democratic society or an abstract democratic model of his own devising that underlies some of his imaginative flights. What I have called his egalitarian interpretation, however, is based on specific comments and judgments that in each case were explicitly made about the United States. Despite the fact that some of Tocqueville's most important insights were based on slight evidence,[5] they were subscribed to by numerous influential contemporaries.

For Tocqueville was not alone in depicting the American society of the 1830s in egalitarian terms. Such Americans as Ralph Waldo Emerson and James Fenimore Cooper, and European travelers as disparate as Harriet Martineau—who smiled at most of what she saw here—and Mrs. Frances Trollope—who frowned—observed the same turbulent, fluid social scene discerned by the brilliant Frenchman. Observers were amazed at a social setting in which the word *servant* was taboo because demeaning, where prisoners could be seen shaking hands with wardens, working people dressed as well as merchants, statesmen proclaiming their humble origins deferred to the masses, and everyone ate huge quantities of foods available in Europe only to the few. The vulgarity of manners—the public slouching, spitting, and rudeness—appeared further to attest to the predominance of the plebeian orders, as did the fact that here "any man's son," in Mrs. Trollope's phrase, could "become the equal of any other man's son." Many articulate persons, particularly those familiar with the traditional society still prevailing in the Old World, leaped to the conclusion that the masses dominated the New.[6] Their joint perception of American society is Tocquevillean, not in the sense that its central propositions were original with Tocqueville, but rather because no one else has formulated the egalitarian thesis as comprehensively, as lucidly, as logically as he. Tocqueville's social portrait is a model of internal consistency.

According to the egalitarian thesis, the United States of the second quarter of the nineteenth century was a society dominated by the great mass of the people, who composed the middling orders. Unfortunate minorities aside, few men here were either very poor or very rich. For that matter, the rich here were rich only by American standards, their wealth not comparing in magnitude to the great fortunes possessed by wealthy European families. The near, if not perfect, equality of condition left little opportunity for the accumulation by individuals of vast surpluses. Material success was available to all men, whatever their backgrounds. What rich men there were in America were typically self-made, born to poor or humble families. Nor did they hold on to their wealth for long. Flux ruled this dynamic society; riches and poverty were ephemeral states in this kaleidoscopic milieu. The limited extent and the precariousness of wealth explained the dwindling influence of its possessors. At a time when the most liberal of European states was grudgingly permitting some wealthy bourgeois to share the suffrage with great landholders, the United States was brushing aside all important restrictions on voting. Deference had given way to the strident rule of the masses, as the beleaguered rich turned their backs on a democratic politics permeated with vulgarity, opportunism, and other loveless expressions of popular power. Social democracy followed on the heels of political democracy; in a civilization that exalted honest work over status, class barriers diminished in significance as they were increasingly breached.[7]

For all its persuasiveness and influence, the egalitarian thesis has not gone unchallenged. A few contemporary men of affairs joined spiritual and secular perfectionists and labor radicals in dissenting from the consensus as a whole or from particular parts of it.[8] A small number of recent scholarly publications have also questioned one or another aspect of the traditional interpretation. It is no disparagement to observe that modern criticisms, my own included, have been less than comprehensive.[9] For the most part, their authors have focused on other themes; in other cases they have either touched on only one facet of the egalitarian thesis or, where the investigation has been broader, examined only one community. And they have been impressionistic in their methodology; that is, their data are random and inconclusive.

The following chapters are based on detailed evidence—what nowadays is called "quantitative data"—gathered in order to subject the thesis of antebellum egalitarianism to the kind of detailed or comprehensive investigation it has hitherto been largely spared.[10] My conclusions rest primarily but not entirely on data drawn from four great cities of the northeast—New York City, Philadelphia, Boston, and the then-separate city of Brooklyn. During the second quarter of the nineteenth century, New York City was the most heavily populated urban community in the nation, with greater Philadelphia second, Boston ranking either fourth or fifth, and Brooklyn rising from perhaps twentieth place in the mid-1820s to seventh by 1840. Containing close to 4 per cent of the nation's population, these cities were centers of great wealth. For most of the period, New York, Philadelphia, and Boston were the leading financial and commercial cities in the nation. By the eve of the Civil War, Brooklyn had joined the big three as an important manufacturing center. The five national leaders in terms of value of manufactured products were these four cities and Cincinnati.[11]

Evidence on southern and western communities, rural as well as urban, has also contributed to my judgments and interpretations. To place my own findings in clearer perspective, I have also compared antebellum American urban society with England and the Continent in the same period and with the United States before 1825 and after the Civil War.

In accord with the fashion popular in historical writing for almost a century now, this book tries to answer questions rather than tell a story. Although the topical arrangement of this account makes clear that I am a child of our own time, with its utilitarian predilections, I am sufficiently an admirer of the great narrative historians of an earlier era to be on guard, at least on the conscious level, against history as sociological treatise. Since it is better, and certainly kinder to the reader, to be intelligible than modish, clear prose and simple mathematical terms have been used wherever possible, in preference to esoteric terminology or equations.[12] Serious historians, even those ancients who had the quaint notion that their purpose was to tell an interesting story well, did after all perform much research. It would be dismaying to think that the amassing of data obliges the scholar to forsake plain English for a mode of communication more suitable to the computer than the historian.

I have focused on the rich because evidence on their fortunes, their backgrounds, their private lives, and their influence clarifies not only their own role but it illuminates also the nature of the broader society during what historians continue to call the "era of the common man." The following pages try to show the extent to which popular myths about that period are corroborated or contradicted by detailed historical evidence.

Notes

1 *On the Penitentiary System in the United States [and Its Application to France]* Philadelphia, 1833).

2 Alexis de Tocqueville, *Democracy in America*, 2 vols. (New York, 1835, 1840). References are to the Phillips Bradley edition (New York, 1954).

3 For recent discussions of the changing political historiography see Alfred A. Cave, *Jacksonian Democracy and the Historians* (Gainesville, Fla., 1964); and Edward Pessen, *Jacksonian America: Society, Personality, and Politics* (Homewood, Ill., 1969), pp. 352–93.

4 Among the modern works that subscribe to one or more of the central tenets of the egalitarian theory are David M. Potter, *People of Plenty* (Chicago, 1958); Carl N. Degler, *Out of Our Past*, rev. ed. (New York, 1970), pp. 144–45; Marvin Meyers, *The Jacksonian Persuasion* (Stanford, 1957); Lee Benson, *The Concept of Jacksonian Democracy: New York as a Test Case* (Princeton, 1961); Marcus Cunliffe, *The Nation Takes Shape, 1789–1837* (Chicago, 1965); John William Ward, "The Age of the Common Man," in John Higham, ed., *Reconstruction of American History* (New York, 1962), pp. 82–97; David Riesman, Nathan Glazer, Reuel Denney, *The Lonely Crowd* (New York, 1953); Rowland Berthoff, "The American Social Order: A Con-

servative Hypothesis," *American Historical Review, LXV* (April 1960), p. 499; and Stuart Bruchey, *The Roots of American Economic Growth, 1607–1861* (New York, 1968).

[5] "Tocqueville scholarship" has become a minor intellectual industry. For discussion of Tocqueville's predilection for deduction or inference from slight or unproven factual data, see Seymour Drescher, *Dilemma of Democracy: Tocqueville and Modernization* (Pittsburgh, 1968), pp. 24–25, 279; Lynn L. Marshall and Drescher, "American Historians and Tocqueville's Democracy," *Journal of American History, LV* (Dec. 1968), p. 517; Edward T. Gargan, "Some Problems in Tocqueville Scholarship," *Mid-America, 41* (Jan. 1959), p. 3–26; Gargan, "Tocqueville and the Problem of Historical Prognosis," *American Historical Review, LXVIII* (Jan. 1963), pp. 332–45; Jack Lively, *The Social and Political Thought of Alexis de Tocqueville* (Oxford, 1962); Marvin Zetterbaum, *Tocqueville and the Problem of Democracy* (Stanford, 1966); and George W. Pierson, *Tocqueville and Beaumont in America* (New York, 1938), pp. 759–60.

[6] For a detailed discussion of the social judgments passed on American society by contemporaries—natives and visitors alike—and the factors that led the latter to exaggerate the extent of equality and social mobility, see Pessen, *Jacksonian America*, chap. 3.

[7] Tocqueville, *Democracy in America*, I:53–54; II:105, 138, 164, 199, 234, 237, 239, 250–51, 258, 263. Tocqueville's comprehensive evaluation of American civilization, stressing as it did the values and beliefs of the people, was of course more complex than the above paragraph suggests. The purpose of this study, however, is not to assess the social philosophy of Alexis de Tocqueville, but rather to consider those elements of his appraisal of America that have been widely subscribed to and that form the egalitarian thesis.

[8] For the ideas of contemporary dissenters see Arthur E. Bestor, Jr., *Backwoods Utopias: The Sectarian and Owenite Phases of Communitarian Socialism in America: 1663–1829* (Philadelphia, 1950); and Edward Pessen, *Most Uncommon Jacksonians: The Radical Leaders of the Early Labor Movement* (Albany, 1967).

[9] Leading examples would include Richard C. Wade, *The Urban Frontier: The Rise of Western Cities, 1790–1830* (Cambridge, 1959), chap. 7; D. Clayton James, *Antebellum Natchez* (Baton Rouge, 1968); Kenneth W. Wheeler, *To Wear a City's Crown: The Beginnings of Urban Growth in Texas, 1836–1865* (Cambridge, 1968); Robert A. Dahl, *Who Governs? Democracy and Power in an American City* (New Haven, 1961); Douglas T. Miller, *Jacksonian Aristocracy: Class and Democracy in New York, 1830–1860* (New York, 1967); Pessen, *Jacksonian America;* Garry B. Nash, "The Philadelphia Bench and Bar, 1800–1861," *Comparative Studies in Society and History, VII* (Jan. 1965), pp. 203–220.

[10] Exceptions to the impressionistic approach are a number of recent quantitative studies of particular communities, some of them yet unpublished. Particularly valuable are Stuart Blumin, "Mobility and Change in Ante-Bellum Philadelphia," in Stephan Thernstrom and Richard Sennett, eds., *Nineteenth-Century Cities: Essays in the New Urban History* (New Haven, 1969), pp. 165–208; Alexandra McCoy, "The Political Affiliations of American Elites: Wayne County, Michigan, 1844–1860, as a Test Case" (Wayne State University Doctoral Dissertation, 1965); and two papers read at the annual meeting of the Organization of American Historians, April 19, 1971, in New Orleans: Robert Doherty, "Property Distribution in Jacksonian America," on New England; and Michael B. Katz, "Patterns of Inequality, Wealth and Power in a Nineteenth-Century City," on Hamilton, Ontario.

[11] For a detailed statistical survey of population, financial, commercial, and industrial rankings, see Elliot A. Rosen, "The Growth of the American City, 1830 to 1860: Economic Foundations of Urban Growth in the Pre-Civil War Period" (New York University Ph.D. diss., 1953).

[12] In dealing with the distribution of wealth, for example, it has appeared to me as sensible and more economical to make simple statements of the proportions of wealth owned by different levels of wealth holders than to use the Lorenz curve to indicate graphically the difference between a perfect equality of distribution and the actual inequality that inevitably obtains. It is more revealing to say that the poorest 90 per cent of Philadelphians owned only 10 per cent of the wealth in 1860 than to

note that the Schutz coefficient of inequality for the same data is .79 (with 0 representing perfect equality and .999 the greatest possible degree of inequality). Similarly, I fail to see the need to refer to the Gini coefficient of concentration, which would be zero in the case of perfect equality of distribution and approaches closer to 1.0 as the area between the diagonal line representing perfect equality of distribution (in a graph in which the vertical pole measures wealth and the horizontal, population) and the Lorenz curve (connecting the points that indicate the proportions of wealth owned by varying percentages of the population—"deciles," where the latter are divided into tenths), enlarges, in an instance in which the richest tenth owning better than 40 per cent of the wealth and the poorest one half less than 15 per cent, produces a Gini coefficient of .54.

PART I

Wealth

2

Were There Truly Rich Americans in the "Era of the Common Man"?

In a democratic society like that of the United States . . . fortunes are scanty. . . . The equality of conditions [that] gives some resources to all the members of the community . . . also prevents any of them from having resources of great extent.

Tocqueville, *Democracy in America,* II:250, 258

To be rich, however honestly riches may have been acquired and however liberally expended, is [considered] a reproach.

Philip Hone, Diary, May 15, 1843, XXI:3

It is no derogation . . . to the Boston aristocracy, that it rests upon money. Money is something substantial. Everybody knows that and feels it. Birth is a mere idea, which grows everyday more and more intangible.

anon., *"Our First Men:" A Calendar of Wealth, Fashion, and Gentility* (Boston 1846), p. 5

One of the chief assumptions of the egalitarian theory is that the preindustrial United States was a society lacking in truly great fortunes. According to an admired modern historian, "sizable fortunes were made but not astronomical fortunes" in America during the era.[1] In asserting that the roughly equal distribution of resources in the United States prevented individuals from amassing great wealth, Tocqueville as always was reasoning flawlessly. The great question is whether his logic is borne out by the facts. It is, of course, impossible to define objectively "resources of great extent" or riches. The terms may be said to contain both a relative and an absolute component. Riches or great wealth will be owned by relatively few, giving each of its possessors a portion of the community's goods that equals or surpasses in value the total wealth owned by hundreds or even thousands of poorer men. And riches make possible lives marked by material comfort, costly—even sumptuous—possessions, servants or retainers to perform menial tasks, much leisure time, and attractive and expensive means of spending or using it. Since a number of contemporary sources indicate the quantity of wealth required to live the life of the rich, the question to be answered concerns the numbers who attained such wealth.

Digging out evidence of this sort is, however, much harder than devising plans to do so. That few scholarly tasks are more difficult than determining the precise wealth owned by individuals at a given point in their lifetimes is made abundantly clear by the admittedly inexact estimates of wealth made by the few outstanding economic historians who have tried to deal with the problem. Authorities in this esoteric field offer, not precise attributions of wealth, but informed estimates.[2]

Nor have many attempts been made by scholars to date to fix the wealth of the great accumulators. Our contemporary *Zeitgeist* may be a contributing factor: an authority on European social history advises that "for the most part social historians have stressed the poor rather than the rich in their studies."[3] Whatever the reasons, the relevant bibliography is a small one. The situation has not changed very much from what it was a half century ago, when Sorokin wrote that "wealthy men as a specific social group have been studied very little up to this time."[4] The supply of authoritative information remains slim, while what is authoritative is unavoidably inexact. But, if precise scholarly appraisals are lacking, there are interesting contemporary publications that, in effect, take up the question "Were there very few or no Americans who had substantial fortunes during the era?"

The answer, according to the estimates made by Moses Yale Beach, publisher of the New York *Sun*, is that there were many. Commencing in 1842 and continuing through 1855, Beach published a dozen editions of a pamphlet that listed the reputedly "one thousand wealthiest citizens" in New York City, together with estimates of their wealth and biographical vignettes claimed to be useful to the business community.[5] Beach's booklets inspired imitators to publish similar listings for Brooklyn, Philadelphia, and Boston and other New England cities during the 1840s and 1850s.[6]

The sums attributed to wealthy individuals in these fascinating publications cannot be credited, however, certainly not at face value; the sources of their estimates are either not given at all or are referred to in undocumented assertions. These monuments to materialism are more useful as reflections of the spirit of the age than as the "credit ratings" some publishers claimed them to be. No more striking testimony exists of the materialism and dollar worship attributed to Americans by articulate observers during the era than these listings, published by men who disingenuously denied that catering to the worship of wealth was their object; even as the title page of one revised edition boldly proclaimed that it listed millions of dollars more than an earlier version.[7]

If Beach's rating for 1845 could be believed, New York City alone had one thousand individuals each worth $100,000 or more. John Jacob

Astor's fortune was estimated at $25 million, while twenty other eminent men were adjudged millionaires.

Unfortunately, Beach's estimates cannot be accepted. Riddled with errors and inconsistencies, they relied heavily on guesswork and anonymous tips supplied by readers of Beach's scandalmongering newspapers. Hints of their publisher's intimate ties with New York City's merchant elite are nowhere confirmed and, in fact, appear to be flatly contradicted by the way in which men of affairs and newspaper editors ignored Beach's pamphlets. Published spasmodically, omitting most of the wealthiest one thousand persons in the city, and filled with biographical tidbits of little value and dubious authenticity, the Beach list is not what it purports to be and cannot be regarded as a reliable estimate of the wealth of New Yorkers.[8] Something better and more solid is needed to provide the underpinnings for a responsible discussion of the dimensions of New York's fortunes during the era. It is indicative of the paucity of materials on the subject and the difficulty of obtaining them that so many excellent scholars have for so long relied on Beach's estimates. One historian recently referred to them as "those exasperating, fascinating, incomplete, and indispensable compendia of the city's economic elite," useful above all for their availability and because the task of drawing up a more accurate list "would involve a lifetime of research in the city directories and tax lists, among other sources."[9]

Tax Records

In view of the unreliability of the "wealthy citizens" lists, the subjectivity of attributions of wealth made in contemporary diaries—not to mention the impossibility of determining their accuracy—the lack of comprehensive lists of corporate officers and bank directors, and the incompleteness of wills and probate inventories, tax assessments appeared to offer the most reliable clues to the era's wealthiest persons and their worth.[10] Undeterred by warnings about the great expenditure of time involved in researching this material and fortified by my conviction that solid evidence of this sort was indispensable to a serious study of wealth, I proceeded to examine the tax assessments of the four northeastern cities for various years, early and late, during the second quarter of the nineteenth century. Much time was indeed required—if fortunately less than a "lifetime"—to construct usable lists of the wealthy and their assessed worth out of the chaotic raw data filed by contemporary assessors.

Urban residents during the era were taxed not on incomes but on the total wealth, real and personal, they owned within the city. The Boston Assessor's Office during the period printed annual lists of all persons taxed "twenty five dollars and upwards."[11] These documents list every taxpayer and corporation and the assessed value of their real and personal estate. From these records it was therefore possible to construct a list of the wealthiest Bostonians and how much they were worth—or, more accurately—how much they were estimated to be worth by the city's assessors. Unfortunately, the other great northeastern cities did not print lists of tax assessments. In order to determine the assessed wealth of New York City's residents, it was necessary to go through tens of thousands of notations made by the city's assessors in the notebooks kept for the city's wards. These volumes contain a block-by-block listing of each piece of real property, its assessed value, and its owner, as well as the assessed value of all personal property, alongside the names of the owners—or the agents, trustees, administrators, or executors of the owners. Since New York City had a population of about 185,000 in 1828 and 371,223 in 1845, ranking its residents for these years according to assessed wealth made it necessary to collect over a hundred thousand separate items and collate them from the unorganized and unalphabetized data in the assessors' notebooks. Compared to this labor, the task of assembling a list of Brooklyn's wealthiest persons, at a time when that city's population was slightly over forty thousand, was child's play.[12]

Philadelphia's tax assessments for this era cannot be used to piece together the total assessed wealth of individuals because real-estate assessments there were levied not on owners, as was the case in the other cities, but on occupants. It was therefore impossible to ascertain the assessed wealth of individual Philadelphians. Fortunately, it was possible to discover the occupations and locate the residential districts (primarily from the city directories) of most of the individuals named in a contemporary listing of Philadelphia's elite. Varied evidence indicates that the persons named in this book were indeed the wealthy of the city—even if their precise wealth cannot be determined. Their occupations were overwhelmingly the high-status occupations associated with wealth.[13] Their residences were for the most part in the city's wealthiest and most exclusive wards. That a house was not located between the Delaware River and 7th Street, running east to west, or between Mulberry and Walnut Streets, north to south, was hardly a sign of poverty, however. By the 1840s, many of Philadelphia's wealthiest and most notable persons lived in "Girard Row," the group of houses on the north side of Chestnut Street between 11th and 12th streets. Although the eastern wards were wealthier, a sharp narrowing of the gap between east and west had begun by 1829 and continued thereafter. In Philadelphia, as in other cities, many a mansion stood in a "poor" ward, the wealth of its occupant not sufficient to change significantly the average per capita wealth of the district's inhabitants.[14] Other data also suggest that the "Wealthy Citizens of Philadelphia" was not a misnomer.

The beauty of the kind of assessment figures available for New

York, Boston, and Brooklyn—and lacking for Philadelphia—is that they make possible fairly objective estimates of the wealth of individuals. Not the least interesting of their features is the light they throw on the accuracy of the various "wealthy citizens" ratings. The New York City tax assessments for 1845 disclose, among other things, that fewer than half of Moses Beach's "wealthiest one thousand" were in fact among the one thousand residents of the great city assessed for the greatest amount of wealth! Beach's imitators in other cities had a far better record.[15]

Not that the evidence of the tax assessments is foolproof. Assessors often made careless mistakes, misspelling names or omitting middle initials that might have distinguished rich men named Smith, Thompson, or Jones from their less fortunate fellows of the same first names. Some entries were incomplete, and others confusing. The tax *collector* collected his proper share when someone's estate was held in trust by someone else. But to a compiler of the list of the wealthy, it is a crucial matter that a sloppy entry by an *assessor* leaves unclear who is administering whose wealth. The typical failure by assessors to indicate the residence of absentee owners of valuable real estate—whose names were too common to be readily distinguishable without further identification—is another example of the kind of human error that reduces the precision of the data. And, inevitably, assessors had unlike standards for estimating the value of property. But the most serious deficiencies of the assessment data for our purposes derive, not from the carelessness or foibles of the men recording them, but from built-in features in the tax laws of the day. Neither in law nor in fact were the assessments designed to record what men were actually worth.

Wealth owned outside the city, for example, did not have to be determined by the assessors. John Jacob Astor, Isaac Bronson, Hezekiah Beers Pierrepont, and their fellow merchants owned much real estate in New York State and in western lands. It is probably impossible to trace the exact value of all the real property owned by the era's great capitalists at any particular point in time. They themselves were sometimes unaware of the precise totals.[16] There can be no doubt, however, that the worth of such property was a substantial portion of the fortunes of the wealthiest residents in the cities. It was also an open secret that residents did not reveal the true worth of their possessions in the city. In the United States of the early nineteenth century, no more than in Tudor and Stuart England, were the rich ready to disclose the actual value of their wealth to assessors.[17]

In Boston prior to 1842 assessors listed both real and personal property at only one-half what they claimed it to be worth. When they subsequently modified their practice by recording the full assessment—which was itself far short of the actual value of the property evaluated—the property tax was halved. According to a special committee appointed by the Boston City Council in 1842, the city's assessors regarded themselves as men whose "interest [was] to keep down the valuation" in their wards.[18] Tax assessors in New York City were required by law to swear that they had assessed real estate at "the true value thereof and at which they would appraise the same in payment for a just debt due from a solvent debtor." Local officials were skeptical, however, stating on a number of occasions that assessors rather made real-estate assessments at the values preferred by their owners—particularly in the wealthier wards. The critics hastened to add that they had "no reason to believe that the assessors of any of the wards have intentionally erred." A comptroller of New York City delicately hinted that "the gentlemen annually chosen as assessors, however conscientiously they perform their trust, may not be acquainted in all cases with the circumstances of the inhabitants of their wards." [19] Assessors were all too human. When appointed, they were widely believed to undervalue real estate in the interests of the large property owners so influential in contemporary local government. When elected, assessors were charged with pandering to the universal desire to pay as little tax as possible. For assessments were not an academic exercise in determining the true value of the property owned by city residents, but rather a preliminary step toward separating potential taxpayers from what they loved dearly. That urban tax rates were low during the era, typically 1 per cent or less of the assessed value of property, did not appear to detract from the disinclination of property owners to reveal their true worth. Contemporary taxpayers, officials, publicists, and scholars alike agreed that real estate was drastically undervalued during the era.[20]

Personal Wealth

Personal property in New York City and Brooklyn, above all the personal property of rich men, was even more glaringly undervalued than was real estate. A number of municipal reports explained why this was so. Personal property was "invisible and incorporeal; easy of transfer and concealment; not admitting of valuation by comparison with any common standards." Since "the nature and character of personal property is so invisible, so migratory, and so changeable," contemporary officials were profoundly pessimistic as to the likelihood of any real improvement in the city's ability to increase and thereby make more accurate its assessments of the personal estates of citizens of "very extensive capital." This pessimism was justified. In many cases, an investigation had noted, wealthy persons had "not been rated at one-tenth part of their personal property." Those with great capital, "in general [paid] . . . far less in proportion than those in moderate and low circumstances." Poorer men were not necessarily more honest; they merely had less to hide. Men of great wealth often made themselves unavailable during the assessment season. When they were at home, they could write their own ticket; throughout the era no assessment of personal property was to be made in "those cases in which the value of said personal estate has been sworn to" by its possessor. Men of substance were evidently quite willing to fabricate in order to save money. (Moses Yale Beach's estate was assessed at $90,000 in 1855, although he listed it publicly at $350,000.) Rufus Story could succeed in changing the valuation of his personal property at Rivington Street from $20,000 to $1,000 on his own say-so. Hundreds of men who were directors—and therefore compelled by law to own substantial portions of the stock of many banks, insurance companies, and other corporations—were assessed for minuscule amounts of personal property or for no personal wealth whatsoever. In Brooklyn, such large real-estate owners and men of corporate affairs as H. B. Pierrepont and his son Henry (the son-in-law of the great and wealthy John Jay), Charles Hoyt, David Leavitt, Joseph D. Beers, Henry C. Murphy, Joseph A. Perry—who two years earlier had personally advanced $25,000 to the faltering Brooklyn Ferry Company—Joseph Sprague, Nathan B. Morse, Seth Low, Samuel Garrison, and many other substantial men were ostensibly worth little or nothing —at least according to the information they gave the assessors.

Some contemporaries attributed the undervaluations in New York City to "the paralyzing influence of politics," which made it "vain [to look] for a reform"; others stressed the alleged influence wealthy men had over the whole process of tax assessments, rates, and collection; still others thought the entire matter so complicated as to doom hopes for reform, no matter how sincere its advocates.[21] Whatever the reasons, it remains true that during the era under consideration, the personal property of New York City and Brooklyn residents was heavily under-assessed.

Unlike their counterparts in New York City and Brooklyn, Boston's assessors assessed personal estate in their city at values close to those they affixed on real property. Yet in Boston too there was a great, if impossible to measure, gulf between the actual value of the property owned by wealthy residents and the values offered by assessors. For most of the era, assessments were based not on direct observations made by assessors but on "true lists" of taxable property brought by taxpayers themselves to special meetings called for the purpose. Officials complained that such lists were neither complete nor true. When these lists were sworn to by the citizens, however, assessors had no alternative but to accept them at face value. By as late as 1848, the city fathers had gone no further than to hold discussions considering the advisability of substituting assessors' visits and direct observations—with all of the weaknesses of the latter method—for the admittedly ineffectual system of depending on tax information volunteered by the taxpayers themselves. Although Bostonians prided themselves, no doubt justifiably, on their lofty public morality, their equally deserving reputation for business shrewdness was evidently regarded by the city's tax officials as explanation enough for why Bostonians—no more than other folk—would not appraise their wealth at anything near full value when doing so would compel them to yield up larger segments of it than otherwise necessary. Mayor Josiah Quincy encouraged nondisclosure, for he believed that "an accurate exhibit of personalty was ruinous to a business man, besides being in many cases entirely impracticable."[22] The niggardly budgets and expenditures of cities before mid-century were powerful indirect testimony of the inaccuracy of the assessments of urban wealth.

In view of their underappraisals, therefore, the most certain value of the tax assessments is in the possibility they afford for creating accurate comparative rankings of the urban rich within a city. For while errors and underestimates were made by assessors, it was unusual for such flaws to have a discriminatory character, favoring one group of rich men at the expense of another. The assessments were a matter of public record, subject to the scrutiny of knowing men. If such reputedly wealthy families as the Hoyts, Brevoorts, Hones, Appletons, and Grays were worth much more than the tax records indicate, there is no reason to think that the ratio between their assessed and actual worth was significantly—if at all—different from the ratio that applied to the fortunes of other wealthy men and families.[23]

For all their inexactness, the assessment data are invaluable. The consoling feature of the sums disclosed by the tax records is that they are solid bedrock on which reliable estimates of the *true* wealth of individuals can be constructed. Rich men were worth at least the sums attributed to them by assessors. Even when the assessed valuations are taken at face value, New York City at the time of Tocqueville's visit had about 100 persons worth $100,000 or more, while Boston had 75 worth at least that sum. A decade later, shortly after the second part of *Democracy in America* appeared, New York's tax data disclosed that John Jacob Astor and Peter G. Stuyvesant were millionaires, while 300 other persons were each worth $100,000 or more. Boston by then had 150 individuals worth the latter sum, in addition to Peter Chardon Brooks, the millionaire. Brooklyn, by 1841 the nation's seventh city, had 26 individuals each assessed for $100,000 or more, although none at one million.

The $100,000 figure, at which many hundreds of northeasterners were assessed, may not appear to be an impressive sum. Yet, even if one makes the most unrealistic assumption that the assessment figures accurately recorded the extent of an individual's wealth, the sums in question were hardly paltry. According to John Jacob Astor's grandson—and he was in a good position to know—a member of the "exclusives" could in 1850 have devoted himself entirely to the good life, including leisurely travel in Europe, on ten thousand a year, in "dollars not pounds," as he hastened to add.[24]

The dollar of the 1830s was capable of wondrous things. William E. Dodge was able to rent a new two-story house on Bleecker Street in New York City for an annual rental of $300, while one or two hundred dollars more could pay for an elegant place on "aristocratic Park Place among the Motts, Hones, Costers, Haggertys, Austins, Beekmans, and Hosacks," the *crême de la crême* of New York City society.[25] Room and board at the new Astor House cost $1.50 in 1836, that sum paying for four meals consisting of "all the delicacies of the season . . . served in a most ample manner." Philip Hone, who was a sufficiently demanding gourmet to have found the famed Delmonico's Restaurant wanting, thought the fare at the Astor House capital; he had never seen "a table better set out, better provided, or a dinner better cooked." A wealthy Philadelphian of mid-century held that fifty dollars "constituted the millionairism of money aristocracy of those days," since this sum enabled a man to keep a carriage. According to Sidney George Fisher, a fashionable Philadelphian of the time, his annual income of less than $3,000 gave him "a comfortable house—servants, a good table—wine—a horse—books—'country quarters,'–a plentiful wardrobe—the ability to exercise hospitality," while an additional one thousand would have enabled him to live like a truly rich man. In view of the prices of other representative goods and services, one understands better why as late as 1852 an informant could advise Carl Schurz that in New York City $150,000 was considered a fortune.[26]

In view of these figures, it is disconcerting to discover that according to the changing wholesale and consumer price indexes from that time to this, the earlier dollar was worth no more than from five to six and one-half times the dollar of 1970.[27] A house comparable to Dodge's today would rent for between 25 and 40 times what he paid. Living and dining at the equivalent of the Astor House, with a menu of like splendor, would cost from 25 to 40 times as much as it did 130 years ago. The good life described by Charles Astor Bristed and Sidney George Fisher would appear to be at least 10 and probably more times as expensive today as then. A changing price index, therefore, is something less than infallible evidence at best, particularly for determining the comparative costs of goods and services consumed, not by the general population but by a particular segment of that population—in this case a small and unrepresentative segment, the wealthy. Yet, even if one accepts the relatively modest devaluation of the dollar pointed to by the changing price indexes, it is clear that the worth of a wealthy person was many times its modern equivalent.

In addition, not one penny was turned over by rich men to a state or federal tax bureau that in our own era may appropriate substantial portions of their wealth. The local tax was minuscule, accounting for perhaps one-tenth of 1 per cent of the wealth of the rich. When the notorious underassessments of the wealth of the rich are taken into account, their probable wealth is still further enhanced.

The value of the estates left by such great Boston accumulators as Gardiner Greene, Peter Chardon Brooks, Thomas Handasyd Perkins, John Parker, and Elias Hasket Derby, was in each case more than six times their assessed worth. The merchant David Sears—who inherited close to $1 million from his father in 1816, married into great wealth, and thrived in commerce and diverse investments over the next generation—was assessed at less than three-quarters of a million dollars at the height of his career; the millionaire several times over, John P. Cushing, was typically assessed for slightly more than $100,000 for any year during the period. In the early 1840s, the wealthy Brooklynite of old family, Henry Boerum, was assessed at a ridiculously low figure—no higher than his annual salary. His neighbor, John Leake, was assessed for less than one-tenth the value of his inheritance. Such wealthy stockholders and eminences as Henry C. Murphy and Henry Evelyn Pierrepont—the latter the son of Brooklyn's richest landowner—were each assessed at roughly $10,000. Evidence on the actual value of only portions of the real property owned by certain New Yorkers strikingly exposes the great disparity between the real value of their estates and the assessors' excessively modest appraisals.

Joel Post, whose properties in downtown New York City alone realized over three-quarters of a million dollars in the 1830s, was assessed for a total wealth of one-quarter that sum. The ratio of the actual value of John Delafield's city real estate to his total assessed wealth was more than six to one. William W. Gilbert sold a fraction of his New York City properties in the early 1830s for a sum three times that of his total assessment. As for the wealthy Henry A. Coster, he left one of his daughters an estate almost ten times the value of the assessment made of his *entire* fortune just prior to his death. Assessed for $85,200 worth of real and personal property in 1828, Henry Rutgers left real estate worth more than $900,000 on his death in 1830. Other New Yorkers whose actual wealth in 1830 dwarfed their modest assessments at least tenfold were the Haight brothers, Robert J. Watts, Ann Rogers, and Peter P. Goelet. The disparities between actual and assessed fortunes continued over the next two decades. Abraham G. Thompson left 15 times as much to charity in 1851 as he had supposedly been worth. Thomas W. Ludlow, owner of valuable properties inside and outside the city, in 1845 threw a party in his upstate villa that cost several thousand dollars more than his assessed wealth for that year! At a time when he was the only New Yorker with a private coachman and footman in livery, Andrew G. Hamersley was assessed for slightly more than $15,000.

Others whose actual worth was barely hinted at in the assessors' records were Henry Brevoort, James Roosevelt, Rufus King, Samuel Leggett, Jordan L. Mott, John Mason, John Rathbone, Jr., Jonathan I. Coddington, William B. Crosby—who, as the beneficiary of almost all of Rutgers' great estate, owned nearly all of the seventh ward but was nevertheless assessed at less than $100,000 in 1845—James A. Hamilton, J. Prescott Hall, John Johnston, and the great diarist—Philip Hone.[28]

The Actual Value of Assessed Wealth

If the assessments offer no more than a modest clue to the total wealth of individuals, contemporary appraisals of the assessments by informed insiders and municipal officials make it possible to construct a formula that transforms assessed values into actual. It goes without saying that no such formula will be foolproof, nor is it likely to apply perfectly to any one individual. When based on reliable evidence, however, a sensible formula has much to recommend it, particularly when compared with the undocumented guesses of wealth that were made by contemporary publicists.

A credible formula must be a conservative formula. The fact that so reputedly wealthy a man as August Belmont—the American agent of the House of Rothschild—was in 1845 assessed for only $25,000 of real estate and for nothing in personal property; or that the successful if uniquely named Preserved Fish had corporate directorships which belied the even lower assessment made of his wealth, tempt one to think in terms of a factor in double figures for converting assessed wealth into actual. A contemporary comptroller's report, hardly an extremist source, had noted that it was above all men of "extensive capital" whose wealth was drastically underassessed; the personal estates of many of them were rated at less than 10 per cent of their real worth. The fact is that for hundreds of New Yorkers who had substantial real estate in 1828 and 1845, and who—like Belmont—were assessed for no personal property whatever, or for the hundreds of others assessed for a few thousand dollars each, the ratio of one to ten appears to be excessively modest. Nevertheless, I would recommend that for most rich men multiplying assessed wealth by six offers a useful estimate of total wealth.

The ratio of one to six for assessed to actual value of property treats real-estate assessments as representing one-third of the actual value of a wealthy person's real estate within and *outside* the city. (New York City officials had estimated that local real estate was evaluated at, roughly, from one-fifth of value to a high, rarely achieved, of three-fifths.) The ratio further treats the personal property of the wealthy as roughly equal in value to their real property, in accord with the judgment of informed contemporary analysts. It should be kept in mind that the latter estimates omitted consideration of the significant fact that slightly

Fashionable New Yorkers at the Park Theatre. Included in the audience in November 1822 were many members of the city's elite. (*Watercolor by John Searles courtesy of the New-York Historical Society.*)

1 Nicholas G. Rutgers
2 William H. Robinson
3 Charles G. Smedburg
4 Robert G. L. De Peyster
5 Alexander Hosack
6 Dr. John Neilson
7 Dr. John W. Francis
8 Castle Rotto
9 Thomas Bibby
10 John I. Boyd
11 Joseph Fowler
12 Francis Barretto
13 Gouverneur S. Bibby
14 Thomas W. C. Moore
15 James Allport
16 Walter Livingston
17 Dr. John Watts
18 James Farquhar
19 James Mackey
20 Henry N. Cruger
21 John Lang
22 William Bell
23 Mordecai M. Noah
24 Hugh Maxwell
25 William H. Maxwell
26 James Seaton
27 Thomas F. Livingston
28 Andrew Drew
29 William Wilkes
30 Charles Farquhar
31 Pierre C. Van Wyck
32 John Searles
33 John Berry
34 Robert Gillespie
35 Edmund Wilkes
36 Hamilton Wilkes
37 Captain Hill
38 Robert Watts
39 George Gillingham
40 Charles Mathews
41 Miss Ellen A. Johnson
42 Mrs. Gelston, *née* Jones
43 Maltby Gelston
44 Mrs. De Witt Clinton, *née* Jones
45 Mrs. Newbold, *née* LeRoy
46 William Bayard, Jr.
47 Miss Ogden
48 Duncan P. Campbell
49 Jacob H. LeRoy
50 Mrs. Daniel Webster
51 William Bayard
52 Dr. Samuel L. Mitchill
53 Mrs. S. L. Mitchill
54 Mrs. James Fairlie
55 Dr. David Hosack
56 James Watson
57 Dr. Hugh McLean
58 John Charnaud
59 Miss Wilkes
60 Mrs. C. D. Colden, *née* Wilkes
61 Mrs. Robert Lenox
62 David S. Kennedy
63 John K. Beekman
64 Robert Lenox
65 Cadwallader D. Colden
66 Swift Livingston
67 Henry Brevoort
68 James W. Gerard
69 James K. Paulding
70 Henry Carey
71 Edward Price
72 Stephen Price
73 Capt. John B. Nicholson
74 Thomas Parsons
75 Herman Le Roy, Jr.
76 William Le Roy
77 Herman Le Roy
78 Mrs. Eliza Talbot
79 Alexander C. Hosack
80 Robert Dyson
81 Mrs. Samuel Jones
82 Judge Samuel Jones
83 Dr. James Pendleton
84 Mrs. Pendleton, *née* Jones

more than 40 per cent of New York City's total assessed *personal* wealth (and an even greater proportion for Brooklyn) was attributed by the assessors to banks, insurance companies, and to other corporations, rather than to individuals. Evidence discussed in the following chapter indicates that the few hundred wealthiest taxpayers in the cities held much of this corporate wealth, which is, in effect, totally masked by the assessment data. In other words, even skeptics who were convinced that personal wealth was egregiously undervalued by assessors, were themselves unaware how badly it was underestimated. Wealthy persons who were assessed for great personal wealth obviously are not covered by the one to six ratio. The latter were rare, however, and do not appear to impair the general usefulness of the suggested formula.

Some Wealthy Individuals

When assessed wealth is thus converted into actual, New York City alone emerges with 113 individuals each worth $1 million or more. This estimate excludes *families*—such as the Schieffelins, Storms, Treadwells, Nevinses, Mildebergers, Mesiers, Kingslands, Lawrences, Duboises, Crugers, Tuckers, Halsteads, Aymars, Beekmans, Bogerts, and Haights—the combined wealth of whose adult members came in each case to $1 million or more. In 1845, when John Jacob Astor's assessed wealth came to $3,074,705, there is good reason to think that he was worth about six times that sum.[29] From a Philip Hone notation that "Mr. Astor once remarked that riches did not bring happiness, a man may be as happy with half a million as if he was rich," one can decide for himself how many times half a million the author of that remark was worth.[30] Astor's fortune placed him on the same financial plateau as Nathan Mayer Rothschild, the redoubtable banker who was widely regarded as the wealthiest man in Europe in the 1840s. Other New York City millionaires were the great merchant's son William B. Astor, Peter Goelet, James Gore King, James Lenox, Peter Lorillard and Peter Lorillard, Jr., Peter G. Stuyvesant, and Stephen Whitney—each of whom was worth about $5 million. The great banking house of Brown Brothers, which had offices in New York City, Baltimore, and Philadelphia—under James Brown, his father Alexander, and his brother John A. Brown, respectively—was one of the greatest international banks, worth at least $6 million.[31]

The will of Stephen Girard, the Philadelphia merchant and banker, disclosed that he was worth at least $6 million at his death, while Jacob Ridgway and Thomas Willing of that city were each worth about half that sum. In Boston, Peter Brooks, the Appleton brothers and the Lawrence brothers each commanded wealth on the same order of magnitude as Ridgway's, with John Bryant, the Parker brothers, Thomas H. Perkins, Jonathan Phillips, David Sears, Robert G. Shaw, Israel Thorndike, the

Welles brothers, the Williams brothers, and John P. Cushing not far if at all behind. Hezekiah Beers Pierrepont, the very successful distiller and land accumulator of Brooklyn, also held property whose value was probably very close to $5 million.

Even before the end of the eighteenth century, Thomas Willing, the Philadelphia financier, and William Bingham of that city, had each accumulated millions.[32] By the 1830s, hundreds of families in the nation's northeastern cities had amassed great fortunes based on commerce, insurance, finance, shipbuilding, manufactures, landholding, real-estate speculation, and the professions. The resources and the style of living enjoyed by the Rhinelanders, Masons, Hendrickses, Beekmans, Lenoxes, Joneses, and Gouverneurs in New York City; the Bownes, Bergens, Howlands, Leffertses, Cortelyous, Trotters, and Hickses in Brooklyn; the Brimmers, Codmans, Cushings, Parkmans, Phillipses, Quincys, Greenes, Derbys, Otises, Searses, Shaws, Welleses, and Williamses in Boston; and the Becks, Copes, Cadwaladers, McKeans, Walns, Shippens, Biddles, Whartons, Wetherills, and Willings in Philadelphia—not to mention the great families of the antebellum South—were very far from scanty and would have been regarded as substantial wealth anywhere in the world.

The wealth of the American rich, unlike that of the contemporary English aristocracy, derived largely from commerce; and when from land, it often took the form of properties relatively recently accumulated, rather than estates held in the family for centuries, as was the case with the Bedfords, Northumberlands, and Devonshires overseas.[33] The American rich were a working class, however, only in a technical rather than an actual sense. The preference shown by many of them for attending to business rather than to entertainment and leisure was a matter of taste rather than necessity and can be compared to the preoccupation shown by some peers with the details of managing their estates. By almost any criterion, opulent Americans lived lives comparable to those enjoyed by their English and continental counterparts and may have been able to do so with significantly smaller expenditures of money.[34]

Lifestyles of the Antebellum Rich

The town houses of David Sears, Nathaniel Prime, William B. Astor, William Bedlow Crosby, Peter Schermerhorn, Samuel Ward, Harrison Gray Otis, or Henry Brevoort would have been adjudged magnificent anywhere. If the lavish country residences of David Hosack, John C. Stevens, or James Gore King did not match the awesome size and cost of the Duke of Northumberland's Alnwick Castle, neither did the mansions and estates of Northumberland's fellow aristocrats in England. Corps of servants, impressive libraries, elaborate furniture (often manufactured by Duncan Phyfe), sumptuous furnishings, stores of the finest wines, and expensive artworks filled the interiors of the houses of the

American economic elite. In the warm weather months, the rich retreated to the delights of the Rockaways and other ocean resorts, or to the waters of Saratoga; they regularly traveled to Havre in ships filled with their own kind, blessed with lavish accommodations, and in Hone's words, with "every day as good a table as the most fastidious gastronome could desire." Their lives at home during the workaday year were enlivened by a constant round of expensive parties, dazzling balls, extravagant fêtes and excursions, binding more closely together the leading families both within and among the great cities. The birthday of the beautiful Elizabeth Willing in 1835 was celebrated on Long Island with a trotting match (won by Robert Goelet), a "splendid ball," and a cotillion. On a sparkling fall day later that year "in the beautiful Bay of Boston," a fishing party was held aboard a pleasure schooner that had once belonged to David Hosack and Robert Hone, among others. New York City's swells joined with the Brookses, Forbeses, Sturgises, and Bryants in sampling chowder and enjoying great quantities of champagne and fine madeira, to compensate for the mere handful of cod and haddock they caught.

A fashionable marriage, such as the one uniting Charles A. Heckscher and the daughter of John G. Coster in late 1834, triggered off a round of balls and parties that left even inveterate pleasure seekers somewhat exhausted and a trifle dismayed at their extravagance. The great ball given by Henry Brevoort on February 28, 1840, excited widespread attention for its opulence; but much space in Hone's more than 10,000 pages is given over to descriptions of many dozens of smaller-scale but equally exclusive and splendid affairs. A "fête champêtre" of unusual elegance, such as that held at Thomas W. Ludlow's villa on the Hudson, in Phillipsburgh near Yonkers, on June 26, 1845, could attract several hundred of the leading "judges, lawyers, merchants, men of leisure and millionaires" of New York City. The occasion provided a "picnic" adorned with "every delicacy," fine band music for outdoors, and waltzes, polkas, and cotillions within the house. The entire scene was enlivened by the presence of several private yachts, which circled the steamer hired by Ludlow to carry his guests to and from the festivities. Theatre, Italian opera, soirées, and elaborate musical evenings also occupied the elite. Although fastidious foreign visitors delighted in mocking the pretentiousness of the American urban elite's high life, there could be no denying its expensiveness.

American as Compared to European Wealth

Those who referred to the paltriness of American fortunes doubtless had European wealth in mind. Aware that European fortunes were far older than American, many contemporaries concluded that the former were much larger as well. Paradoxically, some of the greatest European fortunes, such as those accumulated by the Rothschilds, the Baring

Brothers in England, or the great French financier of the Napoleonic and post-Napoleonic era, Gabriel Julien Ouvrard, were of relatively recent origin. But whether old or new, the wealth of the Old World, where an obvious inequality of condition paralleled an inequality of status that had diminished little since the Middle Ages, was assumed to dwarf the *parvenu* fortunes amassed by rich Americans.

Unfortunately the wealth of the great European accumulators has not been and probably cannot be fixed with precision. For Old World riches as for New, informed estimates rather than precise sums have been offered by scholars. The estate of Nathan Mayer Rothschild, regarded as the wealthiest member of the great family and the richest man in Europe, "was generally assumed to be between £5,000,000 and £6,000,000,"—or roughly between $21,100,000 and $25,700,000—at the time of his death in 1836. Ouvrard, who alone in France dared think of rivaling the Rothschilds as an international financier, could in 1820 "offer a prospective son-in-law a dowry of a million francs." At a high point in Ouvrard's career, his worth has been estimated at slightly more than $5 million.[35]

The Duke of Bedford's great estates in 1839 were worth about $10 million, to judge from his indebtedness of £551,940, an annual net remittance for the preceding seven years of slightly more than £100,000, and the small rate of profits typically earned on his landed property during the period. Only a handful of the three hundred or so families constituting England's landed aristocracy could approximate such wealth; a few others, such as the Earl of Clarendon, were worth closer to $375,000. Sir Francis Baring—whose fortune may have been matched or exceeded in England in the entire nineteenth century by Queen Victoria, Sir Robert Peel, the dukes of Bedford, Northumberland, Bridgewater, Westminster, and Devonshire, and hardly any others—has been judged to have been worth slightly less than $5 million during the period. His son Alexander had real-estate investments worth close to that sum. Lord Overstone, described by a modern authority as the chief figure of Britain's "new commercial aristocracy," had a fortune that at its height, decades after Tocqueville's visit to the United States, has been estimated at about $17 million.[36]

While these were vast fortunes indeed, they appear to have been approximated by those of the wealthiest Americans. John Jacob Astor's wealth was close to Rothschild's. Dozens of American families commanded riches similar to what has been attributed to Ouvrard and the Barings. For that matter, Alexander Baring's fortune had been substantially abetted both by his marriage to the American William Bingham's eldest daughter and by his purchase of Bingham's vast Maine properties. European landed wealth was, of course, much older than American, a fact that led contemporaries to question the extent as well as the vulgarity of Yankee wealth. Herman Thorn, a fashionable New Yorker who, in marrying the niece of William Jauncey had also come into much of the latter's fortune, stayed in Paris during the 1830s. Thorn was said to have "lived in a style of princely splendor that eclipsed all rivalry, to the great astonishment of the French, who failed to comprehend where in America he had acquired such funds." In 1836 he was reported "to have spent $8,000 on a single fancy dress ball in his Paris home [actually, a splendid palace]." According to Philip Hone, his friend Thorn talked "about hundreds of thousands with the air of a man who has been born and brought up in the midst of gold, silver and precious stones." [37] Yet although Thorn was a rich man, there were close to one hundred families in New York City alone whose assessed wealth surpassed his.

The logic of the egalitarian thesis—denying as it does the existence of great extremes of either wealth or poverty here—and what a well-known historian calls the unostentatious style of the American rich and their tendency at all times to "play down their wealth" [38] evidently blinded even the most brilliant contemporary observers to the reality lurking beneath the surface of American life. The notion that antebellum America lacked substantial fortunes is not borne out by the evidence, primarily, as will be noted, because of its faulty assumption concerning the alleged distribution of "resources to all the members of the community."

Notes

[1] Marcus Cunliffe, *The Nation Takes Shape, 1789–1837* (Chicago, 1965), p. 169.
[2] See Ralph Hidy, *The House of Baring in American Trade and Finance: English Merchant Bankers at Work, 1763–1861* (Cambridge, Mass., 1949), pp. 40, 46; Kenneth W. Porter, *John Jacob Astor, Business Man* (Cambridge, Mass., 1931), vol. II, p. 939n.; and Philip L. White, *The Beekmans of New York in Politics and Commerce, 1647–1877* (New York, 1956), p. 214.
[3] Letter from Peter N. Stearns to the author. Mr. Stearns is the author of *European Society in Upheaval: Social History Since 1800* (New York, 1967).
[4] Pitirim A. Sorokin, "American Millionaires and Multimillionaires: A Comparative Statistical Study," *Journal of Social Forces, III* (1925), p. 627. Sorokin's method for determining millionaires, particularly for the nineteenth century, relied heavily on surmise. Robert E. Gallman has recently estimated that there were sixty "millionaire families in the United States in 1840," but unfortunately his estimate is based on undocumented contemporary listings of wealthy citizens. Gallman, "Trends in the Nineteenth Century: Some Speculations," in Leo Soltow, ed., *Six Papers on the Size Distribution of Wealth and Income* (New York, 1969), p. 15.
[5] Published under a variety of labels in its first years, the title of the 6th edition, *Wealth and Biography of the Wealthy Citizens of New York City* (New York, 1845), was with very slight variations the title thereafter used. (See Appendix B.)
[6] Titles include John Lomas and Alfred S. Peace, *The Wealthy Men and Women of Brooklyn and Williamsburgh* (Brooklyn, 1847); "A Member of the Philadelphia Bar," *Wealth and Biography of the Wealthy Citizens of Philadelphia* (Philadelphia, 1845); "A Merchant of Philadelphia," *Memoirs and Auto-Biography of Some of the Wealthy Citizens of Philadelphia [with a Fair Estimate of their Estates—Founded upon a*

Knowledge of Facts] (Philadelphia, 1846); *"Our First Men:" A Calendar of Wealth, Fashion and Gentility [Containing a List of Those Persons Taxed in the City of Boston, Creditably Reported to be Worth $100,000; with Biographical Notices of the Principal Persons]* (Boston, 1846), Thomas L. V. Wilson, *The Aristocracy of Boston* (Boston, 1848); A. Forbes and J. W. Green, *The Rich Men of Massachusetts* (Boston, 1852); and William Armstrong, *The Aristocracy of New York: Who They Are and What They Were* (New York, 1848).

7 According to an editorial in the *Sunday Times*, January 30, 1848, New York City's citizens "manifest much curiosity about [John Jacob Astor's] wealth, and are looking anxiously for the time when they may know its aggregate sum and the manner of its disposal." Cited in Jerome Mushkat, "Epitaph, by Mordecai Noah," *New-York Historical Society Quarterly, LV* (July 1971), p. 257.

8 See Appendix B for a critical discussion of Beach's pamphlets.

9 Frank Otto Gatell, "Money and Party in Jacksonian America: A Quantitative Look at New York City's Men of Quality," *Political Science Quarterly, LXXXII* (June 1967), pp. 238, 240, 241.

10 Wills, while useful, disclose only what a man was worth at his death—if they do even that. In many cases, wills affixed no monetary value to the items they listed. See, for example, Leo Hershkowitz, comp., *Wills of Early New York Jews, 1704–1799* (New York 1967); or the will of William Hamersley, in Lawrence Roth, ed., *Colonial Families of America* (New York, 1946), vol. XXV, p. 16.

While probate inventories are invaluable, they, too, are imperfect, typically omitting real property and transfers of property before death, dependent on the ability of particular valuers, and not existing in sufficient numbers to permit a comprehensive comparison of the relative wealth of diverse individuals and wealth-holding groups in a given community. See "Inventory of the Personal Estate of Peter G. Stuyvesant, December 30, 1847," Stuyvesant Papers, New-York Historical Society. For critiques of the weaknesses of the inventories by scholars who have made effective use of the inventories' strengths, see Jackson Turner Main, *The Social Structure of Revolutionary America* (Princeton, 1965), pp. 288–91; Main, "Trends in Wealth Concentration Before 1860," *Journal of Economic History, XXXI* (June, 1971), pp. 445–46; Richard Grassby, "The Personal Wealth of the Business Community in Seventeenth-Century England," *Economic History Review*, 2nd ser., *XXIII* (1970), p. 220; and Alice Hanson Jones, "Wealth Estimates for the American Middle Colonies, 1774," *Economic Development and Cultural Change, XVIII* (1970), pp. x, 1–172.

11 *List[s] of Persons, Copartnerships, and Corporations Who Were Taxed Twenty Five Dollars and Upwards, in the City of Boston* (Boston, 1832–1850).

12 The New York City assessment books are located in that city's Municipal Archives and Records Center. For a detailed description of how the data were assembled, see Pessen, "The Wealthiest New Yorkers of the Jacksonian Era: A New List," *New-York Historical Society Quarterly, LIV* (April 1970), pp. 145–54. For Brooklyn see Pessen, "A Social and Economic Portrait of Jacksonian Brooklyn: Inequality, Social Immobility, and Class Distinction in the Nation's Seventh City." *New-York Historical Society Quarterly, LV* (Oct. 1971), 321–23.

13 *Memoirs and Auto-Biography of . . . the Wealthy Citizens of Philadelphia.* Guided by the ingenious methodology of Blumin's "Social Mobility in a Nineteenth-Century City," which identified a small number of occupations and residential districts with great wealth, I checked the occupations and residences of the 1,128 individuals listed in this source for accuracy and prestige. Not only was the pamphlet accurate in recording occupations—that is, it was borne out by directories and other evidence—but the occupations were overwhelmingly high-status occupations. Of those listed, 77 per cent were classified as merchants; 11 per cent as lawyers and doctors; 6 per cent as manufacturers; and only 1 per cent as "mechanics"—and some of the latter might well have been entrepreneurs. Compare Main's finding that of Philadelphia's richest hundred in 1765, "more than half . . . were merchants. Nearly one out of five were professional men, mostly lawyers and doctors. . . . Less than one-tenth were artisans or manufacturers." *Social Structure of Revolutionary America*, p. 192.

14 Of the eight hundred wealthy Philadelphians whose residences were located, a majority lived in the wealthly eastern wards whose per capita assessed wealth was more than three times as great as the wealth of most of the other wards in the city.

On the significance of the changing residential pattern, see Willis P. Hazard's revised edition of John F. Watson's *Annals of Philadelphia in the Olden Time* (Philadelphia 1927), vol. III, p. 247, and chap. 9 below. A pattern similar to Philadelphia's existed in Brooklyn: although Brooklyn Heights was clearly the center of fashion and wealth, many wealthy persons continued to inhabit homes put up by their families generations before in what had now become poorer neighborhoods. Another indirect sign of the Philadelphia list's worth is the fact that it contained about 85 per cent of the persons who belonged to the exclusive Philadelphia Club in the mid-1840s.

[15] The Brooklyn elite listing, like the Boston *Calendar of Wealth, Fashion, and Gentility*, appears to have been much more accurate than Beach's compendium. Of the four hundred persons listed in the Boston pamphlet, 85 per cent were among the four hundred most heavily assessed persons in Boston; and most of the Brooklyn estimates were close to the valuations found in the assessors' notebooks, located at the Long Island Historical Society.

[16] The discussion of the value of John Jacob Astor's western real estate and other property in Kenneth W. Porter's authoritative *John Jacob Astor, Business Man*, vol. II, p. 939, illustrates the difficulty, if not impossibility, of fixing a rich man's wealth with precision, in the United States as in Europe; as does Philip L. White, *The Beekmans of New York in Politics and Commerce, 1647–1877* (New York, 1956), p. 214.

[17] See Laurence Stone, *The Crisis of the Aristocracy, 1558–1641* (London, 1965), p. 54.

[18] Lemuel Shattuck, *Report to the Committee of the City Council Appointed to Obtain the Census of Boston for the Year 1845* (Boston, 1846), appendix, p. 59. For discussion of the deficiencies of the Boston assessments, particularly in undervaluing property, see City of Boston, Assessors' Department, *Report of the Committee to Consider and Report Whether any Measures can be adopted that will improve the method of assessing, abating, and Collecting the Taxes of the City*, City Document No. 9 (Boston, 1848), pp. 2–6; and William Minot, Jr., *Taxation in Massachusetts* (Boston, 1877).

[19] New York City Board of Supervisors, "Report of the Special Committee of Supervisors appointed to examine the Assessment Rolls," New York City, Sept. 4, 1829, in City Clerk Filed Papers, Location: 3012; and G. N. Bleecker, Comptroller, "Communication to the Common Council of New York City from the Comptroller on the Subject of the Defective Manner of Assessing Personal Property in this City," City Clerk Filed Papers, Location: 3216, New York City. Municipal Archives and Records Center.

[20] According to a report made by officials appointed to examine the recent history of assessment, New York's valuation of real estate for taxation was typically between 20 and 50 per cent of its real value, in the early decades of the nineteenth century. New York State, *Report of the Tax Commissioners of New York* (New York, 1871), p. 30. See also John Christopher Schwab, *History of the New York City Property Tax: An Introduction to the History of State and Local Finance in New York* (Baltimore, 1890), p. 105; New York City Common Council, *Report of the New York City Comptroller* (New York, 1832); New York City Finance Department, *Communication from the Comptroller for the Year 1842* (New York, 1842); and New York City, Board of Assistant Aldermen, *Report of the Special Committee on the Subject of Equalizing Taxation* (New York, 1846).

[21] See William H. Boyd, compiler, *Boyd's New York City Tax-Book; Being a List of Persons, Corporations and Co-Partnerships, Resident and Non-Resident, Who Were Taxed According to the Assessors' Books, 1856 & '57* (New York, 1857), p. iv. John F. Whitney, introductory remarks, in William A. Darling, comp., *List of Persons, Copartnerships, and Corporations, Who Were Taxed on Seventeen Thousand Five Hundred Dollars and Upwards, in the City of New York in the year 1850* (New York, 1851), pp. iii, iv; Edward Dana Durand, *The Finances of New York City* (New York, 1898), pp. 191, 194; and Schwab, *History of the New York Property Tax*, pp. 73, 105.

[22] Quoted in Charles P. Huse, *The Financial History of Boston* (Cambridge, 1916), p. 39. See also *Report of the Committee to Consider . . . the Taxes of the City*, pp. 14–16, *passim*.

[23] There were, of course, exceptions to this rule. Very wealthy individuals who had recently died left estates that were usually assessed at substantial sums.

[24] Charles Astor Bristed, *The Upper Ten Thousand: Sketches of American Society* (New York, 1852), p. 18. According to Bristed, an upper ten thousand was a great

exaggeration, "for the people so designated are hardly as many hundreds" (p. 271). Bristed was the son of the Rev. John Bristed and of John Jacob Astor's daughter, Magdalen, and the husband of Laura Brevoort. His wife's father, Henry Brevoort, was one of the richest men in New York City.

[25] Abram C. Dayton, *Last Days of Knickerbocker Life in New York* (New York, 1871), p. 97; William E. Dodge, *Old New York: A Lecture (New York, 1880)*, p. 17. To compare the cost of living for a Western merchant, see Daniel Aaron, "Cincinnati, 1818–1838: A Study of Attitudes in the Urban West" (Ph.D. dissertation, Harvard University, 1942), p. 67.

[26] Hone Diary, 13:249; mid-century Philadelphian cited in Elizabeth M. Geffen, "Joseph Sill and His Diary," *Pa. Mag., 94* (1970), p. 303; Diary of Sidney George Fisher, Jan. 17, 1842; R. G. Albion, *The Rise of New York Port, 1815–1850* (New York, 1939), p. 258.

[27] It is impossible to make an exact comparison of the value of the dollar in the 1840s and 1970s. It was possible, however, to work out a rough comparison by using reliable, mainly federal, data on changing wholesale and consumer price indexes that trace the changing value of the dollar. My estimate that the 1840 dollar was worth $6.50 in 1970 is based on Arthur Harrison Cole, *Wholesale Commodity Prices in the United States, 1700–1861* (Cambridge, Mass., 1938); Horace G. Wadlin, Chief of U.S. Bureau of Statistics, *Comparative Wages and Prices, 1860–1897* (Boston, 1898); U.S. Department of Labor, Bureau of Labor Statistics, *Index Numbers of Wholesale Prices on Pre-War Base, 1890 to 1927* (Washington, 1928); Robert A. Sayre, National Industrial Conference Board, *Consumers' Prices 1914–1948* (New York, 1948); U.S. Senate, Joint Economic Committee Report, with U.S. Department of Labor, Bureau of Labor Statistics, *Frequency of Changes in Wholesale Prices: A Study of Price Flexibility;* and information on 1956-1970 furnished me by the U.S. Department of Labor, Bureau of Labor Statistics. Using different data, Alice Hanson Jones has worked out a devaluation from 1774 to 1967, in which a later dollar is worth one-sixth the earlier. "Wealth Estimates for the American Middle Colonies," 127–29. She advises me that in the judgment of the authoritative Jack E. Triplett, neither estimate is right or wrong; different data yield different conclusions; perfection is out of the question in price estimates. See Jack E. Triplett, "Quality Bias in Price Indexes and New Methods of Quality Measurement," in Zvi Griliches, ed., *Price Indexes and Quality Changes,* scheduled for publication in 1971. It is consoling that in Mrs. Jones' judgment the difference between her skilled estimate and my rough effort is not significant. The changing price index undoubtedly underestimates the devaluation that has occurred in the "rich man's dollar." Mrs. Jones, who was formerly with the Department of Labor, informs me that the CPI "is the price of a 'market basket' of goods and services commonly purchased by *wage earners and clerical workers.*" (My italics.)

[28] Much of the above information was drawn from Hone's diary. He regularly listed the sums realized by wealthy acquaintances in the sale of real estate, describing in meticulous detail the boundaries of the properties sold.

[29] The leading student of Astor's finances, Kenneth W. Porter, is skeptical of Astor's claim that his real estate in 1846 was worth only $5,184,340. Porter notes that seven years earlier the great merchant conceded that his real property was worth $5,445,525; subsequently he had amassed more property, while the value of his older properties appreciated. *John Jacob Astor, Business Man,* vol. II, pp. 939, 951–952.

[30] Hone Diary, Jan. 4, 1845, XXII:356.

[31] The Philadelphia "wealthy citizens" list estimated John A. Brown's wealth at a modest $500,000. See the letter of an officer of the firm to the governor of the Bank of England, cited in John Crosby Brown, *A Hundred Years of Merchant Banking: A History of Brown Brothers and Company* (New York, 1909), p. 83.

[32] Burton Alva Konkle, *Thomas Willing and the First American Financial System* (New York, 1937), pp. 120–21; and Robert C. Alberts, *The Golden Voyage: The Life and Times of William Bingham,* 1752–1804 (Boston, 1969), pp. ix, 429.

[33] My view of English landed wealth is derived mainly from F. M. L. Thompson, *English Landed Society in the Nineteenth Century* (London, 1963); David Spring, *The English Landed Estate in the Nineteenth Century: Its Administration* (Baltimore, 1963); and from conversations in which Mr. Spring was kind enough to give me the

benefit of his unsurpassed knowledge of the Bedfords and other English landed families.

[34] The $10,000 per annum said by William B. Astor's nephew to be required for lavish living was evidently from one-third to one-quarter the amount needed to achieve a similar standard abroad. F. M. L. Thompson indicates that in England an annual expenditure of roughly £10,000, or slightly more than $43,000, enabled the fewer than 500 people capable of making it to live like the aristocratic lords many of them, in fact were. *English Landed Society*, pp. 25–26.

[35] David Landes has advised me that it is impossible to determine precisely what Nathan Rothschild was worth, in view of the tangled nature of the great family's finances and the difficulties posed by his will. Bertrand Gille's authoritative *Histoire de la Maison Rothschild, des Origines à 1848* (Geneva, 1965) and *Histoire de la Maison Rothschild, 1848–1870* (Geneva, 1967) focus on the family's corporate assets rather than the personal wealth of its members. For an informed estimate, see Cecil Roth, *The Magnificent Rothschilds* (London, 1939), pp. 25–26. In arriving at the dollar value of the pound for the period I have followed Ralph Hidy's estimate: "calculating the dollar at 4 shillings and 8 pence." "The House of Baring and the Second Bank of the United States, 1826–1836," *Pennsylvania Magazine of History and Biography, LXVIII* (1944), p. 270. The estimate of Ouvrard's wealth in dollars is drawn from Arthur-Lévy, *Un Grand Profiteur de Guerre: Gabriel Julien Ouvrard, 1770–1846* (Paris, 1929), p. 1, and from Otto Wolff's judgment that "during most of Ouvrard's lifetime the rate of exchange was twenty-five francs to the pound." Wolff, *Ouvrard, Speculator of Genius, 1770–1846* (London, 1962), pp. xiv, 148, 187.

[36] Spring, *English Landed Estate*, pp. 35, 41; Thompson, *English Landed Society*, p. 25. Mr. Spring has suggested that multiplying the landed income of the great aristocrats by 30 and then subtracting their indebtedness yields a useful, if rough, approximation of their worth. Thompson uses a similar calculus. Hidy, *House of Baring*, pp. 40, 46; Thompson, *English Landed Society*, p. 39. Overstone had spent £1,670,000 in the purchase of estates, and by his death in 1883 he left £2,118,804 in stocks, shares, and other forms of personal property.

William D. Rubinstein has recently argued that Great Britain had a far greater number of rich men than is suggested here. The evidence he cites, however, is drawn primarily from the late nineteenth century, by which time there had been a great increase in the number of American millionaires and the size of their fortunes. See the exchange between Rubinstein and Pessen in *American Historical Review, 77* (April 1972), pp. 609–612.

[37] Hone Diary, X:76; and *New York Genealogical and Biographical Record, XCI* (1960), p. 91.

[38] Letter from Henry Steele Commager to the author, Jan. 1, 1972.

3

The Distribution of Wealth in the "Age of Egalitarianism"

> Among the novel objects that attracted my attention during my stay in the United States, nothing struck me more forcibly than the general equality of condition among the people.
>
> Tocqueville, *Democracy in America*, vol. I, p. 3

From Tocqueville's time to our own, antebellum America has enjoyed the reputation of being a society marked by an unprecedented economic equality. No one, not even the most inveterate yeasayer, believed that material goods and services were distributed perfectly equally. Blacks and Indians, and the masses of new Irish immigrants obviously were not in on the feast. But it has been widely believed that the cornucopia was almost equally available to all others. Even a modern scholar who has asserted that heavy immigration and industrialization widened the economic gulf between the classes after 1830, concedes that earlier, "there did not appear to be any contradiction between the notion of equality of opportunity and a general equality of condition." [1] A few contemporaries, such as the wealthy philanthropist Mathew Carey, and the radical labor spokesman Seth Luther, dissented from the consensus and attempted to expose the plight of the "laboring poor." [2] Several modern scholarly studies have also questioned, if indirectly, the extent of equality by focusing on the existence of large pockets of poverty, particularly in urban milieus.[3]

The facts that, as reported by the Boston Prison Discipline Society in 1829, 75,000 persons were annually imprisoned for debt in the United States—more than half of them owing less than twenty-five dollars—or that hundreds of private charitable associations sprang up in cities during the period to supplement the work of municipal governments in dealing with poverty, are clear signs that material deprivation afflicted many persons.[4] Congressional reports on debt and debtors, stories in the labor press, and the observations of sympathetic contemporaries, reveal a pattern of want that obviously detracts from the era's reputation for equality. But, if these sources indicate that inequality prevailed in the early nineteenth century, they are not at all precise as to the extent of the inequality. In this chapter, therefore, I shall attempt to work out an estimate that is both more exact and more comprehensive than the impressions yielded by partial and random examinations.[5]

Since the rankings of wealth created from the assessment figures indicate what almost every urbanite was worth during the era, it was possible to determine the distribution of wealth in the great northeastern cities. The fact that other scholars have performed similar quantitative studies for earlier periods, and that relevant evidence exists for the Civil War years and later, enables us to compare the degree of equality in the "age of egalitarianism" with that of other eras in American history.

During the colonial era, wealth had become more unequally distributed with each passing year. This, at least, is the burden of the recent studies of scattered towns and villages. In Chester County, Pennsylvania, the richest 10 per cent of the population owned slightly less than 25 per cent of the wealth in 1693. Over the course of the next century, their share increased to slightly under two-fifths—from 23.8 to 38.3 per cent of the total—at the same time as the proportion owned by the poorest 60 per cent of the population declined from 38.5 to 17.6 per cent.[6] Wealth was even less equally distributed in commercial or seaport towns, and the rate of increasing maldistribution was swifter in such communities. Whereas the wealthiest 5 per cent of property owners in Salem, Massachusetts owned about 20 per cent of its wealth during the quarter century before 1660, by 1681 their portion had risen to about 50 per cent of the wealth of the prospering town's total.[7] In colonial Boston, the wealthiest 1 per cent of the population owned about 10 per cent, the richest 5 per cent about 25 per cent, and the upper 15 per cent about 50 per cent of the city's real and personal estate in 1687. By 1771 the wealthiest 3 per cent of Boston's population held slightly more than 34 per cent of the city's wealth, while the upper 10 per cent owned about 55 per cent of the property of a Boston community that had become "more stratified and unequal." Inequality worsened in Boston during the years of the Revolution, as the share owned by the rich increased, while "the proportion of wealth held by the poor and middling classes declined." [8] More broad-gauged studies found that the richest tenth owned about 40 per cent of the net wealth in the middle colonies of New York, New Jersey, and Pennsylvania on the eve of the Revolution; while in the northeast as a whole the upper tenth owned about 45 per cent of the wealth by the Revolutionary era.[9] Was the inegalitarian trend reversed during the early nineteenth century?

The tax-assessment lists created for New York City, Brooklyn, and Boston make possible a fairly precise answer to this question. I arrived at the distribution of wealth by the following process. The total assessed wealth of the city—corporate and non-corporate—was determined for a given year. Taxpayers were grouped according to the level of their wealth. The total assessed wealth of all members of a given category was then added up to determine the percentage of the city's non-corporate wealth owned by that category. (The significance of the distinction between corporate and non-corporate wealth in this context is discussed below.) In determining the percentage of the city's population represented by the persons in a given wealth category, the denominator used was the number of families in the city, rather than the total population. Not to have done so would have suggested a far more drastic inequality than was actually the case, as it would have converted rich men's wives, children, and other dependents into so many "propertyless" individuals. In view of the fact that some wealthy persons did not have dependents, my methodology exaggerates, if slightly, the extent of equality. Risk for risk, the latter distortion strikes me as more acceptable than exaggerating the degree of inequality.[10] Any procedure is at best doomed to imperfection.

New York City

A contemporary yeasayer wrote that in Jacksonian New York City, "wealth [was] universally diffused." Even the normally optimistic Philip Hone disagreed, noting disconsolately that his beloved New York City late in the era had "arrived at the [unhappy] state of society to be found in the large cities of Europe," in which "the two extremes of costly luxury in living, expensive establishments and improvident waste are presented in daily and hourly contrast with squalid misery and hopeless destitution." [11] The evidence bears out Hone's gloomy assessment. In the year

TABLE 3–1.
The Distribution of Wealth in New York City in 1828

Level of Wealth	*Percentage of Population*	*Approximate Total Non-Corp. Wealth**	*Percentage of Non-Corp. Wealth*
$35,000 or more	1	$25,517,000	29
$7,500 to $35,000	3	$17,520,000	20

*The figures used here for the city's total non-corporate wealth are slightly lower than those given in Thomas F. Gordon's *Gazetteer of the State of New York* (New York, 1836) because I have excluded the assessments on partnerships.

of Andrew Jackson's first election to the presidency, the wealthiest 4 per cent of the population, in owning almost half the wealth, possessed a larger proportion of New York City's wealth than the richest 10 per cent had evidently owned in the urban northeast as a whole half a century earlier. By 1845 the disparities had sharply increased.

To judge from the New York City evidence, the rate or tempo by which the rich got proportionately richer evidently became much more rapid during the nineteenth century than it had been during the seventeenth or eighteenth. As for the city's inequality in 1828 and 1845, its full extent is only hinted at in the assessment figures for these years.

TABLE 3–2.
The Distribution of Wealth in New York City in 1845

Level of Wealth	*Percentage of Population*	*Approximate Total Non-Corp. Wealth*	*Percentage of Non-Corp. Wealth*
$55,000 or more	1	$85,804,000	40
$20,000 to $55,000	3	$55,000,000	26

A committee of the Common Council had reported that persons "of very extensive capital" paid taxes on personal property "far less in proportion than those in moderate and low circumstances." In view of the way in which underassessments masked true wealth—above all of the rich—it is clear that the proportion of the city's wealth owned by a small upper crust was even more inordinate than the figures indicate. If, as municipal officials believed, the richest of the rich owned most of the hidden personal wealth, the proportion of the city's total wealth they controlled goes up by a figure dependent on the percentage of the masked wealth that is attributed to them. Hypothesizing that the personal property of the rich equalled the worth of their real estate and that the wealthiest 4 per cent owned about 90 per cent of New York City's unassessed personal property in 1828, the upper 1 per cent would have owned about 35 per cent; and the next wealthiest 3 per cent about 22 per cent of all noncorporate wealth. In 1845, by this reckoning, the richest 1 per cent would have owned about 47 per cent, while the next wealthiest 3 per cent would have held an additional 32 per cent of the city's wealth. Nor do these estimates take into account the likelihood that the actual worth of the *real* property owned by the greatest wealth holders was also undervalued. Perhaps the latter distortion can be compensated for or cancelled out by an adjustment that takes into account the ownership of *corporate* wealth.

In 1828 corporations, mainly banks and insurance companies, were assessed for $23,984,660 or 21 per cent of New York City's total assessed wealth of $112,019,533 (exclusive of partnerships). In 1845 they were assessed for about 43 per cent of the city's total assessed *personal* wealth of $70,596,629. It is doubtless impossible to track down the individual owners of corporate wealth. Records, inadequate to begin with, have been lost. How trace the varying quantities of shares held by out-of-towners and foreigners? Yet for all the imprecision attending the attribution of corporate capital, certain conclusions can be drawn that affect significantly estimates of the distribution of wealth.

Poor men, and for that matter the great bulk of the city's population, probably owned either nothing or a minuscule portion of such capital. The minimum cost of a share, typically $50 to $100, priced out such people. As Cadwallader C. Colden and Peter A. Jay had pointed out in behalf of the Bank for Savings in 1823, "a depositor is not a stockholder." [12] Among the chief shareholders were the directors, men required by corporate charters to own varying amounts of stock in their corporations. Preserved Fish testified in the case of *City Fire Insurance Company* vs. *Elisha Bloomer* in 1834; in response to the question as to when he had resigned as director, he answered: "I resigned six months ago. The fact is, rather, that I sold out my stock, which precluded my being a Director after that time." [13] According to an insider, himself an officer in several New York City banks during the era, directors usually "own[ed] in the aggregate a considerable portion of the stock" in their companies. They had been chosen in the first place "for their wealth, commercial experience, and influence in attracting to the institution a good class of dealers." [14] The $10,000 worth of shares owned by Samuel B. Ruggles in the Chemical Bank in 1840 was the minimum share that a director could own. Most of the directors of this bank owned more than that amount; the 15 heaviest subscribers owned more than one half of the shares. Precise information available for a number of contemporary banks and insurance companies discloses that a small number of directors owned almost all the capital in their corporations.[15]

The directors of the corporations regularly listed in the annual New York City directories were almost all the same persons ranked as the wealthiest citizens, constituting a merchant elite who formed a kind of interlocking directorate over the banks and insurance companies of the great city. Among the names appearing again and again as directors of different corporations were A. G. Hamersley, Henry Rutgers, Duncan P. Campbell, Peter A. Jay, Henry Eckford, Philip Hone, Chancellor James Kent, S. B. Ruggles, James and Robert Lenox, John Jacob and William B. Astor, Gerard, Henry and John Beekman, Thomas Addis Emmet, Leonard Bleecker, David Hosack, Peter Schermerhorn, Nathaniel Prime, Peter Goelet, John D. Wolfe, A. T. Stewart, Jacob, George, Peter and Peter Lorillard, Jr., David H. Haight, William A. Crosby, Caleb O. Halsted, James Brown, Henry Brevoort, Rufus L. Lord, John T. Irving, and others who were high on the list of the wealthy.

If one half of corporate capital of 1828 is attributed to outsiders—which is probably overgenerous—and the rest to elite taxpayers, the share of New York City wealth owned by the upper 4 per cent (exclusive of the city's wealth owned by rich non-residents) would be 63 per cent of the actual wealth; the top 1 per cent alone would account for 40 per cent of the total. By 1845, under this formula, the richest 1 per cent of the population owned 50 per cent and the upper 4 per cent slightly more than 80 per cent of the city's actual wealth.[16]

Brooklyn

The evidence for Brooklyn is unusually interesting because it permits a comparison of the degree of equality that obtained in the village of 1810[17]—populated by fewer than 5000 persons—with the bustling city of 1841, whose population of about 41,000 placed Brooklyn seventh among the nation's cities. The richest wealthholders of the early-nineteenth-century village held a slightly larger portion of Brooklyn's wealth than had typically been controlled by the upper tenth in the urban northeast late in the Revolutionary era.

TABLE 3–3.
The Distribution of Wealth in Brooklyn, 1810

Level of Wealth	*Percentage of Population*	*Approximate Total Non-Corp. Wealth*	*Percentage of Non-Corp. Wealth*
$15,000 or more	1	$262,400	22
$4,000 to $15,000	7	$383,122	33
$2,500 to $4,000	6	$137,944	11
$1,000 to $2,500	20	$290,000	25
$500 to $1,000	12	$67,500	6
under $500	54	$30,000	3

Although the poorer half of the population owned only a tiny fraction of Brooklyn's wealth in 1810, the fact that seven out of eight families paid taxes on *some* property, even if slight, suggests that few residents of the community could be classified as propertyless proletarians. Actually, most taxpayers whose occupations could be identified were divided among small shopkeepers, skilled and semi-skilled artisans or "mechanics," and unskilled laborers. By 1841 important changes had occurred.

The distribution of wealth in the commercial Brooklyn of 1841 was strikingly similar to the distribution that obtained in its great neighbor

TABLE 3–4.
The Distribution of Wealth in Brooklyn, 1841

Level of Wealth	*Percentage of Population*	*Approximate Total Non-Corp. Wealth*	*Percentage of Non-Corp. Wealth*
$50,000 or more	1	$10,087,000	42
$15,000 to $50,000	2	$4,000,000	17
$4,500 to $15,000	9	$5,730,000	24
$1,000 to $4,500	15	$2,804,000	12
$100 to $1,000	7	$1,000,000	4
under $100	66	—	—

Comfort Sands House, Brooklyn. Sands was one of the city's leading men. *(Watercolor by William Hindley courtesy of the New-York Historical Society.)*

across the East River. By 1841, the poorest 66 per cent of Brooklyn's population owned less than 1 per cent of its wealth, with only about one out of five families (exclusive of non-resident taxpayers) taxed on any property at all. Corporate wealth had come to be a factor of some significance, accounting for approximately 7 per cent of the total wealth. As in New York City, this type of wealth was evidently monopolized by the elite. Data on the holdings and ownership of the Fulton Ferry, the Brooklyn White Lead Company, the Long Island Bank, and the Brooklyn Fire Insurance Company—firms assessed for about 75 per cent of the city's corporate wealth—indicate that the percentage of assessed wealth owned by the richest 1 per cent was closer to 45 than to 42 per cent.

Approximately one-quarter of Brooklyn's corporate wealth belonged to non-residents not readily identifiable, with the great bulk of the remainder owned by Brooklyn's economic elite. As in New York City, the minimum cost of a share was prohibitive to most taxpayers, while corporate charters stipulated that directors had to own substantial shares. In some cases, "the directors monopolized nearly all the stock." In the 1830s, two men, David Leavitt and Silas Butler, obtained "from the scattered stock holders, 44 out of the 60 shares of stock and the controlling influence in the Fulton Ferry Company." The corporate directors were invariably among the wealthiest taxpayers in Brooklyn. Officers of the Brooklyn Savings Bank were Adrian Van Sinderen, David Stanford, Hosea Webster, H. B. Pierrepont, Adam Treadwell, Robert Bach, Daniel Embury, Samuel Smith, Amasa Wright, James S. Clark, and Adrian Hegeman, rich men all. A similar pattern prevailed for other large corporations during the era.[18] Brooklyn's corporate wealth was owned by the men just cited and by such other eminences as Losee Van Nostrand, Parmenus Johnson, Charles Hoyt, Leffert Lefferts, Jacob Bergen, John C. Vanderveer, Jacob Hicks, Samuel A. Willoughby, Henry C. Murphy, August and John B. Graham (who owned one company outright), Joseph Sprague, and R. V. W. Thorne.

In addition, Brooklyn's wealthiest taxpayers for the most part admitted to no personal wealth whatever. If the personal wealth of the richest 1 per cent is treated as though it equalled in value their real estate—and when the underassessment of the latter form of property is accounted for by working into our estimate an adjustment that presumes ownership of three-fourths of corporate capital by Brooklyn's elite (outsiders owned close to one-quarter)—Brooklyn's richest 1 per cent of wealthholders, like their New York City counterparts, emerge with one half of their city's wealth.

Boston

During the "age of equality," wealth in Boston became more unequally distributed than ever before. On the eve of the Revolution, in

1771, Boston's richest 10 per cent had held slightly more than 50 per cent of the city's wealth. Very little change evidently occurred over the course of the next half century; according to a table of Boston's tax payments for 1820 listed in a local census report, the upper 1 per cent of the population controlled about 16 per cent of the city's wealth, while the richest 10 per cent continued to own the slightly more than 50 per cent it had held in 1771.[19] Significant changes occurred over the following decade, since by 1833 the pattern of distribution had been sharply altered.

TABLE 3–5.
The Distribution of Wealth in Boston, 1833

Level of Wealth	*Percentage of Population*	*Approximate Total Non-Corp. Wealth**	*Percentage of Non-Corp. Wealth*
$75,000 or more	1	$19,439,000	33
$30,000 to $75,000	3	$15,000,000	26
$5,000 to $30,000	10	$16,047,400	27
under $5,000	86	$8,331,000	14

*In 1833 Boston wealth was listed at one half its assessed value. In this table, therefore, the sums have been doubled.

The inegalitarian trend continued during the next 15 years. By 1848, the wealthiest 4 per cent in the population had amassed close to the two-thirds of their city's wealth owned by their New York City counterparts. Perhaps the most striking single change between 1833 and 1848 was the decline in the share of assessed wealth held by Boston's poorest taxpayers. By the later year, the poorest 81 per cent of the population owned less than 5 per cent of the city's assessed wealth. They undoubtedly held an even smaller proportion of its actual wealth.

TABLE 3–6.
The Distribution of Wealth in Boston, 1848

Level of Wealth	*Percentage of Population*	*Approximate Total Non-Corp. Wealth*	*Percentage of Non-Corp. Wealth*
$90,000 or more	1	$47,778,500	37
$35,000 to $90,000	3	$34,781,800	27
$4,000 to $35,000	15	$40,636,400	32
under $4,000	81	$6,000,000	4

In Boston, as elsewhere, a small number of rich men appears to have owned most of the capital of their city's great financial institutions.

A careful check reveals that Boston's wealthiest merchants and businessmen were the officers and directors—and therefore the major shareholders—of the city's fifty largest banks and insurance companies. Daniel Parker, the Appleton brothers, David Sears, Abbot and Amos Lawrence, the Lorings, Patrick T. Jackson, the Welleses, the Thorndikes, Ebenezer Francis, the Grays, the Cushings, the Frothinghams, the Winthrops, the Lymans, the Sigourneys, Robert G. Shaw, John Bryant, Henry Lee, the Shattucks, the Amorys, the Otises, Peter C. Brooks, Francis C. Lowell, the Swetts, the Wiggleworths, the Bradlees, the Pickerings, the Perkinses and others of like wealth comprised Boston's ubiquitous financial directorate.[20]

The disparity between the actual proportion of Boston's wealth owned by the city's elite and the share they owned according to the property assessments, is not as great as were the similar distinctions for New York City and Brooklyn. In Boston, banks and insurance companies were assessed only on their real estate, a relatively small component of the city's wealth. The private individuals who owned corporate wealth were evidently assessed for their holdings. The tax records disclose that, in sharp contrast to New York City and Brooklyn, Boston's taxpayers were assessed for personal property almost equal in value to their real estate. My estimate, however, does not attempt to dispose of the wealth owned by so obvious an elite group as the Fifty Associates. The fact that in Boston as elsewhere the undervaluation of property favored the rich above all—assuring that the actual distribution of wealth was less equal than is indicated by the printed records—suggests that the richest 1 per cent in Boston probably owned more than 40 per cent of the city's wealth in 1848.

Philadelphia

Although the intractability of Philadelphia's tax data preclude a precise estimate of the city's distribution of wealth before mid-nineteenth century, a recent study indicates that on the eve of the Civil War, Philadelphia's wealth was distributed according to a pattern similar to those prevalent in the other great northeastern cities. By 1860 the wealthiest 1 per cent of Philadelphia's population evidently owned 50 per cent, while the lower 80 per cent held only 3 per cent of the city's wealth.[21]

Other Cities

The trend toward increasingly unequal distribution of wealth in the antebellum era was not confined to the great cities of the northeastern seaboard. According to data from the manuscript census of 1850, while only 4 per cent of Pittsburgh's families owned real property evaluated at $10,000 or more, 84 per cent "owned no real property of value." [22] While the pattern of distribution in rural communities and small towns was not as skewed as it was in large urban centers, inequality in the former milieus was dramatic and worsening. In Hamilton, Ontario, "a small commercial lakeport almost entirely lacking in factory industry, with a population just over 14,000," shortly after mid-century, the poorest 80 per cent of the population owned less than 4 per cent of the town's property, in contrast to the richest 10 per cent, who owned almost 90 per cent. As small Massachusetts communities, such as Worcester, became increasingly urbanized, the rich became relatively richer, the numbers of propertyless citizens increased drastically, and "patterns of ownership" became "sharply skewed." [23]

Recent research indicates that on the eve of the Civil War the pattern of maldistribution in a number of southern and western cities was quite similar to the inequality that prevailed in New York City, Brooklyn, and Boston in the 1840s. By 1860 in Baltimore, New Orleans, and St. Louis the richest 1 per cent of the population owned about 40 per cent, the richest 5 per cent better than 67 per cent, and the upper 10 per cent more than 80 per cent of the wealth. An impressionistic recent account of Galveston at mid-century finds that the affluent social and economic elite were one hundred times wealthier than their fellow citizens, the wealth of the former group contrasting "strikingly with that of their nearest neighbors." The division of property was not as unequal in rural counties, southern or western, although even in such areas the distribution has been found to have been skewed to a surprising extent. In cotton counties the wealthiest 5 per cent of landholders held more than 40 per cent of the wealth, while the upper 10 per cent owned almost 60 per cent. (According to Gavin Wright, a close student of rural wealth distribution, the actual degree of inequality was greater than the census data indicate.) While wealth was more equally distributed on the northeastern frontier, even there the upper 10 per cent by 1860 held close to 40 per cent of taxable wealth. In the words of two modern students, propertyholdings on the Michigan frontier became "more concentrated" with the passage of time, while the distribution of wealth "scarcely supports the typical American image of the frontier as the land of promise for the poor, ambitious young man." [24]

During the "age of egalitarianism," wealth became more unequally distributed with each passing season. Shared less equally even at the era's beginning than it had been a generation or two earlier in the aftermath of the Revolution, wealth became concentrated in the hands of an ever-smaller percentage of the population. The trend persisted throughout the 1850s, resulting in wider disparities than ever in New York City during the Civil War.[25] Far from being an age of equality, the antebellum decades featured an inequality that appears to surpass anything experienced by the United States in the twentieth century.[26]

According to Gerhard Lenski, the central question in studying social stratification is: "Who gets what and why?" [27] For the era of Tocqueville the answer to the first part of this question is clear enough. The few at the top got a share of society's material things that was disproportionate at the start and became more so at the era's end. Why they did is of course more difficult to explain.

It may be, as Lenski has argued, that in a free market system "small inequalities tend to generate greater inequalities and great inequalities still greater ones." [28] Even if Lenski's comment is true, it is more descriptive than analytical, while leaving unanswered the question: Why? The long-popular explanation that it was industrialization that pauperized the masses, in the process transforming a relatively egalitarian social order, appears wanting. Vast disparities between urban rich and poor antedated industrialism. Commercial wealth, as surely as industrial, enabled its fortunate inheritors to command a disproportionate share of society's good things and the children of the fortunate to hold a still greater share. A massive internal migration, above all of younger, marginal persons of little standing, into and out of the nation's cities increased both the power and the share of wealth commanded by more substantial and therefore more stable elements.[29] It is hard to disagree with Robert Gallman's generalization that "there were forces at work in the American economy during the nineteenth century that tended to produce greater inequality in the distribution of wealth over time." [30] A not insignificant task of future scholarship will be to ascertain as precisely as possible the nature of these "forces." I would venture the judgment that the transportation revolution and the *de facto* single national market it helped create made possible, and indeed decisively fostered, great increases in profit-making opportunities even before the victory of industrialism; while the system of inheritance and the minimal influence of the non-property-owning classes enabled private accumulators to command a larger share of society's product than they would be able to in a later era of vastly greater absolute productivity and profits.

Contemporaries were not and could not have been aware of these trends. A surface equality that contrasted sharply with the inequality that continued to prevail on the Continent evidently blinded many observers to the drastic and worsening maldistribution of wealth that characterized American life before mid-century. Much of the statistical evidence was available at the time, but men convinced that no great disparities existed were hardly disposed to probe the data critically. The era's egalitarian ideology fostered roseate notions about the condition of things in America. What need was there to research the record, in view of the obvious well-being enjoyed here by the masses? Moralistic critics of American society, such as Emerson and James Fenimore Cooper, unwittingly promoted such beliefs; according to their criticism, Americans were in danger of losing their souls precisely because they were gaining too much of the world.[31] Although the European record remains to be examined intensively, it does appear likely that most Americans of light skin were better off materially than their Old World counterparts. It should be noted that a striking pattern of inequality is not necessarily synonymous with massive suffering or misery. If a community is wealthy enough, the fact that a small number of its members own an inordinate portion of wealth, does not doom all others to want. And yet the evidence assembled recently for nineteenth-century cities large and small, as for rural communities in every part of the nation, makes clear that things were not what they seemed in antebellum America. The underlying reality was strikingly unlike the surface equality so widely acclaimed. If the complex actuality is not fully revealed by the statistical data, the data do bring us closer to an accurate appraisal of that reality. They establish that increasing inequality rather than equality was a central theme of American life during the "era of the common man."

Notes

[1] Douglas T. Miller, *Jacksonian Aristocracy*, p. x.

[2] Mathew Carey, *Appeal to the Wealthy of the Land* (Philadelphia, 1833); and Seth Luther, *Address to the Working Men of New England* (Philadelphia, 1836). For a discussion of the contemporary labor argument that inequality ruled the United States, see Edward Pessen, *Most Uncommon Jacksonians* (Albany, 1967), chap. 8.

[3] See Robert Ernst, *Immigrant Life in New York City, 1825–1853* (New York, 1949); Oscar Handlin, *Boston's Immigrants* (Cambridge, 1941); and Raymond A. Mohl, *Poverty in New York, 1783–1825* (New York, 1971), pp. 16, 20, 34.

[4] See Chapter 12 below.

[5] For informed discussions of the different measures that can be used by social scientists see Howard R. Alker, Jr., and Bruce M. Russett, "On Measuring Inequality," *Behavioral Science, 9* (July 1964), pp. 207–18; and Robert R. Schutz, "On the Measurement of Income Inequality," *American Economic Review, XLI* (March 1951), pp. 107–22.

[6] James T. Lemon and Garry B. Nash, "The Distribution of Wealth in Eighteenth Century America: A Century of Changes in Chester County, Pennsylvania, 1693–1802," *Journal of Social History, 2* (Fall 1968), p. 13.

[7] Donald Warner Koch, "Income Distribution and Political Structure in Seventeenth-Century Salem, Massachusetts," Essex Institute *Historical Collections, CV* (Jan. 1969), pp. 54, 58, 59, 63.

[8] The figures for Boston are derived from James Henretta, "Economic Development and Social Structure in Colonial Boston," *William and Mary Quarterly, XXII* (Jan. 1965), pp. 79, 80, 82, 87, 89, 92; and Allan Kulikoff, "The Progress of Inequality in Revolutionary Boston," *ibid., XXVIII* (July 1971), pp. 380–81, 409.

[9] Main, *The Social Structure of Revolutionary America*, p. 42; and Alice Hansen

Jones, "Wealth Distribution in the American Middle Colonies in the Third Quarter of the Eighteenth Century," paper read at the annual meeting of the Organization of American Historians in New Orleans, April 17, 1971.

[10] The figures for numbers of families are by no means foolproof. The 1840 Census data do not invariably indicate the numbers of minors or true dependents for which an adult taxpayer was responsible. Thus in Brooklyn, James Lewis was the head of a "household" of eight persons, but as six of them were adults, it is highly unlikely that the wealth of this family adhered to Lewis alone. Similarly, John Howeth headed a household of sixteen persons, nine of whom were working adults; while seven of the eight persons in Ann Campbell's household were adults under 60 years old. *United States, 1840 Census, Population Schedules,* New York, Kings County, City of Brooklyn; see also David Herlihy, "Computerizing the Manuscript Census—A Comment," *Historical Methods Newsletter, IV* (Dec. 1970), pp. 10–13.

[11] Stephen Girard, *The Merchants' Sketch Book and Guide to New York City* (New York, 1844), p. 6; Hone Diary, XXIV:408. Whoever the author of the *Sketch Book* may have been, he was *not* the great Philadelphia capitalist, who had been dead 13 years by the date of publication of this volume.

[12] Quoted in Charles E. Knowles, *History of the Bank for Savings in the City of New York, 1819–1929* (New York, 1929), pp. 70–71.

[13] New York City Court for the Correction of Errors, *The City Fire Insurance Company of the City of New-York, Respondents, Elisha Bloomer, Impleader with others [including Richard K. Haight and David H. Haight],* 1841, pp. 19–20.

[14] James Sloane Gibbons, *The Banks of New York* (New York, 1858), p. 21.

[15] D. G. Brinton Thompson, *Ruggles of New York: A Life of Samuel B. Ruggles* (New York, 1946), pp. 39–40; *History of the Chemical Bank* (New York, 1913), p. 34; Stephen N. Winslow, *Biographies of Successful Philadelphia Merchants* (Philadelphia, 1864), 197; *Records of Guaranty Trust Company of New York* (New York, nd); Philip G. Hudnut, *The Merchants' National Bank of the City of New York* (New York, 1903), 4; Henry W. Domett, *A History of the Bank of New York, 1784–1884* (New York, 1884); Hone Diary, XIX:93; and *Charter of the Seventh Ward Fire Insurance Company of New-York* (New York, 1839).

[16] The worthwhileness of this formula was confirmed to me by an authority on both statistics and finance, Samuel Richmond, author of *Statistical Analysis* (New York, 1968).

[17] The distribution of wealth was estimated from the data in the "The Assessment Book for the Town of Brooklyn Taken in 1810," Long Island Historical Society.

[18] The Brooklyn directories for the period list valuable data on boards of directors. Also see Henry R. Stiles, *The Civil, Political, Professional and Ecclesiastical History and Commercial and Industrial Record of the County of Kings and the City of Brooklyn New York from 1683 to 1884,* 3 vols. (New York, 1884), I, pp. 143, 154, 436; II, pp. 213, 620–23; "A Director," *A Historical Sketch of the Fulton Ferry* (Brooklyn, 1839), Appendix, pp. 8–11; *History and Commerce of Brooklyn* (New York, 1893); and *Charter and By-Laws and Regulations of the Brooklyn Savings' Bank* (Brooklyn, 1836).

[19] These generalizations are based on computations performed on the figures in Shattuck, *Census of Boston for the Year 1845,* p. 95.

[20] Most of the information on directors was compiled from Boston city directories for the period. Useful on the extent to which Boston's great corporations were owned by the wealthy are N. S. B. Gras, *The Massachusetts First National Bank of Boston, 1784–1934* (Cambridge, 1937), 550–557; and Gerald T. White, *A History of the Massachusetts Hospital Life Insurance Company* (Cambridge, 1955), pp. 12–13.

[21] Blumin, "Mobility in a Nineteenth-Century American City," pp. 46–48.

[22] Michael Fitzgibbon Holt, *Forging a Majority: The Formation of the Republican Party in Pittsburgh, 1848–1860* (New Haven, 1969), p. 28.

[23] Michael B. Katz, "Patterns of Inequality, Wealth and Power in a Nineteenth-Century City," on Hamilton, Ontario; Doherty, "Property Distribution in Jacksonian America," introduction, pp. 2, 4. Doherty found that only towns that languished or stagnated resisted the trend toward greater inequality.

[24] Kenneth W. Wheeler, *To Wear A City's Crown: The Beginnings of Urban Growth in Texas, 1836–1865,* p. 131; Robert E. Gallman, "Trends in the Size Distribution of Wealth in the Nineteenth Century," pp. 1–25; George Blackburn and Sherman L.

Richards, Jr., "A Demographic History of the West: Manistee County, Michigan, 1860."

[25] In New York City by 1863 roughly 61 per cent of all *income* was made by the 1,600 families that constituted the upper 1 per cent of income earners. Computed from figures in *The Income Record, A List Giving the Taxable Income for the year 1863, of the Residents of New York [City]* (New York, 1865). It is likely that wealth was even more badly distributed than this fact indicates, since inheritance accounts for so much of it; by contrast, the democratic rule governing income requires that —in a sense—all people start from scratch, no matter how disparate their earnings. Rufus S. Tucker long ago noted that the 1863 tax record for New York City showed "less concentration and less inequality than actually existed," Tucker, "The Distribution of Income Among Income Taxpayers in the United States, 1863–1935," *Quarterly Journal of Economics, LII* (1938), pp. 561–62.

[26] Modern scholars differ in interpreting the data on wealth and income distribution in our own era. Yet even Michael Harrington and Gabriel Kolko, whose estimates reveal the greatest amount of inequality, attribute percentages of income to the upper brackets that are far smaller than the proportions of wealth owned by New York City's upper 1 per cent or income the upper 1 per cent earned in 1863. See Kolko, "Economic Mobility and Social Stratification," *American Journal of Sociology, LXIII* (July 1957), p. 38; Kolko, *Wealth and Power in America: An Analysis of Social Class and Income Distribution* (New York, 1962); and Harrington, *The Other America: Poverty in the United States* (New York, 1962). Compare the Kolko and Harrington estimates with those in Herman P. Miller, *Income of the American People* (New York, 1955); United States Bureau of the Census, *How Our Income is Divided* (Washington, 1963); and Robert Lampman, *The Share of Top Wealth Holders in National Wealth, 1922–1956* (Princeton, 1962).

[27] Gerhard Lenski, *Power and Privilege: A Theory of Social Stratification* (New York, 1966), p. 3.

[28] *Ibid.*, p. 341.

[29] Doherty, "Property Distribution in Jacksonian America," pp. 4–5; Stephan Thernstrom and Peter R. Knights, "Men in Motion: Some Data and Speculations about Urban Population Mobility in Nineteenth-Century America," *Journal of Interdisciplinary History, I* (Autumn 1970), pp. 29–30; Knights, *The Plain People of Boston 1830–1860;* Michael Katz, "Patterns of Inequality," p. 5; and Blumin, "The Restless Citizen: Vertical Mobility, Migration, and Social Participation in Mid-Nineteenth Century America," a 1970 unpublished version of a paper (on Kingston, New York) presented at the Conference on Social Science Concepts in American Political History, Oct, 24, 1969, at Brockport, New York.

[30] Gallman, "Trends in the Size Distribution of Wealth," p. 11. Jackson Main, "Trends in Wealth Concentration Before 1860," pp. 445–47, offers some useful explanations of the changing trends despite his reliance on estimates that are based partly on Moses Beach's erratic *Wealthy Citizens.*

[31] See Pessen, "Perfectionist Social Thought in the Jacksonian Era," in Robert A. Skotheim and Michael McGiffert, eds., *American Social Thought [Before the Civil War]* (Reading, Mass., 1972), pp. 277–336.

4

The Sources of Antebellum Wealth in the Urban Northeast

All the large fortunes which are found in a democratic community are of commercial growth. . . .

Tocqueville, *Democracy in America*, II:188

The clearest thing about the wealth accumulated by rich men and families in the great northeastern cities during the second quarter of the nineteenth century is the diversity of its sources. Unfortunately, it is impossible to determine with any precision the relative part played in the creation of riches by any one of these varied sources. While useful evidence is abundant, in many cases indicating the full scope of economic interests that engaged successful men of affairs, the data rarely are refined enough to show exactly what proportion of a man's fortune resulted from *this* as against *that* pursuit. Even Kenneth W. Porter's book on John Jacob Astor's finances—a study yet unsurpassed in its mastery of massive relevant data—was prevented by the paucity of evidence from making more than the most general judgments about the relative roles played by investments in western lands, New York City real estate, banking, the fur trade, and shipping in contributing to the famous merchant's total fortune.[1] Part of the problem, as indicated earlier, is that the exact dimensions of fortunes were seldom known; it is devilishly hard to estimate the proportionate part played by each of a number of profit-making activities when the size of the fortune is itself an unknown quantity. Nor are econometric methods likely to be helpful in this instance, in view of the incompleteness of the data and the unreliability of statistical tables drawn from samples and unverified estimates. It would be possible to portray by a graph the number of men engaged in two or three occupations; but the impossibility of ascertaining the dimensions or proportions of such involvements suggests the value —at least in this case—of a word-picture rather than a statistical one. If the evidence is incomplete, it is nevertheless useful and suggestive.

An earlier study, basing its conclusions on an 1846 edition of Moses Beach's *Wealthy Citizens*, held that "finance and industry" had little to do with the amassing of fortunes in antebellum New York City.[2] That

TABLE 4–1.
The Occupations of New York City's Wealthiest Persons in 1828*

Occupation	*Percentage of Rich Population*
Merchants (including brokers, auctioneers, agents)	78
Bank and corporation officers	3
Attorneys	7
Manufacturers	3
Proprietors	2
Physicians	1
Widows	3
Builders	1
Owners of wharves, warehouses, yards	1
Miscellaneous	1
	100

*The wealthiest persons for New York City, Brooklyn, and Boston were drawn from the tax assessments. For Philadelphia they were the persons reputed to be worth $100,000 or more in *Memoirs and Auto-Biography of Some of the Wealthy Citizens of Philadelphia (Philadelphia*, 1846).

finance was insignificant is arguable, but the second part of that judgment is beyond cavil, and not for New York City alone. Very few men among the urban rich depended for their profits upon the manufacture of goods, while fewer still (a mere handful) were managers or heavy investors in factories. The Lowells, Appletons, and Lawrences of Boston were hardly the typical capitalists of their day. More characteristic of the industrial involvement of the rich was Philip Hone's investment in textile mills in New York state. Although Hone derived emotional as well as financial profit from his directorship in the Matteawan Cotton and Machine Company, his business involvements in non-manufacturing concerns engaged much more of his time and capital. Typically, fewer than 5 per cent of the richest men in any of the great cities were described as "manufacturers" in the occupational listings of general and business city directories; and many of these "manufacturers" actually engaged more heavily in the sales than in the production of the goods identified with their names.

The occupations given in directories and other sources are available for almost all wealthy persons. This information is invaluable and when examined for different years—early and late in the era—offers an illuminating glimpse into both the characteristic means by which the rich earned their fortunes and the extent to which trends changed over the course of a generation. As the tables indicate, skilled labor, teaching, farming, and the arts, to name but a few fields, were not the paths to economic preferment during the second quarter of the century.

TABLE 4–2.
The Occupations of New York City's Wealthiest Persons in 1845

Occupation	*Percentage of Rich Population*
Merchants, brokers, etc.	70
Bank and corporation executives	6
Attorneys	9
Physicians	3
Widows	3
Builders, shipbuilders	2
Manufacturers	2
Publishers, booksellers	2
Proprietors	1
Distillers	1
Miscellaneous	1
	100

The occupational data for the northeastern cities are not all of a piece. Urban Brooklyn clearly still had much farm land in 1841. Philadelphia had large numbers of "gentlemen"—although the fact probably testifies more to the vagaries of that city's directory publishers and to the pretensions of some of its retired men of affairs than to a uniquely genteel way of life. For the most part the evidence is remarkably similar for all of the great cities. Equally striking are the signs that little change in the occupations of the wealthy occurred over the course of a quarter of a century. Persons engaged in commerce and business, supplemented

TABLE 4–3.
The Occupations of Boston's Wealthiest Persons *ca.* 1830

Occupation	*Percentage of Rich Population*
Merchants, brokers, etc.	69
Attorneys	11
Widows	7
Bank and corporate officers	3
Physicians	3
Distillers	2
Manufacturers	1
Wharf, yard owners	1
Shipbuilders, sailmakers	1
Officials (state and city)	1
Miscellaneous	1
	100

by attorneys, physicians, and the widows of the rich, constituted roughly nine-tenths of the upper crust of wealth holders late as well as early in the era.

Weaknesses of Occupations as Clues to Wealth

If the evidence on occupations is valuable, suggesting as it does the broad areas of economic activity that appeared to absorb the attention of the rich, it is nevertheless imperfect. The directory information on the occupations of the wealthy—and for that matter of other men as well—is not always what it seems. Occupational designations oversimplified the complex, giving the impression that men of varied affairs were occupied in only one form of economic activity. The arbitrary label, "merchant," could mask the significant non-mercantile practices that might have brought great profit to the individual so described. Even when recorded accurately, an occupation would hardly explain the amassing of a fortune by the "merchant," "shipbuilder," "importer," or "corporation official" whose wealth in fact derived from his wife's dowry and/or his uncle's bequest. The great wealth owned by fortunate heirs has sometimes been misinterpreted as a sign that the fortunes in question were earned in the heirs' occupations. That certain merchants or physicians were very rich men could have been due to the fact that they were merchants and physicians; or it could have been due to their fortunate inheritances, marriages, investments and speculations—or to a combination of factors. The only way to find the answer is to track down detailed evidence for each man. Fortunately, useful data were available for most of the rich. This evidence uncovers a further weakness of occupational labels: the lumping together under a common rubric, as though similarly occupied, persons whose business activities were markedly unlike in scope and quality.

There were Philadelphia "gentlemen" and "gentlemen." Some were very rich, others not; some had worked hard almost all their lives and were architects of their own fortunes, while others had never labored and had experienced material ease from infancy on. Some had achieved their status through selling and buying goods, others through making them. In the case of some, the honorific designation "gentleman" was accepted by their fellows; sometimes the title was self-created. And of course there were "merchants" and "merchants." Since the caption was a prestigious one, a small retail dealer with a capital of a few thousand dollars chose it, as did the shipowner whose vast wholesale operations were pursued by his fleet in ports on every continent; both were "merchants" as far as the directory was concerned. The tables of occupation show that "widows" in every city held much wealth. Yet of course widowhood *per se* was no clue whatever to the riches of the bereaved. For that "occupation," more clearly than for the others, the level of

TABLE 4–4.
The Occupations of Boston's Wealthiest Persons *ca.* 1850

Occupation	*Percentage of Rich Population*
Merchants, brokers, etc.	66
Attorneys	10
Widows	7
Bank and corporate officers	5
Physicians	3
Manufacturers	2
Distillers	1
Shipbuilders, wharves, etc.	1
Ministers, professors	1
Publishers	1
Local officials	1
Artisans	1
Miscellaneous	1
	100

wealth owned by individuals so described was due entirely to factors other than the "occupation" in question. And even nowadays, when public officials' salaries have risen to respectable levels, great wealth accumulated by officeholders is either known to be due to legitimate extraneous sources, or it raises eyebrows. In that earlier age, when local and state offices got little compensation or none whatever, rich men in

TABLE 4–5.
The Occupations of Philadelphia's Wealthiest Persons, 1845–1846

Occupation	*Percentage of Rich Population*
Merchants, brokers, etc.	60
Gentlemen	13
Manufacturers	5
Attorneys	5
Physicians	5
Bank and corporate officers	3
Widows	3
Publishers, booksellers	2
Distillers	1
Stable keepers	1
Artisans	1
Miscellaneous	1
	100

the occupation of public official had to owe their wealth to something other than the occupation.

Particularly misleading was the directory designation that certain prosperous men were artisans or, more precisely, "glaziers," "carpenters," "masons," "chandlers," or "bakers." The reader innocent of details about the individual so described might conclude that the man in question was a skilled craftsman whose wealth had been achieved by working with his hands. Actually, directories, when they did list the names, occupations, business, and home addresses of artisans, generally excluded journeymen.[3] The masters they included typically employed others in shops that sold the finished products made. As for the few rich men whose occupational listings gave an impression that they were solely or primarily skilled craftsmen, the facts were almost invariably otherwise. In Brooklyn, for example, the "stonecutter," David Anderson, was actually the owner of a stoneyard. Jonathan Rogers may have been a "master joiner," but he owed his wealth to the fact that he was a large builder. George Hall, who became mayor, was more an entrepreneur than a "painter and glazier," while the directory designations for Samuel Bouton as "milkman," Peter Bergen as "florist," Moses Reeve as "carpenter," and Adrian Hegeman as "stationer" were equally misleading. Christian Bergh, actually a wealthy shipbuilder, on his death in 1843 was described as "the oldest ship carpenter in the city."

TABLE 4–6.
The Occupations of Brooklyn's Wealthiest Persons, 1841

Occupation	*Percentage of Rich Population*
Merchants, brokers, etc.	57
Widows	7
Farmers	5
Manufacturers	6
Attorneys	5
Proprietors	3
Owners of yards, wharves, warehouses	3
Distillers	3
Bank and corporate officers	2
Physicians	2
Builders and contractors	2
Publishers	1
Local officials	1
Ministers, artists, engineers, accountants	1
Mariners, shipmasters	1
Artisans and miscellaneous	1
	100

The wealthiest persons of the northeastern cities derived their fortunes from diverse activities and interests largely concealed by the designations of occupation. Since the exceptions to this rule were few, any attempt to describe even briefly the economic careers of all these rich persons would, at the least, entail a slim volume. The point can be developed more economically by representative examples drawn from all of the great northeastern cities. Such illustrations both document a general principle and suggest, as statistics alone never could, the unique flavor and economic lifestyle involved in profit-making during the age when rails, factories, and corporations were still in their infancy.

Attorneys

There were many rich attorneys during the era, but it is not clear precisely how much of their wealth was made in practicing law. A number of the most eminent were of rich, usually old, families and owed their fortunes more to inheritance of wealth made in other fields than to their own legal counseling. Some of New York City's most prominent lawyers of the period fit into this category. Daniel Ingraham, nephew of Richard Riker, was the grandson of the wealthy Daniel Phoenix. Riker, himself a prominent attorney, came of a family whose great wealth in land, acquired in the seventeenth century, had been subsequently supplemented by commerce. Francis B. Cutting, active and perhaps too active in the social life of the city's elite, came of a family that had intermarried with the Livingstons and Schuylers, among others. His mother owned a "lucrative ferry lease." Cutting's career indicates that he possessed much personal charm, yet there can be no doubt that his attractiveness and success were enhanced by his name and fortune. The father of Abel T. Anderson had been a "rich boot and shoe maker." Gulian C. Verplanck came of an old, wealthy family, his middle name reflecting its ties with the Crommelins, a "great banking and commercial house in Amsterdam." Isaac Kip's father combined commerce with banking, while the family had long owned valuable estates in the city and been prominent in its commercial life.

The Kanes, great landowners in Dutchess County, contributed several successful lawyers as well as merchants to New York City in the eighteenth and nineteenth centuries. Thomas Addis Emmet was of a leading Irish family, his father a prominent physician in Dublin who moved in that city's highest circles. Joseph Blunt's father was a very successful publisher. David S. Jones's father, the eminent Chancellor Jones, was of course himself a great lawyer; but father, like son, had benefited immeasurably from membership in a family whose ownership of a vast tract of land in Oyster Bay in the seventeenth century grounded a fortune later enriched by whaling and commerce. Evert A. Bancker, like Anthony Bleecker, was of old Dutch family that owned huge landed

Entrance Hall of David S. Kennedy House, New York. Kennedy, whose house stood at 41 Fifth Avenue, was a prominent and socially active lawyer. *(Photograph courtesy of the Museum of the City of New York.)*

estates—the Banckers near Albany, the Bleeckers in Saratoga. John L. Lawrence was the son of the wealthy merchant, Jonathan Lawrence; and the father of William B. Lawrence was the "opulent merchant" Isaac Lawrence—himself the beneficiary of the Lawrence's great landholdings in Flushing, Hempstead, and Newton on Long Island.

Many of Philadelphia's leading lawyers also possessed fortunes created by the non-legal activities of their parents and families. William Rawle, Thomas I. Wharton, Thomas Cadwalader, and a number of Walns came of old, rich families. Isaac Norris's family had been great landholders in Philadelphia since the first Isaac Norris had purchased close to ten thousand acres shortly after William Penn's arrival. The family of Henry C. Townsend, arriving with the first settlers on the *Welcome,* had similarly been great landowners almost from the beginning. Norris's son, the attorney Joseph Parker Norris, received an inheritance that obviously derived only in part from his father's legal fees. George H. Boker, who after the Civil War became minister to Turkey, was the son of the banker Charles S. Boker. Henry D. Gilpin was the son of a rich merchant, Joshua Gilpin, and an equally rich mother, Mary Dilworth. William M. Meredith's father, William, was a bank president as well as lawyer, while his mother was Gertrude Gouverneur Ogden. Joseph W. Paul's wealth came primarily from his father's mercantile success. Charles Biddle Penrose was of a family which profited immensely from shipbuilding and successful marital ties. George S. Pepper was the son of an extremely rich brewer. Eli K. Price's father was a successful merchant; Price himself had been trained for a life in commerce, but when he indicated an interest in law he had been placed in the office of the eminent John Sergeant. Other wealthy Philadelphia lawyers whose fathers and families were exceedingly rich or prestigious were Charles Ingersoll (the grandson of the illustrious Jared Ingersoll), Thomas McKean Pettit, Richard Rush (son of Dr. Benjamin Rush), George M. Dallas, Benjamin Chew, Jr.; and Joseph Hopkinson (son of the eminent Francis Hopkinson, whose own father had studied under Benjamin Chew).

In Boston, Charles P. Gray's "lucrative [legal] business" had been made possible by his "extensive family connections." If Francis C. Gray was an attorney who hardly practiced, it was because his father was the very rich "Billy" Gray. The father of Ebenezer Smith, Jr., was a successful speculator in lands, while most of William P. Mason's wealth had been left him by his extremely wealthy father, Jonathan Mason. Charles G., Francis C., and Ellis Gray Loring, legal eminences all, were the children of the wealthy merchant, Caleb Loring. Josiah Quincy, Mayor of Boston and later President of Harvard, was the grandson of the wealthy William Phillips and the son of a wealthy merchant and shipbuilder. If Quincy's own son, Josiah Quincy, Jr., accumulated a large fortune on his own by holding "many lucrative trusts and guardianships," his success was compounded of personal ability, a prestigious family name, kinship ties, and a substantial inheritance.

With its smaller population, Brooklyn had fewer lawyers whose wealth was due to the non-legal pursuits of family than did its sister cities; but the pattern was similar. Perhaps the wealthiest lawyer in Brooklyn, John A. Lott, was of an old Dutch family, great landholders as early as the seventeenth century. Gabriel Furman had a similar background. John Greenwood's success was largely due, if not to fortunate blood ties, to the fact that he had been taken up by Aaron Burr when he was still a young law student. Samuel Smith, one of Brooklyn's most prominent judges, came of an old Plymouth, Massachusetts, family that after the early seventeenth century was prominent in Huntington, Long Island.

Many wealthy lawyers supplemented valuable inheritances by marrying well. Dowries and property acquired through wedlock rivalled commerce and landholding as routes to "success in law." In New York City, John Anthon, the son of a successful doctor, married the daughter of the wealthy John Hone, a step that marvelously enhanced the quality of his social life as well as his material situation. John T. Irving took as a bride the daughter of Gabriel Furman. The social prominence of John Ireland's own family no doubt abetted his entry through marriage into the wealthy Floyd family.

Richard Vaux of Philadelphia, son of the renowned gentleman, humanitarian, and man of culture, Roberts Vaux, married into the estimable Waln family, living in circumstances so affluent that in the words of one biographer, he was "relieved from the drudgery of early [law] practice." Vaux's wealth, like his later success in politics (for he was to become mayor of Philadelphia) had little to do with either legal acumen or hard work. William J. Duane, best known for his removal from cabinet office by Andrew Jackson, in addition to being the son of a famous newspaper editor and a member of the Markoe family, was the husband of a Bache. John K. Kane's ascension to the attorney generalship of Pennsylvania as well as to great wealth, owed much to his family's kinship to such great New York lineages as the Van Rensselaers and to his own marriage to the daughter of Thomas Leiper. Another wealthy Philadelphia lawyer who owed much to a New York connection was William Meredith, husband to the niece of Lewis and Gouverneur Morris. James Dundas, heir to the fortune of an old Scottish family, married Anna Maria, daughter of the wealthy Henry Pratt. The prestigious judge, John I. C. Hare, the son of the wealthy Dr. Robert Hare and Mary Willing, married the daughter of Horace Binney. The wealth she brought to Hare was indubitably derived in part from a law practice, but it was her father's rather than her husband's.

Boston had a large contingent of rich lawyers who supplemented parental, mainly mercantile, fortunes with wealth drawn from marriage.

Henry Codman, son of a wealthy merchant, married the daughter of Jonathan Amory; while the great William Hickling Prescott—nominally an attorney and known to the world as an historian—also married an Amory. Lucius Manlius Sargent, whose "inheritance of a fortune precluded the drudgery of a practice," married into the Binney family of Philadelphia. Theodore Sedgwick married a granddaughter of Governor William Livingston of New Jersey, while Nathaniel L. Bowditch, son of the famed mathematician, married the daughter of the very rich Ebenezer Francis. William H. Gardiner married the daughter of Thomas Handasyd Perkins, one of Boston's greatest and of course richest merchants. Jonathan Chapman married a Dwight, of the "wealthy Springfield family." William F. Otis, son of the great social lion Harrison Gray Otis, married if not the wealthiest of women, perhaps the most beautiful, Emily Marshall—the "toast of Boston" and "the greatest belle in American history." Franklin Dexter, rich from his father's inheritance, came into a fortune left him by his wife's father, Judge Prescott. Elias Hasket Derby, son of a commercial giant, married the daughter of the wealthy George Washington Strong of New York City. John C. Gray, another attorney who had no need to practice, had inherited one mercantile fortune from his father William Gray and married into another by taking the hand of Samuel P. Gardner's daughter.

Other Boston lawyers, the bulk of whose wealth appeared to come from matrimony, included Benjamin Guild, husband to Samuel Eliot's daughter; Samuel D. Parker, whose wife was the daughter of Jonathan Mason; Russell Jarvis, married to a daughter of Thomas Cordis; James Savage, whose first wife had left him a sugar plantation; William D. Sohier, son-in-law of Thomas Amory; and Thomas G. Cary, the fortunate husband of Thomas H. Perkins's daughter. Benjamin Gorham came of a family given to successful marriages—considering his own connection to a Lowell and his sister's marriage to the richest man in Massachusetts, Peter Chardon Brooks.

In the case of wealthy men who never practiced the law, the designation "attorney" may have attested to the formal education they received in their early adulthood at Harvard, Columbia, or the University of Pennsylvania; certainly it offered no clue whatever to the sources of their wealth. In Boston, Harrison Gray Otis and David Sears headed a list of successful non-practicing lawyers that includes, as we have seen, the Grays, Lucius M. Sargent, and William H. Prescott. Philadelphia gentlemen who were only nominally lawyers included George H. Boker, Richard Vaux, Thomas I. Wharton and John K. Kane. New York City's best example of a man who studied law but never practiced it was Andrew G. Hamersley, the possessor of two fortunes—one bequeathed by his father, Lewis C. Hamersley, the other accruing from his marriage to Sarah Mason, daughter of the great merchant, John Mason.

A number of lawyers were men of diverse interests that combined with inheritances and dowries to account for their fortunes. In Brooklyn, Cyrus P. Smith was a heavy investor in financial and other corporations, as was John A. Lott, who also owned much real estate. Lott's colleague—the refined and versatile Henry C. Murphy—was able to pursue his varied cultural and political tastes because of financial success only partly explained by the undeniable success of his law firm. Samuel Smith was another attorney active in business and real estate, while the versatile Gabriel Furman combined an elegant social life with the writing of local history and the presidency of the Brooklyn Fire Insurance Company, among other activities. A leading example of sometime New York City lawyers, rich from a variety of other interests, was Samuel B. Ruggles, whose success in marriage, business, speculation, and in relentlessly accumulating New York City real estate made it unnecessary for him to practice law through the prime of his life. Two children of great Revolutionary era figures were James A. Hamilton and James Gore King. In Hamilton's own words, from his 37th year on he "devoted attention to making money by dealing in real estate in New York City and Brooklyn and building homes with very marked success." King, son of Rufus King and son-in-law to the wealthy Archibald Gracie, was a broker, merchant, banker, an ubiquitous corporate director, and for many years head of what was perhaps New York City's greatest mercantile house.

Among Philadelphia lawyers previously mentioned in other connections, Thomas Wharton and Charles Ingersoll were active in real estate, James Dundas, William Meredith, and Joseph P. Norris were bank presidents. A number of wealthy Bostonians might best be described as "lawyer-capitalists." Richard S. Fay profited from his many investments in corporations as well as his own business enterprises, as did Russell Jarvis. Thomas G. Cary owned a quarry, while Francis C. Gray owned extensive iron works. Alexander Townsend, in addition to being a hotel proprietor, owned much real estate, as did the younger Elias H. Derby and Ellis Gray Loring—both were successful land speculators. Perhaps the most versatile profit-makers among Boston's attorneys were Henry B. Rogers, merchant, corporate investor and director, owner of valuable real estate; Henry Codman; and the towering social figure, Harrison Gray Otis. If Otis was a master of high living, a fastidious gourmet and connoiseur of fine wines, and perhaps the most sought after guest among the interurban social elite, his exalted status rested in part on the inheritance and marriage earlier alluded to and in part on his own success, particularly in real-estate speculations.

All of this is not to say that the law could not be a financially rewarding field in its own right. Attorneys to the mighty—in roles such as William Duane played in behalf of the fabulous merchant Stephen Girard or Josiah Quincy, Jr., held as trustee and executor to many great estates—obviously thrived. It is well to remember however that few men listed in city directories as attorneys were fortunate enough to be sought out by the Shimmins or the Stuyvesants as legal advisors or as guardians of their great fortunes. This was an era when a prosperous small town lawyer could consider himself fortunate if he "cleared between $800 and $1500 a year" during the inflationary 1830s.[4] Even in the great cities, rich men usually classified as lawyers appear to have derived most of their wealth from fields other than the law. During the second quarter of the nineteenth century, lawyer-capitalists may have been attorneys in terms of their identifiable occupations. As wealthholders however they were primarily merchants, investors, corporate officers, and real estate owners—in addition to being sons and sons-in-law to the rich.

Physicians

Medicine was the other great profession of the era, commanding a status similar to that enjoyed by the law.[5] In medicine as in the legal profession outstandingly successful or wealthy men owed their fortunes more to other sources than to fees charged for treatment. Such great figures as Dr. David Hosack of New York City or Dr. Philip Syng Physick of Philadelphia evidently each earned about $20,000 annually at the height of his career, which was a highly unusual income for physicians of that period. Yet, as will be indicated, even these nonpareils of the profession profited substantially from other business or worldly involvements. Given the particular nature of the medical profession —the special intellectual commitment it required of its devotees, as well as the absence of the direct connection between its central practices and the needs of business that obtained for law—it is not surprising that fewer doctors than lawyers were preoccupied with the marketplace over profession. There is nonetheless a remarkable similarity in the pattern of background and pursuits of *wealthy* doctors and lawyers during the period.

George Parkman, son of the wealthy Boston merchant, Samuel Parkman, was a highly successful if unusual physician who devoted his time more to real-estate speculation and the renting of cheaply built tenements than to medicine. Dr. James Jackson's fine style of living in Waltham was evidently made possible by the riches of his then-successful manufacturer brother, Patrick Tracy Jackson. Other Boston physicians who inherited wealth made in commerce were Dr. John Odin, son of a prominent merchant and himself a local political activist, and Dr. Henry Gardner, one of that interesting group who although "bred a physician, did not [have to] practice."

Philadelphia had doctors similarly advantaged. If Dr. John H. Weir was wealthy, it was due to the fortune accumulated by his father, the well-known auctioneer Silas E. Weir. Dr. Thomas C. Henry was the son of the wealthy Alexander Henry. The eminent surgeon, Dr. George W. Norris was the son of the rich merchant Joseph P. Norris; while Dr.

Caspar Wistar came from an esteemed Philadelphia family whose fortune had originated with what was perhaps the first glass factory in the country. The father of Dr. Henry S. Patterson was the rich merchant John Patterson. Edward and Isaac Parrish were wealthy doctors both but their fortunes came largely from the successful practice of their father, Dr. Joseph Parrish, rather than from their own.

Philadelphia physicians famed for their broad scientific interests, as well as their private medical practices, were also beholden to family wealth carved out in commerce. Dr. James Mease, humanitarian, author, man of culture, and leader of the Philosophical Society, was the son of an Irish immigrant who, from the mid-eighteenth century on, had been an "eminent shipping merchant in Philadelphia." The philanthropist, Dr. Caspar Morris, dispensed benefits made possible by the wealth of Anthony Morris, his merchant father. Dr. Isaac Hays, President of the Academy of Natural Sciences, had been brought up "with culture and luxury," as befitted the son of a wealthy merchant married to a Gratz.

The eminent Dr. John A. McVickar of New York City was the son of the substantial shipowner and importer, John McVickar. Dr. Marinus Willett (1801–1840), latest bearer of the name, came of an old and wealthy New York family, his father having amassed riches through land speculation in general (and the purchase of confiscated Tory estates in particular), the founding of a ferry to Long Island, commerce, and shipowning. David Hosack's father too had been a successful man of diverse business affairs, including valuable New York City real estate. If Hosack's home in the city was lavishly outfitted, while his suburban mansion and estate on the east bank of the Hudson was a magnet to the elite of the northeast, it was due largely to the estate he came into in 1823 on marrying Magdalena, the widow of the very rich Henry A. Coster.

Successful marriages were often made by men whose status as socially prominent physicians of good family made them highly attractive to the daughters of the rich and the fashionable. Such liaisons had more to do with the wealth of the physicians entering into them than did their skill in surgery or diagnosis. Dr. John Collins Warren, who as Boston's most eminent physician stood on the same plane with Hosack and Physick, and was himself the son of a rich surgeon, made two exemplary marriages: the first to a daughter of the rich Jonathan Mason, the second to a daughter of Lieutenant Governor Winthrop. Dr. George C. Shattuck's riches derived largely from his marriage to the wealthy Miss Derby, as well as from a splendid maternal inheritance; while Dr. Benjamin D. Greene too benefited from having a rich father and making a most successful marriage to the daughter of Josiah Quincy. Dr. Edward H. Robbins married the daughter of the wealthy Barnabus Hedge of Plymouth.

Philadelphia's most famed physicians owned wealth derived from

Silhouette of Family and Guests of the Wealthy Dr. John Cheesman. The occasion was a reception in 1840 at his home on Broadway, New York City. *(Painting by August Edouart courtesy of the New-York Historical Society.)*

the classic combination of personal inheritance and marriage. The great Philip Syng Physick received one fortune from his father and another in the form of his wife Elizabeth Emlen's dowry. The marriage of Physick's own daughter to Dr. Jacob Randolph enhanced the career and the fortune of that descendant of a prominent Philadelphia Quaker family. Dr. Samuel G. Morton, holder of a chair in anatomy in the University of Pennsylvania, was the son of George Morton, successful merchant, and husband to Rebecca G. Pearsall, also of a prominent Quaker family. Dr. George McLellan's career also demonstrated the classic pattern of eminent parentage and in-laws, as did Dr. Robert M. Patterson's. Patterson's wealth was based both on a medical fortune—albeit one compiled by his father—and on his marriage to the daughter of Thomas Leiper. Dr. Thomas D. Mütter married a niece of Richard Alsop, although most of his wealth came from the fortunes bequeathed him by a rich uncle and his merchant father. The proportions were reversed in the case of Dr. Robert Hare's estate; for although he profited immensely from his rich brewer father's inheritance, he did even better by marrying Margaret Willing. Dr. John Forsyth Meigs, who came of an old, respected, landed family, married the daughter of Charles J. Ingersoll. As for Dr. Joseph Hartshorne, whose family had owned several thousand acres of Long Island real estate in the seventeenth century before moving to Philadelphia, it was said that his marriage to Anna Bonsall resulted in a great boost to his medical practice.

As was true of their brethren in the legal profession, rich physicians also devoted themselves, if in smaller numbers, to other profit-making pursuits. Dr. R. V. W. Thorne of New York City actually engaged in business with his brother, John Thorne. In Philadelphia, Dr. Hartshorne was preoccupied with real estate, while Dr. David Jayne was a successful drug manufacturer and wholesale drug merchant. A number of Boston physicians mentioned earlier also pursued profit in the marketplace. The group included Drs. Shattuck and Warren, known for their "good investments," and Dr. Edward H. Robbins, an active real-estate speculator. Dr. John Ware owned much property; Dr. Benjamin Shurtleff speculated successfully in western lands; while Dr. Amos Binney's M.D. —earned from Harvard in 1826—had less to do with his wealth than his real estate and diverse business ventures. And as was earlier noted, Dr. George Parkman devoted more time to real-estate speculation and to renting out tenements than to medical science.

The level of wealth associated by census returns or other data with the occupation of physician, therefore, cannot be attributed to the field of medicine. Rather physicians in general had inordinate wealth because a few of their number—including most of the rich ones—inherited portions of mercantile fortunes, married into wealth, and made shrewd investments. Lucrative medical practices existed, of course, but they rewarded men already rich from a variety of sources.

Other Professions

Wealthy ministers, "officials," and military and naval officers during the era owed their wealth to sources other than these occupations. This was so even more clearly than for law and medicine, as the income possible from the ministry was strictly limited and to most modest sums. State Supreme Court Justices at the time typically earned under $3,000 a year. If the Reverend Evan M. Johnson of Brooklyn was rich, it was not because he presided over hundreds of marriages (as he was known to have done), but because he was born rich, married into wealth, and became a great accumulator of real estate. Boston's wealthy ministers had quite similar backgrounds. The Reverend Joseph Tuckerman was the son of the founder of the first insurance company in New England and husband, successively, to daughters of Samuel Parkman and Colonel Samuel Gray. Thomas Thompson and Samuel A. Eliot, like some of their counterparts in the other professions, were ministers who never preached. Thompson's father, like Eliot's, bequeathed his son a great fortune. Eliot took his bride, the daughter of Theodore Lyman, Jr., to the fine house at 31 Beacon Street built for him by his father and went on to a career in local politics and cultural activities more congenial to him than the ministry. General Jeremiah Johnson of Brooklyn used his large inheritance as a basis for a successful career in politics, the arts, and business. Naval Captain William Spencer was of an old landed family whose wealth and status were enhanced by his marriage to a Lorillard. Herman Thorn was an Army colonel, but his wealth was based in part on his familial inheritance and even more on his marriage to Jane Mary Jauncey, whose wealthy uncle willed Thorn a great fortune. As for the rich Captain Turner Camac of Philadelphia, he benefited both from the wealth of his parents and his marriage to a woman so rich (she was a member of the Penn family) that Camac was able to devote his life primarily to looking after his wife's extensive estate. General John C. Pemberton came of a family which, at the time of settlement, were part of the "Quaker merchant oligarchy." Consular officials such as Henry Bohlen and Adolph Borie were wealthy men because of family inheritance, and owed their diplomatic status to the prestige accruing from their surnames.

Merchants

The great preponderance of rich men in the antebellum northeast were classified as merchants, as were almost all of the "richest of the rich"—the men assessed for a quarter of a million dollars or more. Certainly this was the designation usually applied to each of the individuals who was the richest man in his city during the era: John Jacob Astor in New York City, Peter Chardon Brooks in Boston, Stephen Girard in

Philadelphia, and Hezekiah Beers Pierrepont in Brooklyn. That Pierrepont's wealth was primarily in real estate in Brooklyn Heights and northern New York State, Girard's in ships, banks, and a variety of investments, Brooks's founded in marine insurance, and Astor's in a fur empire, finance, an array of commercial activities—and above all in New York City real estate—suggests the heterogeneous mix that underlay the deceptively simple categories "commerce" and "merchant." To understand the sources of the era's fortunes, it is necessary to probe beyond these rubrics and to attempt to disentangle the varied elements that accounted for contemporary riches.

Much merchant wealth which was ostensibly created in the dynamic decades surrounding the Panic of 1837 and 1839 and the early 1840s—when the effects of the Panic were shaken off—was in fact founded earlier in mercantile and other pursuits. Many contemporary merchant capitalist fortunes in Boston followed such a course. The wealthy William Parsons received much property from his similarly named uncle, a wealthy merchant, and from his father, Chief Justice Theophilus Parsons. Henderson Inches inherited substantial real estate, while Frederick Tudor and Thomas Lamb benefited from fortunes of heterogeneous origin. Samuel Frothingham, himself prominent in commerce and finance, came of a family whose diversified interests included a "large factory for building coaches." Just as there were lawyers, doctors, and ministers who did not have to practice, so too were there merchants in this enviable situation. One of the chief of these was Charles R. Codman, the beneficiary of a great inheritance in real estate.

Philadelphia merchants whose fortunes consisted heavily of wealth bequeathed by old, rich families included John Welsh, Thomas Pym Cope, and Robert W. Waln, who benefited from the successful career of his lawyer-capitalist father, Nicholas Waln. Other commercial notables whose inheritances included valuable real estate were Charles Massey, William Crump the shipbuilder, and a number of successful Logans and Leas, the latter eminent publishers. Charles Humphreys was the son of the lumber merchant and shipbuilder who had been appointed by George Washington as Constructor of the Navy of the United States, and later designed the frigate *Constitution.* The chemical merchant and manufacturer John P. Wetherill had received a large fortune from his father. In a reversal of the usual pattern, the successful merchants Henry and Thomas Pratt had benefited from the fortune earned by their father Matthew Pratt, a famous artist.

John A. Willink of Brooklyn was the son of a wealthy banker in Holland, while a number of Sandses, the sometime merchant George Rapelye, the "painter and glazier" George Hall, Losee Van Nostrand, E. J. Whitlock, and the coal merchant Nicholas Van Brunt were typical of Brooklyn capitalists who were beneficiaries of old wealth, much of it in land. Andre Parmentier, proprietor of a successful "garden" which like John Contoit's in New York City offered refreshments and a social center for the "exclusives," had profited in youth from a not inconsiderable sum from his merchant father's estate in Belgium. The publisher Samuel Fleet came of a family which even in the seventeenth century had owned forty vessels and much valuable land.

A large group of New York City's commercial capitalists had fortunes that had been initiated with parental or family wealth variously accumulated. The great merchant William B. Astor began his business life with $1 million bequeathed by his uncle, Henry Astor, and by his father out of the latter's diversified fortune. Vast real properties were inherited by Peter P. Goelet, Jacob B. Herrick, Joel Post, and Lispenard Stewart—the latter the twice-blessed son of the wealthy merchant Alexander L. Stewart and Sarah Lispenard, of the great New York City family whose landholding formed the basis of the wealth of a number of contemporary merchants. The rich merchant Jonathan Thompson was the son of Mary Gardiner of the Long Island family whose "manorial" estate dated back to the first Lion Gardiner in the seventeenth century. Henry Brevoort's father had by the mid-eighteenth century held a "huge tract of land" along the Bowery in lower Manhattan. John Church Cruger, whose seventeenth-century ancestor had been a successful merchant and slave trader, lived on his inheritance on Cruger's Island in the Hudson. William B. Crosby was the son of a successful doctor and a woman of an old, prestigious New York family, Catherine Bedlow. Even more fortunately, his mother was the niece of Colonel Henry Rutgers, whose lavish mansion on Rutgers Place near Clinton Street and great land holdings and other wealth were on his death transferred to Crosby.

New York City merchant wealth of the era had in many instances drawn on earlier fortunes constructed elsewhere. Samuel, Thomas, and William Leggett came of a great landed family of Westchester. Gould Hoyt's family had been large landowners in Connecticut, as had been the family of John Drake. Philip Lydig inherited a large estate on the Bronx River in Westchester from his parents; his mother was the daughter of the wealthy Peter Mesier. Josiah Macy's father had been a wealthy shipowner of Nantucket. John Delafield's was a distinguished London family, which owned much wealth in land there. Archibald Russell, who became eminent in New York City's commerce and philanthropy soon after he arrived in 1836, was the son of James Russell, President of the Royal Society in Edinburgh; while George Douglass came of a Scottish family of large landowners that had emigrated to North America.

Contemporary merchant fortunes were also composed substantially of dowries accruing from well-chosen marital partners of wealthy but by no means entirely mercantile family. If Edmund Dwight was one of the favored group who "did not have to toil in drudgery of active business," it was due primarily to his marriage to a daughter of Samuel Eliot.

Typically, successful marriages in Boston were made by successful men who had already been enriched materially and intangibly by successful parents and families. John D. Bates, whose family was connected with the great house of Baring Brothers, married a daughter of the wealthy "Beau Bill" Boardman. William Lawrence too greatly increased his wealth through marriage to a daughter of "Gentleman Bill." Benjamin W. Crowninshield married Mary Boardman, while his son married a daughter of the great merchant David Sears. Sears, whose own inheritance had been close to $1 million, married into the family of Jonathan Mason. The "provisions dealer" William P. Winchester, on the other hand, got nearly a million dollars through marriage to supplement the large fortune left him by his father, Edmund Winchester. Thomas Dixon, of a rich Scottish family, married the wealthy daughter of Benjamin P. Homer. Other examples of the happy cycle of wealth aligning with wealth were George W. Lyman, Robert G. Shaw (son-in-law to Samuel Parkman), and John L. Gardner, whose father-in-law was Joseph Peabody of Salem. A successful Boston merchant—if less eminent than the latter trio—who married strategically was William Shimmin, whose vast estate owed much to his marriage to the only daughter of John Parker.

Others in this category were H. H. Hunnewell, of the Paris trading house of Samuel Welles, father of his bride; Aaron Baldwin, commission merchant and president of the Washington Bank, who quite properly married the daughter of Philip Marrett, President of the New England Bank; John T. Apthorp, who as the president of the Suffolk Insurance Company and the Boston Bank won the daugter of William Foster, Samuel Swett, most of whose property accrued from his marriage to the daughter of "Billy" Gray; Ebenezer Chadwick, whose property was sharply increased by his marriage to a daughter of John Coffin Jones; John Bray, who wedded a daughter of Samuel Eliot; and Nathaniel P. Russell, who married a daughter of Samuel Hammond. The broker John A. Thayer became the son-in-law to the wealthy Ebenezer Francis, while the latter great capitalist had himself earlier mingled his fortune with that of his father-in-law, Israel Thorndike.

In Philadelphia, as has been noted, Silas E. Weir profited by becoming the son-in-law of the rich Alexander Henry, a form of augmenting wealth that was hardly unique in that city. Mayor Benjamin W. Richards, whose own family had owned extensive land since the late seventeenth century, married into the Lippincotts, proprietors of a great auction house; while Joshua Lippincott of the prominent New Jersey landowning family married Sarah Wetherill. The wealthy dry goods merchant Alexander Benson married well, as did Robert Ralston. Coming into the fortune left by his father, the lawyer-capitalist John Ralston, Ralston married the daughter of the famous New York merchant, real-estate owner and bearer of an eminent family name, Matthew Clarkson.

Wealthy Brooklynites who married well included the sometime

"grocer" Lyman Betts—himself of a seventeenth-century family—who won the hand of a descendant of the old and even more prestigious family of Lambert Suydam. The wealthy Edgar Bartow married the daughter of Brooklyn's richest man, H. B. Pierrepont. Parmenus Johnson, of an old Oyster Bay family, married the daughter of the rich and renowned Tunis Joralemon. The great merchant and financier Samuel A. Willoughby acquired valuable properties in the Borough Hall area through marriage, supplementing the estate left him by his shipowning father.

As shall be noted in a subsequent chapter, most of New York City's elite forged matrimonial alliances with quality families within and without the metropolis. The rich and newly-arrived Archibald Russell found it unnecessary to occupy himself with business after he married Helen Rutherford Watts. John Watts, Jr., whose own family owned vast estates in upper New York City in the Rose Hill district, married into Rutherford Watts. John Watts, Jr., whose own family owned vast leather merchant was vigorously abetted by his marriage to Lydia Ann Corse, daughter of the successful leather merchant Isaac Corse. The auctioneer Joseph Sampson married the daughter of John W. Livingston; the merchant Frederick Schuchardt, the daughter of the wealthy Swiss merchant Frederick Gebhard; the merchant and financier John Adams, the daughter of John Glover; while Henry White married into the Van Cortlandts and Philipses. The great estate left by Monsieur F. Depau owed much to his marital alliance with the daughter of the great Count DeGrasse.

In addition to expanding through inheritance and dowries, the stream of commercial wealth was fed by the real estate and nonmercantile investments and interests of the era's merchant capitalists. The great Philadelphia merchant Jacob Ridgway probably held most of his vast wealth in real estate, as did a number of Whartons and John Stoddart. Business versatility was the characteristic of many of the city's leading merchants, including its outstanding figure, Stephen Girard. Thomas P. Cope owned ships and land, as did the banker and merchant John Welsh and the great shipping merchant Manuel Eyre. Samuel Bispham was wholesale grocer and commission merchant, while Robert W. Waln, also active in politics, owned a cotton factory in Trenton and an ironworks at Phoenixville, Pennsylvania. The famous Robert Ralston and Hyman Gratz headed insurance companies, among their varied business pursuits. It should be noted, however, that merchant involvement in the insurance business was commonplace. The Wainwrights were block and pumpmakers; in addition, Jonathan Wainwright was president of the Kensington Bank and William, president of the Commercial Bank.

Boston merchants not previously mentioned who owned profitable real estate included the great wine merchant John D. Williams, Matthias P. Sawyer, Joshua Bennett, Andrew Carney, and Benjamin Humphrey.

Gardiner Brewer, the distiller, was also a large real estate owner, a speculator in lands, and a wholesaler of domestic goods. Peter C. Brooks, President of the New England Insurance Company, was also an owner of real estate and an officer in diverse corporations, as were the very rich merchants Robert G. Shaw and Rufus Lamson. The iron merchant Jeffrey Richardson owned ropewalks in addition to real estate. Nathaniel D. Goddard was an underwriter, large shipowner, holder of valuable real properties and wharves, as well as a merchant and president of the New England Bank. James Bartlett was another merchant interested in wharves. The distiller, Addison Gilmore, was president of the Western Railroad Company, while the importer of British dry goods Thomas Cordis became a large hardware merchant. Elijah Loring was, among other things, a wharf owner, commercial agent, and a director in the Eagle Bank.

Few wealthy Bostonians were great manufacturers in the sense that the Appleton brothers, John A. and Francis C. Lowell, or Abbot and Amos Lawrence were. Of the latter, a contemporary wrote in 1840: "late a drygoods merchant of Boston, and at present a cloth manufacturer of Lowell." Nonetheless, varying investments in manufacturing enterprises were made by a sizable number of capitalists. The versatile merchant Ebenezer Francis, who held many directorships and much real estate, was for a number of years treasurer of Harvard, the president of the Suffolk Bank as well as the head of a New Hampshire textile mill. David Sears held stock in many manufacturing corporations, as did Patrick Tracy Jackson, whose manufacturing interests possibly superseded his investments in railroads, commerce, and land speculation. The merchant Horace Gray owned a large iron works, and the editor David Child, a beet sugar manufactory; while the merchants John Bumstead and Ebenezer Chadwick combined investments in manufacturing and commerce. Among his other activities, Henry Oxnard was an agent for the Lowell Manufacturing Company in New Orleans. The merchant Nathaniel P. Russell was an insurance broker, secretary of the New England Marine Insurance Company, and shareholder in several New England manufacturing enterprises. Josiah Dunham was a rope manufacturer as well as a builder.

A significant economic fact not always apparent from the general biographical and genealogical accounts of the era's wealthy men is the extent to which their fortunes consisted of insurance company shares. Most great merchants were investors in this form of enterprise. In Boston, for example, in one year in the mid-1840s, approximately one-half of the three hundred wealthiest persons were found to hold *substantial* amounts of the capital of the city's insurance companies. Such investments earned a very high rate of profit at a time when risks, particularly of fire on land and disaster at sea, remained very great.[6] Whatever the reasons, the wealth of the great merchants and men of affairs of the era was heavily invested in companies created to provide safeguards against commercial disaster. Attracted to such wealth were the Shaws, Bryants, Appletons, Lorings, Lawrences, Pratts, Mays, Dorrs, Borlands, Blakes, Sargents, Curtises, Gardners, Wards, Stedmans, Waleses, Sigourneys, Cordises, Lowells, Chadwicks, Thorndikes, Pickerings, Parkers, Binneys, Armstrongs, Sturgises, Bangses, Lambs, Bacons, Lees, Henshaws, Amorys, Shattucks, Bradlees, Prescotts, Lamsons, Trains, Trulls, Shimminses, Otises, Everetts, Jacksons, Quincys, Searses, Tildens, Loverings, Francises, Grays, Peabodys, Hubbards, and Brookses.

Most of Brooklyn's wealthy merchants, such as H. B. Pierrepont, the Rapelyes, the Sandses, the Hickeses, Parmenus Johnson, Charles Hoyt, Stephen Halsey, the Cornells, and the Boerums held valuable real estate in Brooklyn Heights along the waterfront, in the then-outlying areas of Flatbush and Gravesend, in Manhattan, or elsewhere in New York state. As typical were merchants of diversified interest such as Nicholas Van Brunt, landowner and investor; Henry P. Waring, shipowner, bank and corporate director as well as collector of Brooklyn Heights real estate; and Samuel A. Willoughby, who owned ships as well as real estate, founded banks, and played a prominent part in many corporations. Other bank presidents and chief officers included Leffert Lefferts, of an old landowning family, Joseph Sprague, Samuel Smith, Daniel Embury, John Schenck, and Jonathan Trotter. The latter was also a factory owner and active in insurance companies, as was Sprague who, in addition to sitting on the boards of several fire insurance companies, was president of the Long Island Insurance Company. Joshua Sands, whose family had owned valuable real property, was a land speculator who acquired Tory estates, invested in a variety of enterprises, and manufactured cordage, rigging, and other naval products. Edgar Bartow combined commerce with paper manufacturing. Alden Spooner, Brooklyn's foremost newspaper publisher and the city's chief directory publisher, invested heavily in ferry, banking, and insurance companies. Of the merchant Conklin Brush it was said that "from 1816 to 1840 [he was] at the head of nine successful mercantile firms, no one of which ever failed . . . all highly prosperous."[7] His record of unbroken success was much more unusual for the era than the wide variety of his interests.

The actual economic interests of New York City's merchants were as heterogeneous as those of their counterparts in the other great cities. Kenneth W. Porter long ago noted that by the 1840s John Jacob Astor's investment in the city's real estate was greater than in any other general source. The roster of substantial owners of Manhattan lots and real properties included by far most of the city's richest men. As was true elsewhere, New York's merchants did not confine their business activities to the particular firm or even the particular pursuit with which they were usually identified. In view of his more than a dozen simultaneous diverse business affiliations after his retirement from the family auction business—some in finance, some in transportation, some in manufacturing, some in mines, some in insurance, all in addition to his real-estate investments—it is hard to say precisely what Philip Hone's chief occupation may have been. Jordan L. Mott of the old Long Island landed family was part landowner, part iron manufacturer, and part wholesale merchant; but he is probably most accurately described as a "gentleman," in view of the little attention his great wealth permitted him to devote to business. Abraham Van Nest of an old landed family that had intermarried with the Rapelyes and other adornments of New York state's elite, was a New York City merchant, owner of substantial property on Bleecker Street, corporate officer, and president of the Greenwich Savings Bank. The leather merchant Jonathan Thorne owned tanneries and large tracts of land in Pennsylvania. Another merchant whose interests extended to the source of the products he traded in, was Harmon Hendricks, whose Soho Copper Works in Belleville, New Jersey, manufactured and rolled the copper used in his extensive carrying trade. The drug merchant Al[l]ison Post was a heavy investor in the Delaware and Hudson Canal Company, while Benjamin Strong was a director in the Merchants Bank and the North River Insurance Company, and president of both the New York Sugar Refining Company and the Seaman's Bank for Savings. Strong's investments in insurance and banking were typical of the period.

Relying too heavily on the erratic information provided in Moses Beach's vignettes of the rich, an older authority had written that finance lagged far behind commerce and real estate as a source of New York City's merchant elite's wealth.[8] Actually, finance and banking attracted most of the city's leading men (although unfortunately it is impossible to ascertain precisely what proportions of their wealth were so invested). It is instructive that in the mid-1840s the assessed value of such capital approximated one-fifth of the city's wealth. Presidents and vice-presidents of the city's banks, with the heavy investment such leadership entailed, included such leading merchants as Herman LeRoy, Philip Hone, Peter A. Jay, Nathaniel Weed, Leonard Kip, Preserved Fish, Stephen Allen, John Q. Jones, John Mason, James and Albert Gallatin, Effingham Schieffelin, Walter Bowne, Cornelius W. Lawrence, Matthew Clarkson, Jonathan Thompson, Jacob Lorillard, Henry Remsen, John G. Coster, Moses H. Grinnell, in addition to those mentioned earlier. A list of bank officers for Philadelphia and Boston would be similarly representative.

Astor, as Porter had noted, although he "could not be classed as a banker . . . like most moneyed men of his time . . . was necessarily somewhat interested in banking." [9] The necessary interest was heightened by the great opportunity for profit banking then offered. The biographer of the Philadelphia iron merchant Nathan Trotter reports that, "beginning in 1840 commercial-paper discounting was to employ the largest part of Trotter's capital. It had taken him thirty years as a merchant and investor to make $350,000. It would take but thirteen as a commercial-paper specialist to gain an additional $600,000." Trotter discounted paper. Many wealthy men doubtless shared the insight of George Brown of the Baltimore branch of the great house of Brown Brothers, when he wrote in the late 1830s that were he to give up his business and start over again, he "would employ [his] . . . capital in discounting and doing a private banking business."[10]

"Gentlemen"

A final "occupation" missing from contemporary directories, was perhaps most closely alluded to in the Philadelphia category of "gentleman." I have in mind persons of old, usually seventeenth-century, families that had long been prominent in the political and social affairs of their communities, possessed of great landed estates, and were typically active in commerce as well. Their genealogical tables show an intermeshing network of ties with families of similar distinction in their own or outlying locales. No matter how described in general or business directories, contemporaries of such background were rich primarily because they belonged to a "great family." Such were the Deforests, the Gardiners, the Hickses, the DePeysters, the Livingstons, the Van Rensselaers, the Bayards, the Stuyvesants, the Jays, the Schermerhorns, the Bergens, the Beekmans, the Bokers, the Walns, the Shippens, the Whartons, and other families which in the early nineteenth century—and for that matter in the later twentieth century—continued to command the status that in most cases they had first carved out in the seventeenth. If more often than not the members of this elite only dabbled in particular occupations, their capital was active in investments that ran the gamut of the era's possibilities. Real estate, shipyards and shipbuilding, sawmills, flour bleaching (supervision of all of which had occupied Henry Rutgers), wharves, corporate directorships, speculations in western lands occupied their capital, as lives of refinement, opulent uses of leisure, and in some cases the professions and suitable humanitarian and artistic endeavor occupied their minds.

As was noted at the outset, the wealth of the northeastern urban economic elite was swelled by varied sources during the second quarter of the nineteenth century. The business leaders of the time engaged in commerce, but this involvement took diverse forms. The situation was not one in which one clearly defined group of men were merchants, others shipbuilders, others brokers, other financiers, others real-estate purchasers or speculators. Rather, the typical merchant of the time was involved in a number of these and other forms of profit-making. Manufactures still appeared to attract relatively little investment capital in the northeast as a whole. At a time when the president of the American Mutual Insurance Company earned a salary of $3,500 per annum, as Philip Hone did in 1843, men were not "bankers" or "insurance executives" in the sense that they invested most of their time or drew most of their income from positions in such organizations.[11] But the very great rewards obtainable from participation in such enterprises explain why most wealthy men invested and were ready to be directors in them. The "lucrative professions" were lucrative less in the sense that their practice was a significant source of contemporary wealth than that they were favored by young men who were otherwise rich. Law and medicine alike possessed a prestige born of the relatively expensive and cloistered higher education needed to prepare properly for them; and the law was of particular significance to men of substance because of their reliance on its unique services. The most striking revelation afforded by the economic case histories of the era's wealthiest individuals is the extent to which their riches were the product of the dead hand of the past, primarily in the form of landed estates and mercantile fortunes first accumulated in earlier centuries.

Notes

[1] Kenneth W. Porter, *John Jacob Astor, Businessman*, 2 vols. (Cambridge, 1931).
[2] Robert G. Albion, "Commercial Fortunes in New York: A Study in the History of the Port of New York About 1850," *New York History, XVI* (April 1935), p. 159.
[3] See Blumin, "Mobility in a Nineteenth-Century American City: Philadelphia," p. 58.
[4] See Thomas J. Curran, ed., "The Diary of Henry Van Der Lyn," *New-York Historical Society Quarterly, LV* (April 1971), p. 122.
[5] See Daniel Calhoun, *Professional Lives in America: Structure and Aspiration, 1750–1850* (Cambridge, 1965), for an interesting discussion of law, medicine, and the ministry. The latter profession, of course, could confer great prestige as well as power on individuals; but since its practitioners were not "dependent on something resembling market transactions" or as fully "implicated in a [worldly, acquisitive] social order," and perhaps too because it demanded a commitment too strenuous and inimical to the tastes of the well-born, it attracted far fewer rich young men to its ranks than law and medicine.
[6] See Mark Anthony DeWolfe Howe, *Boston: The Place and the People* (New York, 1907), p. 77; and Freeman Hunt, *Lives of American Merchants*, 2 vols. (New York, 1857), I, pp. 420–21. The latter notes the very high rate of profit earned by the Atlantic Mutual Insurance Company in the 1840s while under the leadership of Walter R. Jones, of the ancient and wealthy family of Cold Spring, Long Island.
[7] Henry R. Stiles, *The Civil, Political, Professional and Ecclesiastical History and Commercial and Industrial Record of the County of Kings and the City of Brooklyn* (New York, 1884), vol. I, p. 153.
[8] Albion, "Commercial Fortunes," p. 159.
[9] Porter, *John Jacob Astor*, II, pp. 955–56.
[10] Elva Tooker, *Nathan Trotter, Philadelphia Merchant, 1787–1853* (Cambridge, 1955), pp. 157, 177.
[11] Hone Diary, Dec. 4, 1843, XXI:296.

[illegible] At a time when the president of the [illegible] Mutual Insurance Company received a salary of $[illegible] per annum, as [illegible] did in 18[illegible], however, no "natural" [illegible] tended to [illegible] that they [illegible] of [illegible] day matter [illegible] meet in [illegible] organizations [illegible] they were great [illegible] from [illegible] to explain why [illegible] men [illegible] and [illegible] would be [illegible] of them. [illegible] in the sense that in fact [illegible] than that they were favored by [illegible] to [illegible] the [illegible] experience and fostered [illegible] needed to prepare properly [illegible] [illegible] of their [illegible] revolution [illegible] by the [illegible] individuals [illegible] the product of the [illegible] and [illegible] to [illegible] accumulate [illegible] great fortunes.

[illegible] Robert G. Albion [illegible] New York [illegible]

[illegible] American [illegible] Philadelphia [illegible]

[illegible] (April 1840), p. 122.

[illegible] Daniel [illegible] and the [illegible] The latter [illegible] great [illegible] as well as power [illegible] individuals [illegible] were not [illegible] medicine.

[illegible] New York [illegible] New York, [illegible] very [illegible] of prominent [illegible] wealthy family of Long Island.

[illegible] Commercial [illegible] New York [illegible] vol. [illegible] p. 13[illegible].

[illegible] Albion, Commercial [illegible] p. [illegible].

[illegible] Pessen, [illegible]

[illegible] Nathan [illegible] (Cambridge, [illegible]

[illegible] Diary [illegible]

PART II

Social Mobility

General Reflections on Social Mobility

Who would discuss social mobility must first make clear what he means by the term. As a vast modern literature attests, no topic exerts greater fascination for sociologists than social mobility. Fifteen years ago Bernard Barber noted that about a hundred articles and books on the concept were appearing each year.[1] Even a hasty glance at the articles and book reviews in the *American Sociological Review* of the past decade indicates that the pace of publication on social mobility has, if anything, quickened. The clearest point made about the topic in the literature is its complexity; for as Reinhard Bendix and Seymour Martin Lipset have observed, "the concept of social mobility is ambiguous," depending among other things on men's subjective perception of changes in that most elusive phenomenon, their status.[2] Few students would dissent from the conclusion reached by Thomas Fox and S. M. Miller that "there are a host of different ways of measuring mobility," or that "mobility has many varied contours." Another study finds that at least twenty-two different ingredients of social mobility have been used by scholars.[3] Nor was this list exhaustive. In view of the varying definitions given the concept and the unlike aspects of it emphasized by different scholars, one appreciates Ralf Dahrendorf's judgment that "the concept of social mobility is too general to be useful."[4]

The chapters in this section, therefore, consider not social mobility in general but three significant facets of antebellum mobility: the social and economic situation of parents and families of the rich (or intergenerational social and economic mobility); the extent to which fortunes rose and fell during the era (or intragenerational economic mobility); and the classic issue of equality of opportunity. If the discussion will not reveal or even purport to reveal the full extent of social mobility in antebellum America—an impossible task given the elusiveness of that topic and the diverse ways of measuring it—its purpose is more modest and therefore perhaps more useful. The evidence illuminates important aspects of American social development that have been obscured in myth and neglect.

Although much has been written about social mobility in general and its prevalence or non-existence for *other* periods in American history, very little has been done on the "age of egalitarianism." To be more precise, little has been done that is based on substantial evidence.[5] Lipset and Hans Zetterberg concluded some time ago that since "enough descriptive material has now been collected" on such matters as the "background of members in certain elite groups," the time had come for a shift from descriptive to theoretical studies.[6] This judgment does not, in fact, apply to the second quarter of the nineteenth century in America. Historians have often referred to the "fluidity" of the era and have evidently convinced sociologists that the facts are known, for this as for other periods. But, as shall be seen, prevailing beliefs concerning the era's mobility have rested primarily on logical but undocumented assumptions. The few scholars who have expressed awareness of the flimsy basis of the belief in antebellum mobility are precisely those historians who have studied in depth the materials for a particular city. Stuart Blumin, author of a dissertation on occupational and residential mobility in antebellum Philadelphia, has pointed out that the "proposition that nineteenth-century American society was highly fluid . . . has all but escaped evaluation." Stephan Thernstrom, student of intergenerational occupational mobility in Newburyport, Massachusetts, advises that "systematic studies of social mobility in nineteenth-century America are still woefully absent." [7] The chapters that follow attempt to respond to this deficiency.

Most previous studies of social mobility have been "almost exclusively concerned with occupational mobility." [8] This preoccupation is explained less by the superiority of occupational evidence than by its availability.[9] As the previous chapter indicates, occupations can sometimes be quite misleading as clues to wealth and status. Charles Westoff, Marvin Bressler, and Philip C. Sagi have found that neither intergenerational nor intragenerational occupational mobility correlates significantly with a number of other indices of social mobility.[10] A recent study of vertical mobility in rural Michigan during the mid- and late-nineteenth century suggests that the "direct measurement of wealth mobility is no doubt preferable to the inferential method" that relies on occupational mobility.[11] Such direct measurements are rare because the wealth of individuals has usually been inaccessible to sociological students. Fortunately, the availability of data on the wealth of thousands of persons in antebellum cities—complemented by primary evidence both on their own occupations and status and on the wealth, occupations, and prestige of their parents and families—makes possible an investigation of social mobility that combines "direct" with "indirect" measurement.

Notes

[1] Bernard Barber, *Social Stratification* (New York, 1957), *passim.*
[2] Bendix and Lipset, *Social Mobility in Industrial Society* (Berkeley, 1963), p. 112.
[3] Fox and Miller, "Occupational Stratification and Mobility," in Bendix and Lipset, eds., *Class, Status and Power* (New York, 1966), p. 581; Charles F. Westoff, Marvin Bressler, and Philip C. Sagi, "The Concept of Social Mobility: An Empirical Inquiry," *American Sociological Review, 25* (June 1960), pp. 375–85.
[4] Dahrendorf, *Class and Class Conflict in Industrial Society* (Stanford, 1959), p. 220.
[5] C. Wright Mills, "The American Business Elite: a Collective Portrait," *Journal of Economic History,* Supplement ["The Tasks of Economic History"], *V* (1945), pp. 20–44, makes sweeping generalizations about the social mobility experienced by politically eminent businessmen in antebellum America, on the basis of the thin accounts in the *Dictionary of American Biography.* Also relying on this secondary literature is P. M. G. Harris's provocative "The Social Origins of American Leaders: The Demographic Foundations, "*Perspectives in American History, III* (1969), pp. 159–344.
[6] Lipset and Hans L. Zetterberg, "A Theory of Social Mobility," in *Class, Status, and Power,* p. 561.
[7] Blumin, "The Historical Study of Vertical Mobility," *Historical Methods Newsletter, I* (Sept. 1968), p. 1; Thernstrom, "Notes on the Historical Study of Social Mobility," *Comparative Studies in Society and History* (Jan. 1968).
[8] Fox and Miller, "Occupational Stratification and Mobility," p. 574.
[9] For that matter, the methodology employed in many mobility studies has been severely criticized lately. See Natalie Rogoff, *Recent Trends in Occupational Mobility* (Glencoe, Ill., 1953), p. 13; Otis Dudley Duncan, "Methodological Issues in the Analysis of Social Mobility," in Neil J. Smelser and Seymour M. Lipset, eds., *Social Structure and Mobility in Economic Development* (Chicago, 1966), pp. 51–97; Saburo Yosuda, "A Methodological Inquiry into Social Mobility," *American Sociological Review, 29* (Feb. 1964), pp. 16–23; and Gosta Carlsson, *Social Mobility and Class Structure* (Lund, 1958), chaps. 5 and 6.
[10] "The Concept of Social Mobility: An Empirical Inquiry," p. 378.
[11] Gordon W. Kirk, Jr., "The Promise of American Life: Social Mobility in a Nineteenth Century Immigrant Community: Holland, Michigan, 1847–1894" (Ph.D. diss., Michigan State University, 1970), p. 232.

NOTES

[illegible] (New York, 1957), [illegible]
[illegible] and Lipset, Social Mobility in Industrial Society (Berkeley, 1959) [illegible]; Fox and Miller, "Occupational Stratification and Mobility: Intra-country Variations," [illegible] Lipset and Bendix [illegible] Social Mobility [illegible] the [illegible] "The Concept of Social Mobility," Empirical Inquiry [illegible] (1960), pp. [illegible]
[illegible] Dahrendorf, Class and Class Conflict in Industrial Society (Stanford, 1959), p. [illegible]
[illegible] "The American [illegible]" [illegible] "Fernand [illegible]" "The Tasks of Social History" [illegible] about [illegible] social mobility [illegible] the basis of [illegible] in the [illegible] American [illegible] Also [illegible] on this secondary literature [illegible] Handlin [illegible] The Social Origins of [illegible] The [illegible]
[illegible] pp. [illegible]
Lipset and Bendix [illegible] "[illegible] of Social Mobility [illegible]"
[illegible] p. [illegible]
[illegible] "The Historical Study of Vertical Mobility," Historical Methods Newsletter [illegible] (1968) [illegible] Thernstrom, "Notes on the Historical Study of Social Mobility," Comparative Studies in Society and History [illegible] (1968).
[illegible] and Miller, "Occupational Stratification and Mobility," p. [illegible]
[illegible] methodology [illegible] many mobility studies [illegible] [illegible] Duncan [illegible] Social Mobility [illegible] and [illegible] M. Lipset [illegible] Social Structure and Mobility in Economic Development (Chicago, 1966), pp. [illegible] Social Mobility [illegible] Mobility and Class Structure [illegible]
[illegible] "The Concept of Social Mobility [illegible]"
[illegible] of American [illegible] Social Mobility in a [illegible] [illegible] (Ph.D. diss., Michigan State University, 1970), [illegible]

5

Were Rich Americans in the "Era of the Common Man" Self-Made Men?

In America most of the rich men were formerly poor. . . . They have felt the sting of want; they were long a prey to adverse fortunes.

Tocqueville, *Democracy in America*, I:54; II:138

In a speech to the United States Senate on February 2, 1832, Henry Clay advised his colleagues and the nation that almost all of the successful factory owners of his acquaintance were "enterprising self-made men, who have whatever wealth they possess by patient and diligent labor." Made in the context of a pro-tariff argument, Clay's remarks were hardly original, nor did they purport to be. The Kentuckian was merely proclaiming a social belief he had reason to think was held by most of his countrymen.[1]

The Contemporary Mythology

The notion that not only factory owners but almost all wealthy Americans were self-made men came close to being a secular article of faith during the "era of the common man," so widely did it appear to be subscribed to. There is, of course, no way of determining either the extent of its acceptance or the depth of conviction of those who did adhere to it. Certainly the idea was persistently propagated by orators and publicists. In this instance, at least, the Tocquevillean conclusion that rich Americans had been born poor only confirmed what his American audience evidently believed it already knew.

Moses Beach and the other compilers of the lists of wealthy citizens reminded their readers that the great fortunes they immortalized through publication were characteristically self-made. Boston's "first men" ostensibly "were once poor themselves, or their fathers were;" their wealth "came to them through toil and labor. . . ." Many of New York City's Midases too had "by honest and laborious industry . . . raised themselves from the obscure and humble walks of life, to great wealth and consideration." The anonymous editor of the Philadelphia rating reported that most of the city's "wealthy citizens are plain men . . .

[who] pride themselves for having made their own money." Such contemporary historians of successful merchants as Freeman Hunt and Stephen N. Winslow glorified their subjects above all for having risen to the top through heroic struggle. "Philadelphia," wrote Winslow, "is remarkable for the number of self-made merchants and manufacturers in it; men who feared not 'those twin-jailors of the aspiring soul low birth and misfortune.' " To the question, what is a self-made man? he responded: "the reply is easy. A man who, without any extraordinary family or pecuniary advantages at the commencement of life, has . . . by indomitable industry and unwavering integrity achieved both character and fortune." The nation was told that such men abounded here. Not long after Clay's tariff speech, the respected Calvin Colton affirmed that "this is a country of self-made men," whose wealthiest citizens had started "from an humble origin and small beginnings," and whose success was "the reward of merit and industry." These roseate judgments were confidently uttered by men who gave the impression of harboring no doubts concerning their accuracy.[2]

The great merchant William E. Dodge even offered a detailed estimate as to the proportion of his wealthy mercantile contemporaries who were self-made. "If the history of our citizens of wealth were written," he advised a lecture audience, "we should find that full three fourths had risen from comparatively small beginnings [with little or nothing] to their present position." [3] Neither Dodge nor the other contemporary purveyors of the rags-to-riches myth reached their conclusions on the basis of detailed factual investigation into the origins of wealthy men. Drawing on a few examples, which they evidently had no difficulty in convincing themselves represented a universal American tendency, they said, above all, what they wanted the American people to believe. As ideologists of a sort, they were less concerned with the accuracy of their sunny social judgments than with their popularity. This is not to impugn their sincerity; for few men are more sincere than those who seek to convince others of what they themselves know intuitively. What is in question is not the motives of these contemporary yeasayers but their accuracy.

It is well known that Tocqueville, one of the influential architects of the rags-to-riches belief, was at times prone to spin his marvelous social theorems by recourse more to logic than to pedestrian data. What is fascinating is the extent to which scholars ordinarily skeptical of unverified observation have relied on it in discussing the origins of the rich in the "age of the common man." If few modern historians would commit themselves to a precise ratio, as did William Dodge, many have nevertheless agreed that a remarkable movement up the social and economic ladder, did take place during the second quarter of the nineteenth century.[4] The author of an influential modern interpretation of voting behavior in antebellum New York State, in explaining why economic class allegedly influences voting less than does ethnic and religious identity, states that "since the United States is highly heterogeneous, and has high social mobility, I assume that men tend to retain and be more influenced by their ethnic and religious group membership than by their membership in economic classes or groups." [5] One marvels that so significant a theory would be based on a premise of high social mobility that is merely asserted rather than demonstrated.

Modern factual studies have been undertaken to test the validity of the rags-to-riches thesis for most periods in American history. The twentieth century, the post–Civil War decades, the colonial and the Revolutionary eras have all been subjected to detailed investigations of varying intensity. The "age of egalitarianism," however, has heretofore escaped inquiries of similar scope.[6] One surmises that a major reason for this neglect is that constant repetition of the theme of fluidity has convinced scholars that for the Jacksonian period the facts are in: intergenerational economic and occupational mobility were the rule.[7] Actually, it is not the facts that are in, but rather a continuing series of firmly-stated generalizations that essentially do nothing more than assume that the facts bear them out. I have, therefore, gathered evidence on the wealth and status of the parents and families of the several hundred wealthiest persons in each of the major cities of the northeast during the era in order to subject the belief that typically they were born poor to the kind of empirical test it has previously been spared.

Social Mobility Before and After the "Era of the Common Man"

Before considering the results of this investigation, it would be useful to summarize recent findings on the surrounding decades. A clearer perspective is thus afforded that makes possible a comparison of social or vertical mobility patterns over the course of several historical eras, revealing whether the trend for the entire span was uniform or followed a broken course.

Modern studies of the family status and backgrounds of five hundred big business leaders of 1900 and the 1870s disclose that they were overwhelmingly of high status and from unusually successful families. Discovering that "poor immigrant boys and poor farm boys actually made up no more than 3 per cent of the business leaders" of 1900 whose backgrounds he studied, William Miller concludes wryly that poor boys "who become business leaders have always been more conspicuous in American history books than in American history." [8] But that the validity of the Horatio Alger legend has been called into question for the post–Civil War era appears to have weakened not at all belief in the companion idea that the successful and wealthy men of the antebellum era were self-made. A "new industrialism" had supposedly reversed the egalitarian trend that came to a climax in the antebellum decades.

The social landscape of the two centuries after Jamestown has not

Jacob Patchen (1759–1840), Wealthy and Eccentric Brooklyn Butcher. *(Courtesy of the New-York Historical Society.)*

been as intensively researched as have the last hundred years; the evidence that has been uncovered, however, points to the very much greater social mobility of the earlier period. A recent study of seventeenth-century Salem, Massachusetts, finds a mixed picture, in which although "some members of the rapidly emerging elite began their careers propertyless and benefited from the opportunities for investment . . . more often they emigrated with considerable wealth which was further augmented by fortuitous investment."[9] Jackson Main has concluded that there were "remarkable opportunities for the man of modest property to become rich" by the late eighteenth century. His data on the three greatest cities of the northeast—although admittedly imperfect—are of special interest. About one-third of the sixty wealthiest Bostonians of 1771 had started with little or nothing. By 1789 only one-half of a small number of the city's very wealthiest merchants had been born into wealthy or well-to-do families, with the rest scattered among middling or lower-status occupations. (In his more recent study of social mobility in Revolutionary Boston, Allan Kulikoff finds a "moderate" rate of movement from one occupational category to another between 1771 and 1790.) Of a group of a hundred wealthy Philadelphians, "about one third had made their own fortunes." And between "one third and two fifths of the merchants in pre–Revolutionary New York City [actually, the members of the Chamber of Commerce] were self-made men." In the years immediately after the Revolution, the already high "mobility rate" actually went up: "probably 60 per cent at the least [of a number of merchants in 1786] were self-made men," while in 1791 50 per cent of the wealthiest citizens of the "east ward" had risen from humble origins. Main's data lend credence to Cadwallader Colden's contemporary statement that in eighteenth-century New York City, the most opulent families had risen from the lowest rank of the people.[10]

A recent study of post–Revolutionary New York City concludes that for the period ending in 1815, "the evidence of upward social mobility is marked. Almost two thirds of the attorneys and merchants in public office had risen above the occupational level of their fathers who were mechanics or farmers."[11] Partial and random though it may be, the evidence does indicate that many successful and wealthy northeasterners in the eighteenth and early nineteenth centuries had begun in humble circumstances. Did this evidently high rate of intragenerational mobility continue during the "age of the common man?" Were "most of the era's rich men formerly poor?"

Sources on the Family Backgrounds of the Rich

My answers to these questions are based on detailed evidence gathered on the wealthy in New York City, Brooklyn, Boston, and Philadelphia. Ordinarily such documentation would be relegated to footnotes; but in view of the importance of the supporting data to an argument whose main claim to significance is precisely that its conclusions follow the evidence, a brief explanation of the material relied on—and rejected—is called for.

Since several sources were consulted for each of close to two thousand individuals, and useful material (albeit sometimes in snippets) was obtained from still other, general writings, any attempt even to list all of the sources would run into dozens of pages. What follows therefore is not a description of all the evidence used but rather a discussion of the most important material.[12]

Unless their data were confirmed by reliable contemporaries, little stock was placed in the evidence of the famous biographical encyclopaediae, primarily because of their thinness but also because of their unreliability. Even the rightly admired *Dictionary of American Biography* sometimes lapsed, although its deficiencies for a study such as this one stem more from its principles of selection and the slight interest of its authors in the parental status of their subjects than in its outright errors.[13] I have discounted entirely Moses Beach's *Wealthy Citizens* pamphlets, since Beach's cavalier methods of publication disqualify his listings as reliable sources.[14] I also agree with a former editor of the authoritative *New York Genealogical and Biographical Record,* who said of Joseph Scoville's well-known contemporary account, *The Old Merchants of New York,* that "the character of this entertaining, gossipy work is not such as to entitle it to any weight," for all its author's ability and experience.[15]

Genealogical evidence was heavily relied on. These data, however, are hardly foolproof, even when drawn from such reliable sources as the *NYGBR,* the *New England Historical and Genealogical Register*—which for a short period after 1869 was entitled the *NEHGR and Antiquarian Journal*—the *Publications of the Historical Society of Pennsylvania,* and the *Pennsylvania Magazine of History and Biography.* Every item in every issue of these journals was scrutinized for useful leads, commencing with the first issue of the *NEHGR* in January, 1847. The researcher using these publications, arising from his work after consulting an early volume confident that he has secured accurate data, would be disappointed to discover that subsequent volumes sometimes modify drastically previous biographical statements. As for family genealogies, one must be wary of the habit of some genealogists of attributing too exalted a status to the families of their subjects. This form of exaggeration is perhaps cancelled out by the opposite tendency to attribute humble origins to substantial men. As one contemporary noted: "it was long deemed inconsistent with the self-reliance and humanitarian sentiment of republican and democratic faith, to lay much stress upon genealogical claims," in tracing the lives of the eminent.[16]

The private papers of many wealthy families were examined. Such evidence is invaluable, although it yielded better information on the contemporary activities of eminent persons than on either the wealth or status of their parents and families—the latter information seldom being explicitly referred to. Among the papers consulted were those of such families as the Stuyvesants, Hendrickses, Fishes, Hones, Grosvenors, Beekmans, Lorillards, Schermerhorns, Suydams, Van Rensselaers, Tillotsons, Strongs, Brinckerhoffs, Astors, Hallocks, Kings, Bennets, Livingstons, Griswolds, Brevoorts, Dodges, Allens, Phelpses, Enos, Whitneys, Aspinwalls, Emmets, Bories, Fishers, Careys, Brimmers, Appletons, Searses, Lawrences, Brookses, Everetts, Furmans, and many others of the great northeastern cities.

Local histories were excellent, particularly when written by competent men who knew personally the elite families they described. Such an author was John Latting, an early editor of the *NYGBR*, who had studied law with Francis B. Cutting and Caleb S. Woodhull.[17] Another was Henry R. Stiles, friend to many of New York City's and Brooklyn's elite and their descendants. Stiles founded the Long Island Historical Society, was the first president of the New York Genealogical and Biographical Society, and wrote a massive, sprawling, utterly indispensable book on nineteenth-century Brooklyn and its leading families.[18] That Henry Simpson, mid-nineteenth century biographer of Philadelphia's elite, was aided in his researches by such eminences as Horace Binney, Samuel Breck, Henry W. Gilpin, Charles J. Biddle, and Thomas Balch, adds greatly to the credibility of his *Lives*. John F. Watson's personal encounters with some of the elite whose family histories he sketched similarly induce respect for his portrayals.[19] The value of Abraham Ritter's charming anecdotal account of *Philadelphia and Her Merchants* is enhanced by the evidence that many of the early nineteenth-century merchants he discusses respected his judgments. Dozens of substantial volumes, including histories of the great cities, memorial histories, histories of bench and bar and of the other professions, histories of the great universities and their graduates, histories of streets and homesteads, as well as many hundreds of smaller-gauged histories of individuals, societies, business organizations (particularly banks), memoirs, funeral orations, club minutes and records, also yielded invaluable data.[20] A number of modern scholarly biographies provide reliable sources of information on eminent individuals and families, as do recent essays in the scholarly journals.[21]

Contemporary diaries and private journals were also a precious source. Of outstanding value are the manuscripts kept by George Templeton Strong and Edward Neufville Tailer of New York, Samuel Breck of Boston and Philadelphia, Sidney George Fisher of Philadelphia, and Gabriel Furman and John Baxter of Brooklyn. Standing alone as the nonpareil of such sources are Philip Hone's twenty-eight folio volumes, a treasure trove of information on the second quarter of the nineteenth century.[22] The well-known published excerpts from this diary—focusing on national politics or material of obvious public interest—only hint at the amazingly rich data on families and ancestors, business, private life, medicine, the arts, society, and the uses of leisure, contained in Hone's meticulously kept daily journal. An unusual source is the 160 scrapbooks located in the Long Island Historical Society, a storehouse of much trivia side-by-side with invaluable manuscript and other material on the Cortelyou, Hoyt, Gerritson, Couwenhoven, Martense, Rapelye, Schermerhorn, Remsen, Hicks, Willoughby, and other elite families of Brooklyn and the then-outlying districts of Flatbush, Flatlands, Gravesend, Bushwick, and Williamsburgh.

These are the chief factual sources for the discussion that follows on the status and condition of the parents and families of the rich.

Family Wealth and Status of the Antebellum Rich

Some of the best known among the wealthy citizens did, in fact, have the kind of background ascribed to them by the egalitarian thesis. Although John Jacob Astor's story is perhaps improperly described as "rags to riches," there is some question as to the precise wealth or status of his father. Whether the latter was a "very worthy" minor officeholder, as some described him, or a poor man devoted more to tippling than to industry, as others saw him (and it is not clear that the two judgments are mutually exclusive) it seems fairly certain that the great merchant was indeed a self-made man of humble origin. The same can be said with even more certainty of his sometime partner, Cornelius Heeney, who migrated from Ireland apparently with less than a dollar in his pockets and went on to become one of the wealthiest residents of Brooklyn.[23] Lewis A. Godey, publisher of the popular *Ladies Book*, John Grigg, and Joseph Sill were wealthy Philadelphians of humble beginnings. In Boston, Daniel P. Parker, Ebenezer Chadwick, John R. Adan, and the three Henshaw brothers also appear to have been of poor or humble birth. Anson G. Phelps, Marshall O. Roberts, Gideon Lee, Saul Alley, and possibly the Lorillard brothers were New York City eminences whose backgrounds appear to have been plebeian, as was John Dikeman's in Brooklyn. Stephen Girard's claim that he too had been a destitute youth was evidently accepted by most contemporaries, although there is some doubt as to whether it was well founded.[24] No matter how Girard's family is finally appraised, evidence is not lacking that some rich men had in fact been born poor. The most interesting feature of such evidence however is its uncommonness.

During the age of alleged social fluidity, the great majority of wealthy persons appear to have been descended of parents and families that combined affluence with high social status. The small number of these families that had been less than rich had typically been, not poor, but well-to-do. (My treatment, in differentiating the rich from the well-to-do, contrasts somewhat with Jackson Main's handling of a similar problem in the Revolutionary era. In dealing with vertical mobility, Main treated children of "well-to-do though not wealthy" family as persons who were *not* self-made, also concluding that men who "inherited *part* of their wealth cannot really be considered mobile." [25] But what if the part inherited were extremely small?) In terms of occupation, the well-to-do or the middling category was composed of less-than-rich ministers, professionals other than very successful lawyers and doctors, petty officials, shopkeepers, skilled artisans who doubled as small tradesmen, and independent or moderately prosperous farmers. Included in the middle are the families of Peter Cooper, William E. Dodge, Gerard Hallock, Joseph Sampson, Cornelius Vanderbilt, Moses Yale Beach, Peter Chardon Brooks, Amos and Abbott Lawrence, Thomas Handasyd Perkins, George C. Shattuck, George Hall, Thomas Everitt, Jr., Samuel R. Johnson, Cyrus P. Smith, and Samuel Smith, all of whom appeared to have been both better off and of higher-status occupations than the mechanics, cartmen, milkmen, and laborers who predominated in the cities. The evidence for these generalizations, inevitably imperfect, requires elaboration.

TABLE 5–1.
The Wealth and Status of Parents and Families of the Richest Persons in Antebellum Northeastern Cities (by percentage)

Cities	*Rich and/or Eminent*	*Middling*	*Poor or Humble*
New York City	95	3	2
Brooklyn	81	16	3
Philadelphia	92	6	2
Boston	94	4	2

It was, of course, impossible to obtain reliable information on the family status of all rich persons. Fortunately, abundant evidence exists on the backgrounds of most of the very wealthiest persons in the great cities. Data were secured on 90 per cent of the more than 100 New Yorkers who in 1828 were assessed for $100,000 and upward and in 1845 at $250,000 or more; on 85 per cent of the more than 100 Bostonians worth $100,000 or better in 1833 and $200,000 or more in 1848; and on about 90 per cent of the 75 Brooklynites who in 1841 were evaluated at $60,000 or more. For Philadelphia, as indicated earlier, the nature of the tax records does not permit them to be used to disclose the total assessed wealth of individuals. One can differentiate the "super rich" of that city from other wealthy persons only by accepting at face value the sums attributed in the anonymous *Memoirs and Auto-Biography of Some of the Wealthiest Citizens of Philadelphia.* Varied evidence does point to the credibility of that document.[26] Information was obtained on 75 per cent of the 365 persons each claimed by the *Memoirs* to be worth $100,000 or more. As Table 1 indicates, the pattern of the social backgrounds of the urban rich was strikingly similar for the four leading cities. If the families of Brooklyn's smaller number of rich persons were more often than elsewhere of middling or well-to-do rather than wealthy status, an explanation may lie in Brooklyn's more recent origins as an independent city, its much smaller population, its lesser wealth, and its more limited economic development. It appeared to be easier for newcomers to the city proper (or to its most envied ranks) to find a niche in Brooklyn's elite than in larger cities richer in both wealth and tradition.

Evidence was not as freely available for the lesser rich of the great cities. Data were obtained on about 70 per cent of the more than 450 New Yorkers assessed at between $25,000 and $100,000 in 1828, and for 63 per cent of the 950 New Yorkers who in 1845 were worth between $45,000 and $250,000; on about 60 per cent of the 260 Bostonians evaluated at between $50,000 and $200,000 in 1833, and on the same percentage of the 400 Bostonians similarly appraised in 1848; and on 63 per cent of the 100 Brooklynites assessed in 1841 at between $30,000 and $60,000. These are not unsubstantial proportions, yet it is possible that the backgrounds of the missing persons were unlike those of the much larger number of individuals for whom information was obtained. It can be fairly argued that the omissions concern less-eminent persons whose families probably were neither as wealthy nor of as high status as the families whose careers and records are better publicized.[27] Yet a significant feature of the evidence is its disclosure that there appeared to be no difference in the social origin patterns of the lesser wealthy as against the "super rich"; nor did the patterns of family background of the relatively little-known rich for whom information was obtained differ from those of the eminent rich. Vastly rich or fairly rich, celebrated or obscure, it mattered not: the upper 1 per cent of wealthholders of the great cities—the rich of their time—almost universally were born to families of substance and standing.

These are amazing findings. Startled at the great disparity between previous beliefs and actuality, I went over the evidence for each wealthy person a number of times, assessing it as conservatively as possible in order to make certain that the delights neither of revisionism nor iconoclasm would affect the evaluations made of family rank. Determining relative wealth and standing involves judgment, in contrast, say, to determining religion or date of birth. Among the chief factors that went into the appraisal of a family were wealth (actual and alleged), occupation, reputed standing in the community and the period of time during which they had status, religious denomination, kinship ties, and the kind of material life and opportunities provided the eminences of the 1820s, the 1830s, and the 1840s in their youth.[28] That, for example, a young person attended so prestigious an institution as Harvard, Columbia, or the University of Pennsylvania in an era when only one-tenth of 1 per cent of the population attended any college at all was a significant fact.[29] For all their unevenness and inevitable deficiencies, the data are so abundant that even concise descriptive summaries alone would require a substantial volume. More than a thousand case histories are involved in all. The following chapter contains representative examples of the leading "patterns of social origin" of the era's wealthiest persons. Such material conveys more forcefully than the statistical analysis derived from it the characteristic social routes taken by the rich. Impervious to the mood of the interpreter, the evidence stands, sharply refuting prevalent views about the backgrounds of the wealthy in the "era of the common man."

Reasons for Persistence of the Myth of Social Mobility

What accounts for the popularity of this false notion? How could so many intelligent and informed persons have been so wrong? A number of explanations come to mind. Men of conservative persuasion such as Moses Beach, Calvin Colton, and Edward Everett evidently hoped that popular acceptance of the "sound doctrine" of rags to riches would have happy social consequences: unfortunates would be deflected from radical thought and action. The Malthusian teaching so popular with social conservatives here and abroad—that "the poor are the authors of their own misery"—was thus complemented by its corollary—that "the rich are the authors of their own success or happiness." [30] Successful men, eager to convince their less fortunate countrymen that their successes were due to innate ability, virtue and honest labor—rather than to mere luck or unfair advantages, such as inheritance—had little trouble in convincing themselves in the process. Nor was it entirely a matter of the wish being father to the thought.

Contemporary writers, particularly the small army of European visitors who toured the United States during the era, were for the most part convinced that in the society of the fabled young republic the social ladder was easily climbed. That most of the visitors actually found little evidence of upward social movement hardly detracted either from their own conviction that such mobility was a reality or from their

American audience's acceptance of a conclusion both logical and comforting. These same visitors also agreed, in the words of one of them, that "the most striking circumstance in the American character was the constant habit of praising themselves." Not the least of the features of their civilization that Americans boasted of was the alleged opportunity it afforded ordinary men to rise to the top.[31]

The rags-to-riches ideology had so penetrated American thought during the era that men whose own publications contradicted the thesis, nevertheless insisted it was true, often reaching conclusions at odds with their evidence. (Even if biographical sketches in the "wealthy citizens" pamphlets are taken at face value, men born rich far outnumbered those born poor.) One Boston publicist described as a "poor boy" Robert G. Shaw, whose family was a prosperous one; another, overlooking the connections and the wealth accumulated by the eminent Huguenot family, the Sigourneys, wrote that Henry Sigourney amassed his wealth by his "own industry" alone.[32] The eulogists of Philadelphia's merchants were also prone to this form of self-delusion. Overlooking the "respectability and wealth" of the Beck family in Germany, old Ritter wrote that Paul Beck, Jr., "was the architect of his own fortune." Winslow, after noting that the parents of Isaac R. Davis were in "moderate circumstances" and that a prosperous friend to the family took interest in the lad, wrote that Davis began "without a single dollar." John Hare Powel, an ornament of the Philadelphia elite, could assert that "influence and standing should be won and maintained by individual merit," as though his own life illustrated this wholesome principle.[33] This comment came from a man whose father, Robert Hare, was an eminent Englishman and speaker of the Pennsylvania Senate; whose mother was Margaret Willing of the fabulously wealthy family; who before he was 21 years old managed to earn $20,000 in one commercial voyage alone—undertaken while he was with the counting house of his relatives the Willings—; who on attaining his majority took the Grand Tour "for improvement and pleasure," his tastes catered to in the most opulent manner by his paternal relatives in England; who had his surname changed in order to gratify—and become the heir to the fortune of—his aunt Elizabeth (herself the wife of Major Samuel Powel, and the daughter of Charles Willing and Anna Shippen of the great Philadelphia family); and who as an adult lived a refined and elegant life made possible by his inheritance!

Perhaps the most Pollyannaish contemporary [mis]interpreter of biographical evidence was Freeman Hunt, devoted and enthusiastic admirer of America's merchants, whom he extolled in his charming *Merchants' Magazine*. According to Hunt, Stephen Girard had left his "native country . . . in the capacity of a cabin boy, without education, excepting a limited knowledge of the elements of reading and writing." From this description one would hardly guess that the great merchant's father was a shipping merchant who "piled up a good-sized fortune," and left a substantial inheritance to young Girard, or that "there had never been the slightest thought that Stephen Girard would remain a junior officer." [34] Mathew Carey, we are told, landed "at the wharf at Philadelphia . . . with scarce a dozen guineas in his pocket," information that does not quite convey either the wealth that had been accumulated by this great publisher's father in Ireland as an "extensive contractor" or the kind of education the latter had provided for the younger Carey and his fortunate brothers. Hunt could also somehow describe Walter Restored Jones of the old, eminent, and wealthy family of Cold Spring, Long Island—truly one of fortune's favorites—as a "self-taught and self-made man." [35]

Of course, evidence that one form of social mobility was absent in antebellum cities by no means rules out the possibility that other forms flourished. That, in technical terms, an "in-flow" study of a social and economic elite reveals little upward movement is no assurance that there was equally small "out-flow" movement from society's low and middle levels upward. (A subsequent chapter on the rise and fall of fortunes will focus more closely on this matter.) In the absence of the requisite data, we know very little at this time about the later fate of the poor and the middling. A recent statistical investigation of upward and downward mobility among different socioeconomic strata in antebellum Philadelphia does disclose relatively slight movement; and that the changes that occurred were confined to contiguous rather than to widely separated categories. As it relies chiefly on the criteria of occupation and residence, that study is admittedly not definitive for Philadelphia, let alone for other cities.[36] But if the need for continued exploration of early-nineteenth century mobility patterns—particularly among the poor—reduces the universality of generalizations drawn from the careers of the rich, it in no sense detracts from their importance.

Why so many historians accepted the rags-to-riches version of antebellum success is a fascinating question, a problem in psychology and intellectual history which is beyond the scope of this essay. One suspects that unwitting yeasaying, nationalism, a belief in American exceptionalism, and unwillingness to tamper with a historical belief that was both comforting and logical, among other reasons, played a part. Whatever the ultimate explanation, it seems clear that historians' belief in this most dramatic form of social mobility—the alleged leap from the bottom to the top in one generation—is untenable. The detailed evidence, illustrations from which follow in the next chapter, indicates that the "self-made man"—recently shown to have been more fantasy than fact in the post–Civil War decades—was similarly a creature of the imagination a generation earlier, at the very time when the great Henry Clay was asserting the phantom's corporeality and ubiquitousness.

Notes

[1] Clay's speech is cited in Irvin G. Wyllie, *The Self-Made Man in America: the Myth of Rags to Riches* (New York, 1966), p. 10. Wyllie's book is an interesting examination of the history of an ideology; it does not deal with the accuracy of the "myth" but rather with its persistence and modifications over the course of time.
[2] Preface, *Memoirs and Auto-Biography of Some of the Wealthy Citizens of Philadelphia*; "Prefatory Notice," *Wealth and Pedigree of the Wealthy Citizens of New York City* (3rd ed., New York, 1842); Introduction, *"Our First Men:" A Calendar of Wealth, Fashion and Gentility* (Boston, 1846); Stephen N. Winslow, *Biographies of Successful Philadelphia Merchants* (Philadelphia, 1864), pp. viii, 111, 137; Freeman Hunt, *Lives of American Merchants*, 2 vols. (New York, 1857), *passim;* and Calvin Colton, *Junius Tracts, VII* (New York, 1844), p. 15.
[3] Dodge, *Lecture on Old New York* (New York, 1880), pp. 38–40. The context makes clear that Dodge's conclusions were meant to apply as much to the rich of an earlier generation as to the post–Civil War period.
[4] One well-known textbook states that "of the successful businessmen of the period before the Civil War, almost 50 per cent came from the lower social and economic strata of society." Dexter Perkins and Glyndon G. Van Deusen, *The United States of America: A History*, 2 vols. (2nd ed., New York, 1968), I, p. 446. For variations on the theme of the self-made Jacksonian rich see Carl R. Fish, *The Rise of the Common Man: 1830 to 1850* (New York, 1927), p. 9; Rowland Berthoff, "The American Social Structure: A Conservative Hypothesis," *American Historical Review, XLV* (April 1960), pp. 499–500; Marcus Cunliffe, *The Nation Takes Shape, 1789–1837* (Chicago, 1959), p. 164; Morton Borden, *The American Profile* (Lexington, 1970), p. 114; Samuel Eliot Morison, *Oxford History of the American People* (New York, 1965), p. 475; Stuart Bruchey, *Roots of American Economic Growth 1607–1861* (New York, 1968), pp. 201, 207; and P. M. G. Harris, "The Social Origins of American Leaders: The Demographic Foundations," p. 218.
[5] Lee Benson, *The Concept of Jacksonian Democracy: New York As a Test Case* (Princeton, N.J., 1961), p. 165.
[6] In recent years a few studies have been undertaken of the backgrounds of successful men of the antebellum period, which, while useful, are fragmentary. See Bibliography.
[7] For examples of sociologists' belief that the social mobility of the era has been established see Lipset and Zetterberg, "A Theory of Social Mobility," p. 561; Harold M. Hodges, *Social Stratification: Class in America* (Cambridge, 1964), p. 1; and Leonard Reissman, *Class in American Society* (New York, 1959), pp. 11, 243.
[8] Miller, "American Historians and the Business Elite," in *Men in Business*, edited by Miller (New York, 1962).
[9] Donald Warner Koch, "Income Distribution and Political Structure in Seventeenth-Century Salem, Massachusetts," Essex Institute *Historical Collections, CV* (Jan. 1969), p. 51.
[10] Main, *Social Structure of Revolutionary America*, pp. 167, 163, 189–93; and Kulikoff, "The Progress of Inequality in Revolutionary Boston," pp. 404–408.
[11] Edmund Willis, "Social Origins of Political Leadership in New York City From the Revolution to 1815" (Ph.D. diss., University of California, 1967), p. 171.
[12] See the Bibliography for a fuller treatment of the chief sources.
[13] See Allan Nevins, *The Gateway to History* (Boston, 1938), p. 202, for a discussion of the actual invention of material in Appleton's *Cyclopaedia of American Biography*. [The pagination is from the reprint of a portion of Nevins' essay in Robin Winks, ed., *The Historian as Detective: Essays in Evidence* (New York, 1969).] See also Daniel Scott Smith, "Cyclical, Secular, and Structural Change in American Elite Composition," *Perspectives in American History, IV* (1970), p. 370, for a brief discussion of some of the *DAB* material, For an example of an actual inaccuracy, see the discussion in Nicholas B. Wainwright, ed. *A Philadelphia Perspective: The Diary of Sidney George Fisher Covering the Years 1834–1871* (Philadelphia, 1967), p. iii.
[14] See Appendix B.
[15] *NYGBR*, III:180. Specific Scoville errors are pointed out in *ibid., LXI*, pp. 341–43.

[16] Henry T. Tucker, Introduction to John W. Francis, *Old New York* (1857), p. ix. A similar criticism is made in Benjamin D. Silliman's, "Personal Reminiscences of Sixty Years at the New York Bar," I, pp. 226–43; and John F. Watson, *Annals of Philadelphia in the Olden Time*, 2 vols. (Philadelphia, 1842).
[17] For an idea of Latting's finicky perfectionism in tracking down genealogical data, see the correspondence between Latting and the historian of contemporary Long Island, Henry Onderdonk, Jr., in the Onderdonk papers, the Long Island Historical Society.
[18] *Civil, Political, Professional and Ecclesiastical History . . . of Brooklyn* (1884).
[19] See the comment in J. Thomas Scharf and Thompson Westcott, *History of Philadelphia, 1609–1884*, 3 vols. (Philadelphia, 1884), II, p. 1169.
[20] For a discussion of the more important of these works see Pessen, "The Egalitarian Myth and the American Social Reality," pp. 1031–34.
[21] See Bibliography.
[22] The diary is located in the New-York Historical Society.
[23] Kenneth W. Porter, *John Jacob Astor, Business Man*, I, pp. 4–5; John William Leonard, *History of the City of New York, 1609–1909* (New York, 1910), II, p. 500; Thomas F. Meehan, "A Self-Effaced Philanthropist: Cornelius Heeney, 1754–1848," *Catholic Historical Review, IV* (1918), p. 4; and Stiles, *Civil . . . History of Brooklyn*, II, p. 990.
[24] According to his most recent biographer, who had access to papers not available to earlier commentators, "the facts do not support the myth" propagated, above all by Girard himself, as to his boyhood poverty. Harry Emerson Wildes, *Lonely Midas: The Story of Stephen Girard*, pp. 4, 5, 10–11, 319. Girard's status before emigrating to America was junior officer rather than cabin boy. Cf. *Memoirs and Auto-Biography of Some of the Wealthy Citizens of Philadelphia*, appendix.
[25] Main, *Social Structure of Revolutionary America*, p. 184. If some of the wealthiest men of the antebellum era had greatly expanded the fortunes left them, the fact remains that they did start out with what in their time were indeed fortunes. Among such "augmenters" were Hezekiah Beers Pierrepont, Edgar J. Bartow, William P. Winchester, Gardiner Greene, Elias H. Derby, and John L. Gardner.
[26] The occupations given in that document, like its biographical information, were found to be almost totally accurate. A check of the residences of the persons listed shows that overwhelmingly they lived in the wealthy and high-status wards in the middle and eastern part of the city. The fortunes it attributes to A. E. Borie, Manuel Eyre, Joseph Sill, Nathan Trotter, and Stephen Girard, among others, appear to have been modest estimates in the light of other reliable evidence.
[27] For the argument made in a different context, that persons, data on whose families are lacking, were not necessarily of lower status than those for whom the data are available, see Lipset and Bendix, *Social Mobility in Industrial Society* (Berkeley, 1963), pp. 125–26.
[28] Where the evidence on a family was inconclusive, I treated it as nonexistent.
[29] Shattuck, *Census of Boston for the Year 1845*, p. 74.
[30] See Joseph Dorfman, *The Economic Mind in American Civilization, 1606–1865*, 2 vols. (New York, 1946), particularly Vol. II; and Edward Pessen, *Most Uncommon Jacksonians* (Albany, 1967), pp. 129–34, for the influence of Malthusian conservative social dicta on American thought.
[31] For a discussion of the role played by influential European visitors in winning acceptance for the rags-to-riches myth, see Pessen, *Jacksonian America: Society, Personality, and Politics*, chap. 3.
[32] Wilson, *The Aristocracy of Boston*, p. 30; and *"Our First Men:" A Calendar of Wealth, Fashion and Gentility*, p. 41.
[33] Abraham Ritter, *Philadelphia and Her Merchants*, pp. 66–67; Stephen N. Winslow, *Biographies of Successful Philadelphia Merchants*, pp. 121–23; Henry Simpson, *Lives of Eminent Merchants*, p. 810.
[34] *Hunt, Lives of American Merchants*, I, p. 227; cf. Wildes, *Lonely Midas*, pp. 9, 319, and McMaster, *Stephen Girard*, I, p. 3.
[35] *Lives of American Merchants*, I, pp. 428, 307–13.
[36] Blumin, "Mobility in a Nineteenth-Century American City."

6
The Backgrounds of the Urban Rich: Characteristic Life Histories

That oft quoted, though rare class, known as self-made men.

Winslow, *Biographies of Successful Philadelphia Merchants*, p. 24

[Philadelphia society has] few whose families have not held the same status for several generations.

Diary of Sidney George Fisher, February 9, 1837

The social origins of rich men in the cities of the northeast were remarkably similar, more than 90 per cent of them coming from wealthy, eminent, or successful families. A close analysis focusing on details and subthemes not immediately apparent in the larger pattern, reveals additional uniformities, suggesting that all of the great cities made up one homogeneous urban locale. And yet the unique histories of the cities, their varying age, size, wealth, their slightly unlike national, ethnic, and religious makeup, as well as their diverse recent pasts—New York City was in the midst of a dynamic expansion, Boston was trying hard to make an economic comeback, Brooklyn in 1841 had been an independent city for only seven years—gave to the social mobility pattern of each of them a special cast. What follows are sketches designed to illustrate typical family histories of the rich in each of the great cities. If the chapter is a fairly long one, it is because I believe concrete vignettes convey more vividly than statistical summaries the backgrounds characteristic of successful men in the cities.

New York

As the national leader in wealth and population, New York City had the largest number of rich men and women during the era. While typically born to good fortune, as were their counterparts in the other cities, the elite of the metropolis had diverse and unique family backgrounds. A major motif was a lineage that went back two centuries or more in this country—eminent almost from the city's beginnings in the days of Peter Stuyvesant and thereafter sprinkled with individuals who achieved wealth while maintaining or enhancing family status. Peter Gerard Stuyvesant, who in 1845 shared with John Jacob Astor the distinction of being the only New Yorker with real and personal property in the city assessed at more than a million dollars, was the fortunate inheritor of a name and estates whose value had almost constantly appreciated.

The Beekmans were a New York City family which, according to their modern biographer, had "maintained for more than two centuries a high position among the interrelated families whose ability and wealth made them the aristocracy of New Netherlands and New York." Wealthy adults of this family who lived during the period included James, John, and Gerard, sons of the successful merchant James Beekman who died in 1807. James William Beekman, the son of Gerard, on his father's death in 1833 inherited an estate worth close to $100,000 "exclusive of a considerable extent of land in Beekmantown, near Lake Champlain"; his father's fortune, when supplemented by the shares left by wealthy uncles and a childless aunt, left the young man at age twenty-one possessed of "real property, stocks and bonds to the value of nearly $300,000." It was truly said that he had been brought up with "every luxury and comfort of life."[1]

The Remsens were another family whose fortune was interwoven with the commercial and financial history of New York City from the seventeenth century on. As in many other families, the repetition of Christian names over the generations bedevils the student of the Remsen genealogy. A Peter or a Henry Remsen must be identified by century or more precisely by generation. In the 1840s there were at least nine wealthy adult members of this family who owned property in the city, exclusive of the young and wealthy Simeon Remsen. The latter, although assessed for no New York City estate whatever, left more than $250,000 on his untimely death in 1846. Prominent in politics as well as finance during the eighteenth century, this family's fortune also waxed through successful intermarriages, such as the one contracted by the Henry Remsen of the Revolutionary era with the daughter of Abraham DePeyster.

Alexander Phoenix had emigrated to New Amsterdam from England in 1640, commencing another successful New York City line that persisted through the antebellum era. As indicated in the discussion on sources of wealth, Nathaniel Ingraham married Elizabeth, the daughter of Daniel Phoenix; the latter was prominent in politics and one of New York City's most eminent and wealthy merchants in the late eighteenth century. The Quackenbosses, owners of substantial if not awesome properties in different sections of the city, were descendants of a family that since its arrival in New Amsterdam had intermarried with the Bogarts, the Van Schaicks, the Kortrights, the Gardiners, the Gansevoorts, the Wynkoops, the Greenleafs, and the Leggetts, among others.

According to Philip Hone's diary notation of February 4, 1835, George Rapelye had "lately taken it into his head to furnish his house handsomely and give splendid dinner parties." When he died later that year Rapelye left an "immense estate" which, to Hone's annoyance, was not left as it "should have been to his nephew David C. Colden." Rapelye was the rich son of a rich father, descended of a family that after the Civil War was perhaps the oldest living in New York City, a Rapelye having arrived there "with the first band of Walloons in 1623." The first Van Nest arrived a generation later; Peter Pieterse (the suffix "se" signifying that he was the son of Pieter) Van Nest in fact married Judith Rapelye, daughter of Joris Janse Rapelye, the pioneer of 1623. Abraham Van Nest, successful merchant and corporate officer of the antebellum era, was of this admired family; the Van Nests were longtime owners of valuable Manhattan properties in what is today the West Village. The Van Zandts were another family of "pure Holland origin,"—although the first Wynant Van Zandt in America, a supporter of Charles I, arrived only in the reign of James II—the success of their nineteenth-century representatives owing much to the achievements of their ancestors a century earlier. The latter were said to have held a "leading position not only in the business world, but also in the social, civic, and church history" of the city.[2]

Even more prestigious than the Van Zandts were their contemporaries the Gouverneurs. Abraham Gouverneur played a prominent part in city politics during the time of Jacob Leisler late in the seventeenth century. Samuel Gouverneur, the wealthy attorney of 1828, who married the daughter of President James Monroe, was the descendant of a family that "ranked among the best families of New York for nearly two centuries" and was tied by blood with the Ogdens, the Kembles, the Kortrights, and the Morrises. The latter family hardly requires mention in view of the political fame earned by Gouverneur Morris and by General Lewis Morris, signer of the Declaration of Independence. Together with Richard Morris, judge of the Admiralty Court, they were the grandsons of Colonel Lewis Morris. Colonel Morris, a great English landowner, had emigrated to New York City in 1674 and by 1691 owned a large estate in the area which earlier belonged to Joseph Bronck. A family whose fortunes closely paralleled and were intertwined with the Gouverneurs were the Kortrights. James Monroe himself married the daughter of Lawrence Kortright. N. Gouverneur Kortright, whose New York City properties were assessed at close to a quarter of a million dollars in 1845, came of a family that had amassed great wealth and prestige since its first members had arrived in New Amsterdam from Flanders in 1663. Connected to the Cornells, the Aspinwalls, and, with "hoops of steel," to the Gouverneurs, the Kortright family owned large tracts of land outside the city—wealth that was omitted in the assessments.

Five members of the "honourable and distinguished Kip family" were among the richest New Yorkers of the era. It was said that a "DeKype" had explored the shores of the North (Hudson) River before Hudson. Later descendants built on the valuable lower Manhattan property granted Isaac Kip early in the seventeenth century, to which were added tracts along the Hudson north of the city. Included in their holdings were the areas that later became City Hall Park and Nassau Street, which was first known as Kip Street. Of course, there were dozens of streets in Manhattan and Brooklyn named in honor of the great accumulators of the time: Rutgers, Crosby, Beekman, Astor, Pierrepont, Middagh, Sands, Brevoort, Ludlow, Remsen, Schermerhorn, Constable, Lefferts, Halsey, and many others, in addition to Isaac, Jacob, Leonard, and Lewis Kip. Other Dutch families that achieved success almost immediately on arrival in New York in the seventeenth century and maintained it through the antebellum decades were the Duyckincks, the Abeels, and the Bensons.

A number of English families became prominent in New York City shortly after they emigrated in the late seventeenth and early eighteenth centuries. In 1824 Lafayette was entertained at a ball given in his honor, "long regarded as the most magnificent social function New York had witnessed up to that time." The locale was the "celebrated Ludlow mansion in State Street, facing the Battery," built by the merchant Cary Ludlow, grandson of Gabriel Ludlow (founder of the American branch of the family). Descended from what one genealogist described as "the oldest gentry in Great Britain,"[3] Gabriel Ludlow quickly launched a successful career in shipbuilding and overseas commerce, amassing immense real properties that included a tract of four thousand acres of land in Rockland County. He became a vestryman of Trinity Church—as did so many of the city's financial and social elite—and married the wealthy Sarah Harmer. A partial list of the wealthy and eminent families that intermarried with the Ludlows during the eighteenth and early nineteenth centuries would include the Strongs, Hoffmans, Goelets, Morrises, Gouverneurs, Crommelins, Ogdens, Verplancks, Mortons, Glovers, LeRoys, Wrights, and Hones.

Pursuing a course of wealth, influence in Trinity Church, and intermarriage with exalted families, that closely matched the career of the Ludlows, were the many wealthy descendants of William Hamersley, said by one source to be "of the same baronial family as Sir Hugh Hamersley," and by another, to have founded a family than which no other was more distinguished. Equally eminent and of roughly parallel achievements were the Crugers. Among the five hundred richest New Yorkers in the 1840s were Harriet Cruger and John Church Cruger, great-granddaughter and great-grandson respectively of John Cruger, who came to New York City late in the seventeenth century. A Cruger ancestor may or may not have accompanied Richard I on his crusade, but there can be no question that during the eighteenth century John Cruger and his descendants were active in politics, commerce, and the acquisition of substantial real estate. Miss Cruger's father, Nicholas Cruger, was a great merchant who, before his death in 1800, owned a large estate in Rose Hill, a northern suburb of the city. Not the least of his achievements was the patronage he extended to Alexander Hamilton.

A number of the families of wealthy New Yorkers of the antebellum era had originally made their fortunes outside the city before moving to New York City in the seventeenth and eighteenth centuries. In some cases they quickly became so prominent in New York's commercial and political life that they are usually identified with the city; yet the wealth of their nineteenth-century descendants who lived in New York owed much to estates originally carved out in neighboring areas. The narrow, sprawling territory known as "Long Island" (exclusive of Brooklyn and its satellites, then considered a part of it) was the first or close to the original home, on this continent, of a number of wealthy New Yorkers. Typically they were beneficiaries of ample land grants or prescient purchases, which provided the solid underpinnings to their local prominence; their descendants subsequently invested portions of their capital in the great city's commerce and shipping, and built or moved into townhouses, the better to oversee their business ventures and to participate in the city's fascinating social world.

A number of wealthy Gardiners were nineteenth-century members of the family that subsequent to 1667 reigned over Gardiner's Island "with all the customary feudal privileges" (as, for that matter, does the present-day descendant to a large extent). The first "lord of the manor," Lion Gardiner, was a British officer who first stayed in Boston—building fortifications under Winthrop—before purchasing Gardiner's Island from the Indians. In the early nineteenth century John Lion Gardiner, the seventh lord of the manor by direct descent, continued to rule over the island which he had received by entail. The niece of the seventh lord married John Tyler—another manifestation of the matrimonial interest of Virginia-born chief executives of the era in the daughters of the New York elite. One dozen New Yorkers named Jones, on the "New List" of wealthy New Yorkers for 1828 and 1845, were descendants of Major Thomas Jones, an English officer under James II; late in the seventeenth century Jones had acquired a manorial estate of five to ten thousand acres near Oyster Bay on the south shore of Long Island. The brick mansion he built there stood until David S. Jones, a wealthy attorney of Jones Street in the city, replaced it with a more magnificent residence in the nineteenth century.

John Burling Lawrence, a leading antebellum merchant, was a descendant of the Flushing, Long Island branch of this eminent family. Captain William Lawrence, who had arrived in New England at the same time as Lion Gardiner, subsequently became one of the incorporators of

Flushing. The family was thereafter influential, maintaining its status through land, commerce, and intermarriage. Effingham Lawrence, brother of John B. Lawrence, and Watson Effingham Lawrence, John's son, were leaders in the nineteenth-century wholesale drug business. Another original patentee of Flushing was William Thorn[e], the founder of one of the leading families of the era. Thorn also became a proprietor of Jamaica, Long Island. Jonathan Thorn, a successful leather merchant of the early nineteenth century and father of seven wealthy members of the family who lived in the antebellum period, was a grandson of the founder and the son of Samuel Thorn and Phoebe Dean. Colonel Herman Thorn was reputed to be so rich that Hone on May 11, 1835, said of him he had "the air of a man who has been born and brought up in the midst of gold, silver, and precious stones." The description may well have been true of this family as a whole, which in the eighteenth century had ties with the Livingstons, Beekmans, Schuylers, Bownes, and Haights.

Another great New York City family that originated on Long Island were the Thompsons. The successful merchants Jonathan and Abraham Gardiner Thompson were the sons of the wealthy Judge Isaac Thompson and Mary Gardiner of East Hampton, granddaughter of the fourth lord of the manor. Isaac was a descendant of William Thompson, who came to America in 1634 and became owner of a "large amount of real estate," and of his son John, who moved to Suffolk County in the middle of the seventeenth century and became a proprietor of the town of Brookhaven. The vast fortune that permitted Abraham Gardiner Thompson to bequeath about $350,000 to charitable and religious institutions in 1851 was based largely on his successful business partnership with James Boggs and Joseph Sampson. Yet clearly, its creator had never been a poor boy, let alone a poor man.

The Motts were another wealthy New York City family whose career in America followed the classic course: the pioneer Adam Mott came to New England in 1635, swiftly moved on to become a founder of a Long Island town (Hempstead), and a large landowner, officer, and prominent individual. His descendants intermarried with other great families, such as the Lawrences, and by the eighteenth century were active in New York City commerce, as were the two Jacob Motts, grandfather and father of the wealthy iron manufacturer and merchant of the second quarter of the nineteenth century, Jordan L. Mott. It was said of the latter that "the ample fortune of his father rendered application to business unnecessary." To fill the cup, finally, in honor of the political as well as the commercial eminence of Jacob Mott, "Mott Street perpetuates his name upon the map of the city" (later immortalized in Rodgers' and Hart's song "Manhattan").

The wealthy drug merchants, Al[l]ison, Joel, and Jotham Post were also descended of an old family, originally established in Southampton by

Richard Post in 1640. Their father, Jotham Post, left this Long Island town for New York City in the mid-eighteenth century and thrived in business. A scholar who has recently written that Post "never rose above the middle class in his lifetime," nonetheless concedes that he had accumulated capital, "lived in a very substantial house," and in 1785 owned property assessed for an amount that in fact placed him in the richest 1 per cent of the city.[4] Dr. Marinus Willett was the son of the famous Colonel Marinus Willett, Liberty Boy, vestryman of Trinity Church, mayor of New York City at the beginning of the nineteenth century, ferry proprietor, and "merchant of means and considerable property owner" (largely of confiscated Tory estates in New York City and Jamaica, Long Island). The Willetts were descended of Thomas Willett, described as a wealthy Dutch merchant and shipowner who had settled in Flushing after first entering the country via New England. The eminent lawyer, Richard Riker, city recorder in Philip Hone's New York, was the wealthy descendant of Abraham Riker, a Dutch emigrant to New Netherlands. Riker's Island belonged to this family, whose American ancestor specialized in receiving large land grants: Governor Kieft in 1638 gave him " a large tract at the Wallabout," while Peter Stuyvesant sixteen years later allotted him "one fourth of the township of Newtown on Long Island." Richard Riker's father had been a wealthy and prominent citizen married to Anna Lawrence of the Long Island family. Other New York City eminences descended of successful Long Island families that traced back to the seventeenth century included Clement C. Moore, David Cromwell, John Suydam, and the great merchant Comfort Sands.

A substantial contingent of wealthy New York City residents were descendants of old families whose first successes were achieved north of the city in New York State. Anthony Bleecker—one of the most prestigious lawyers in New York City during the first third of the nineteenth century—came of a Dutch family whose pioneer in America, Jan Jansen Bleecker, was one of the seven patentees of the Saratoga grant. Building on this estate of more than forty square miles on both sides of the Hudson near Mechanicsville, the Bleeckers developed close ties with the Schuylers, the Livingstons, and the Wendells to become one of the most eminent as well as the most wealthy families in the Saratoga area. James Bleecker removed to New York City in the mid-eighteenth century, marrying a daughter of the prominent Anthony Lispenard, and acquiring valuable city real estate. Their son, Anthony Lispenard Bleecker, the father of Anthony Bleecker, became "one of the wealthiest and most influential citizens of New York. He was the proprietor of the Bleecker estate through which Bleecker Street [immortalized in the somber opera by Gian Carlo Menotti] runs and to which he gave his name; he was long a vestryman of Trinity Church and a member of the Tontine Society," [5] the coffee house and social center established by and for the city's merchant elite late in the eighteenth century. Anthony Bleecker was one of the thirteen children of this man and Mary Noel, daughter of a prominent minister of Elizabethtown, New Jersey. The younger Bleecker was a good example of a "gentleman lawyer," able to devote much time to the writing of poetry, the fashionable Drone Club, the affairs of the city dispensary, and the New York Society Library, as befitted a man born into wealth and eminence.

The equally wealthy and eminent Peter R. and Maturin Livingston, the early nineteenth-century possessors of Christian names carried over the generations by other members of the family, were sons of Robert James Livingston—a grandson of the nephew of the "first lord" of Livingston Manor, who was also an original Saratoga patentee. Robert J. Livingston had wed Susan Smith, daughter of the famous lawyer and judge, the Honorable William Smith. Maturin Livingston, their son, married Margaret Lewis, daughter of the wealthy and renowned General Morgan Lewis and Gertrude Livingston. His mother-in-law was herself the daughter of Judge Robert Livingston and Margaret Beekman, and the great-granddaughter of the first lord. Another wealthy contemporary Livingston, Edward, a mayor of New York, law-giver, author, and statesman, among other things, was Gertrude Livingston's brother and uncle to Margaret Lewis and Maturin Livingston.

In a diary entry he made in April, 1845, Philip Hone noted the marriage of his ward, Adeleine Coster, to Peter Augustus Schermerhorn, son of the very rich Peter Schermerhorn. The Schermerhorn family had been prominent in New York City since the time Symon Jacobse Schermerhorn had come to the city in 1691 to establish himself as a shipping merchant. Descendants subsequently accumulated valuable real estate in Brooklyn (in order to build a summer home) and water lots and a wharf on Queen (later Pearl) Street, between Beekman and Fulton Streets. Jacob Janse Schermerhorn had moved to Beverwyck (Albany) in 1636 and quickly built a fortune in trade, leaving a great estate—for that time—of $25,000, including much real estate in Albany and Schenectady. The family was long prominent in the affairs of Rensselaerwyck before it achieved prominence in New York City. Samuel Leggett, also a friend of Hone's, was the wealthy son of Thomas Leggett, a great landholder of Westchester County who had survived his Tory sympathies to make a fortune in New York City's commercial life after the Revolution. The Leggetts had been rich and influential in Westchester County following the migration of Gabriel Leggett in 1661. This English family—some of whose members liked to think that "their family name was derived from an ancestor who was a papal legate"—prospered in the eighteenth century through real estate, commerce, and intermarriage with Beekmans, Whites, Suydams, and Bayards. Other luminous New York City commercial families whose fortunes had commenced with Dutch ancestors in the Albany region and thrived thereafter through the classic blending of real-estate accumulation, commerce, and prestigious marriage were the Banckers and the Clarksons.

Some of the most wealthy members of the New York City elite were descended from families that landed in New England and instead of moving on to Long Island, built their fortunes in New England. Included in the sizable group whose ancestors had "made it" in seventeenth century Connecticut were the eminent New York City merchant John Drake, direct descendant of Samuel Drake, owner of much real estate, and ancestor of many influential descendants. The wealthy and fashionable naval officer, William Spencer, who married first one, then another Lorillard, was a son of the successful lawyer, Ambrose Spencer, and a descendant of William Spencer, a landed proprietor of Hartford; the family had arrived in 1633. The rich merchant and corporate executive, Courtlandt Palmer, was the son of Captain Amos Palmer, a prominent citizen of Connecticut, and descendant of the Englishman Walter Palmer, successful landowner and a political figure in Connecticut after his arrival there in 1629. Daniel Lord, described by an informed nineteenth-century contemporary as "for many years the leading commercial lawyer in [New York] City,"[6] was the son of a very successful doctor and Phoebe Crary, of an eminent commercial family. The Lords had been prominent in Connecticut throughout the eighteenth century, after Thomas Lord had migrated (first to Massachusetts) early in the seventeenth century. The great merchant and financial figure James DePeyster Ogden was of a family that had been among the original settlers of Stamford in the seventeenth century and which thereafter contracted marriages with elites in and out of the state. Samuel B. Ruggles, who played so vital a part in New York City's business and political affairs in the second quarter of the nineteenth century, was the son of a leading lawyer of Milford and a mother, Ellen Hubbell Bulkley, of equally prominent family. The Ruggleses had migrated to Connecticut in 1635. Through land holdings, an iron works, and intermarriage they attained the "first rank in society." Three of the most successful lawyers in New York City at mid-nineteenth century were Samuel, William, and John Lawrence, sons of the wealthy merchant Jonathan Lawrence. This branch of the distinguished family had intermarried in the eighteenth century with the Woodhulls, Sacketts, and Livingstons, and been eminent since Henry Lawrence had received a large land grant in Connecticut. Robert Chesebrough, wealthy merchant and banker, was the son of a successful drygoods merchant and descendant of a family that settled in Massachusetts in the time of Winthrop and shortly thereafter achieved eminence in Hartford. The great merchants, George Griswold and his brother Nathaniel Lynde Griswold, were descendants of perhaps the most prestigious of the early Connecticut families that ultimately produced wealthy New Yorkers—the Griswolds attaining an eminence that transcended the boundaries of the "state of steady habits."

Many New York City fortunes were begun in Massachusetts during the seventeenth and eighteenth centuries. The large shipping merchants Gardiner Greene Howland and Samuel Shaw Howland were the sons of that "fine old gentleman," Joseph Howland. The latter was born in Boston in 1749 and went on to become one of the leading shipping merchants in the northeast. John Howland, the American ancestor of this family, had arrived on the *Mayflower*. Jonathan Goodhue, another leading antebellum merchant, was the son of the Honorable Benjamin Goodhue, twice elected to the United States Senate from Massachusetts, and husband to the daughter of the prominent General Mathew Clarkson. The wealthy Gould Hoyt, one of those several hundred merchants privileged to move in Hone's social circle, was descended of a family prominent in Massachusetts in the seventeenth century and Connecticut in the eighteenth. In the eighteenth century Samuel Hoyt (son of the rich father of the same name and Hannah Go[u]ld) became "a large landholder, inheriting the larger part of his father's estate," as did his son Gould Hoyt in turn. Benjamin L. Swan was a very rich merchant whose early success in New York City permitted him to retire from business at the age of thirty-three, almost a half century before his death in 1866. He was a direct descendant of the Richard Swan who, after coming to Massachusetts in 1634, became an original proprietor of the Narragansett land grant; Benjamin's father was an eminent Revolutionary figure, Major Samuel Swan. Edward Prime, wealthy son of a fabulously rich father, Nathaniel Prime, and of a rich mother, Cornelia Sands—herself the daughter of the longtime mighty merchant and financial leader, Comfort Sands—was the sixth-generation descendant of the English settler of Rowley, Massachusetts, Mark Prime. The latter was an "influential citizen [who] owned considerable property," as did his sons and grandsons. The great shipping and commission merchants, Josiah Macy and his son William, were of an old and substantial family. Thomas Macy had come to Massachusetts in the middle of the seventeenth century and was one of the purchasers of Nantucket. Josiah Macy's father was a substantial shipowner and merchant of that island, possessing "considerable wealth for the time and place in which he lived." Robert Bowne Minturn, of the great shipping house of Grinnell, Minturn and Company, was named after his maternal grandfather, the famous New York merchant Robert Bowne. His father, William Minturn, Jr., was a large shipowner. The latter's father, husband to a niece of General Nathaniel Greene, was also a shipping merchant who, before removing to New York City, had prospered in Newport, Rhode Island. Another child of Rhode Island was Jonathan Inslee Coddington, a wealthy New York City merchant until his death just after the Civil War, as were his successful brother Joseph, his son J. I. Coddington, Jr., and Jonathan Q. Coddington; the latter was regarded by his friends as a good sort despite his "locofoco" (actually Democratic) political leanings.

An ancestor was William Coddington, a collaborator of Roger Williams and the first governor of Rhode Island. The family was thereafter a prominent one. Jonathan I. Coddington's father James Coddington was a Revolutionary officer said to have served in Lafayette's bodyguard at Brandywine. His mother, Experience Inslee, was herself of a prominent family and the widow of another Revolutionary officer killed in battle.

Influential in New York City in mid-nineteenth century were many descendants of French, mainly Huguenot, families. The harsh religious policy of Valois France in the sixteenth century and Louis XVI in the seventeenth, redounded to the commercial advantage of America's greatest city. Matthew Grinnell came first to Newport, and his immediate descendants thrived in New Bedford, Massachusetts. Joseph, Henry, and Moses Hicks Grinnell, "the first shipping merchants in America" during the early nineteenth century (associates of John Howland, Robert B. Minturn, and Preserved Fish) were sons of one of the "wealthiest shipmasters and merchants of his time." An even more prestigious family were the Bayards, who for two centuries following their migration to New Amsterdam in the mid-seventeenth century moved in the first rank of the city's leadership, intermarrying with DeLanceys, Livingstons, Schuylers, Jays, Stuyvesants, Van Rensselaers, and like eminences in and out of New York City. William Bayard, who at his death in 1826 was one of the wealthiest men in the city, was born in an "atmosphere of wealth and culture." He became a partner in the great mercantile house of LeRoy, Bayard and Company, in addition to serving as president of the Chamber of Commerce and officer in financial and charitable institutions and the Tontine Coffee House. Cornelius Dubois, a director or officer in no less than thirteen corporations and charitable organizations, was a descendant of Jacques Dubois, the founder of the eminent family who arrived in New York *circa* 1654. The wealthy merchant Amos R. Eno was the son of a Connecticut legislator and man of prominence, descended from a family that arrived in America before 1650. James and John Jauncey were shipowners who came to New York before 1750. The eldest son of James Jauncey was the wealthy William Jauncey, most of whose great fortune was inherited by his niece's husband, Herman Thorn. The Lispenards of New York City, great landowners of valuable Manhattan lots early in the eighteenth century, were descendants of a seventeenth-century Huguenot refugee, as were wealthy families such as the Gouverneurs, mentioned earlier.

The DePeysters, whose New York founder Johannes was "a gentleman of noble blood, who was distinguished among the original colonists of New Netherlands by his wealth and business ability,"[7] were in a sense a Dutch family; but they were also Huguenots who had evidently relocated in Holland soon after the St. Bartholomew's Day massacre. The wealthy Frederic DePeyster, who was born in 1796 "at the town house of his parents on Hanover Square . . . then one of the most fashionable localities" in New York City, belonged to one of the great families of the seventeenth and eighteenth centuries. He married Mary Watts of the prominent Scottish family that had owned Rose Hill and had ties with the Nicolls, the DeLanceys, the Schuylers, and the Van Cortlandts; she was a fit partner for a young man whose own family had intermarried with Van Cortlandts, Phillipses, Reeds, and Beekmans. If John Watts DePeyster, son to Frederic DePeyster and Mary Watts, was one of the fortunates included on the list of the wealthiest New Yorkers of 1845 and could devote his young manhood to leisurely travel, finding his "chief recreation . . . in the execution of mock battles," it was because of wealth amassed over many generations. The several Deforests who were among the city's wealthiest shipping merchants were descendants of Isaac Deforest, a Huguenot who came to New Netherlands early in the seventeenth century. The Lockwood Deforest prominent in antebellum commerce had the Christian name of his prominent grandfather. The extremely rich Rhinelanders of the early nineteenth century, who were among the several dozen leading wealthholders in New York City, were direct descendants of the Huguenot Philip J. Rhinelander, who in 1686 "sought refuge in America from the persecutions caused by the revocation of the Edict of Nantes." The second William Rhinelander, who died in 1825, was trustee of the family's large estate in Westchester County and, like his ancestors and descendants—particularly his sons William Christopher Rhinelander and Frederick William Rhinelander—was an extensive landowner.

The most eminent of all Huguenot families in America was undoubtedly the Jays, given the national prominence achieved by John Jay. The famous patriot was the grandson of the family founder in America. His grandmother was Anna Maria Bayard, while his parents were Peter Jay and Mary Van Cortlandt. The wealthy sons of John Jay, William and Peter Augustus Jay, and his nephew Peter Jay Munroe were descendants of a family that had from its beginnings in this country aligned itself with "the most prominent representatives of social importance and culture in the city." Henry Evelyn Pierrepont, refined son of Brooklyn's chief property owner in 1841, was a proper match for the daughter of Peter A. Jay.

Much New York City wealth had been relatively recently accumulated. If it had not been created by the successful men of the antebellum era themselves, it had originated not in the seventeenth century but in the eighteenth. That a number of families of such history could have been dealt with earlier—as Dutch, long prominent, originating in another part of America, or French—only points up the arbitrariness of all rubrics, on the one hand, and the complexity of most family histories, on the other. If Henry Brevoort, Jr. and the other heirs inherited about $500,000 on Henry Brevoort's death in 1841, the substantial hereditary ingredient in the latter's wealth was the huge tract of land along the

Bowery in the vicinity of 14th Street left him by his father Elias Brevoort. The Brevoorts were, of course, an old Dutch family. Cornelius Van Schaick Roosevelt, grandfather of Theodore Roosevelt, was one of New York's most important merchants and in 1844 a founder of the re-chartered Chemical Bank. Together with three other children, he was willed several hundred thousand dollars by his father James I. Roosevelt, a merchant whose large hardware and glass business was located on Maiden Lane next door to the family's residence late in the eighteenth century. Dr. James Renwick, chosen in 1838 as one of the commissioners to explore the northeastern boundary between Canada and the United States, was the son of William Renwick and the grandson of James Renwick, wealthy merchants who controlled the first packet ships that sailed from New York City to Liverpool.

The prominent financial figure Maltby Gelston was the descendant of Hugh Gelston, who came to Suffolk, Long Island, early in the eighteenth century and prospered both as a merchant and as a judge. Gelston married Mary Maltby, daughter of a seventeenth-century family that even before arriving in New Haven around 1670 "held the rank of gentlemen and were merchants" in Yorkshire. Delancey Kane, a wealthy man of affairs in New York City before 1850, was another who was descended of a prominent Irish family. His great-grandfather, John O'Kane, who came to America in the middle of the eighteenth century, was a well-known Tory during the Revolution and owner of a large estate in Dutchess County. Benjamin McVickar was among the wealthiest New Yorkers, while his brother John, the celebrated professor of moral philosophy at Columbia College, was one of the most eminent men of the antebellum era. Their father was a rich merchant of Scotch-Irish extraction, their mother, the daughter of John Moore, "a patriarch of Newton, Long Island." Their grandfather had become a successful importer and shipowner, accumulating a large fortune and serving as vestryman in Trinity Church shortly after the family's arrival in the city in the eighteenth century. Cadwallader D. Colden, mayor and prominent New Yorker before his death in 1834, was the son of Dr. David Colden and grandson of Cadwallader Colden who migrated from Scotland to Philadelphia in 1710. The latter became a prominent figure both in New York City and the colony of New York, procuring large estates and the lieutenant-governorship in the latter and coveted eminence in Trinity Church in the former. He left a "lavish will" for his children. William A. Duer, president of Columbia, was descended of a successful English family that had made successful marriages to equally prominent families since its arrival in the eighteenth century.

Among the more prominent German families that migrated to America in the eighteenth century were the Wolfes and the Schieffelins. John David Wolfe, Trinity Church vestryman and wealthy partner with Japhet Bishop in the commercial house of Wolfe and Bishop, had inherited the hardware business left by his father David, a successful figure from before the Revolution until his death in 1836. The pioneer was the original John David Wolfe who at his death in 1759 left "a comfortable property to his wife and four children," one of whom was David Wolfe. Henry H., Richard L., Jacob, and Effingham Schieffelin were four prosperous brothers who early in the nineteenth century inherited the wealth and the great wholesale drug house established in the 1790s in the city by their father, Jacob Schieffelin, and his brother-in-law, John Burling Lawrence. This Jacob (the third of the name in America, the first having stayed briefly in Philadelphia around 1740 before returning to Germany) had married Hannah Burling Lawrence of the "notable Long Island family of that name."

Another successful German family were the Berghs. Christian Bergh and his sons Edwin and Henry were wealthy shipbuilders in the antebellum period—third- and fourth-generation descendants of the first Christian Bergh, who had migrated from Germany to New York in 1710. Hone on June 23, 1843 referred to the Christian Bergh of his own era as "the father of that great system of naval architecture which has rendered the city of New York famous throughout the world. He was the first to send on the great waters the models of packet ships." The Arculariuses were another wealthy German family, their successful bakery and grocery business deriving from pre–Revolutionary days. Even more successful in the latter line were the Biningers. The Swiss-born Abraham Bininger had come to America as a boy early in the eighteenth century (on the same ship that carried John Wesley) and for some years lived in the Moravian settlement in Pennsylvania. The family moved to New York City just before the Revolution. The Abraham Bininger of the post–Revolutionary era and his son Jacob Bininger established a grocery business that by the early nineteenth century was regarded as the largest in the city. On the death of Jacob Bininger in 1837 Hone wrote, "few men have disposed as great an amount of good drinkables, eatables and smokables to the people of New York as these gentlemen." (April 15, 1837.)

Moses Taylor, wealthy merchant of the nineteenth century, was the son of Jacob Taylor (successful merchant and longtime business associate of John Jacob Astor) and the grandson of the Moses Taylor who before the Revolution was already a man of considerable wealth. The first Moses Taylor in America was a London merchant who had arrived in New York City in the 1730s and prospered thereafter. Few English families did better than the Kings. John Alsop King—governor of New York just prior to the Civil War—, Charles King, successful journalist and, from 1849 to 1864, president of Columbia College—, and James Gore King—fabulously successful figure in commerce and finance in the antebellum era—, were the sons of the Revolutionary hero Rufus King and Mary, daughter of the wealthy merchant John Alsop. At his death in 1836 Rufus King was worth the then-great sum of $140,000. If there was a self-made man in the family it was Rufus' father Richard King who, starting out as a carpenter and housewright in New England, managed to buy lands, become a successful shipbuilder and the most prominent merchant in his Maine community, engaging in trade with England and the West Indies.

Thomas Buchanan, a rich contemporary of James Gore King, was the son of a wealthy merchant of the same name who, before his death in 1815, owned warehouses in lower New York City. Peter and Robert Goelet were among the "super rich" of New York City in the generation before the Civil War (as for that matter they were in the decades following it). Their father Peter P. Goelet, who died in 1828, was a wealthy hardware merchant and real-estate owner, as was his father before him. "Old" Peter Goelet had long before the Revolution "laid the foundation of his business success in his Hanover Square hardware store, known far and wide as the 'Sign of the Golden Key.' " Before he died in 1811 he had branched into many other articles—making it "in many ways the prototype of the modern department store"—and amassed valuable real properties in the lower city.[8] Francis B. Cutting, the society attorney, was the son of Gertrude Livingston of the great New York family. Her "iron determination" as administratrix and guardian of her husband's estate and her ownership of a ferry lease enabled the young Cutting to be brought up in comfort and style. Cutting's grandfather Leonard Cutting had left England for America in the eighteenth century to become a leading Episcopal minister at Hempstead and Oyster Bay, Long Island, while his father William Cutting, was a successful lawyer. Many other wealthy New Yorkers derived their wealth, as Cutting did, from parents and ancestors prosperous in a variety of lines, as discussed in Chapter 4.

In numerous instances, wealthy New Yorkers of the early nineteenth century simply followed in the economic or occupational footsteps of a rich father, practicing the same line in the city. John H. Contoit, wealthy purveyor of sweets and delicacies to the rich, had been left a fortune by his father, also a "confectioner." Herman LeRoy, of the commercial house of LeRoy, Bayard and Company, one of the greatest in the country, was the son of Jacob LeRoy, wealthy head of his own house. Harmon Hendricks, great copper merchant, was the son of Uriah Hendricks, who initiated the business in the city in 1760. William Frederick Havemeyer, successful sugar refiner, was the son of William Havemeyer, who was a sugar refiner in London after he emigrated from Germany. Dr. Isaac John Greenwood was a successful son of a successful father, Dr. John Greenwood. George Templeton Strong, prominent attorney and keeper of an invaluable diary, was the son of George Washington Strong, one of New York City's most successful commercial lawyers. Strong's grandfather was Judge Selah Strong of the Court of Common Pleas in Suffolk County. Bradish Johnson, prominent merchant

A View of Brooklyn in the Nineteenth Century. (*Wash drawing by Alexander Anderson courtesy of the New-York Historical Society.*)

and social figure, was the son of the wealthy merchant, manufacturer, and real-estate accumulator, William M. Johnson.

In many cases, the rich fathers of rich New Yorkers of the antebellum era had made their mark in the same line but outside the city. The eminent Dr. Samuel Bard, head of the College of Physicians and Surgeons, was the son of Dr. John Bard of Philadelphia. The great Dr. Valentine Mott, described by his peers as "admittedly the most distinguished surgeon of his day," was the son of Dr. Henry Mott, a prominent practitioner of Newton, Long Island. Descended from Adam Mott, the great New York City physician belonged to the same family as the prominent merchants alluded to earlier. Dr. Hugh McLean, admired both as physician and as social figure, was the son of Dr. Alexander McLean, a surgeon in the British Army.

Many successful New Yorkers of the antebellum period were recent immigrants, sons of wealthy parents or families. John Delafield, whose New York City real estate alone realized over $250,000 at auction in 1834, came to New York from London in 1783, married Nancy Hallett, daughter of a prominent merchant, and quickly established himself as one of the city's leading merchants and social figures. His Long Island mansion was one of the grandest of its day. His prominent sons, Dr. Edward, Henry, and Mayor Joseph Delafield were descended, as was their father, of a very old and distinguished English family. The wealthy Richard Mortimer, who earned a "high rank in the New York commercial community," after coming from England in 1816, was the son of William Mortimer, a politically prominent man of independent means. Archibald Gracie was a wealthy merchant who left England for America shortly after the Revolution. He was descended from a well-to-do Scottish mercantile family. Also born in Scotland of a "landed family of rank and renown" was George Douglas, who emigrated to America early in the nineteenth century to establish one of New York City's most successful trading companies with the East Indies. George Bruce, a successful typefounder in the city, was born in Edinburgh to John Bruce and Janet Gilbert. His mother had received a considerable fortune from her father. The first Thomas Addis Emmet in America came to New York City from Ireland in 1804, going on to become one of the city's leading lawyers before he died in 1827. His father was a leading Dublin physician, while the family was famous for its political role in Ireland. August Belmont came to this country as a young man in the 1830s, to establish his own banking firm as a branch of the House of Rothschild. Belmont, who at the age of fourteen had been placed in the Frankfort branch of the great Jewish firm, was the son of a landed proprietor, a man possessed of great wealth in the Rhenish Palatinate.

Such were the backgrounds of New York City's wealthiest persons of the second quarter of the nineteenth century.

Brooklyn

Brooklyn's rich had achieved their wealth almost without exception as a result of a great boost given them at birth by wealthy or comfortably situated parents or relatives. The essential division was not between persons born rich and others born poor, but rather between those whose riches dated back to the mid-seventeenth century and those whose families' wealth was more recently acquired. Of course, Brooklyn could not match its great neighbor across the East River in population, either of ordinary men or of the rich.

The most prestigious families in Brooklyn were those whose ancestors had received tracts of land and played active social and political roles in Brooklyn itself or in such neighboring villages as Flatbush, Flatlands, and New Utrecht, or in eastern Long Island during the seventeenth century. For Brooklyn, old family with few exceptions meant Dutch family. Great families of the era when "Breuckelyn" was founded that continued to be the great families of antebellum Brooklyn included the Rapelyes—owners of the "largest estate in Brooklyn before the Revolution"—the Remsens, the Schermerhorns—who owned the oldest house in Brooklyn—the Schencks, the Suydams, the Bergens, the Polhemuses, the Boerums, the Cornells, the Cortelyous, the Middaghs, the Martenses, the Lotts, the Leffertses, the Johnsons of Oyster Bay—from whom the rich real estate owner Parmenus Johnson was descended—the Gerritsons, the Hickses, the Co[u]wenhovens, the Van Brunts, the Voorheeses, the Willinks, and the Wyckoffs. Old families of other than Dutch extraction included the Fleets and Halseys of England, the Warings of Ireland, the Zabriskies of Prussia, and the Debevoises, French Huguenots who played a prominent part in the history of Ridgewood and New Utrecht. Daniel Embury, a wealthy merchant and banker, came from a prominent German family more recently established; while Henry C. Murphy—a prominent attorney, refined man of letters, community activist and politician—was the son of a man whose enterprise after emigrating in the eighteenth century was not unusual for successful men, but whose Irish ancestry was most uncommon.

Many of the newcomers to Brooklyn's economic and social aristocracy were children of New England and upper New York State, sometimes of Huguenot but more often of English and Scottish extraction. Edgar John Bartow, wealthy paper manufacturer and son-in-law of H. B. Pierrepont, was born in Fishkill, New York, of a wealthy and prominent Episcopalian family descended from the Bertrants of Brittany, who had fled to England late in the seventeenth century. The successful merchant Robert Speir was the son of a Scottish-born importer who, after arriving in New York, became a "successful businessman, attaining a high position in mercantile and social circles." Dr. Matthew Wendell, successful antebellum doctor, came of an "old and highly respectable family of Albany County." John H. Prentice was born in New Hampshire in 1803. Prentice was a fur merchant in Albany before he came to Brooklyn Heights, and was descended of an English family that had migrated to America in the seventeenth century. Alden Spooner, Brooklyn's eminent publisher, was born in Vermont into a family that had been prominent editors and printers for several generations in Connecticut. Other Connecticut Yankees who attained further success in Brooklyn were Nathan B. Morse, Peter Morton, Joseph A. Perry, and Hezekiah Beers Pierrepont, who were all cited earlier for building fortunes in occupations different from those of their fathers.

A number of successful Brooklynites were children of prominent Massachusetts families. Joseph Sprague, ubiquitous director and officer in Brooklyn's banks and insurance companies, who was elected mayor of the city in 1843, was born in Massachusetts, the son of a wealthy farmer. The abolitionist and wealthy silk merchant and real-estate accumulator, Arthur Tappan, was descended from Abraham Tappan, an artisan and small tradesman who had emigrated from Yorkshire to Massachusetts in 1637. Over the course of the following century and a half, the Tappans—uniquely for the families of the later rich—achieved modest respectability and middling wealth rather than eminence and riches. Arthur's father Benjamin Tappan was a goldsmith who for a time ran Northampton's only general store. According to a modern historian, Benjamin Tappan was "a freeman and pewholder [and] a respectable merchant" with no great ambition to amass wealth.[9] Alanson Trask's family, on the other hand, was a distinguished one from the time of its seventeenth-century progenitor Captain William Trask. Abiel Abbott Low, son of Seth Low (ancestor of the prominent reform mayor of the same name), also came of a relatively successful Massachusetts family. The Reverend Evan M. Johnson and John Greenwood, successful and wealthy minister and lawyer, respectively, were born into well-to-do Rhode Island families. Dr. John Haslett, who came to Brooklyn after graduating from Harvard and the University of Pennsylvania Medical School in 1822, was the descendant of a well-to-do family in Charleston, South Carolina. And André Parmentier, whose horticultural garden made him wealthy because of the popularity of its food, beverages, and atmosphere with Brooklyn's elite, was the son of a successful Belgian merchant who bequeathed Parmentier a substantial sum prior to the latter's departure for Brooklyn in 1824.

Boston

That the families of many wealthy New Yorkers had originated in New England, whereas few rich New Englanders had begun in New York, was one of the facts that differentiated the family backgrounds of

Bostonians from New Yorkers. The Dutch, prominent in the one city, were insignificant in the other. These and other variations, including the earlier establishment of the New England community as an English city, may have accounted for the widely noted feelings of cultural superiority expressed by Boston's elite in the nineteenth century. The latter emotion may have been due as well to defensive feelings occasioned by the obvious and widening commercial supremacy established by New York City during the antebellum decades; its dynamic growth made it a magnet even to men successfully established in New England. Yet Bostonians could console themselves that if their upstart urban rival was gaining the world at a much swifter pace, Boston excelled in the arts and the intellectual realms that manifested man's soul.

Bostonian pride in the greater antiquity or renown of its most prestigious families was not without foundation. What New York family could compare with the Winthrops? Who in New York could match such distinguished patriotic families as the Hancocks, the Warrens, the Prescotts, the Reveres, the Otises, the Adamses? What merchants ranked, in the prestige conferred by antiquity, with such Boston and Salem names as Peabody, Codman, Loring, Higginson, or Endicott? As the following sketches reveal, however—unique variations notwithstanding—the parents and families of antebellum Boston's economic elite fall into patterns markedly similar to those obtaining for their New York City counterparts. In the interests of economy, the discussion for both Boston and Philadelphia will touch on selected family careers that typified many others.

Dozens of the richest Bostonians of the 1830s and 1840s were descendants of families that had migrated from England to Massachusetts two centuries earlier, attaining prominence immediately on arrival or soon after and maintaining it almost unbroken thereafter. Heading this list, in prestige if not in the magnitude of his fortune, was the undeniably rich Robert Winthrop, direct descendant of the first governor of Massachusetts Bay colony. In the interval between John Winthrop and Robert, the family intermarried with the most respected families in their own community and with such as the Bayards and Stuyvesants outside, never faltering from its original exalted position. The second Theodore Lyman, wealthy merchant and mayor of Boston in the mid-1830s was the son of a similarly named father. The latter was a prosperous shipping merchant, and a sixth-generation descendant of Richard Lyman, an immigrant of 1631. After graduating from Harvard, a classic act in the careers of the Boston rich, the second Theodore Lyman made the Grand Tour, traveling also to eastern Europe—as uncharacteristic an act in 1810 as it was later. The wealthy merchant William Sturgis and his successful cousin Russell Sturgis were descendants of Edward Sturgis, who in 1635 came to Charlestown and played a leading part in the General Court for most of the seventeenth century. The prominence of the Lowells was, of course, due largely to the business success achieved by Francis Cabot Lowell prior to his death in 1817; the family was an old one, however, dating back to the arrival of Percival Lowell in the 1630s, and prominent thereafter. Successful in commerce and the professions, Lowells intermarried with Cabots, Higginsons, and, of course, Russells, before the antebellum period.

The several Theodore Sedgwicks, spanning three generations between the mid-eighteenth and mid-nineteenth centuries, were the successful descendants of Robert Sedgwick, a prominent commercial, political, and military figure in Charlestown, Massachusetts, after his arrival in 1635. The second Theodore, husband to the granddaughter of Governor William Livingston of New Jersey, was, like his father, a prominent attorney and a Yale graduate. The latter fact testified not to disloyalty to Harvard but to the family's long sojourn in Connecticut prior to the first Theodore Sedgwick's move to Great Barrington, Massachusetts. It has been said that the ramifications of Elizabeth Saltonstall's descendants "would fill a book by itself." She was the daughter of Nathaniel Saltonstall, one of the wealthiest men in Boston in the 1830s, and a descendant of Sir Richard Saltonstall, a pioneer of the Bay colony. One of the latter's sons was in the first Harvard class. Thomas Loring, who arrived in 1634, was of a distinguished English family. A Caleb Loring was prominent in almost every subsequent generation, first in Plymouth, and after the late seventeenth century in Boston, together with numerous other Lorings. They won eminence at Harvard, in the ministry, medicine, commerce, art, science, and of course the law. The marriage of Celia Loring to Peter Sigourney in 1769 was interpreted by one genealogist as an example of the Lorings' penchant for marrying into "other interesting and distinguished families," such as the Curtises, Putnams, and Goddards. Michael Wigglesworth migrated to New England in 1638, graduated from Harvard, and launched a family that became prominent in theology, politics, and law. Matthew Cushing arrived the same year. Robert Cushing, eighteenth-century member of this prominent family, married the sister of the great merchant Thomas Handasyd Perkins. Their son was the immensely wealthy China trader of the nineteenth century, John Perkins Cushing, regarded by contemporaries as a millionaire several times over. In addition to their ties with the Perkinses, the Cushings also married into the Higginson and Cotton families.

The wealthy Abigail Phillips was the daughter of Governor William Phillips and descended from the original settler who came over with Winthrop in the seventeenth century. Members of this "Harvard family" were prominent in religion; by the eighteenth century they had achieved great success in commerce, made numerous advantageous marriages, and insured their immortality by founding the academies at Andover and Exeter. The Artemus Ward of the antebellum era, together with his brothers, were descendants of William Ward, one of the founders of

Marlborough, Massachusetts. His grandson, the father of the first Artemus Ward, was by the early eighteenth century a militia colonel, a magistrate, a representative to the General Court—"altogether a substantial man." The Reverend Joseph Tuckerman's wealth derived not from the ministry but from his father, Edward, "founder of the earliest fire insurance company in New England." The family had been prominent in the Boston area since the arrival of John Tuckerman from Devonshire in 1650 or 1651; successful merchants of that name flourished thereafter in almost all ensuing generations. Stephen Higginson, the organizer of the Massachusetts First National Bank, was a wealthy merchant in Boston until his death in 1828. He came of a long line of merchants and hardy sea captains, who had intermarried with the mighty following the arrival in Salem of the Cambridge graduate, Reverend Francis Higginson, about 1629. Samuel Frothingham, a leading banker in the nineteenth century, was a descendant of a prominent family that had owned much land ever since the first settler William Frothingham had arrived from Yorkshire in 1630. The Codman family had a similar history, extending back for almost precisely the same period of time; these extremely wealthy merchants of the 1840s were the sons of prosperous merchants and real-estate accumulators. John Codman, of the post–Revolutionary generation, married the daughter of the eminent and wealthy Jonathan Amory.

John L. Gardner, wealthy son of the successful merchant Samuel Gardner and husband to the daughter of Salem's leading merchant Joseph Peabody, belonged to a family which became eminent in Salem shortly after the arrival of the planter Thomas Gardner in the 1620s. No family surpassed the Gardners in making proper marriages: the Putnams, Crowninshields, Bowditches, Cabots, Pickerings, Lowells—in addition to the Peabodys—were only a few of the families with whom they forged ties in the seventeenth and later centuries. Joseph Peabody, the great antebellum merchant, was descended from Francis Peabody, who arrived in Massachusetts *circa* 1635. The wealthy attorney William Minot was the son of Judge George R. Minot, a Harvard graduate and a founder of the Massachusetts Historical Society, and the grandson of Stephen Minot, a successful merchant. They were descendants of George Minot who, after arriving in Dorchester around 1630, built a house there that stood for two centuries.

David Sears, whose great mercantile fortune enabled him to build one of the finest houses in the entire northeast, had early in the nineteenth century inherited a huge estate from his father, also named David Sears, a great shipping merchant and land speculator, and from his mother, Anne Winthrop, of the great family. The first settler, Richard Sears, had come to Yarmouth in 1630 to found a family whose sons were successful in the eighteenth century, although none amassed wealth comparable to the fortunes of the two David Searses. But *their* fortunes were equalled by few men anywhere. Augustus Hemenway, wealthy taxpayer of 1848, prominent in the West Indies trade and a large shipowner even when he was a very young man, was the sixth-generation descendant of Ralph Hemenway, who in 1638 "was one of the largest taxpayers and landholders of Roxbury." The Hemenways of the intervening generations were invariably successful men. John Swett, one of the original grantees of Newbury in the early 1640s, was the American ancestor of a family prominent two centuries later, following a series of intermarriages with leading Massachusetts families in and out of Boston. The rich lawyer James Savage was one of eleven Savages who attended Harvard between the time of Major Thomas Savage's arrival in 1635 and 1850. The son of a wealthy merchant, James came into valuable property that had been in the family for almost two centuries. The wealthy William F. Weld, one of the greatest shipbuilders of the nineteenth century, was the son of a shipping merchant. The fact that Weld evidently had to forgo Harvard may indicate that eleven children were a strain on his father's resources. Captain Joseph Weld, the ancestor who settled in Massachusetts Bay colony in the early 1630s, was said to have been the richest man in the colony at his death. The interesting figure Patrick Tracy Jackson was the son of Jonathan Jackson, who had inherited a vast property from his father Edmund Jackson and his mother Dorothy Quincy, and from Hannah Tracy, daughter of "the rich and successful Patrick Tracy." The Jacksons forged marital ties with the Lees, the Cabots, and the Lowells, in addition to the Tracys and the Quincys, as befitted a family whose sons played a prominent part in the commercial and political life of Newton and Boston throughout the seventeenth and eighteenth centuries following the arrival of Edward Jackson *circa* 1643. Patrick Tracy Jackson's great-grandfather had left a fortune estimated at £24,000.

The Quincys were an old family but their greatest prominence was earned by the several Josiah Quincys of the late eighteenth and the nineteenth centuries. Of course, one Quincy daughter was the mother-in-law of President John Adams, while another married John Hancock. The second Josiah Quincy, Jr., was the wealthy son of Josiah Quincy, mayor of Boston in the 1820s and subsequently president of Harvard until 1845. The latter was the son of the wealthy lawyer Josiah Quincy, Jr. and Abigail daughter of William Phillips, and the grandson of Josiah Quincy, rich merchant and shipbuilder of mid-eighteenth century Boston. Earlier Quincys descended from Edmund Quincy, who came to Boston in 1633. The name Parkman is known to the world primarily because of Francis Parkman, the historian grandson of Samuel Parkman, an "eminent and opulent merchant." The latter was evidently a self-made rich man, but his success preceded by one generation the period under study here. If earlier descendants of Elias Parkman were not rich, many were prominent. Elias arrived in Dorchester in 1633. Other rich Bostonians of the nineteenth century whose families were among the earliest settlers in Massachusetts were Josiah Dunham; Samuel Cobb; Benjamin, Alpheus, and Jacob Bigelow; Benjamin and George W. Bangs; Joseph Coolidge; and Rufus and John Lamson.

The great manufacturing families, the Appletons and the Lawrences, were also descended from early settlers, the ancestors of both lines arriving around 1635. Amos, Abbott, and William Lawrence were the sons of Major Samuel Lawrence, a "man of note," and the grandsons of an earlier Amos Lawrence, a prominent political figure in Groton, as other Lawrences had been for several generations. If the later Lawrences were largely self-made men, they had hardly been poor. The great merchants and later manufacturers Samuel and Nathan Appleton stressed the poverty of their upbringing, as did most contemporary publicists. It is probably more accurate to say that their father Isaac Appleton was a man of moderate circumstances, "one of the most respected citizens" of his community (Ipswich, New Hampshire), a man capable of sending his son Nathan Appleton (one of twelve children) to Dartmouth College. The family genealogy confirms the judgment of one contemporary, that Nathan "was by no means without advantages of family and education." A number of Appletons achieved some substance and eminence in the generations after the arrival of the first Samuel Appleton in 1635. In any case, the relatively modest circumstances of the parents of the famous brothers were most atypical for the families of rich men during the era.

Another large group of wealthy Bostonians of the nineteenth century were born into families that, while successful and in some cases in the top rank socially, had come to North America relatively late in the seventeenth century or early in the eighteenth. The first Thomas Amory in this country did not come to Boston until 1720, yet what family was more successful? The son of a Dublin merchant, Thomas Amory used the profits from his trade with Portugal, Holland, and America to buy land, build a wharf, and establish a business in Boston that his descendants expanded over the generations. Successful marriages with the Coffins, Lymans, and Greenes added both to the status and the wealth of the family. The children of the great merchant of the turn of the century, Thomas Coffin Amory, perpetuated this invaluable tradition, William marrying a daughter of David Sears, Susannah wedding William H. Prescott, and Charles taking the daughter of Gardiner Greene—Boston's wealthiest merchant in the early years of the nineteenth century. Although Thomas Welles became prominent in the colony of Connecticut shortly after arriving in the 1630s, the family did not attain comparable renown in Boston until almost a century later. The very rich merchant Benjamin Welles, who lived until the eve of the Civil War, was the son of Samuel Welles, prosperous eighteenth-century merchant, and Isabella Pratt, daughter of the chief justice of New York. Dr. Amos

Binney, prominent man of letters and science, was the son of a successful business man and the descendant of a family that came to Massachusetts in the late 1670s. The wealthy Henry Oxnard, a southern agent of the Lowell Manufacturing Company (among other interests), was the grandson of the rich merchant Thomas Oxnard, who moved with the elite of Boston in the early eighteenth century. The elder Oxnard was associated in business ventures with Samuel Sewall, Edmund Quincy, Edward Hutchinson, and James Bowdoin. The wealthy Derbys of Boston in the antebellum era were actually the children of a great Salem family that had come to that port late in the seventeenth century. Their father was the preeminent merchant and shipowner Elias Hasket Derby who, prior to his death in 1799, was reputed to be the richest man in this country. Derby only added to the fortune accumulated by his father, the great merchant Richard Derby, who built a mansion in the Georgian style for his famous son. Derby's mother, the wife of Richard Derby, was Lydia Gardner of the great mercantile family.

The great antebellum merchant and amasser of real estate, Robert Gould Shaw, was the nephew of Samuel Shaw—a pioneer in the lucrative China trade. After the untimely death of his brother, Francis Shaw, Robert Gould's father, Samuel Shaw looked after the young man. The first Shaw had come to this country from Scotland, late in the seventeenth century. The family prospered almost immediately; Francis Shaw of the second generation—the father of the great China trader—was himself an eminent merchant. Franklin Dexter, a wealthy Harvard graduate of the nineteenth century, was the son of John Adams' secretary of war and child of a family prominent since the days of Richard Dexter, seventeenth-century immigrant. Dexters intermarried with Sigourneys, Bradfords, and Wards. George W. Gerrish, one of the richest of the rich before 1850, was descended from Captain William Gerrish, who arrived in Boston in 1678 to found "a conspicuous Boston family of the eighteenth century." The pioneer's grandson Captain George Gerrish was a wealthy shipping merchant and "one of the original proprietors of Long Wharf." The equally rich Hollis Hunnewell, assessed at over one quarter of a million dollars in 1848, descended of a family that had come to Maine shortly after the Restoration. In 1681 Richard Hunnewell was one of the wealthiest Bostonians. His brother Charles, who amassed valuable real estate in Charlestown, was the ancestor of successful children who intermarried with the Frothinghams and the Lamsons. Hollis Hunnewell married Isabella Pratt Welles, daughter of the great merchant Samuel Welles, whose Paris house the young Hunnewell had entered. The Eliots were another famous family whose Massachusetts origins traced back to the 1660s and whose marriages with the Ticknors, the famous Dwight family of Springfield, the Guilds, the Nortons, and the Lymans—as well as their early success in commerce—culminated in the selection of Samuel A. Eliot as mayor of Boston in 1837.

The wealthy merchant Henry Lee was the son of the merchant and shipowner Joseph Lee, husband to Elizabeth Cabot and partner to her immensely prosperous brother George Cabot. Thomas Lee, Joseph's father, after graduating from Harvard in 1722, became a successful merchant in Salem. The first George Cabot in this country had come here with his brothers John and Francis early in the eighteenth century—a rather late beginning for a family that attained such elevation. Great success at sea and marriages with such families as the Ornes and the Higginsons quickly vaulted the family onto the highest social plateau, and subsequent ties with the Gardners, Winthrops, Lowells, and others of that stature helped keep them there. Several Grays, wealthy lawyers in Boston before 1850, were descendants of another extremely rich Salem family, if one lacking the social eminence of the Cabots. The great-grandfather of Harrison Gray Otis, Edward Gray, was a rich rope manufacturer in seventeenth-century Boston who in 1699 married Susanna Harrison. Martin Brimmer, wealthy merchant and mayor of Boston in 1842, was the third-generation bearer of that name, the first Martin Brimmer having immigrated from Germany early in the eighteenth century. Mayor Brimmer, husband to Susanna Sigourney, married his daughters into the Sohier, Green, and Inches families. George Odin, a successful merchant, was also of an eighteenth-century family, Captain John Odin having come to Boston in 1745. Among George Odin's sons-in-law was Joseph Dorr.

While the families of many wealthy Bostonians had been eminent for upwards of three generations, the evidence for a number of others is not clear. What is not in dispute is that the parents of the latter were almost invariably rich or successful. The wealthy John H. Bird was the son of the landowner Jonathan Bird and Ann V. Woodward, whose father looked after his grandson when Jonathan Bird died. The rich importer John Bumstead received a large property from his parents Josiah Bumstead and the sister of Governor Gore. The wealthy Dr. Benjamin D. Greene received a substantial inheritance from his father, the great merchant Benjamin D. Greene. Jonathan Mason also got a large inheritance from his similarly named father, who was a partner to the wealthy William Phillips. The rich and prominent lawyer William P. Mason was the son of the younger Jonathan Mason. The father of Robert C. Mackay, shipping merchant, was the city treasurer of Boston, while Robert Hooper, President of the Boston Bank, and Samuel Hooper, partner to William Appleton, were sons of a leading Marblehead merchant. Dr. George Parkman, who was victimized in a notorious murder that shocked antebellum Boston society, was the son of the great merchant Samuel Parkman. The bank president William Parsons profited from property left him both by his uncle, a successful merchant, and his father, Chief Justice Theophilus Parsons. Another bank president, Benjamin T. Reed, was the son of a niece of the rich William Gray. Reed's father, although aided by Gray, evidently did not himself prosper. The prominent Dr. Edward H. Robbins was the son of a lieutenant-governor of the state. Henry B. Rogers was a wealthy man who inherited much property from his father, a successful merchant. The great jurist Lemuel Shaw was hardly born rich, yet he did have advantages. He attended Harvard, and the second marriage of his father, to Susanna Hayward, made it possible for the young Shaw to gain valuable legal experience in the office of David Everett, a friend to his uncle. The learned and rich George Ticknor was the son of a successful business man. Judge Peter O. Thacher and the successful broker John A. Thayer were sons of prominent ministers. Thayer's marriage to a daughter of Ebenezer Francis was more instrumental, however, in accounting for his fortune than his elite birth. If Frederic Tudor, prosperous ice merchant, did not attend Harvard, it was not because his family lacked the resources. Brought up in almost lavish comfort by his father William Tudor, who had studied law under John Adams, the young Tudor simply preferred business, leaving Harvard to his three brothers and all those others who would put off life's real work. The wealthy merchant Moses Grant inherited a large property from his father.

Many rich Boston businessmen and professionals followed in the footsteps of their fathers. Cyrus Alger, President of the South Boston Iron Company, was the son of a man who was in the foundry business. The father of John D. Bates, wealthy Boston merchant, was a merchant of Concord. Frederick H. Bradlee was the super rich son of the great commission merchant Josiah Bradlee. If the richest Bostonian, Peter C. Brooks, was the son of middling parents, the same could hardly be said of his own son, the agent of his vast real-estate holdings Edward Brooks. Daniel Franklin Child was another successful son of a successful father. Benjamin W. Crowninshield–not nearly so successful in national politics as he and his family had been in commerce—was the very rich son of the wealthy Salem merchant George Crowninshield. The great provisions merchant William P. Winchester, assessed for close to $350,000 in 1848, was the son of the rich butcher Edmund Winchester. Thomas Lamb, president of banks, insurance companies, and a wharf corporation, got his start in business in the firm of his wealthy merchant father. Richard S. Fay, a businessman, politician, and sometime lawyer, was the son of Judge Samuel P. P. Fay of Middlesex County. Charles Cunningham was a wealthy merchant in partnership with his father Andrew Cunningham. Also in business together were George Pratt and Captain John Pratt, successful merchants both. Dr. George Hayward inherited a substantial estate from his father, also a successful doctor, as did the eminent physician George C. Shattuck from his physician father (in addition to an inheritance from his grandmother). Fitzhenry Homer's father, Benjamin P. Homer, was the largest general insurance underwriter in Boston in the early nineteenth century. The wealthy Robert Bennett

Forbes thrived when he was taken under the tutelage of his uncles, James Perkins and the great Thomas H. Perkins. Thomas B. Curtis and Charles P. Curtis were the wealthy sons of Thomas Curtis, partner in the firm of Curtis and Loring. James Dalton, bank cashier, was the son of a cashier of the branch of the Bank of the United States. Edmund P. Tileston was, like his father, a wealthy paper manufacturer (of a very old Dorchester family). Jeffrey and James B. Richardson were iron merchants, as were their father and grandfather before them. The brothers Weston were the sons of Ezra Weston, described in *Our First Men* as reputedly the "largest ship-owner in the world." Numerous other wealthy men of commerce were sons of men who could be similarly described.

The Boston tax records for the quarter century between 1825 and 1850 disclose that a large number of the greatest wealthholders in the city were the heirs of wealthy deceased relatives. While many of these fortunates were men, the distinctive feature of this category was the extent to which it was composed of women. Elizabeth and Susan Inches, Anna P. Grant, Anna Jones, Caroline Mackay, Anna Parker, Sarah Perkins, Anna D. Perkins, Mrs. William Pratt, Caroline Putnam, Mrs. Shelton (the daughter of Benjamin P. Homer), Mrs. William Shimmin (the daughter of the wealthy John Parker), Mrs. T. Swett, Eliza and Mary Townsend, Sophia Tuckerman (daughter of Samuel Parkman), Mrs. Gardiner Greene (widow of the fabled merchant and daughter of the eminent painter John Singleton Copley), and Laura D. Welles were among the richest 1 per cent of the city because they were widows and daughters of the rich.

A unique category of wealthholders were the children of great Revolutionary figures. Their riches by no means emanated entirely from prestige and opportunities accruing from well-publicized heroism, but certainly their fortunes were enhanced by fame. Paul Revere's father was a goldsmith, but Revere's son, the very rich Joseph Warren Revere, was the offspring of a man whose occupation was similar but whose reputation was golden. The great historian William Hickling Prescott, of course, made his own reputation; yet the status of his father, an eminent lawyer, was perhaps enhanced more by the fact that he was the son of a hero of Bunker Hill than by the fact that the family belonged to "the original Puritan stock and blood of New England." The great and wealthy physician John Collins Warren was the son of an eminent surgeon, descended from a John Warren who had come on the *Arabella* in 1631. The family was by no means least known for the exploits of Dr. Joseph Warren, another hero of Bunker Hill. The great John Hancock's uncle, Thomas Hancock, was a wealthy merchant and shipowner; although he left his famous nephew a substantial portion of his estate of about £100,000—a great estate indeed for 1764—it is likely that later members of this family profited as much from the great renown of the patriot as from the far superior wealth of his uncle. Ebenezer Francis' great fortune was abetted by his own acumen, his marriage to Elizabeth Thorndike—daughter of the wealthy Israel Thorndike—and his father's fame as a Revolutionary martyr, killed in battle in 1778. That Harrison Gray Otis was the nephew to a number of eminences of the Revolution, including James Otis, added to his prestige and promoted his political career. His wealth, it must be conceded, derived from his own efforts, not the least of which resulted in the acquisition of a share of the increasingly valuable Copley estate and his marriage to Sally Foster, daughter of a wealthy merchant. Otis' father, a prominent merchant, went bankrupt—but not before his son had experienced an opulent youth and graduated from Harvard, thus building the essential foundations of his later fortune.

Philadelphia

The backgrounds of the Philadelphia rich of the early nineteenth century were markedly similar to those of the New York City and Boston elites. As in its great urban rivals to the north, the most prestigious families were, with few exceptions, the oldest families; these had either accompanied William Penn on the *Welcome*, come at the same time, or arrived soon enough afterwards to be associated with the city's beginnings. Thomas, George, and John Cadwalader, wealthy Philadelphians of the 1840s, were descendants of what Cleveland Amory has described as "perhaps the most aristocratic of all Philadelphia families." The first John Cadwalader became politically prominent, a large landowner, and "immensely wealthy" after accompanying Penn on the latter's second voyage to the city at the end of the seventeenth century. Marriages with other admired families, the achievements of Dr. Thomas Cadwalader, son of the family founder, and the exploits of his own son, General John Cadwalader, a "hero of the Revolution," helped maintain the status of the family.

The several wealthy Walns of the early nineteenth century were also descendants of a great family that had all of the characteristics associated with eminence in Philadelphia. The founder, Nicholas Waln, was a Friend, an original settler with Penn, a purchaser of a large and valuable tract of land within the city, a member of the general assembly, and a holder of various offices of trust and honor in the colony. In the eighteenth century and the early nineteenth, another Nicholas, Richard, Jesse, Jacob, and several Robert Walns were vastly successful in commerce and law. Although not represented by any males in the Philadelphia lists of the rich in the mid-1840s, the wealth and prestige of the Shippens were indirectly present through the marriages contracted by its daughters to the Burds, Willings, and other prominent families. Edward Shippen was a wealthy merchant in Boston shortly after his arrival there early in the Restoration period. If his Quaker faith was reason for his expulsion from Boston, it was, of course, no bar in Philadelphia, where he quickly rose to a "place of social importance and political power." In addition to being appointed the first mayor of Philadelphia by William Penn, he held the highest offices in the province of Pennsylvania, while living in perhaps the most splendid style of any individual in the city. His long-lived son, also Edward Shippen, attained great prominence as a lawyer, becoming chief justice of Pennsylvania before his death early in the nineteenth century. The prominent lawyer, Thomas I. Wharton, was a descendant of another first family. Descendants of the first Thomas Wharton held great estates, built elaborate homes (General Howe held his strange fête, the "Meschianza," in the Wharton mansion), thrived in commerce, politics, and law, were active in community affairs, and singlemindedly married with their own kind. They transmitted great wealth to their heirs; William Wharton of the fourth generation, for example, received so large an inheritance from his father, the wealthy merchant Charles Wharton, on the latter's death in 1838, that he "engaged in no business, but was active in many trusts and charities . . . and in simple hospitality." [10]

Thomas Pym Cope, eulogized in Hunt's *Lives of American Merchants*, was one of half a dozen wealthy nineteenth-century bearers of the Cope name, all descended from Oliver Cope; "one of William Penn's first purchasers in England," he settled in the colony in 1682. The Vaux family, whose reputation for public-spiritedness came to a climax with Roberts Vaux in the nineteenth century, was another Friends family that was prominent, if not magnificently wealthy, from early in the city's history. Not that Roberts was ever in need. Recipient of a fine education made possible by the wealth of both his parents, he quickly gave up the countinghouse for the higher life of humanitarianism, not only because of inner conviction but also because his comfortable circumstances permitted him to do so. The wealthy nineteenth-century merchant Joseph Parker Norris and his family were descendants of Isaac Norris, who became one of the wealthiest men in early Philadelphia after marrying Mary Lloyd, daughter of the president of the provincial council. Amassing a vast landed estate, which later became known as Norristown, Isaac was the last of the Norrises who was truly a self-made man; and he lived a century before the type allegedly flourished.

The eminent lawyer Henry D. Gilpin was descended of a Quaker family that by the 1690s owned a sizable tract of land in the province. His father, Joshua Gilpin, had been compelled to forgo his own plans for practicing law in order to devote himself to supervising the family's large properties in Delaware, Maryland, and Virginia, as well as Pennsylvania. Anthony Morris, an original settler who built a substantial mansion on his ample estate, was the ancestor of a family that was prominent thereafter; Morrises intermarried with the Cadwaladers and had several wealthy descendants in antebellum Philadelphia, including Anthony Morris, the merchant and political figure, and Dr. Caspar Morris. George M. Coates and Samuel Coates were wealthy descendants of another early settler, Thomas Coates. The founder accumulated much property, which served as the bulwark to the fortunes of family members over the next two centuries. The Sellers family also traced its fortune to a man of 1682, Samuel Sellers, whose large estate was the foundation of the success of ensuing generations. William Rawle, Attorney General of the United States for Pennsylvania and an eminent lawyer (as was his son William Rawle, Jr.) was a descendant of Francis Rawle, a Quaker who escaped persecution under Cromwell by settling in Philadelphia near a large tract of land purchased from Penn. Successful marriages abetted the subsequent status enjoyed by later generations of Rawles. The rich lawyer John Ashmead was descended from an ancestor who came to Germantown even before Penn came to Philadelphia. The first Ashmead founded a family whose sons in the eighteenth century were prominent in medicine, commerce, and the patriot cause. The wealthy antebellum shipping merchants John Welsh and his three sons John, William, and Samuel were descendants of William Welsh, who represented New Castle county in 1684. Enriched by his large estate, his heirs intermarried with prominent families, enabling the first-named John Welsh, from his "wharf below Walnut Street," to become the greatest shipowner in Philadelphia by the close of the War of 1812. His contemporaries, the prosperous merchants Thomas Fisher Leaming and Jeremiah Fisher Leaming were the sons of the successful lawyer-capitalist Thomas Leaming. Their father had studied law under John Dickinson and was descended from a family wealthy since its establishment in Philadelphia shortly after the *Welcome*'s arrival.

The prominent nineteenth-century lawyer Eli K. Price—who, when he thought he would go into business, joined the house of Thomas Pym Cope, and, when he transferred to law, entered the office of the redoubtable John Sergeant—was able to move in such exalted circles because he came of an eminent Quaker family that had come to the colony in 1682. Like Prescott and Parkman in Boston, the great historian Henry Charles Lea was descended from a seventeenth-century landowning family—in this case of Friends—which flourished in commerce over the next 150 years. The Mifflins of the nineteenth century were a family whose success dated back to the arrival of George Mifflin in Philadelphia around 1700 and to the successful marital connections the family made thereafter. Other nineteenth-century successes who were descended of seventeenth-century, usually Quaker, settlers were Morris Longstreth; the great shipping merchant Charles Massey of the firm of Eyre and Massey; the descendants of the very rich Samuel Richardson; James W. Paul; the famous painter Matthew Pratt and his wealthy sons, the merchants Henry and Thomas Pratt; a number of members of the Stille family; the socially prominent if not very wealthy Sidney George Fisher

—described by Nicholas B. Wainwright as the "scion of an aristocratic and notable merchant family of early Philadelphia;"[11] and the prosperous iron merchant Nathan Trotter. The latter's background was unusual in that his father was merely a small businessman, and the family, if old, was hardly prominent. His mother's brother, who became Trotter's guardian, was, however, a timber merchant and wharf builder.

A number of Philadelphia families that were in or close to the first rank socially had established themselves first outside the city before coming to Philadelphia, swiftly earning wealth and eminence there. Such were the Biddles. The first William Biddle had purchased land from William Penn prior to the founding of Philadelphia; but the tract, a very extensive one, was in West New Jersey. Subsequent to the arrival of his grandson, William Biddle, in Philadelphia in the eighteenth century, and to young Biddle's marriage to the daughter of the wealthy Nicholas Scull, the family thrived and was represented by many luminaries in each generation prior to the Civil War. The prominent Balch family, which intermarried with the leading families of Philadelphia, also came to the city late, making its fortune first in Maryland. James Balch and his son Stephen, the progenitors of the Philadelphia branch, lived in various areas in the eastern seaboard before coming to Philadelphia. The Ingersoll family has recently been described as "one of America's oldest"; but Jared Ingersoll established the Philadelphia branch of the family only in 1771.[12] The latter, the son of the prominent Connecticut lawyer of the same name, was himself the father of two leading Philadelphia lawyers of the antebellum period. Benjamin Chew, Jr., the very rich Philadelphian who before his death in 1844 had entertained Lafayette "in great splendor," was the son of a wealthy lawyer and a descendant of the prominent family that had arrived with Lord Baltimore in 1671. The Chews' early success was achieved in Maryland; it was Dr. Samuel Chew, a Friend, who established the Philadelphia branch early in the eighteenth century.

The eminent Pemberton line was descended from the wealthy and influential Quaker Israel Pemberton, who came to Philadelphia early in the eighteenth century. John Sergeant was descended of an old and successful family that had made its mark in Connecticut before Sergeant's father moved to Philadelphia in the eighteenth century. John Price Wetherill headed the great drug-and-chemical firm that had been in the family for four generations prior to the Civil War. His ancestor Christopher Wetherill was "a man of substance [who] speedily became the owner" of considerable West New Jersey real estate in the seventeenth century. His son Samuel Wetherill, the founder of the firm, moved to Philadelphia before the Revolution.

Charles Humphreys, a successful merchant of the mid-nineteenth century, was the son of a famous shipbuilder and the grandson of Joshua Humphreys, the lumber merchant who first came to Philadelphia in 1758—75 years after the family's migration from Wales to America.

Samuel Breck, as prominent in public affairs as in commerce, was born in Boston in 1771 and accompanied his father to Philadelphia when he was eleven. The family had been almost continuously successful since the arrival of Edward Breck in Massachusetts in 1635. Samuel Breck was himself brought up amid luxury and gentility. The eminent Dr. Nathaniel Chapman, who studied in London and Edinburgh after graduating from the University of Pennsylvania in 1801, was descended of a family that had been among the earliest settlers of Fairfax County, Virginia. In view of the great prestige they attained in Philadelphia even before the end of the eighteenth century, it would no doubt have surprised many Philadelphians to know that James Tilghman came to the city only in 1760. A successful lawyer, his son William and his grandchildren attained even greater eminence in this field and intermarried with the leading families of the city. The Philadelphia founder's father and grandfather, both Richard Tilghman, were very rich and politically prominent in Maryland after 1661. The Lippincotts, another great Quaker family, had been prominent in New Jersey and New England long before young Joshua Lippincott migrated to Philadelphia shortly after the Revolution. Joshua Lippincott, a wealthy citizen of the 1840s, was the son of this prosperous merchant and of Sarah Wetherill. Prominent Philadelphians whose long-successful families did not come to the city until the nineteenth century were Thomas Earle, John K. Kane of the great New York family, and Dr. Charles Meigs.

A number of families that had come to the United States only in the eighteenth century swiftly achieved wealth and fame of great magnitude in Philadelphia, enabling them to gain entry into the economic elite (if not always into the most charmed social circle). Described by old Simpson as "one of the oldest and most distinguished families," the Willings may not have been the former but they were the latter. Their great wealth and ties with the city's leading families earned for them a status that matched their riches. Charles Willing, a wealthy Bristol merchant, came to Philadelphia only in 1728, "to take charge of the Willings' American business." In 1730 he married Anne Shippen. Thomas Willing, who was possibly the wealthiest man in America during the Revolutionary era, was born to the couple the following year. The Willings of the mid-nineteenth century were the fortunate inheritors of the vast wealth and lofty standing of the family. The valued Scottish family, the Leipers, were descended from Thomas Leiper, who came to Philadelphia shortly before the Revolution and made an immediate success as a tobacco merchant. Trained originally for the ministry and "educated at the best schools of Glasgow and Edinburgh," Leiper had found his cousin's offer of a lucrative partnership irresistible. Charles Biddle Penrose, a prominent attorney and politician before the Civil War, was the son of rich parents and a descendant of a wealthy shipbuilder who had come to the city at the beginning of the eighteenth century and almost immediately married into the family of "one of the large landed proprietors of the province." Governor Thomas McKean, the most prominent member of the McKean family, came to Philadelphia only two years before the Revolution, after a successful legal career in Delaware. Almost overnight he became one of the chief political actors in the next generation.

Benjamin W. Richards, Mayor of Philadelphia in 1830, was the son of a wealthy New Jersey landowner. He was a descendant of Owen Richards, who arrived in Pennsylvania during the second decade of the eighteenth century to amass extensive landholdings. Paul Beck, who left a great estate on his death in 1844, was the son of a wealthy German merchant who migrated to Philadelphia around 1752. No Sansoms appeared in the wealthy citizens listings of the 1840s, since the wealthy William Sansom had died in 1840. The fortune of his daughter Eliza, however, abetted that of her husband George Vaux. Samuel Sansom, a Friend, had come to Philadelphia in 1732 to become a successful dry goods merchant. Over the course of the following century, Sansoms intermarried with the Callender, Perot, Biddle, Vaux, and Morris families. The famous surgeon John Rhea Barton was the extremely wealthy son of the sister of David Rittenhouse and the very rich Thomas Barton, who came to Pennsylvania *circa* 1750. The rich as well as politically eminent William J. Duane was the son of a successful publisher, who came to Philadelphia only in 1796, and a wealthy mother. The prominent lawyer John Read was the son of George Read, one of the Founding Fathers of the nation, and the grandson of John Read, who came to America in 1728. John Ralston, a wealthy attorney, and Robert Ralston, a wealthy merchant, were the sons of the rich lawyer-capitalist Robert Ralston, who came to Pennsylvania early in the eighteenth century.

Some of the richest men of the antebellum period were themselves first- or second-generation Philadelphians. John Bromley, who came from England *circa* 1840, almost immediately became a successful manufacturer of carpets; he was the son of a Yorkshire manufacturer of woolen products. John Haviland, an eminent English architect and engineer, was the nephew of a count. John Powel Hare, mentioned earlier in another connection, was the son of Margaret Willing and the wealthy Robert Hare, who came over from England in 1772. Joseph L. Moss was the son of the wealthy merchant John Moss, who arrived from London around 1793. The rich Dr. Jonas Preston was the son of a similarly named Welsh doctor who came to Delaware County before the Revolution. David Landreth "the younger" moved into the successful seed-and-nursery-business established by his father shortly after the latter migrated from England after the Revolution.

A number of successful men were descended from recently arrived Scottish families. Joseph and Thomas Dundas became successful merchants shortly after they arrived in the mid-eighteenth century, their descendants flourishing thereafter both in society and business. John McAllister, Jr., who was noted for his unparalleled personal library, his interest in local antiquities, and his public-spiritedness, was able to cultivate these tastes because of the wealth accumulated by his father after emigrating from Glasgow in 1835. Charles Macalester, a successful banker of the 1840s, inherited much wealth from his Scottish-born father of the same name. Macalester, Sr. became a wealthy merchant and was associated with William Bingham and the Baring Brothers.

Possibly the most eminent Irishman in the city was Alexander Henry, who came to America when not yet twenty; he had already been established in Ireland as a successful merchant. Orphaned at age two, he was essentially a self-made man. Yet his father had been well established, his brother saw to it that Henry received a good education, and his way was smoothed in Philadelphia by "valuable letters of introduction." Henry's daughter married the prominent businessman Silas E. Weir. The humanitarian and author, Dr. James Mease, was the son of John Mease, who became a leading shipping merchant after arriving from Ireland *circa* 1760. The wealthy merchant Robert Meade, who came to Philadelphia around 1731, was the founder of a prolific and successful family. The Civil War general George Meade was his great-grandson. Dr. Samuel George Morton was the son of a successful Irish merchant who came to Philadelphia in the late eighteenth century. Captain Turner Camac had come to town in 1804 to oversee the extensive estate of his wife, a sister of Mrs. Penn. The captain left a "splendid fortune" to his heirs.

Heading the French contingent in the city was Peter Duponceau. Arriving in Pennsylvania during the Revolution as an aide to Baron Steuben, Duponceau stayed on to become one of the most admired men in Philadelphia, sought out for his wisdom and knowledge by the young Alexis de Tocqueville. He had been born of a "rather distinguished French family and had the opportunities of a competent education in French and classical culture." At age fifteen this young man, a friend to Beaumarchais, gave a class in Latin at the Episcopal College of Brussière. The wealthy Perot brothers, John and El[l]iston (who married Sarah Sansom), migrated to America in the later eighteenth century. Their extensive business profited six sons who lived in antebellum Philadelphia. Adolph E. Borie, a wealthy and prominent graduate of the University of Pennsylvania, was the son of John Joseph Borie of an "old mercantile family" that migrated to the city from Villeneuve, France in 1805. The wealthy Peter Bousquet was descended from a prosperous mercantile family. John Bouvier, a legal protegé of John Kennedy(!) and friend to Roger B. Taney, was the wealthy son of a prosperous father and of Marie Benezet, of the well-known Quaker family. Bouvier arrived in Philadelphia with his father at the beginning of the nineteenth century. Miss Crousillat, the woman who sold the city of

Philadelphia the area of Point Breeze in the Schuylkill River used for the erection of a city gas works, was the daughter of Louis Crousillat, a shipping merchant who was prominent in the "French trade" at the start of the nineteenth century.

Of the German families in Philadelphia, probably none had a higher status than the Wistars. Following Caspar Wistar's arrival in the city from Heidelberg in 1717, the family thrived in business, science, and the arts. Particularly eminent in the early nineteenth century were Richard Wistar, husband to Sarah Morris, and his brother, Dr. Caspar Wistar, who after graduating from the University of Pennsylvania, studied in London and Edinburgh. The Gratzes were eminent in business and politics following the arrival first of Barnard Gratz around 1754 and then his brother Michael to found a successful mercantile house. By the Jacksonian era, Simon Gratz was one of the founders of the Pennsylvania Academy of Fine Arts, Jacob was a president of the Union Canal Company, Joseph was prominent in "social circles"–Jewish and other—and Hyman Gratz was president of both the Pennsylvania Insurance Company and the Academy of Fine Arts. John Frederick Lewis, a great Philadelphia merchant, associate of the Willings, partner to Silas E. Weir, and possessor of an ample fortune, was descended of a German "patrician" family. His father, who was prominent during the Revolution, had anglicized the family's original surname, Ludewig. William Wagner, who had been a supercargo under Stephen Girard before becoming a wealthy merchant on his own and marrying Louisa Binney, was the son of John Wagner, a successful merchant who came to Philadelphia in the late eighteenth century. The wealthy Hartman and Charles Kuhn were descended of a long-prominent Philadelphia family of German descent. Zachariah Poulson, publisher of *Poulson's American* and *Daily Advertiser*, was the third-generation descendant of a family that had had a successful printing establishment in Philadelphia since Nicholas Poulson left Copenhagen in the early nineteenth century. The wealthy Bohlens of the nineteenth century were the children of Bohl Bohlen, a Dutch immigrant of about 1754 who became a successful importer in Philadelphia.

Whether of old family or new, most wealthy Philadelphians of the antebellum decades were quite simply the sons of relatively rich parents. The great merchant Manuel Eyre was the son of a prosperous shipbuilder and patriot. Edward W. Clark, whose family first settled in Massachusetts in 1639—and who therefore could have been otherwise categorized—was a leading Philadelphia banker whose father had been a successful New England banker. Charles S. Boker, who was a leading merchant and for a time president of Girard's bank, was the son of a merchant, albeit one whose means were not extensive. Henry Carey, the publisher and writer, and his brother-in-law Isaac Lea, each received a substantial share of the stock in Carey's father's firm; the elder Carey was the eminent publisher and philanthropist Mathew Carey. Charles Marshall and Charles Marshall, Jr. inherited the prosperous wholesale drug business initiated by Christopher Marshall. The mother of Josiah Dawson, the philanthropist, was the daughter of the rich Jeremiah Elfreth, who was himself the beneficiary of a sizable dowry.

Richard Somers Smith, successful in the insurance business, was aided by a father who was a "hero of the Revolution" and a mother, Elizabeth Shute, whose uncle had been the mayor of Philadelphia in the middle of the eighteenth century. Edmund A. Souder launched his business career with the financial aid of a relative, after first working in the countinghouse and transportation business of his father Thomas M. Souder—"an energetic business man." The financier Alexander Benson got started in his father's dry goods and later carpet trade. The substantial leather merchant William Musser began in the business as a young boy by working in a relative's countinghouse. The successful wholesale grocers John, Edward, and Francis Jordan were the sons of a shrewd businessman who gave his family a comfortable independence. Alexander G. Cattell and his brother Elijah were the sons of a longtime merchant. The lumber merchant Henry Croskey inherited the business of his father. His mother was the daughter of the prominent Revolutionary figure, Captain John Ashmead. William F. Potts started his successful iron business with his own capital, but only after first working in the same business in the firm of his father, William L. Potts. Isaac Jeanes, a commissions dealer in the fruit business as well as a shipbuilder, was the son of a prosperous merchant. The wealthy William J. Maitland was the son of the successful distiller John Maitland.

In contrast to those professionals whose wealth actually derived from a variety of sources—some of them having little to do with their professions—some wealthy Philadelphians in the professions had followed in the footsteps of their fathers. Frederick Carroll Brewster, a successful lawyer after graduating from the University of Pennsylvania in 1841, was the son of a man who "for many years carried on a large practice." Judge Robert T. Conrad, an editor as well as a lawyer, was the son of a publisher. Dr. James B. Rogers, who became a professor of chemistry at the University of Pennsylvania, was the son of the successful Dr. Patrick Kerr Rogers. And Dr. D. Hayes Agnew, who according to old Morris, "quickly gained a lucrative practice" in Philadelphia after graduating from the University of Pennsylvania in 1838, was the son of Dr. Robert Agnew, "a physician of high repute."

If these are success stories, their plots do not conform to the story line widely assumed to be true, both then and later. The urban rich of the antebellum era appeared to be successful above all in inheriting wealth and status that contributed significantly to their material fortunes.

Notes

[1] Philip L. White, *The Beekmans of New York in Politics and Commerce, 1647–1877* (New York, 1956), pp. 556, 562.
[2] *New York Genealogical and Biographical Record, LXI*, pp. 317, 343, 346.
[3] Martha Lamb and Mrs. Burton Harrison, *History of the City of New York* (New York, 1877–96), III, p. 446.
[4] Willis, "Social Origins of Political Leadership in New York City," p. 155.
[5] *NYGBR, XXXIV*, pp. 231–34.
[6] Benjamin Silliman, "Personal Reminiscences of 60 Years at the New York Bar," in David McAdam *et al*, eds., *History of the Bench and Bar of New York* (New York, 1897), I, p. 241.
[7] Horace Lyman Weeks, *Prominent Families of New York* (New York, 1897), p. 170; James G. Wilson, *Memorial History of the City of New York* (New York, 1893), V, pp. 167–68.
[8] Weeks, *Prominent Families*, p. 231; *History of the Chemical Bank* (New York, 1913), pp. 102–03.
[9] Bertram Wyatt-Brown, *Lewis Tappan and the Evangelical War Against Slavery* (Cleveland, 1969), p. 3.
[10] Jonathan Wharton Lippincott, *Biographical Memoranda Concerning Joseph Wharton* (Philadelphia, 1909), p. 10.
[11] Wainwright, ed., "Diaries of Sidney George Fisher," *Pa. Magazine, LXXVI* (April 1952), p. 177.
[12] Irwin F. Greenberg, "Charles Ingersoll: The Aristocratic Copperhead," *ibid., XCIII* (April 1969), p. 190.

7
Did Fortunes Rise and Fall Mercurially During the "Age of Fluidity?"

> In no country in the world are private fortunes more precarious than in the United States. It is not uncommon for the same man in the course of his life to rise and sink again through all the grades that lead from opulence to poverty.
>
> Tocqueville, *Democracy in America,* II:213

If the second quarter of the nineteenth century has long been known as an age of egalitarianism, its reputation has rested largely on the mercurial rise and fall in fortunes believed to be characteristic of the era. In America, wrote Tocqueville, fortunes were both "scanty and insecure . . . wealth circulate[d] with inconceivable rapidity. New families [were] constantly springing up, others . . . constantly falling away, and all that remain change[d] their condition." According to the brilliant French visitor, if Americans were aggressively boastful, yet insecure and addicted to an unlovely conspicuous display of their material possessions, it was because "their wealth had been only recently acquired and at any instant these same advantages might be lost." [1] These striking generalizations continue to command scholarly support. In his well-received recent treatise on American economic development, Stuart Bruchey wrote that "before approximately mid-century, class lines fell lightly over the contours of an essentially fluid society. It was a highly speculative age in which fortunes were made and lost overnight, in which men rose and fell with . . . dexterous agility." [2] The belief thus persists that flux was the rule during the second quarter of the nineteenth century.

As is true of other Tocquevillean social concepts, this one too owes more to the deductive flair of its originator than to the facts of American economic life. In view of the paucity of contemporary evidence underlying the belief in antebellum intragenerational economic mobility, the purpose of this chapter is to subject the thesis to a detailed empirical test, based primarily on data from New York City and Boston and, to a lesser extent, from Brooklyn.[3] Stuart Blumin's recent study indicates that in Philadelphia upward economic mobility was slight during the period 1820 to 1860 and that the little vertical mobility in evidence was confined chiefly to moves between contiguous rather than widely separated levels of wealth and income. His conclusions were based on the pattern of change in the occupations and residences of hundreds of randomly selected individuals.[4] If Blumin had to resort to an ingenious methodology —which, among other things, tried to fix a relative hierarchical position for over fifty occupations and an absolute money equivalent of the wealth or income associated with each of them—it was because he was compelled to do so by the vagaries of Philadelphia's tax-assessment data. The city's practice of levying assessments against occupants as well as owners of real property makes it impossible to use the assessment rolls as an indicator of the total wealth owned by individuals within the city. The fact that Boston, New York City, and Brooklyn listed assessments alongside the names of the owners of real and personal property makes it possible to create lists of thousands of property owners and to trace the course of their upward or downward economic movement by comparing their wealth early and late in the era.

The tax assessments, as has been shown, are an imperfect clue to wealth. An additional drawback for purposes of this chapter, is that the assessments were mostly on real estate, a form of wealth less fluid than personal property. The study of real property over time might, therefore, suggest slightly greater stability than was in fact the case for wealth as a whole. Counteracting this possibility would be the vaunted speculation in city lots that characterized the era. Of course, tax-assessment records for great and populous cities cannot tell us anything about the subsequent fate of persons who fled, possibly to smaller communities of greater opportunity; such persons were several times as likely to leave Boston, Brooklyn, and New York City as rich men.[5] And, although assessors were guided by uniform theoretical standards of evaluation, they inevitably offered differing appraisals, influenced by subjective considerations. Yet for all the deficiencies of the tax data, there is nothing better for measuring changes within an era. In effect, all men were underassessed, but they are underassessed according to a common rule of thumb. Valid comparisons could, therefore, be made of the worth of different individuals in a given year, as well as the amount of change in their fortunes over a period of time. Despite the era's reputation for inflation, the value of the dollar changed only slightly during the era; of course, what change there was affected similarly the dollars held by all persons within a city.

No claim is made here that these cities were the ideal specimens for a study of this kind, nor that they were typical of other cities. But certainly they were not selected simply because their data were available: Boston did publish printed lists of taxable wealth during the era; New York City and Brooklyn, alas, did not. New York City lists had to be created, as explained earlier, by taking note of over 100,000 separate and unindexed items in the manuscript assessment rolls. New York City was the largest and fastest growing of the nation's great cities, as well as the wealthiest. Boston had a far smaller population, yet was vitally important to New England as its businessmen faced up to the challenge posed by its relative decline as an entrepôt by vigorous involvement in transportation and manufacturing projects. Brooklyn's special relationship to and dependence on its great neighbor were unique among cities of the second rank, but its rapid growth both in population and enterprise was typical of the recent experience of other bustling small towns. Above all, these cities met the fundamental requirement for an investigation of the rise and fall of fortunes. They all contained inordinately large numbers of wealthy men.

Boston

This chapter is essentially a comparison of the wealth and relative standing enjoyed by several thousand individuals early and late in the "era of the common man." For Boston this era shall include the years 1833–1848. In 1833, when the city's population was about 70,000, approximately 1,815 Bostonians paid taxes on real and personal property worth $6,000 or more.[6] It is these persons whose subsequent wealth has been traced.[7] The notion that rich men regularly and suddenly lost their possessions could have been checked by reference to a much smaller number of taxpayers; but in view of the ampleness of our data bank, I decided to investigate the subsequent situations of the large number of persons who were less than rich at the beginning of the era, in order to compare the course of their careers with patterns that emerged for their wealthier neighbors.

Boston's taxpayers of 1833 have been broken down into categories according to wealth. Group I includes the 83 individuals worth $100,000 or more—the "richest of the rich" or the "super rich" of that year; Group II contains the 54 individuals whose property was valued at roughly between $70,000 and $100,000; Group III consists of the 166 individuals whose wealth was assessed at between $40,000 and $70,000; Group IV contains the 317 persons worth between $20,000 and $40,000; and Group V is made up of the 1,195 individuals whose property was assessed at between $6,000 and $20,000. Although the latter group was part of the wealthiest 2½ per cent of Boston's population, its members were hardly rich. Such classifications, of course, can never be exact but it would appear sensible to regard Groups I–III as comprising not only the 303 wealthiest persons in Boston but also the "truly rich" of the city: that is, those capable of living in comfort, of amassing costly possessions, and of securing expensive housing and uses of leisure. Group IV can be described as the "not quite rich," while Group V was perhaps the upper-middle level of wealthholders; of course, many younger members of wealthy families were to be found in the latter two groups.

By 1848, when Boston's population had risen by about 70 per cent since 1833 and the city, in common with the rest of the country, was in the midst of economic prosperity, the minimum value of estate required for membership in the wealthiest group had gone up to $50,000. In 1848 Boston's rich numbered 477 individuals. From the top down they have been divided into three groups for that year. Group I, the "richest of the rich," contained the 52 Bostonians worth $200,000 or more; Group II the 137 persons worth between $100,000 and $200,000; and Group III the 288 individuals worth between $50,000 and $100,000. Table 7–1 provides answers to the questions: what had happened to the rich, the "not quite rich," and the upper-middle wealthholders of 1833 by the year 1848?

TABLE 7–1.
The Category of Wealth in 1848 of the Wealthiest Boston Taxpayers of 1833

Boston taxpayers of 1833 according to level of wealth		*In the rich of 1848 (≥$50,000)*		*In 1848 tax list but not among the rich*		*Not in 1848 tax list**	
Group	No.	No. from 1833 group	% of 1833 group	No. from 1833 group	% of 1833 group	No. from 1833 group	% of 1833 group
I. ≥$100,000	83	62	74	4†	5	17	21
II. $70,000–$100,000	54	31	57	4‡	8	19	35
III. $40,000–$70,000	166	81	49	36	22	49	29
IV. $20,000–$40,000	317	104	33	105	33	108	34
V. $6,000–$20,000	1195	80	7	655**	55	460	38

*Individuals could disappear from the list because of death, departure from Boston, poverty, or an assessor's lapse.
†Includes the heirs of two fortunes: Andrew Brimmer's and Gardiner Greene's. The only severe declines in Group I were experienced by Thomas Lee, whose worth dropped from $122,000 to $26,000 and Nathaniel Goddard, who fell from $157,200 to $24,800. The Goddard family, however, continued to be very rich.
‡Includes Abigail Salisbury, whose own wealth was assessed at $35,000 and whose husband was worth $60,200.
**Of this number, 71 were worth between $30,000 and $45,000 in 1848. The other 584 persons were worth less.

The Boston evidence hardly points to any dramatic rise upward during the period 1833–1848. Very few persons of Group V, the upper-middle level—only 7 per cent of the total—moved into the rich class of 1848. Not shown in Table 7-1 is the fact that an additional 6 per cent of the large number of persons in this category rose slightly in wealth; more than half of the group experienced no change to speak of; and 38 per cent dropped out of the later tax list. The group of "not quite rich,"

(Group IV) although only about one-quarter the size of the upper middle, sent a larger number of its members upward to the rich of 1848 than did Group V. The 1833 Group IV fifteen years later had dispersed almost equally into three categories: the rich, the wealth group below, and those who had disappeared from the records. As for the rich of 1833, Groups I-III considered as a whole, 57 per cent of them were in the rich of 1848, not quite 15 per cent were just below, and not quite 29 per cent had disappeared from the list. Yet, only a handful of the 137 Bostonians worth $70,000 or more in 1833 and still alive in 1848 were *not* among the rich in the later year. Interestingly, the rate of disappearance from the 1848 tax list did not differ markedly for the three wealthiest categories of 1833: death appeared to be no respecter of slight wealth barriers. That the disappearance rate for the upper middle, however, was almost twice that for the richest of the rich, points to the higher rate of departure either from the city or from the class of property owners experienced by the former group.

Like all statistics, these can be variously interpreted. Of the almost endless generalizations that can be drawn from them is the not-insignificant one that the "rich class" of Bostonians in 1848 were drawn about equally from the 1,500 persons in the two 1833 categories owning between $6,000 to $40,000 in property and from the 300 persons earlier assessed for $40,000 or more. The tabular data by themselves are unrevealing of many things, including the great extent to which the later rich were composed of Bostonians of great or wealthy family whose earlier low assessments testified not to their poverty but to their youthfulness. The pattern that is most clearly discernible from the evidence is that the extent of an individual's wealth in 1833 was the major factor in determining whether or not he would be among the rich in 1848.

Another fact not apparent from Table 7-1, which measures movement by groups or categories, is that in terms of the absolute change in the worth of individuals, most Bostonians owning $20,000 or more in 1833 became richer in subsequent years. Yet here too a significant disparity manifested itself. Two-thirds of the persons originally worth $20,000 experienced increases in their fortunes, with only two individuals from this group suffering any kind of decline. For all groups below the "super rich" the trend prevailed almost without exception: the greater the original wealth of members of the group, the greater was the percentage of individuals from the group whose wealth increased. Moreover, during this exuberant period, decline occurred for only a small percentage of the members of any group that in 1833 had been worth $20,000 or more. In contrast to the fact that about half the individuals in the $20,000 to $40,000 bracket had made gains of some sort over the fifteen-year period, only about 16 per cent of the group suffered declines.[8]

Although the evidence indicates that it was primarily the rich men

Residence of Harrison Gray Otis, Boston. Otis was a leading member of Boston's elite. This magnificent mansion at 85 Mount Vernon Street was the second of two houses built for him by architect Charles Bulfinch. (*Photograph by Samuel Chamberlain courtesy of the Print Department, Boston Public Library.*)

of early in the period who became the rich men at the era's end, it does not show the extent to which the fortunes of the wealthy may have followed an erratic or zigzag course during the cycle. The Tocqueville thesis assumed that the rich who suddenly fell might just as suddenly rise. Such things could and of course did happen.[9] The question is, how often? Fortunately, the Boston tax data permit observation of the variation in the fortunes of wealthy persons over five-year periods. Table 7-2 makes clear that in the short run there was significantly less change in the wealth or standing of the rich than over the entire period of fifteen years. In other words, in those few instances in which the worth of a rich Bostonian declined significantly, in all but a handful of cases the drop was a gradual rather than a sudden one.

The evidence on the subsequent situations of the holders of different categories of wealth of 1833 in large part answers the question as to the backgrounds or earlier position of the rich Bostonians of 1848. As has been related 75 per cent of the 477 persons worth $50,000 or more in 1848 had been among the wealthiest 2½ per cent of the population in 1833. Of the 52 members of the super rich of 1848 (Group I, $200,000 or more), more than half had been worth over $100,000 in 1833, 75 per cent came from the rich of the earlier year, while only four were new men. While only 18 per cent of the next lower category—Group II, whose individual members were each worth between $100,000 and $200,000 in 1848—had been worth $100,000 or more in 1833, more than half of the remainder had been in the rich groups of the earlier year; fewer than 10 per cent were new men. *No one in the two highest categories of 1848 who had paid taxes in 1833 had paid them on less than $20,000 of estate.* As might have been expected, the so-called lower rich of 1848 (Group III, worth between $50,000 and $100,000) had the most disparate earlier status of the rich as a whole. Slightly less than 25 per cent of the lower rich had been among the rich of 1833, with just over half of the group having earlier been located in the "not quite rich" and the upper middle levels of 1833. Of this group, 15 per cent were new Boston taxpayers. When the 1848 rich are treated as a whole, it is found that about 40 per cent had been of the three rich groups of 1833: and about another 20 per cent had been in the "not quite rich" group. Of the 22 per cent who were newcomers to the tax list, more than half were from wealthy families.[10]

Working backward over short-run periods to discover the *earlier* wealth categories of the rich Bostonians of 1838, 1843, and 1848, yields results that are almost identical with the findings on the *later* standing of the rich Bostonians of 1833, 1838, and 1843. (See Table 7-2.) Eighty-three per cent of the rich men of 1838 were among the rich of 1833, with 12 per cent in the "not quite rich" group of the earlier date. Only two of the eight persons new to the tax list of 1838 came of new family. Since the number of rich in 1843 had risen more than 20 per cent since 1838,

TABLE 7–2.
Changes in Wealth Experienced by Rich Bostonians in the Short Run (5-year periods)

1838 wealth category reached by the rich of 1833 (303 persons)					
In the rich of 1838 ($50,000)		*In 1838 tax list but not among the rich*		*Not in 1838 tax list*	
No. from 1833 group	% of 1833 group	No. from 1833 group	% of 1833 group	No. from 1833 group	% of 1833 group
252	83	37	12	14	5
1843 wealth category reached by the rich of 1838 (303 persons)					
In the rich of 1843 ($50,000)		*In 1843 tax list but not among the rich*		*Not in 1843 tax list*	
No. from 1838 group	% of 1838 group	No. from 1838 group	% of 1838 group	No. from 1838 group	% of 1838 group
242	80	37	12	24	8
1848 wealth category reached by the rich of 1843 (404 persons)					
In the rich of 1848 ($50,000)		*In 1848 tax list but not among the rich*		*Not in 1848 tax list*	
No. from 1843 group	% of 1843 group	No. from 1843 group	% of 1843 group	No. from 1843 group	% of 1843 group
341	84	27	7	36	9

the figures on the earlier status of the rich of 1843 inevitably disclose that the percentage who had been rich five years earlier had fallen off. Yet even here the decline was slight: 77 per cent of the rich of 1843 had been rich in 1838, and another 15 per cent were earlier in the upper 2½ per cent bracket. Better than 75 per cent of the 450 persons worth $60,000 or more in 1848 had been among the smaller rich class of five years before. Only a handful of the new rich of 1848 were of families not previously wealthy.

During any year in the 1830s and 1840s the great preponderance of Boston's wealthy citizens were found to have been rich five years earlier. Most of the small number who were new to the economic elite came of families that were old. Very few Bostonians rose from the lower depths or from outside the city to reach the top. Mercurial rises and falls of fortune were striking only because of their rarity.

Another interesting piece of Boston evidence is an 1837 list prepared by the assessor—evidently for his own edification—of "Individuals and Firms whose aggregate tax for 1837 amounts to $800 or upwards." (As I opened the printed tax list for that year, this handwritten document, neatly folded up inside the tax list, fell to the ground.) Only two firms—Dana, Fenno and Henshaw, and A. A. Lawrence and Company—appeared on this list. For the rest, it was a listing of the forty wealthiest Bostonians of 1837, no doubt the "truly rich" to the man who prepared this special rating. The question arises: who were these persons and what was their standing in the other years of the era? Table 7-3 provides an answer.

With the single exception of William Sawyer, whose 1833 estate just failed to qualify, every member of Boston's "super rich" of 1837 had been a member of the rich class in 1833. Only three other men had been worth less than $100,000 in the earlier year, none of them by very much. The "super rich" of 1837, in fact, contained the names of the majority of persons who made up the "super rich" of every other year examined during the period: close to 90 per cent of the 1833 elite; two-thirds of the larger 1843 group; while better than 85 per cent of the 1837 elite who survived to 1848 were still in the "super rich" of that year. It is a striking fact that the list of the "super rich" I have drawn up for 1843 also contained the name of only one person—Abijah S. Johnson—who had not been rich both in 1833 and 1838. Only William J. Walker of the more than fifty persons who by 1848 were assessed at the $200,000 or more that qualified them for a place in the "super rich," had not been a rich man earlier in the era: in 1843 he belonged only to the "not quite rich."

It is possible that when contemporaries spoke of "fortunes" they meant wealth of the magnitude here ascribed to the "richest of the rich" or to the "super rich." The evidence for Boston indicates that such wealth, far from circulating with "inconceivable rapidity," tended rather to remain in the hands of the small number of men and families who had managed to accumulate it in the first place. During the antebellum years, few new great wealthholders sprang up, while fewer still fell away. The rapid change in condition attributed by Tocqueville's hypothesis to most persons was confined to very few families in Boston during the period.

New York City

Inasmuch as New York City printed no official tax lists during the era, this study relies on the lists of taxpayers for 1828 and 1845 created by the author from the manuscript assessment rolls, and on a tax list for 1856–1857 published by William H. Boyd.[11] If the time span covered by the New York City data is somewhat asymmetrical and does not include evidence on the short run, the relatively long period it represents adds to its usefulness. In any case, the chronological limits for the "era of the common man" for New York City will be 1828 to 1857.

1828–1845

In 1828, New York City had 1,341 persons assessed for $7,500 or

TABLE 7–3.
The Wealthiest Taxpayers (Forty) of Boston in 1837 and Their Wealth in 1833, 1838, 1843, and 1848*

Taxpayer	*Wealth in 1837 ($)*	*Wealth in 1833 ($)*	*Wealth in 1838 ($)*	*Wealth in 1843 ($)*	*Wealth in 1848 ($)*
Appleton, Samuel	247,200	220,000	257,200	309,000	416,000
Appleton, William	227,400	135,400	249,600	265,000	336,000
Appleton, Nathan	166,000	115,000	186,000	221,000	413,000
Blake, Sarah	182,600	119,400	167,600	157,800	—
Andrews, Ebenezer T.	228,400	155,000	228,400	246,300	305,000
Boardman, William H.	211,800	139,400	211,000	119,600	133,000
Bradley, Thomas D.	185,200	134,000	184,000	—	—
Borland, John	177,000	169,000	193,000	115,600	114,000
Brimmer, Martin (heirs)	243,000	186,000	243,000	243,000	283,000
Brooks, Peter C.	873,000	343,600	891,000	1,026,000	1,324,000
Bussey, Benjamin	164,200	122,000	164,200	98,800†	105,500
Codman, Charles R.	169,400	124,000	169,400	197,000	254,000
Codman, Henry	284,200	226,200	289,000	305,000	352,000
Coolidge, Joseph	163,000	206,000	161,000	48,000	131,500
Crowninshield, Benj. W.	261,800	210,000	320,800	271,000	308,100
Eliot, Samuel A.	149,000	106,400	65,000	110,000	162,000
Ellis, David	163,000	144,000	152,000	56,400	—
Francis, Ebenezer	422,000	177,600	422,800	191,800	213,900
Goddard, Nathaniel	182,600	157,200	169,600	246,000	24,800
Hammond, Samuel	210,400	240,000	220,400	—	—
Homer, Benjamin	271,400	195,200	192,400	—	—
Hubbard, John L.	169,600	232,000	—	—	—
Jackson, P. T.	202,600	76,000	264,400	22,000	15,500
Lyman, George W.	163,000	170,000	163,000	158,000	88,000
Otis, Harrison Gray	329,800	291,200	314,600	324,800	416,300
Parker, John	664,000	238,000	685,600	510,000	—
Phillips, Jonathan	422,400	433,600	437,600	470,000	663,000
Pratt, William	310,000	58,400	318,000	323,000	132,000†
Sawyer, William	173,000	31,000	173,600	171,000	71,000
Sears, David	409,200	225,800	453,000	483,600	727,500
Shattuck, George C.	251,200	189,200	258,200	275,000	349,100
Shaw, Robert G.	235,200	211,000	248,000	600,200	716,500
Thompson, Thomas	166,800	110,600	191,400	229,400	300,000
Thorndike, John P.	212,800	100,400	231,600	176,200	229,500
Trull, John W.	163,400	92,000	176,400	179,800	222,300
Tucker, Richard D.	164,600	123,000	167,600	—	—
Tuckerman, Edward	267,600	218,800	286,600	284,600	202,600†
Welles, John	316,000	260,000	327,400	411,400	551,500
Williams, John D.	421,000	364,400	469,000	580,400	785,200
Winthrop, Thomas L.	242,400	142,000	323,600	220,800†	—

*The assessor's handwritten list cites only the tax dollars to be paid in 1837 by the individuals listed. The tax rate for that year was an even 1 per cent.
†Heirs.

more of real and personal property, individuals who were thus in the wealthiest 1 per cent of the city's population of approximately 185,000. With 1828 treated as the base year, the city's taxpayers have been divided into categories according to wealth: Group I contains the 59 individuals worth $100,000 or more—New York City's "richest of the rich"; Group II, the 36 persons worth between $70,000 and $100,000; Group III, the 116 persons worth between $50,000 and $70,000; Group IV, the 309 persons worth between $25,000 and $50,000; and Group V, the 821 individuals worth between $7,500 and $25,000. The first four of these categories will be described as the "rich" of 1828. The 135 persons in Group V who were worth between $20,000 and $25,000 will be considered analogous to Boston's "not quite rich," with the remaining 686 members of that category regarded as the upper middle level.

By 1845, New York City's population had doubled, then totalling 371,223. The number of rich persons had also doubled. From the top down, the highest category (Group I) contained the 55 persons worth $250,000 or more—the "super rich" of 1845; Group II, the 238 New Yorkers worth between $100,000 and $250,000; and Group III, the slightly more than 700 individuals whose wealth was assessed at between $45,000 and $100,000. Table 7-4 indicates what had happened by 1845 to the wealth of New York City's wealthiest taxpayers of 1828.

In New York City, as in Boston, the relative worth of persons at the beginning of the period appeared to be the most significant factor in determining their chances of belonging to the rich by the mid-1840s. New York City's more dynamic economic growth was reflected by the greater ease with which individuals from each of the five categories were able to remain in or move slightly upward within the rich class. The greatest disparity between the two cities in this respect was the rate of increase in absolute wealth made by New York City's lower-wealth categories. Nonetheless, in New York City as in Boston, the few persons who rose from the "upper middle" level at the beginning of the period to the rich of the 1840s were more often than not from families of great wealth. New York City's supremely rich suffered no sudden loss of fortune during the era. Not one of the dozen families that contained individuals worth $200,000 or more in 1828 dropped below $100,000 by 1845. Only William Jauncey, of the almost fifty persons valued between $100,000 and $200,000 in 1828, fell from the class of the rich by 1845; and even he barely failed to qualify.

When the earlier—1828—status of New York City's wealthiest taxpayers of 1845 is investigated, the results yield a pattern quite similar to Boston's during the same period. Just under 50 per cent of the 55 New Yorkers worth $250,000 or more in 1845 had been assessed for $75,000 or more in 1828, and 76 per cent of the group as a whole had been among the rich in the earlier year. (For Boston's "super rich" of 1848 the comparable figure is 75 per cent.) The twelve newcomers to

TABLE 7–4.
The Category of Wealth in 1845 of the Wealthiest New York City Taxpayers of 1828

New York City taxpayers of 1828 according to level of wealth		The rich of 1845									
		$200,000 in 1845		*$100,000–$200,000 in 1845*		*$45,000–$100,000 in 1845*		*$25,000–$45,000 in 1845*		*Not in 1845 tax list*	
Description	No.	No. from 1828 group	% of 1828 group	No. from 1828 group	% of 1828 group	No. from 1828 group	% of 1828 group	No. from 1828 group	% of 1828 group	No. from 1828 group	% of 1828 group
I. ≥$100,000	59	23	39	13	22	9	15	1	2	13	22
II. $70,000–$100,000	36	7	20	13	36	6	17	3	8	7	19
III. 50,000–$70,000	116	11	10	30	26	29	25	15	13	31	26
										Not in 1845 tax list or worth less than $25,000†	
IV. $25,000–$50,000	309	17*	6	51*	16	92	30	44	14	105	34
VI. $7,000–$25,000	821	—	—	26*	3	124	15	118	14	553	68

*Most of these persons were members of well known wealthy families.
†The list drawn up for 1845 does not include taxpayers on very small amounts of property.

New York City's "richest of the rich" included members of the Gilbert, Hendricks, Janeway, Douglass, Jones, Lenox, Lorillard, and Roosevelt families. Probably only William Niblo and James Phalen can be properly classified as "new men." Of the 238 persons in the lower category, those worth between $100,000 and $250,000 in 1845, 56 per cent had been among the rich of 1828—a figure slightly higher than that obtained for the corresponding Boston category in 1848. While close to one-third of this New York City group were new taxpayers in 1845, most of the newcomers came from such wealthy families as the Barclays, Andersons, Crugers, Douglasses, Gihons, Grinnells, Grosvenors, Hendrickses, Holbrooks, Hones, Joneses, Kennedys, Lawrences, Mesiers, Murrays, Palmers, Posts, Storms, Pecks, Targees, Taylors, Wards, Van Rensselaers, and others of like distinction.

Nearly 40 per cent of the New Yorkers who were worth $70,000 to $100,000 in 1845 had been among the rich 17 years earlier, while another 17 per cent had been slightly below the rich in 1828. As was true of the wealthier New York City categories, most of the new 1845 taxpayers in the $70,000 to $100,000 bracket were of wealthy families. The list of new taxpayers in this category includes such eminent names as Aspinwall, Bogart, Bronson, Cadwallader, Cutting, DePeyster, Grinnell, Havemeyer, Hoffman, Kennedy, King, Kingsland, Morris, Murray, Ogden, Palmer, Pentz, Post, Remsen, Rogers, Russell, Schieffelin, Thorn, Valentine, Wagstaff, Van Zandt and Ward. New York City's wealthiest 500 in 1845 were slightly more likely than their Boston counterparts to have been among the "not quite rich" a decade-and-a-half earlier, but in the one city as in the other, the later rich derived overwhelmingly from the earlier rich.

1845–1857

The existence of the New York City tax list for 1856–1857 permits a further check of the fluidity thesis. It will be recalled that the "rich" of 1845 had included approximately one thousand persons, divided into three categories or groups according to wealth. For purposes of comparison, a fourth category is now added to the 1845 list: this Group IV includes the 1,103 individuals who paid taxes on property that was worth roughly between $15,000 and $45,000. Table 7-5 records the changes in fortune experienced by the four groups between 1845 and slightly more than a decade later. These figures are of special interest since they relate to what was becoming the industrial era, the terminal date falling just short of the Civil War. Did the economic mobility pattern change as industrial capitalism moved to replace commercial capitalism at the apex of the American economy?

It is difficult to compare the patterns disclosed for New York City from 1845 to 1856–1857 with those for the period 1828 to 1845. In view of the shorter time span of the former, a precise comparison is out of

TABLE 7–5.
The Category of Wealth in 1856–1857 of the Wealthiest New York City Taxpayers of 1845*

New York City taxpayers of 1845 according to level of wealth		The rich of 1856–1857													
		$500,000 in 1856–57		*$250,000–$500,000 in 1856–57*		*$100,000–$250,000 in 1856–57*		*$50,000–$100,000 in 1856–57*		*$25,000–$50,000 in 1856–57*		*under $25,000 in 1856–57*		*Not in 1856–57 tax list*	
Description	No.	No. from 1845 group	% of 1845 group	No. from 1845 group	% of 1845 group	No. from 1845 group	% of 1845 group	No. from 1845 group	% of 1845 group	No. from 1845 group	% of 1845 group	No. from 1845 group	% of 1845 group	No. from 1845 group	% of 1845 group
I. ≥$250,000	55	16	29	16	29	10	18	3†	6	1	2	2†	4	7	12
II. $100,000–$250,000	238	3	1	36	16	97	41	52	21	15	6	12	5	23	10
III. $45,000–$100,000	707	2	—	15	2	116	17	270	38	109	16	115	16	80	11
IV. $15,000–$45,000	1103	—	—	2	—	32	3	155	14	250	23	351	32	313	28

*The absence of addresses, the occasional misspellings, and the regular use of a first initial instead of a first name, among other characteristics of Boyd's *Tax-Book*, suggest that the matching of names from that list with those obtained from the assessment entries of 1845 carries the risk of occasional cases of mistaken identity.
†All members of wealthy families.

South Street from Maiden Lane, 1828. An illustration of the lively waterfront activity that was the source of many New York City fortunes. (*Aquatint by William I. Bennett from the Edward W. C. Arnold Collection of the Metropolitan Museum of Art. Photograph courtesy of the Museum of the City of New York.*)

the question; for that matter, even two periods of equal length are by no means necessarily similar. One may have been marked by a relatively unbroken inflationary trend, the other by countervailing tendencies. Perhaps serving to equalize the two periods under consideration is the fact that the first, and longer, one featured a financial panic and a general economic setback that persisted for half a decade or more, while prosperity in the second, and shorter, period was almost unbroken.[12] Nonetheless, whatever the qualitative differences in the two periods, the patterns of upward, horizontal, and downward movement for comparable categories of wealth were markedly similar.

The persistence rate for the "super rich" of the 1845–1856 period was slightly greater, although the addition of six years to its shorter time span would no doubt have reduced the disparity. The few individuals from the "super rich" of 1845 who fell below the upper one thousand in 1856 were—with the single exception of Laurent Salles—from families whose other members were thriving. In the industrial era of the mid-1850s, the very rich of the previous decade remained as impervious to disaster as their counterparts during the 1820s, the 1830s, and the early 1840s. The groups representing middle wealth also had roughly parallel careers, whether between 1828 and 1845 or between 1845 and 1857. As for the large numbers who both in 1828 and 1845 failed to qualify as the "rich," the course of their subsequent careers was amazingly similar. In no case did any of these persons advance to the "richest of the rich." If 18 per cent of the former group of 1828 had managed to ascend to the "lower rich" seventeen years later, 17 per cent did so between 1845 and 1857.

The 1845–1857 picture does differ from that for 1828–1845 in two respects. Although not many persons suffered calamitous declines in wealth, during the later period a larger percentage of wealthy persons did experience a decline in their absolute wealth, even though the drop was characteristically slight. The most striking difference between the two periods was the greater rate by which the wealthy of 1828 subsequently disappeared from the later list. It seems probable, however, that the addition of five or six years to the second period would have shown an increase in deaths that would have erased most of this difference.

Fluidity is hardly suggested by the results of an examination of the earlier standing of the very rich of 1856–1857. Not one of the individuals worth half a million dollars or more that year had risen from the lower orders of 1845. In fact, only two of these "richest of the super rich" had been assessed for less than $100,000 in 1845: Amos R. Eno and Cornelius Vanderbilt, each of whose New York City wealth was estimated at about $80,000. As for the other members of the top 100 of 1856—persons worth $250,000 or more—only two had *not* been among the rich a dozen years earlier: James R. Whiting and Gerard Stuyvesant, of the great Dutch family. The 10 newcomers in this group included members of the Hoffman, Townsend, and Phelps families, as well as the estate of W. Kent, which was administered by the eminent Henry Parish. Sixty-seven per cent of the 340 New Yorkers worth between $100,000 and $250,000 in 1856–1857 had been among the rich of 1845, while another 10 per cent had earlier been "not quite rich." More than 20 per cent of this substantial group had evidently been too young to pay taxes or had paid them on very small estates in 1845. As was generally the case with rich new taxpayers, most of them were new only as taxpayers; they came of such old families as the Astors, the Hoffmans, the Kips, the Langdons, the Morgans, the Phelpses, the Phoenixes, the Lorillards, the Spencers, the Stewarts, the Swans, the Van Pelts, the Whites, and the Wolfes.

Perhaps the most interesting question that the New York City data make it possible to answer concerns the status in 1828 of the city's richest men of 1856–1857. Table 7-6 throws light on the matter.

The figures in Table 7-6 provide perhaps the most powerful refutation of the thesis that fortunes were made and lost overnight and circulated with inconceivable rapidity in antebellum America. For the passage of time involved here was not a five-year period or a ten-year or seventeen-year period but more than a quarter of a century. More than two-thirds of the entire group of persons worth $100,000 or more in 1857 had been from among the rich or the "not quite rich" families of a generation earlier. About 75 per cent of the 100 members of the "super rich" of pre–Civil War New York City turn out to have been from the rich families of the city in the year when Andrew Jackson waged his first successful presidential campaign. The families constituting New York City's plutocracy early in the industrial era were for the most part the families which comprised the plutocracy of the merchant-capitalist era.

Brooklyn

Brooklyn's tax data are imperfect for this kind of comparative study because the city's assessments are known for only one year in the second quarter of the nineteenth century. The list of Brooklyn assessments in 1810 is a short one, containing only handfuls of "rich" persons in the lightly populated village community of that year. And yet, if the earlier date falls before what even the most flexible classification would consider the Jacksonian era, that fact hardly detracts from its value. If anything, the earlier starting point permits those so inclined to draw conclusions about economic fluidity between the Jeffersonian and Jacksonian periods. Brooklyn's wealthiest families of the early nineteenth century remained among the wealthiest families of 1841. Only one member of the truly

TABLE 7–6.
The Category of Wealth in 1828 of the Families of the 440 Richest New York City Taxpayers of 1856–1857*

New York City taxpayers of 1856–1857 according to level of wealth		The rich of 1828								*Not in 1828 tax list*	
		$100,000 in 1828		*$50,000–$100,000 in 1828*		*$25,000–$50,000 in 1828*		*$15,000–$25,000 in 1828*			
Description	No.	No. from 1856–57 group	% of 1856–1857 group	No. from 1856–57 group	% of 1856–1857 group	No. from 1856–57 group	% of 1856–1857 group	No. from 1856–57 group	% of 1856–1857 group	No. from 1856–57 group	% of 1856–1857 group
I. ≥$500,000	21	7	33	3	14	6	29	1†	5	4	19
II. $250,000–$500,000	79	13	16	17	22	27	34	5	6	17	22
III. $100,000–$250,000	340	27	8	37	11	85	25	66	19	125	37

*Families rather than individuals.
†C. V. S. Roosevelt.

rich of 1810 fell by the wayside—not because of poverty but because of death. In Brooklyn, as in its mighty neighbor, riches achieved by early in the nineteenth century appeared to be the surest guarantee to the possession of wealth a generation later. The many wealthy persons of 1841 who were relative newcomers to the city had achieved their success almost without exception as a result of a great boost given them at birth by wealthy or comfortably situated parents or relatives.

The pursuit of wealth in the antebellum decades was marked not by fluidity but by stability. Great fortunes earlier accumulated held their own through all manner of vicissitudes. The Panic of 1837, for example, appeared to have no effect on the minuscule rate by which the mighty fell or the puny rose during the years surrounding that economic convulsion. The Boston tax records disclose that of the owners of the modest property assessed at between $5,000 and $7,000 prior to the Panic, fewer than 1 per cent became significantly wealthier in its wake, while slightly more than one-third were badly hurt by the cataclysm. In contrast, only two of the nearly one hundred Bostonians worth $100,000 or more each suffered substantial losses; about 23 per cent of them enjoyed gains of $20,000 or better in the immediate aftermath of the crisis.

Although the evidence on economic in-flow indicates that the wealthy categories of a later year were composed of individuals who were earlier rich or well-to-do, much work remains to be done on the out-flow of the poor. Since the poor left the city at an inordinate rate, serious research will face the imposing task of tracing the course of their careers in other, smaller communities. Partial but interesting modern studies have revealed that on the Michigan frontier, too, the antebellum rich came almost entirely of the rich of the previous generation, and that poor, recent immigrants in rural towns and counties had little weight—socially, politically, or economically—in the affairs of their new communities.[13] The New York City and Boston data on the out-flow of the medium or upper middle wealthholders show that between 80 and 90 per cent of them remained in the same category throughout the period. As for the rich, the record is clear.

Dramatic accounts of sudden failure or success rose to the surface, catching the fancy of contemporaries precisely as did the companion notion that most of the era's successful men were self-made. In the one case, as in the other, the data—mute, undramatic, but unyielding—disclose an actuality most unlike the "reality" accepted by most articulate contemporaries. In the antebellum decades, urban fortunes tended, not to rise and fall overnight, but rather to persist. If the logic of the egalitarian myth pointed to economic fluidity, the facts of American economic experience indicate that stability, if not rigidity, characterized the situation of most wealthholders.

Winter Scene in Brooklyn. View is of Fulton Street in 1820 when Brooklyn was a small village. *(Oil painting by Francis Guy courtesy of the Brooklyn Museum.)*

Notes

[1] Tocqueville, *Democracy in America*, I:53; II:105, 234, 237, 250, 251.
[2] Bruchey, *The Roots of American Economic Growth, 1607–1861*, p. 206.
[3] Robert G. Albion, "Commercial Fortunes in New York," pp. 167–68, bases its generalizations about the alleged precariousness of the careers of New York City's merchants on a pessimistic remark attributed to one wealthy merchant—the account by Joseph Scoville of his own business failure—and on Moses Beach's publication, *Wealth and Biography of the Wealthy Citizens of New York* (New York, 1846).
[4] Blumin, "Mobility in a Nineteenth-Century American City: Philadelphia, 1820–1860."
[5] Peter R. Knights, *The Plain People of Boston 1830–1860*, pp. 106, 108; Raymond A. Mohl, *Poverty in New York 1783–1825*, p. 21.
[6] There are no exact population figures for 1833. My estimate is based on the census figures for Boston of 61,032 for 1830 and 78,603 for 1835.
[7] See *List of Persons, Copartnerships and Corporations who were Taxed . . . in the City of Boston for the year 1833* (Boston, 1834). I have not included corporations or most partnerships in my estimates because of the changing and often hidden personnel they represented. The published lists for 1833 and later years were, of course, far from perfect: the same names were variously spelled; assessments on real property were arbitrarily changed to assessments on personal estate; valuations are listed alongside the names of executors or administrators of estates (in some cases also giving the names of the owners, in other cases omitting them). Where the owner is not listed I felt compelled to omit the listing, since otherwise the later coming of age of an heir could be construed as signifying a loss of wealth by its executor or administrator.

All those who use the Boston data will be struck by the sudden leap experienced by all fortunes, large and small, after 1841. This rise was not what it seemed. Shattuck has explained that before 1842 "the valuation was entered on the assessors' record at half its real value, and the taxes assessed on that amount." *Census of Boston for 1845*, appendix, p. 59. I have therefore doubled the assessment figures for 1833 and all others years prior to 1842.
[8] The foregoing generalizations are based on an examination of the subsequent assessments for about 700 individuals listed in the tax list for 1833. Cf Knights's way of measuring "success." *The Plain People of Boston*, p. 81.
[9] According to Hone, merchants had great resilience. "Throw down our merchants ever so flat," he confided to his diary, and "they roll over once and spring to their feet again. Knock the stairs from under them and they will make a ladder of the fragments and remount." Hone Diary, 23:165. Hone was in an ebullient mood because of the amazingly rapid recovery the city made after a terrible fire in July, 1845.
[10] These estimates are based on the tax lists of 1848 and 1833.
[11] See Pessen, "The Wealthiest New Yorkers of the Jacksonian Era: A New List," fn. 12, for a discussion of the strengths and weaknesses of William H. Boyd, ed., *Boyd's New York City Tax-Book, 1856 and 57* (New York, 1857). When compared to the assessments cited in assessors' notebooks for that year, Boyd's list appears to be reliable.
[12] Peter Temin's *The Jacksonian Economy* (New York, 1969) sharply challenges older versions of the causes, extent, and economic consequences of the panics that punctuated the 1830s, noting among other things that the price decline of the early 1840s was not accompanied by a fall in productivity. For a clear statement of the orthodox interpretation, see Reginald C. McGrane, *The Panic of 1837* (Chicago, 1924).
[13] Alexandra McCoy, "The Political Affiliations of American Elites: Wayne County, Michigan, 1844–1860, as a Test Case" (Ph.D. diss., Wayne State University, 1965); Michael B. Katz, "Social Structure in Hamilton, Ontario," in Thernstrom and Sennett, eds., *Nineteenth-Century Cities: Essays in the New Urban History*, pp. 209–44; Blumin, "The Restless Citizen"; and Kirk, "The Promise of American Life: Social Mobility in a Nineteenth Century Immigrant Community," p. 85.

8

Equality of Opportunity?

The only feature in American society that [is] indicative of the equality they profess [is that] any man's son may become the equal of any other man's son.

Frances Trollope, *Domestic Manners of the Americans*, p. 121

He who is diligent at school will take his station accordingly, whether born to wealth or not. [Where common schools are universally established] the carer of each youth will depend upon himself.

Samuel Breck, *Report of the Joint Committee on Education* (of the Pennsylvania Legislature), 1834

It has long been argued that equality of opportunity prevailed in antebellum America. If wealthy men were, supposedly, self-made, it was because in this country ability ranked over privilege in accounting for success. The belief was widespread that in the United States the "humble mechanic" had available to him "all the facilities in business and every means of winning independence which are extended only to rich monopolists in England."[1] The inequality of condition that actually characterized American life, far from contradicting equality of opportunity, was believed to confirm and even to result from it.

James Fenimore Cooper was one of the few admired contemporaries who did not deny that material things were maldistributed in antebellum America. Yet, he believed, equality of opportunity was "in a social sense the very means of producing the inequality of condition that actually exists. By possessing the same rights to exercise their respective faculties the active and frugal become more wealthy than the idle and dissolute."[2] In this view, equal rights were not an unmixed blessing; they permitted the gifted to outdo their inferiors. The matchless appeal of equality of opportunity, however, was the fairness it imposed on social competition. In the language of a leading modern historian, in this country equality did not mean the possession of uniform wealth so much as "parity in competition."[3] That in the race for success some men reached the finish line while others fell by the wayside was due to the natural superiority of the winners. But all men were believed to have started the contest together, with equal opportunity for success and without artificial impediments that favored some competitors over their rivals.

One of our most cherished social beliefs has been that throughout American history "the positions at the top are open to those who have the talents" (and the corollary, that "those who do not reach the top do not deserve to").[4] Like other comforting social theorems, this one has rarely been carefully analyzed or subjected to a detailed factual check. What follows is a discussion of equality of opportunity in the antebellum decades that, on the one hand analyzes the concept and its logical implications, and on the other examines contemporary evidence for signs of correspondence between the concept and the reality of American life. That the analysis may at times make points that appear too obvious to dissent from will, I trust, be accepted as unavoidable in any attempt to dissect an idea that for all its previous usage has rarely been subjected to close examination.

The discussion, while based on a close look at several thousand personal histories, does not take the form of a statistical report. There are certain questions beyond the power of quantitative studies to answer precisely. Equality of opportunity is one of these. As will be seen, *immeasurable* variables must be considered; these defy—if they do not make ridiculous—any attempt to deal with the issue in the empirically testable form that provides the most certain answers to questions. But that a question cannot be dealt with in such form is no reason it should go undiscussed, particularly when the question is an important one; conclusions that do not rest on statistical tables do not thereby rest on sand. There is value in subjecting so influential a concept to close critical scrutiny. In view of the paucity of treatment it has heretofore received, the ensuing discussion should at least provide a point of departure for further consideration.

Equality of opportunity means that an individual's chances of success in a given field are limited only by his innate shortcomings or deficiencies and by the vagaries of fortune. Good or bad luck can affect his career significantly, but since fate operates impersonally it does not improve his neighbor's chances at the expense of his own. Cooper was correct, of course, in assuming that inequality of material condition was no contradiction of equality of opportunity. Men differently endowed would achieve different degrees of success even if they strived with equal diligence to reach the heights. It might be argued, for example, that a mind better able than another to grasp the complexities of the law gives its possessor a superior biological inheritance that constitutes an advantage over his less fortunate competitor, thereby detracting from the latter's opportunity to succeed: the "opportunity" of the innately weaker contestant is not equal to that of his stronger or more capable rival, all other things being equal. As used in our civilization, however, the concept of equality of opportunity discounts or excludes natural, genetic, or biologically grounded distinctions or advantages. In effect, it assumes that an individual's opportunity is impaired only when *artificial* disadvantages deprive him of a chance of achieving success that is equal to the chance of his neighbor not burdened by such disabilities. That the fat fellow, whose obesity and slow reflexes are congenital, runs far behind his lean, well-coordinated rival is a sign, not that the overweight man was denied equal opportunity to win the race, but rather that he showed poor judgment in even running it. Were one runner to beat another, however, because the winner alone had the opportunity to learn techniques of starting and sprinting, it could then be fairly concluded that the loser was denied equality of opportunity. Where success or failure in a social activity is determined by such artificial circumstances as money and family standing, then opportunity is less than equal.

Cooper assumed, at least in the quoted passage, that worldly success came to those who took advantage of opportunities equally available to their unsuccessful neighbors. Those who failed to achieve wealth were the "idle and dissolute"—in contrast to the "active and frugal" who amassed it. One suspects that different work habits may indeed have accounted for some dissimilar careers; but the judgment is an unproven one and assumes as true what in fact must be proven to be. Similarly, in the famous tenth *Federalist*, Madison argued not merely that factions arise out of differing interests resulting from different types of property, but that disparities in wealth result from the differing talents men have for amassing it. Madison, like Cooper, attributed to talent or industriousness what might have been due to inheritance. The only way to find out whether they are right is to go to detailed evidence on individuals.

As is true of other questions whose answers depend on facts rather than logic, the clearest thing about the question whether equality of opportunity was prevalent in antebellum America is the impossibility of finding a precise answer to it. The factual evidence is inevitably insufficient or deficient. It might appear that since successful accumulators of wealth had almost invariably been born rich, the well-born had a far greater opportunity to amass great fortunes than their poorer contemporaries; but this is not necessarily true. It is possible that the young man who rose from wealth to even greater riches had innate talents that would have brought him commercial success even in the absence of his original advantages. The details of his career must be collected, sifted, and evaluated to try to separate out the comparative roles played by different elements in his background and personal makeup in accounting for his success. Information on such details is bound to be imperfect.

We have learned that IQ tests do not measure intelligence but only certain abilities which may or may not reflect "native intelligence" but which surely do reflect the environmental influences on the test taker. We do not know how to determine native intelligence. Only God knows and He does not disclose. It is impossible to ascertain the true natural ability of individuals, let alone groups of men, whether for the "era of the common man" or for any other period. This is particularly so with regard to the race for economic and social success, a competition so much more complex than the footrace—which tests swiftness and physical prowess alone. It is difficult and probably impossible, even with the best of evidence, to isolate and to assign a fixed weight to the part played in a successful man's career by innate ability, persistence, and luck, as against family wealth, high standing, and reputation. And yet the attempt must be made.

For, if the only permissible generalizations were those doomed to perfect accuracy, men could only state quantitative descriptions or deal in questions whose answers are built into the "language" they are derived from, as with questions of grammar, mathematics, or logic. The great historical and social questions require not only a search for evidence in the world "out there" beyond the limits of a restricted logical system, but the evidence they rely on must be appraised or interpreted rather than merely recorded or counted. Since men—even when they are scholars—are subjective creatures, their evaluations reflect their biases. To be specific, the "facts" bearing on the kinds of opportunity available to those who succeeded and failed in the antebellum decades will be variously appraised. If there is no such thing therefore as an absolutely true interpretation (as against a false one), there does remain a distinction between a good explanation and a poor one. A good judgment is based on relevant factual data rather than surmise, and its conclusions follow reasonably from the data. That is, the conclusions flow not from the ideology or the preconceptions of the subjective observer but from the evidence he has assembled. Inasmuch as Jacksonian equality of opportunity has heretofore been assumed or accepted on the basis of slight factual data, the discussion that follows may be helpful, if only because it attempts to make its case on the basis of much historical evidence—rather than on logic alone.

According to a contemporary, William B. Astor's nephew Charles Astor Bristed, membership in New York City's social and economic elite was conferred on young men who, possessed of "fair natural abilities, add to these the advantages of inherited wealth, a liberal education, and foreign travel."[5] Bristed's may have been yet another subjective judgment, but in his case it was very much the judgment of an informed insider who was familiar with the values of New York City's elite. It also appears to have been an astute judgment free of partisan rancor. His appraisal pays its respects to the importance of advantages both natural and artificial in achieving social success: neither genius nor venerated family were demanded of aspirants to the highest social ranks, according to his definition. The evidence on hundreds of wealthy families appears to bear out his conclusions. The brilliance of a Nathaniel Bowditch in mathematics, William Hickling Prescott in history, or Washington Irving in literature were not asked for, let alone required, of the rich and the prominent. The quick social leadership conferred on such relatively *nouveaux riches* as the Delafields, the Hones, the Cabots, and the Astors suggests the acuity of Bristed's insight that the dimensions of wealth counted for more than family antiquity in determining social success.

The "inherited wealth," education, and travel cited by Bristed were hardly available to the common man during the era. Substantial estates were inherited only by that fortunate few known as the rich. The leisurely travel done by young fortune's favorites in western Europe was probably not akin to the undoubted horizontal mobility displayed by large numbers of poor young people who moved in and out of northeastern cities during the era.[6] The inarticulate poor did not, it is true, leave records explicitly denying that they periodically traveled along the Thames, the Rhône, the Rhine, and the Danube, seeking identification with the cultural glories of the Old World. In such matters the absence of negative evidence is not nearly so persuasive as the presence of ample positive evidence, indicating that many wealthy young Americans did, in fact, make the Grand Tour. Let us say, in sober understatement, that the costs of such travel appeared to be beyond the power of all but relatively wealthy families. As for "liberal education," its benefits appeared to be even more unequally distributed than material fortune during the era. According to the great contemporary statistician Lemuel Shattuck, only one-fifth to one-tenth of 1 per cent of the Boston population attended college during the 1830s and 1840s.[7] In view of the very great proportion of wealthy young men who went to Harvard, Columbia, and the University of Pennsylvania during the period, it is clear that attendance at these prestigious institutions depended heavily on the means of the students' families. If Bristed's criteria are reliable, it is obvious that the opportunities to achieve social prominence were highly unequal; "fair natural abilities" alone were within the grasp of men of low social or economic station. The other three ingredients, wealth, travel, and liberal education demanded artificial advantages unknown to most men and therefore excluding them from the urban elite. The opportunity to attain social prominence in the "age of egalitarianism" appeared to be far from equal.

Did equal opportunity obtain in the pursuit of what was perhaps the most coveted of all successes in this country, wealth? Money, as we have seen, went to money. But as I have earlier noted, it is theoretically possible that the era's great accumulators owed their worldly success more to innate business abilities—whatever they might have been—than to their original fortunes. The detailed record, however, does not support this logical possibility. The chief "natural ability" required for successful moneymaking appeared to consist above all of blood ties with previously wealthy parents and families. The ability to make a successful marriage was an important asset to the ambitious man. But as will be noted in a subsequent chapter on the matrimonial ideas and behavior of the rich, this ability had much more to do with the wealth and reputation of a young man's family than with his mere interest in marrying rich. (It can be assumed that many poor young men shared that ambition.) A search of the record fails to disclose more than a handful of cases in which a genius for accumulation appears to have been the factor that enabled a young man blessed with it to succeed. As for the many rich adults of the 1840s who had been rich young people in the 1820s, their careers in acquisition followed a progression that seemed largely impervious to their unique personal traits. Such traits either did not obtrude or they went undiscerned by the biographers of the antebellum rich. Of course, some men born rich went under. Who could control social and natural catastrophes such as the panics of the late 1830s or the great fires that gutted Wall Street in the 1830s and 1840s? Some rich men's sons turned out to be failures, erratic men incapable of maintaining their positions. The great preponderance of wealthy men and women, however, appeared to possess no distinctive traits so congenial to acquisition that they overshadowed their material advantages.

The career of William Wharton, son of the great Philadelphia merchant Charles Wharton, was typical. "Having by inheritance a sufficiency of the world's goods, which was supplemented by the considerable inheritance of his wife," William Wharton did not have to engage in business, let alone display an affinity for the ways of commerce. The great merchant John Murray Forbes had what one genealogist called the "very good luck" to be enrolled at one of Boston's most prestigious private schools as a boy, and perhaps the better fortune to be accepted into the countinghouse of the great Thomas Handasyd Perkins. What caught Perkins' eye was the fact that young Forbes was his nephew. Thomas H. Perkins, Jr.'s path to success was even smoother than Forbes's. One suspects that the fact that young Perkins' home was a great social center to Daniel Webster, Judge Story, Lothrop Motley, as well as to many prominent business men in Boston, had more to do with his family's success than his own unusual charm. The latter trait he undoubtedly possessed but it appears to have been a product less of his unique nature than of his privileged nurture. Horace Gray, inheritor of a great fortune from a father who was worth millions and a mother who was the niece of Peter Chardon Brooks—the richest man in Massachusetts—first married Harriet, daughter of Phineas Upham; on her death he acquired another fortune by marrying Sarah Russell Gardner, the daughter of Samuel Gardner. Gray, who invested heavily and almost always successfully—first in overseas trade and then in the iron industry—seemingly owed his success to his inheritance and to his family's repute. His wealth appeared to be no more due to any intuitive financial wizardry than his youthful attendance at Harvard betokened any unusual intellectual prowess.

Andrew Gordon Hamersley, a rich young New Yorker of the era, was one of the great city's most dazzling social figures. Certainly his wealth owed nothing to unusual moneymaking ability, inherited or acquired, for Hamersley came of an old, rich, and eminent family. His father was an important merchant, while his grandfather had been a vestryman of Trinity Church who lived in a mansion of "costly elegance" and attracted some attention by having a servant in livery accompany him on his travels through the city. Hamersley was one of those fortunate young men who studied law but was too rich to have to practice it or any other occupation. He married Sarah Mason, "a lady noted for her striking beauty and great personal charms." Adding to her appeal was the great wealth of her father, the famous merchant John Mason, who bestowed a fortune on Hamersley. The young man cut a dashing figure, which no doubt enhanced his social position. He was said to have a "tall, erect form, high forehead," and was "noted for his entertaining conversation and courtly manners." While he resided in Paris, his "graceful, easy" dancing made him a "great favorite of the court balls and other entertainments." He also "fully enjoyed and appreciated the refined life and culture of the light-hearted city on the Seine," doubtless imparting some of its sparkle to the New York City salons he graced.[8] It is not facetious to note that laboring men who were tall and possessed high foreheads found these excellent attributes insufficient for breaking into the social elite. As to the other refinements that enabled Hamersley to attain his great social success, it is no disparagement to observe that they were what cultural anthropologists call "learned behavior" rather than instinctive or natural aptitudes. One must sadly conclude that poorer men of less magnificent inheritance lacked the opportunity to master the varied social skills that permitted Andrew Gordon Hamersley to rise to the top of the social ladder.

Great riches, like social prominence, were most accessible to the fortunate few who from the beginning possessed the artificial advantages of wealth and the education and refinement wealth made possible. The political scientist Robert A. Dahl has contended that in New Haven the era was marked by a "cumulative inequality: when one individual was much better off than another in one resource, such as wealth, he was usually better off in almost every other resource," particularly political influence.[9] Cumulative inequality elsewhere gave the wealthy opportunities to amass still more wealth and attain high status that were not available to ordinary men.

Nor were opportunities in the arts uninfluenced by social advantage. After discovering that a successful career in law was closed to him because of an accident that had impaired his eyesight while he was a Harvard undergraduate, William Hickling Prescott was able to devote himself to historical research and writing because "he was in possession of ample means." (It is perhaps a sign of our own era's greater opportunities that now one who is in possession of nothing more than a tenured professorship can pursue Prescott's interests.) One suspects that in the absence of his social advantages, his great intellectual powers might have gone unnoted. Certainly he could not have done and had done for him the massive research on which he built his great narrative of the Spanish Empire had he not been wealthy. His fellow Bostonian, Henry Tuckerman, prevented from graduating Harvard by ill health, devoted his life to literature, largely because as a rich man's son he was able to visit and live in Italy long enough "to form and develop a decided taste for literature and art." George Ticknor became an eminent professor of literature at Harvard and the son-in-law of Samuel Eliot after studying at the University of Göttingen and traveling extensively in Europe; there he met Goethe, Byron, Scott, and Wordsworth. His background, it need hardly be added, was a function of social rather than genetic gifts, even granting that he put his individual stamp on the raw material of his experience.

Was there equal opportunity to succeed in the professions? If the backgrounds of many lawyers and doctors were obscure, the careers of the most successful and acclaimed physicians and attorneys fortunately are available in some detail. William Beach Lawrence became the wealthy and successful law partner to Hamilton Fish. Young Lawrence was a precocious lad who entered Rutgers at the age of twelve; but such "early entrance" was by no means uncommon in the era, and Lawrence's success appears to have been much abetted by the fame of his great Long Island family and the wealth of his father, Isaac Lawrence. That wealth, among other things, provided him a Columbia law school education. The interaction between "fair natural abilities" and unusual wealth and family status was characteristic of most successful lawyers in New York and other cities.

Robert C. Winthrop, prominent Boston lawyer and politician, dispenser of lavish hospitality, friend to culture and the arts, and owner of a fashionable town house and an estate in Brookline, was what he was not because of his dazzling mental traits but because of his matchless family status and an inheritance that permitted him to cultivate his scholarly tastes. David Sears, a most successful lawyer indeed, after studying in the law office of Harrison Gray Otis went on to amass great wealth. Of course, Sears' wealth had little to do with law as he was one of those attorneys who never practiced. But where others in that fortunate situation cultivated elegant uses of leisure, Sears pursued wealth through commerce. His mentor's son, William Foster Otis, was another eminent Bostonian "counsellor-at-law" whose success appeared to be grounded in factors other than his natural abilities. John C. Gray and Francis C. Gray, fortunate heirs to a millionaire father, were other highly successful Boston "lawyers" equipped with no discernible innate legal or mental peculiarities. Their great wealth was the product of

Residence of the Hon. David Sears. Boston Common.

Residence of David Sears, Boston. Sears Beacon Street house faced the Frog Pond (foreground) on Boston Common. The mansion was regarded by many as the finest in the North, if not in the nation. *(Photograph courtesy of the Bostonian Society.)*

inheritance, commerce, manufactures, and in the case of the former, marriage to Samuel P. Gardner's daughter. Before mid-century, Russell Sturgis joined the house of Baring Brothers; he ultimately became its senior partner. This most successful attorney was the son of the wealthy Nathaniel Russell Sturgis and Susan Parkman, and had been "early placed in the best schools [and] fitted for Harvard." The career of Lucius Manlius Sargent is particularly interesting.

Sargent was a young man of unusual physical and mental gifts. At Harvard he was said to be "an elegant horseman, an expert charioteer . . . a swift and powerful swimmer, and . . . a good fencer with the broad sword. He loved the classics, wrote Latin verse and prose with great facility, and was probably the best Latin scholar in college." In maturity he was said to have "a finely formed and uncommonly large head, oval face, grey penetrating eyes, well favored mouth and a Roman nose." In addition, his manners were attractive: "though a man of fortune, he was affable in his address, and genial in conversation," never assuming "in his intercourse even with persons of inferior rank, that coldness of reserve and distance which chill the soul." [10] This innate charm and intellect did not lead to great achievements in his profession, however. For although Sargent studied law with Samuel Dexter—who is described in the *New England Historical and Genealogical Register* as standing "at the head of his profession when New England had a constellation of great lawyers"—Sargent remained in practice only three years after being admitted to the bar. Born in the "splendid mansion" his wealthy father rented in Boston, Sargent was brought up in comfort. That the inheritance of a fortune led Sargent to forgo "the drudgery of a practice" indicates that whatever his potential in legal studies, his zest for the law was slight. He subsequently devoted himself to "deep antiquarian research." On closer scrutiny, Sargent's traits, even in the obviously smiling description of them cited here, reflect refined breeding rather than natural intellectual superiority. And yet, he achieved great if flawed "success."

The eminent Philadelphia lawyer John I. C. Hare was a rich man's son who chose the profession of law and made valued contributions to it as teacher, writer, and judge. His career appears to have been enhanced by the fact that he studied in the office of William M. Meredith and married Horace Binney's daughter—"cumulative advantages" that owed more to the repute of the Hare name than to anything else. Other prominent Philadelphia attorneys also had better than equal opportunities to achieve the success they did, including the historians' friend, Sidney G. Fisher, keeper of the invaluable diary. The impression formed by a close reading of Fisher's private thoughts is that he had a much greater interest in the good life success at law might bring than in the law itself. Nor was his one of those rare instances in which seeming disinterest in a field of work was accompanied unaccountably by unusual powers to perform it. George H. Boker, who later became minister to

Turkey in the Grant administration, became a lawyer shortly after graduating from Princeton. Nothing in his career, including his extended tour of Europe or his literary dabbling, indicates that the chief explanation of whatever success he managed to achieve was not the fact that he was the son of the wealthy financier, Charles S. Boker. Richard Vaux, Mayor of Philadelphia in the mid-nineteenth century, was another of those successful lawyers whose "affluent circumstances relieved him from the drudgery of practice." These circumstances, it need hardly be noted, were not of his own doing but rather were made possible by his eminent father and his respected Quaker family.

Like their eminent legal brethren, the prominent doctors of the era were, for the most part, men blessed with wealth and acquired advantages. Dr. James Jackson of Boston was successful from any standpoint. He studied at Harvard and abroad, married Elizabeth Cabot, was an intimate of the great John Collins Warren, taught at Harvard, and had a lucrative practice. After 1825 he traveled to Boston from his home in Waltham, which was built on land acquired by his wealthy brother Patrick Tracy Jackson. Most of these good things stemmed from the fact that he was the son of Jonathan Jackson and Hannah Tracy.

Philadelphia's most successful doctors had similar backgrounds. Henry S. Patterson died before he could make a great mark. His eminence and his interest in humane activities reflected his sensibilities, but his excellent general and scientific education reflected the wealth of his father, the merchant John Patterson. As though anticipating the focus of this chapter, old Simpson noted that in studying with his eminent father, Dr. Joseph Parrish, the wealthy Isaac Parrish "enjoyed many and peculiar advantages over students in nearly all other situations." [11] Dr. Nathaniel Chapman had a brilliant career as a Philadelphia practitioner and professor at the University of Pennsylvania, where he succeeded to the chair of Dr. John Rhea Barton. Chapman's great success was made possible by private study with a variety of outstanding teachers, including Dr. Benjamin Rush and other eminences at London and Edinburgh; it was a course of training befitting a young man born into one of "the best families of Virginia." Dr. Jacob Randolph's career was enhanced by his marriage to the daughter of Philadelphia's outstanding surgeon Dr. Philip Syng Physick, while Randolph's medical education was made possible by his family's wealth.

Physick's own career displays a blending of great natural gifts with favorable family situation. His father was a wealthy and strong-minded man, who, despite his son's interest in another kind of career, insisted that the young Physick become a doctor; his wealth and influence succeeded in placing Physick as a student of the redoubtable Dr. Adam Kuhn after graduation from the University of Pennsylvania. If Philip Syng Physick came to be known as the "father of American surgery," it was due to his own achievements. And yet, in the absence of the direction and opportunities given him by his father, that successful career in medicine might never have been launched. His contemporaries, John Collins Warren in Boston, and Valentine Mott and David Hosack in New York City were, like Physick, brilliant physicians all and men who from childhood had moved in the most rarified circles, attended the greatest universities and studied with the most learned masters at home and abroad. They accumulated much wealth, primarily because they had much to start with, and attained great eminence, largely because of opportunities created by their family wealth.

Nor was there equality of opportunity to be treated by physicians of such exalted reputation; means rather than need gave one access to the services of these eminences. When Philip Hone's brother John was seriously ill in 1832 he was attended by Hosack, Mott, and the admired Dr. Hugh McLean. For that matter, the hospitalized sick received significantly different types of treatment, dependent on the wealth of the patients.[12] Is it exaggeration to conclude that in view of their advantages, the rich and well-to-do had a better opportunity to recover from illness than their socioeconomic inferiors?

The most successful men in the professions, like the leaders in society and in accumulating wealth, were typically men who had extraordinary opportunities. Such opportunity for the few meant less than equal opportunity for the many. The absence of legal disabilities did not mean that most men started the race for success on equal terms with their more favored contemporaries. The race was indeed to the swift, but the requisite swiftness was beyond the power of ordinary men to attain. For this swiftness was of a special sort. Unlike the speed of thoroughbred horses—which is a rare but a natural if inbred gift—the ability to cover great ground in the race for material or social success appears to have depended less on the possession of innate abilities than on the inheritance of the artificial gifts of wealth and standing. During the "age of egalitarianism" opportunity was hardly more equal than material condition.

Notes

1 See the editorials in *New York Sun*, June 8, 11, 13, 18, 1845.

2 James Fenimore Cooper, *The American Democrat* (New York, 1838), p. 73.

3 David M. Potter, *People of Plenty* (Chicago, 1965), p. 92. Douglas T. Miller has recently written that in antebellum America, "a democracy of opportunity helped create an aristocracy of achievement." *The Birth of Modern America* (New York, 1970), p. 118.

4 Leonard Reissman, *Class in American Society* (New York, 1959), p. 293.

[5] Bristed, *The Upper Ten Thousand: Sketches of American Society*, p. 9.
[6] See Stephan Thernstrom and Peter R. Knights, "Men in Motion: Some Data and Speculations About Urban Population Mobility in Nineteenth-Century America," *Journal of Interdisciplinary History, I* (Autumn 1970), pp. 29–30; and Stuart Blumin, "The Restless Citizen: Vertical Mobility, Migration and Social Participation in Mid-Nineteenth Century America."
[7] Shattuck, *Census of Boston for the Year 1845*, p. 74.
[8] Wilson, *Memorial History of New York City*, V, pp. 159–61.
[9] Dahl, *Who Governs*, p. 85.
[10] *New England Historical and Genealogical Register, XXV*, pp. 209–17, 220.
[11] Henry Simpson, *Lives of Eminent Philadelphians*, p. 758.
[12] Hone Diary, IV:121; Gerald N. Grob, *The State and the Mentally Ill: A History of Worcester State Hospital in Massachusetts, 1830–1920* (Chapel Hill, N.C., 1966), pp. 71–72, 92–93.

PART III

Class

The Problem of Social Class

The chapters that make up this part are concerned with what nowadays would be called the "lifestyle" of the urban social and economic elite. This is precisely the subject matter modern sociologists have in mind when they discuss class. Since "class" and "social class" are among the trickiest terms in the vocabulary of social scientists—the number of definitions of these concepts almost matching the number of scholars who have formulated them—a brief explanation of my own viewpoint may be helpful.[1]

We have come a long way since Aristotle described the classes that inhabit all states as the rich, the poor, and those in between, and since Marx defined a class as a group having a distinctive relationship to the means of production. The modern discussion has moved toward increasingly complex definitions. Not only have our classes increased in number —from Marx's exploiters and exploited or Aristotle's three to the six classes cited by W. Lloyd Warner[2]—but modern definitions also include many ingredients in addition to wealth and economic power. They invoke not only a variety of social and religious factors but also such intangible considerations as status, prestige, reputation, and the subjective perceptions of the class under observation and those who are observing it. Such complexities explain why a scholar recently asserted that "the ambiguity of the term 'class' makes it difficult to find one's bearings among the divergences between the different viewpoints involved."[3] There are many sociologists who would agree with Joseph Schumpeter that, in view of its dependence on the subjective predilections of the individual who does the classifying, "class is a creation of the researcher."[4] The sophisticated are well aware that definitions of class will vary, revealing above all the interests and values of those who formulate them.

While class is one of those abstractions that enables us to better understand concrete reality, in Leonard Reissman's phrase, it "is not simply an abstraction devised by the social analyst for his own convenience." Few sociologists would take issue with his contention that "class is part of social reality, part of the fabric of society." [5] Classes existed in antebellum America as elsewhere; by almost any definition the urban rich were an upper class. Their wealth, the means by which they accumulated it, and the standing of their families placed them on a lofty plateau high above the social terrain occupied by the great majority of their contemporaries, envied and admired by the mass of men who looked up to them from below.

Class also is as class does. Twentieth-century discussions of social class have stressed the ways in which class influences individual behavior. Social class is said to express itself in the unique quality of education, intimate associations, uses of leisure, social and public activities, style of life, and political roles played by the members of a particular group. According to Edward Shils, deference is evoked by an upper class not only because of its great wealth but also by the kinship connections, the distinctive level of educational attainment, the political power, and the style of life its members follow.[6] These are the matters considered in the remaining chapters of this book.

The purpose of these chapters is not to add yet one more set of generalizations to the theoretical discussion of class so vigorously waged by American sociologists, but rather to provide a detailed *historical* account of behavior—in this case behavior of the urban upper class. Such detail on a neglected era should be valuable to those theorists who hold tentatively to their abstract formulations, always prepared to modify them in the face of new data. The evidence underlying much of the modern thinking about class is quite general and drawn primarily from studies of twentieth-century class behavior; when social scientists invoke earlier history they sometimes make large assumptions about the alleged "inner directedness" of personality or the "egalitarianism and mobility of pre-industrial society,"—assumptions that turn out to be unfounded. What follows is historical detail on the uses of leisure, the social lives, the marital behavior, and the residential patterns of the urban rich. When this information is added to the data from the foregoing chapters—on the scope and sources of their wealth, the proportion of the community's riches they owned and the tenacity with which they held on to it, the material situation and status of their parents and families, and the unusual opportunities available to them—the nature of the urban upper class in antebellum America is illuminated perhaps more brightly than it would be by a theoretical discussion whose abstractions are based primarily on data drawn from other periods.

The focus of the discussion that follows is on the extent to which considerations of class appear to have influenced the social behavior of the rich. Inevitably, therefore, certain issues and questions—by no means insignificant ones—will be neglected, if not entirely bypassed. For I have gathered data on *measurable* behavior, data that perhaps accentuate uniformities in the actions of a mass of men—in this case the small mass of wealthy persons. When the rich are broken down into the individuals who composed their group, homogeneity is immediately replaced by diversity. I take it as axiomatic that each member of a group sharing a common material situation and social standing has his unique complex of reasons for participating in one or another of the group's overt actions —actions or behavior that a later researcher is likely to label "the uniform actions of a class." The nuances of individual motivation are beyond the scope of this study. I have come across fascinating material on the rebelliousness of some of the children of the rich, pointing to intergenerational tensions and to signs of hostility dividing one renowned family from another on grounds more complicated than merely old against new. Such data, however, are in short supply, and while important, as well as interesting in their own right, their existence detracts not at all from the significance of the observable actions taken by the rich as a whole. Uniform social behavior by a distinctive group or class indicates that shared feelings of class solidarity or class consciousness ultimately prevailed over the inevitably heterogeneous feelings of the group's individual members.

Insight into the role of class, whether in antebellum cities or for any other time or place, is made possible above all by examining the social *actions* of class.

Notes

[1] As with the related concept of social mobility, the literature on class is vast, containing many titles also cited for the former topic. See Bibliography.

[2] Warner's six classes are the upper-upper, lower-upper, upper-middle, lower-middle, the upper-lower, and the lower-lower. *The Status System of a Modern Community* (New Haven, 1947).

[3] Stanislaw Ossowski, *Class Structure in the Social Consciousness* (London, 1963), cited in Bendix and Lipset, *Class, Status, and Power*, p. 87.

[4] Schumpeter, *Imperialism and Social Classes* (New York, 1951), cited in Bendix and Lipset, *Class, Status, and Power*, p. 42.

[5] Reissman, *Class in American Society*, p. 169.

[6] Shils, "Deference," in J. A. Jackson, *Social Stratification* (Cambridge, 1968), p. 106.

9

The Streets Where They Lived: The Residential Patterns of the Rich and Elite

> By our modes of life—our houses–our dress–our equipage; in short by what is strictly external to us . . . men detach themselves from their neighbors–withdraw themselves from the human family.
>
> Walter Channing, *An Address on the Prevention of Pauperism* (Boston, 1843), *p. 18*

In recent years, the physical or geographical mobility of northeastern populations, above all of the urban poor in the antebellum United States, has been subjected to detailed and fruitful investigation. This chapter will attempt to broaden our understanding of antebellum cities by examining the changing residential choices made by an equally important if more neglected social stratum, the urban rich. The housing site selections made by the wealthiest men and families in New York City, Brooklyn, Philadelphia, and Boston have been closely investigated as part of our larger inquiry into the wealth, family backgrounds, lifestyles, values, and influence of the urban elite.

Since this chapter also assesses the significance of the spatial patterns revealed by the evidence, it is, willynilly, a venture into social ecology. The latter is defined by one authority as a field whose concern is with "explaining the territorial arrangements that social activities assume," and whose task is "to discover and to explain the regularities which appear in man's adaptation to space." [1] I have tried to take Charles Glaab's advice, that "in writing about cities in the past, historians should take into account the findings of social science concerned with the present day city." [2] If the requirements of the new urban history have not produced a formal partnership between those wary sometime collaborators, historians and sociologists, practitioners in the one field have been increasingly impelled to try to benefit from the techniques utilized by their colleagues in the other. Urged by one of their number recently to "seek out strategic negative cases with an eye to refuting existing notions and replacing them with more tenable generalizations," [3] urban sociologists may find value in the abundant historical data presented here. That my tentative generalizations will be more "tenable" is problematical. What is more certain is the usefulness of the new evidence to adherents of whatever generalizations, old or new.

Historians have only recently begun to show an interest in urban residential and spatial expansion—or for that matter in any but the descriptive aspects of urban development.[4] The fruitful generalizations that have provoked the liveliest discussion in this area have been contributed by such scholars as Ernest W. Burgess, Homer Hoyt, Walter Firey, Leo F. Schnore, Norman J. Johnston, David Ward—sociologists, students of city planning and urban architecture, non-historians all—or by such economic historians as George R. Taylor and Charles J. Kennedy. As historians come to be more at home in the study of spatial expansion, they will doubtless become more adept at creating generalizations from the data their persistent research uncovers and at building on the as-yet simple theoretical scaffolding they have to this point constructed.[5] Since this chapter is intended as an exercise in neither the historiography nor the theory of urban growth, it will consider illuminating concepts of urban expansion only insofar as the data on antebellum elite residential patterns appear either to confirm or to require modification of them. The direction taken by the discussion that follows has been shaped primarily by my curiosity about the extent to which the antebellum urban rich sought to live in a restricted social world guided by ideals of class exclusiveness rather than social egalitarianism.

Significance of Residential Locations

Residence is an important ingredient of lifestyle and manifestation of status. Whether class lines are rigid or fluid—the idiosyncratic behavior of some individuals aside—the rich can be expected to live well, putting sizable portions of the material wealth whose accumulation so absorbs them into comfortable, even opulent housing. Where social exclusiveness is not on their minds, their expensive homes might conceivably be located almost anywhere within a city other than in the most poverty-stricken neighborhoods. Such dispersal appears to have been the case in a number of early-nineteenth-century cities. According to the modern student of antebellum Texas cities, the residential "egalitarianism" of Houston's upper crust was not devoid of an element of shrewd calculation: "scattering themselves throughout the [city's] wards, they more easily maintained their position of political as well as economic leadership in the community."[6] In Galveston and in other western cities, on the other hand, increasingly "the homes of the well-to-do pre-empted the choice spots while other people moved to less desirable areas." On the basis of a contemporary's later reminiscence that in St. Louis, "all the rich people lived on Main Street," and a Pittsburgh correspondent's comment that "most of the fashionable residences" in that city were located on attractive Penn Street, the modern historian of these and other cities on the urban frontier concludes that "by 1830 social lines could be plotted on a map of the city."[7] These social lines were evidently not a random consequence of the pursuit of attractive locations, but rather a byproduct of a policy of upper-class exclusiveness followed not only in housing but in other activities as well.

A few studies have in fact plotted out social maps of northeastern cities, ward by ward.[8] This procedure relied on printed lists of tax-assessment figures for every ward or local political district in a city and the population figures for each ward. The wards with the highest per capita assessments, such as the first, second, and third wards in Brooklyn and New York City or the seventh ward in Boston, were regarded as the wards that contain the rich and well-to-do. This was a logical procedure, the good sense of which is confirmed by evidence that many wealthy families did indeed live in the wards of heaviest per capita assessments.

The latter evidence is by no means mere confirmation of the obvious; for, as some of the historians using the method that equates the wealth of a ward with high per capita assessments have known, it is far from foolproof. The presence in a lightly populated ward of a few banks or great warehouses could result in a high figure of assessed wealth that is most misleading; it proves not that the district's residents were rich, but rather that certain of its real properties were valuable. The great disparity between the per capita "wealth" of New York City's first ward and the "wealth" of all other wards, for example, was due primarily to the great financial institutions located in the former. Even when unusual forms of real property had not skewed the figures, a "wealthy" ward typically contained many poor persons. A ward was a large area, usually not identical with a residential district. Then as now, adjacent areas might enclose families of drastically dissimilar wealth and income. The line or street dividing rich from poor might be located, not at the boundary, but within the ward. The high mean average or per capita wealth of such a ward would hardly indicate that located within it were many poor families. Even in cities in which the difference between the per capita assessed wealth of rich and poor wards was most extreme, the disparity did not come close to matching the disparity between the mean average of wealth owned by the wealthiest families in the city as against the wealth owned by the poorest 50 per cent. The richest 1 per cent typically each owned several hundred times as much wealth as the families at the bottom half of the wealth ladder. And yet, the most extreme ratio between so-called wealthy and poor wards was typically on the order of only ten to one.[9]

The discovery of the names of the wealthiest persons in New York City, Brooklyn, Philadelphia, and Boston made possible a much more precise study of the housing patterns of the rich than that afforded by per capita assessments of the cities' wards. For by going to the manuscript assessments and to the annual city directories one could locate the addresses and indeed plot out on a map the streets and neighborhoods where the rich lived. Not the least value of this evidence is that the residential patterns it discloses provide a further empirical testing of Ernest W. Burgess's theory of concentric zones, Homer Hoyt's concept of growth by sectors, and George R. Taylor's interpretation of the decisive role of innovations in antebellum urban transport in moving elites away from the central city.

New York City

In 1828 the 500 wealthiest families in New York City lived on about 100 of the city's streets.[10] They could be found in each of the city's then 14 wards. And yet the distribution of wealthy residents was not as scattered as this evidence might indicate. Over half of the rich lived on only eight of New York City's more than 250 streets.

TABLE 9–1.
Where the New York City Rich Lived in 1828

Street	*% of city's rich*	*Average wealth of rich families*
Broadway	23.0	$80,000
Greenwich St.	7.0	51,000
Chambers St.	5.0	48,000
Pearl St.	5.0	50,000
Beekman St.	4.0	34,000
Hudson St.	2.5	28,000
The Bowery	2.5	56,000
Park Place	2.0	43,000
Cliff St.	1.75	29,000
Cortlandt St.	1.75	51,000
State St.	1.75	41,000
Warren St.	1.75	57,000
Bowling Green	1.5	92,000
Broome St.	1.5	37,000
Fulton St.	1.5	51,000
Cherry St.	1.5	42,000
Laight St.	1.5	63,000
Varick St.	1.25	35,000
Whitehall St.	1.25	48,000
Maiden Lane	1.25	36,000
Washington St.	1.25	47,000

New York City's wealthiest residential districts were by no means identical with the wards of greatest per capita assessment. For all the reputation of the first three wards (located near the southern tip of Manhattan) as the area preferred by the rich, these heavily assessed wards contained only slightly more than half of the 500 wealthiest families: 53 per cent to be precise. Even with a per capita assessment that was

Residence of William B. Crosby, New York. Crosby, whose house stood at Rutgers Place, was one of New York City's richest men. *(Photograph courtesy of the I. N. Phelps Stokes Collection, Prints Division, the New York Public Library, Astor, Lenox, and Tilden Foundations.)*

greater than the combined assessments of the second and third wards, the first ward did not attract greater numbers of rich families; roughly equal numbers of the wealthy lived in each of the three wards. Nor were the rich of the first ward richer than their fellows in the "poorer" two wards. The wealthiest residents of Broadway, for example, lived not on that avenue's southernmost portion in the first ward, but further north, where Broadway bisected the second and third wards, and on that part of the great thoroughfare lying between Canal Street and Fourteenth Street—the latter street the sparsely settled northern outpost of substantial numbers of dwellings. This is not to say that the lower Broadway numbers housed petty wealthholders; for occupying the addresses One through Five Broadway were Nathaniel Prime, Peter Remsen, John Watts, John Suydam, and Isaac Bronson, respectively. But living on the western side of the avenue that provided the eastern boundary of the third ward were John Jacob Astor, John G. Coster, Philip Hone, and Henry Laverty. And further north resided Peter A. Jay, William Rhinelander, Isaac Lawrence, and Peter G. Stuyvesant. Such presences indicate that the contemporary verdict that "Broadway was the great aristocratic thoroughfare" was indeed well founded.[11]

Neither for Broadway nor for the other residential centers of the opulent was the ward the vital consideration that attracted them. The chief criteria appeared rather to be the combined utility, appeal, and repute of a particular street or section, irrespective of whether it chanced to fall in the first, the sixth, or the ninth ward. Bowling Green in the first ward was a lightly populated, beautiful, and prestigious location near the Battery; its residents included John Hone and the fabulously wealthy Stephen Whitney. The Bowery, on the other hand, although known as the "great democratic thoroughfare" as it meandered north from the sixth ward, intersecting the populous tenth and fourteenth wards, contained such wealthholders as Henry Astor, Stephen Allen, and the widow Spingler. Jacob Lorillard, Alexander Stewart, and Laurent Salles were neighbors on Hudson Street in the fifth ward, just south of Canal Street—the thoroughfare that divided the fifth from the eighth ward. Similar concentrations of the rich could be found on other streets, in close proximity to masses of their poorer neighbors who lived within the same wards. The burden of the New York City evidence for 1828, however, is not the random dispersal of the rich as a whole, even if individual families did live in widely scattered locations, but rather their strong tendency to cluster together in a handful of streets and residential districts, veritable plutocratic enclaves in the early nineteenth-century city.

Little about the New York City evidence gives comfort to the influential theories of urban morphology. The rich of 1828, while concentrated for the most part in a small number of blocks and streets, formed no distinct part of any of the concentric circles posited in Burgess's model. Concentric zones or sectors radiating from the alleged business center are not to be found in Manhattan. The island's business district was located, not at Hoyt's center, but at the southern tip. Even when interpreted figuratively, the notion of the business center is not very helpful for the great northeastern cities in the early nineteenth century, since in fact their business activities were centered at the edge of the city: the south for New York, the west for Brooklyn, at first the north for Boston, and the east for Philadelphia. As Map 1 indicates, in the "walking city" of 1828, New York's wealthy families lived on streets located in diverse areas, districts manifesting no pattern other than the desire of the elite to reside in proximity to one another, whatever sector they happened to choose.[12]

During the next two decades this residential concentration declined somewhat. Although inordinate numbers of wealthy families continued to live on Broadway in 1845, Table 9–2 makes clear that the percentage who did so decreased; the richest five hundred were to be found in a larger number of locations and areas than earlier.

A striking change was the sharp decline in the percentage of rich families that by 1845 lived in the three southern wards. The latter continued to have by far the highest per capita assessments of all the wards in the city; but where more than half of the richest 500 had lived in the first three wards in 1828, only a quarter of the elite resided in these wards by 1845. For with the doubling of the population, the city's dynamic economic expansion, and the carving out of new wards north of 14th Street, many rich families joined in the northward movement, building homes closer to the city's moving frontier. Such residences were more like palatial mansions than log cabins, since this frontier brought its occupants in close proximity, not to hostile savages, but to greater speculative opportunities. The continued improvement and proliferation of the horse-drawn omnibus, its quick availability to the well-to-do—who alone could afford the fare—and its promptness of response that evoked praise even from the normally captious Philip Hone, enabled wealthy New Yorkers to move beyond the confines of the walking city, well to the north of the chief business area.[13]

Undiscouraged by the Panic of 1837, Philip Hone built an elegant home on the corner of Broadway and Great Jones Street, north of Houston Street in the ninth ward and well north of his earlier mansion on Broadway near City Hall Park in the third ward. This move placed him in closer proximity to his wealthy friend John G. Coster. In 1834 Coster had moved from 227 Broadway, next door to Hone's earlier residence, to the "noble granite house, furnished in the most elegant style," at 539 Broadway near Mercer Street in the eighth ward. Hone was struck by similar moves made by other of his intimates. A decade later he remarked on William H. Aspinwall's new "beautiful and commodious mansion" at University Place, "one of the palaces which [had] been lately erected

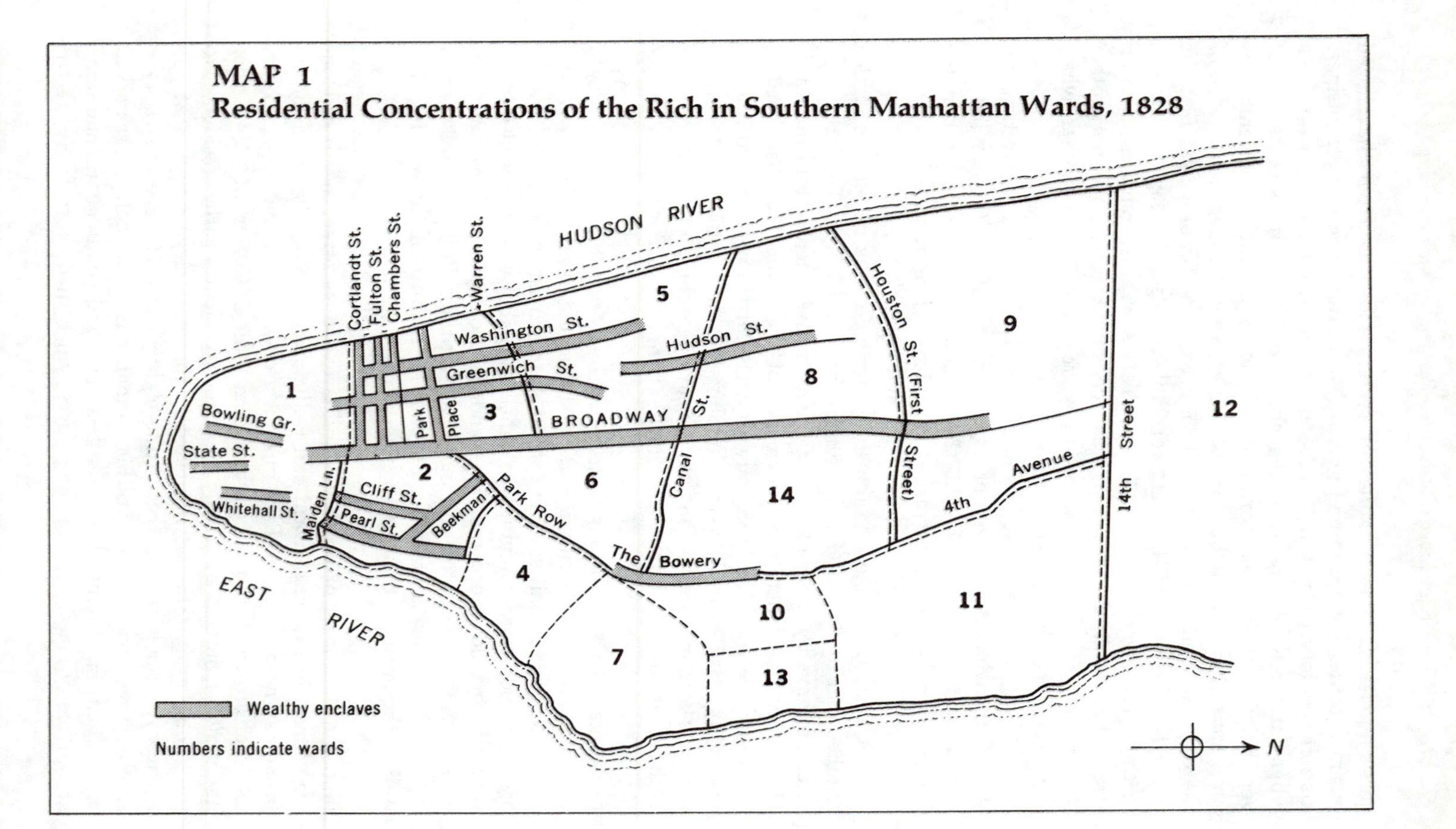
MAP 1
Residential Concentrations of the Rich in Southern Manhattan Wards, 1828
HUDSON RIVER
EAST RIVER
Cortlandt St.
Fulton St.
Chambers St.
Warren St.
Washington St.
Greenwich St.
Hudson St.
Park Place
BROADWAY
Canal St.
Houston St. (First Street)
14th Street
4th Avenue
Bowling Gr.
State St.
Whitehall St.
Maiden Ln.
Cliff St.
Pearl St.
Beekman
Park Row
The Bowery
1
2
3
4
5
6
7
8
9
10
11
12
13
14
N
Wealthy enclaves
Numbers indicate wards

TABLE 9–2.
Where the New York City Rich Lived in 1845

Street	*% of city's rich*	*Average wealth of rich families*
Broadway	17.0	$205,000
Washington Square	3.5	185,000
Waverly Place	3.5	128,000
Greenwich St.	3.5	66,000
Bleecker St.	2.5	135,000
Fifth Avenue	2.5	135,000
St. Mark's Place	2.5	95,000
Chambers St.	2.5	$128,000
East Broadway	2.0	87,000
Union Place	2.0	129,000
Second Avenue	2.0	250,000
Fourth St.	2.0	105,000
Brooklyn	2.0	100,000
14th St.	1.7	86,000
Bond St.	1.7	135,000
Lafayette Place	1.7	235,000
College Place	1.4	148,000
State St.	1.4	100,000
Washington Place	1.4	140,000
Bowling Green	1.4	225,000
Barclay St.	1.4	110,000
Beach St.	1.4	105,000
Madison St.	1.4	112,000
The Bowery	1.4	85,000
Franklin St.	1.4	85,000
Great Jones St.	1.3	171,000
Hudson St.	1.3	67,000
Murray St.	1.3	83,000
Rutgers St.	1.3	89,000
Warren St.	1.3	123,000
Water St.	1.3	73,000
Ninth St.	1.3	76,000
10th St.	1.3	90,000

in this part of the city." In January, 1847, Hone attended a party at the new home of Robert Ray, "away up" at the corner of 28th Street and Ninth Avenue, in what was by then the sixteenth ward. His comments are instructive. The Ray house, he wrote, was "one of those palaces which have lately sprung up in places where a few years earlier cattle grazed . . . this magnificent abode of costly luxury, now the town residence of my good friend Mr. Ray, stands on the very spot where his father's garden [then] away out of town [stood]." [14]

In moving north, Hone and his rich friends were conforming to the behavior of most families in their privileged position. Of several hundred randomly selected families that were among the richest 1 per cent of New Yorkers both in 1828 and 1845, 25 per cent of the group did not change their residences during the period, while another 10 per cent moved to a location very close by. While only 4 per cent moved to a prestigious location to the south of their earlier addresses, 61 per cent moved to a more northern location within the city.

In 1828 more than half of the rich who lived on Broadway had been located in the lower three wards; by 1845, more than 60 per cent of Broadway's wealthy residents lived north of Houston Street in the eighth, ninth, fourteenth, and fifteenth wards. Heading these opulent migrants were John Jacob Astor, James H. Roosevelt, Isaac Carow, Dr. Benjamin McVickar, Stephen B. Munn, a number of members of the Post family, John Beekman, Andrew G. Hamersley, Bernard Rhinelander, C. V. S. Roosevelt, John D. Wolfe, Stephen B. Munn, Cornelius Dubois, George Lovett, and the Schieffelin brothers. The pattern was similar on other streets popular with the rich: addresses moved northward. For the elite as a whole, the center of residential gravity shifted from the area bounded roughly by Maiden Lane and Liberty Street to the south and Chambers and Beekman Streets to the north (see Map 1) to an area several miles further north. The new center of population density for the wealthy fell between Houston (or First Street) and Union Square, thirteen blocks north. This was a significant change that, among other things, explodes any notion that the rich clung to their early nineteenth century homes. Unlike the poor, the rich remained in the city; but they did not stay in the same place.

Yet no more in 1845 than in 1828 did the rich of New York City simply build or move into homes anywhere within the city. In a city whose land area and populated streets were both increasing steadily in number, wealthy citizens created new enclaves, in some cases in districts that shortly before had been lacking not only in status but in residents of any sort. If Washington Square was an example of a newly fashionable center, its youthfulness did not betoken social democracy. Stephen Allen, George Griswold, John C. Green, Robert Ray, James Boorman, William and William C. Rhinelander, Gardiner Greene Howland, and Lyman Denison were neither less wealthy nor more *nouveaux* than John Gihon, Elisha Riggs, and Ferdinand Suydam, Jr., of Bowling Green to the south. James C. Roosevelt, Dr. Edward Delafield, Uriah Hendricks, and Abraham Van Nest, who lived on Bleecker Street, were neither more egalitarian nor less eminent than David S. Kennedy, Robert Goelet, and John Q. Aymar of State Street. Certainly Henry Brevoort, Henry Remsen, Myndert Van Schaick, W. W. Deforest, and John R. Livingston, residing on Fifth Avenue just south of 14th Street, were the social peers of Jonathan Goodhue, Hugh Maxwell, and Stephen Storm of Whitehall Street near the Battery. In New York City, as in Houston, the scattering of at least some wealthy residents in almost every one of the city's wards made possible, if it did not assure, the political domination of the city by men of wealth. Random site selection, however, was hardly the practice of New York City's social and economic elite during the second quarter of the nineteenth century. Although they were flexible rather than rigid in responding to the city's continual expansion, inhibited not at all by any sense of veneration toward real estate earlier settled or homes earlier occupied, the wealthy families of New York City did continue to seek the proximity of families of wealth and standing.

It seems clear that Philip Hone and members of his large circle were very much concerned about living near their friends and intimates. Sentiment was thus a consideration in the residential moves of the elite. But if the social circle of the wealthy was composed almost entirely of their own sort, moves induced by emotional considerations had the same result as moves resulting from feelings of class exclusiveness. The manuscript tax assessment rolls and New York City directories during the era disclose that while many of the rich lived in wards inhabited by families of modest means, with plebeian alleys, streets, and blocks typically bordering the neighborhoods of the wealthy, the addresses of the latter were clustered together on contiguous blocks rarely infiltrated by social or economic outsiders.[15]

Brooklyn

In Brooklyn the rich also lived more luxuriously than ordinary people and went out of their way to live apart from them as well. Great homesteads, some of them dating back to the seventeenth century, could be found in every section of the city and its immediate environs. The Debevoises, the Bergens, the Willinks, the Boerums, and such old families as the Gerritsons, Ditmases, Lotts, and Leffertses, were not about to tear down their mansions because the latter were not located in Brooklyn Heights. Yet there can be no doubt that the Heights had become the great center of the rich and the fashionable by the 1840s. According to Gabriel Furman, a respected member of Brooklyn's elite, in the late 1830s Fulton Street was the great dividing line. To its east, stretching out over most of the city, lived the masses, while "on the westerly side, reside[d] the . . . silk stocking gentry," as their detractors called them.[16]

An area of natural beauty and cool ocean breezes and blessed with a matchless view of and easy accessibility to lower Manhattan, even before the Revolution Brooklyn Heights had caught the eye of wealthy New Yorkers searching for a nearby summer resort. In the 1790s its champions sought to have it designated the nation's capital, asking, "where could a situation be found for the capitol and other public buildings comparable to the Heights of Brooklyn?" It was the judgment of the greatest historian of Brooklyn that the charms of Brooklyn Heights

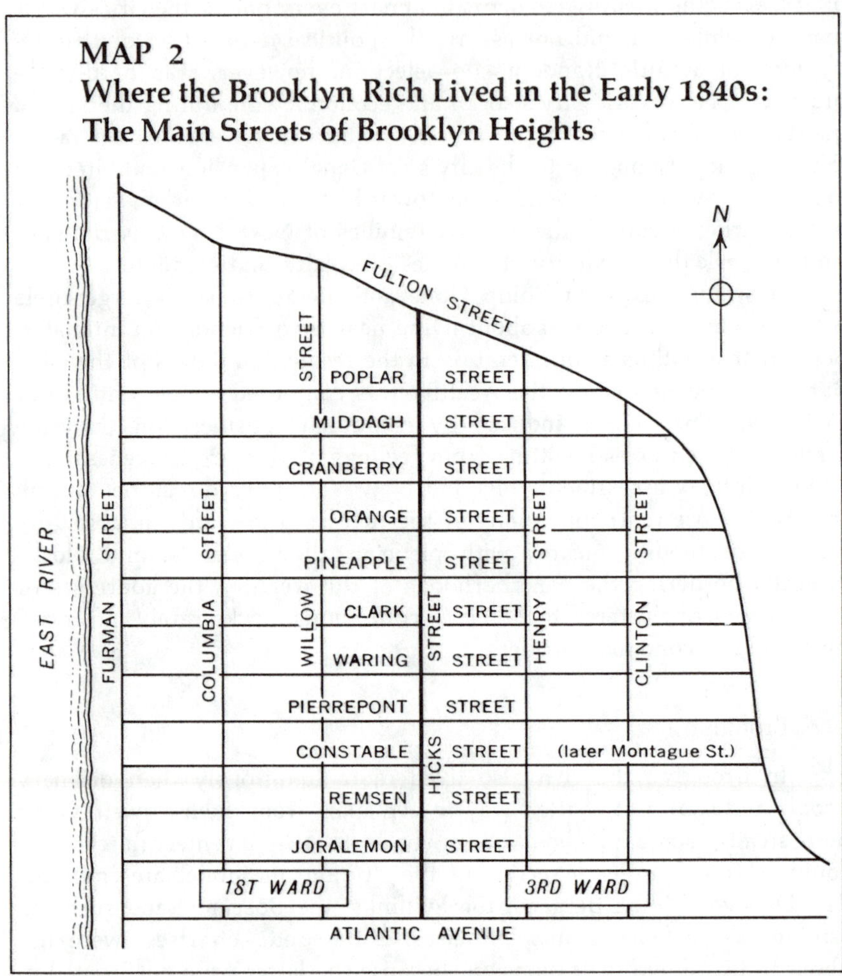

appealed above all to "that higher strata of culture and intellect to be found in a 'limited circle' " of New Yorkers.[17] That may or may not have been true. Whatever their cultural pretensions, such successful New York merchants as Thomas W. Birdsall, Conklin Brush, Peter C. Cornell, Robert T. Hicks, Fisher How[e], Charles Hoyt, George, E. D., and John Hurlbut, C. N. Keirstead, David Leavitt, Joseph Sands, Arthur Tappan, Henry P. Waring, Asa Worthington, and Henry Young chose to live in Brooklyn Heights. In this sense, Brooklyn Heights was a suburb for a small but significant number of New York City's wealthiest merchants; the Heights was available to them because of the excellence and efficiency of a ferry service that by the mid-1840s cost two cents one way for a three-to-five-minute trip from Fulton Street in Brooklyn to lower Manhattan, with a wait of no more than three minutes for a boat.[18]

View of New York from Brooklyn Heights. The Heights, shown here about 1837, was the site of Brooklyn's most fashionable residences. *(Engraving by William I. Bennett courtesy of the New-York Historical Society.)*

By the 1840s some of the most splendid homes in the nation were said to have been put up by Brooklyn's merchant and professional elite on the streets of Brooklyn Heights. Of the 250 wealthiest families of Brooklyn in 1841 65 per cent lived in a small area of the city that a walking tour discloses occupied only a fraction of a square mile. Although some eminent families continued to live in areas of declining prestige, on sites established by their ancestors generations before, by far the majority of the Brooklyn rich lived in that relatively tiny enclave "west of Fulton Street." According to New York State census figures for the period, the Heights contained only about 2 per cent of the city's still substantial livestock population, but about 16 per cent of its human population. The area's prestige stemmed from the fact that it also housed about 67 per cent of the city's wealthiest citizens.

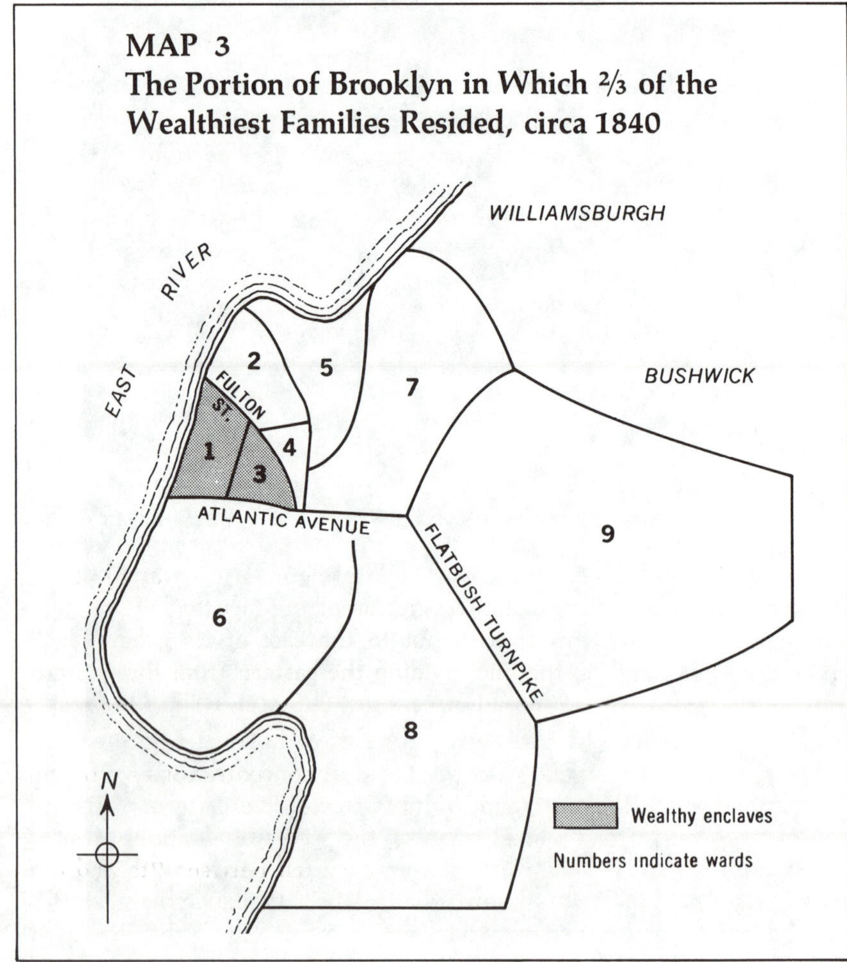

Philadelphia

A modern student of Philadelphia has written that during the period 1830–1860, "social and economic heterogeneity" characterized most of its districts, with "occasional class and ethnic enclaves" atypical of the "spatial patterns of the city." [19] Ethnic concentration is beyond the reach of this essay, although impressive evidence has been presented by Norman Johnston indicating that color did indeed create enclaves in antebellum Philadelphia. Johnston's study also demonstrated the tendency of selected wealthy and high-status Philadelphians, particularly Presbyterians, to cluster together in neighborhoods restricted to their own kind.[20] The main point of this section is to present broader evidence on the residential choices made by wealthy Philadelphians of varied denominations in the mid-1840s.

In the early nineteenth century, according to the impressionistic accounts written by contemporaries and later scholars, "the smart quarter of the city was that in the vicinity of Third and Spruce Streets. In the circle of a few blocks, around the spot where Thomas Willing had fixed his home, there were now a number of fine houses. Many substantial Quaker families were settled in Arch (or Mulberry) Street. . . . Chestnut Street was early spoken of as the city's fashionable promenade ground." [21] To those not familiar with the geometric layout of Philadelphia, Spruce, Arch, and Chestnut were (and are) streets parallel to one another, running from the Delaware River, the city's eastern boundary, to the Schuylkill River, slightly more than two miles west.

Under William Penn's plan, the east/west avenues, typically named after plants and trees, were intersected by two dozen numbered streets running north to south.[22] Water Street, and then First or Front Street paralleled and were closest to the Delaware, with 2nd through 13th streets extending westward; Broad or 14th was roughly the halfway point between the two rivers; and High or Market Street bisected the city into north and south streets. The political boundaries (wards) of the city were early drawn in realistic recognition of the fact that the population center was not identical with but to the east of its geographical center. As Map 4 shows, the line dividing the eastern from the western wards in the 1840s was not Broad Street but 7th Street, well to the east.

Until the 1830s, the elite were supposed to have been located primarily in the eastern wards, with the heaviest concentrations by far on Mulberry, Market, Chestnut, and Walnut Streets. Thereafter a westward movement toward Broad Street enhanced the status of locations west of Washington Square (whose western boundary fell between 7th and 8th streets.) By the 1840s it was known that many of Philadelphia's wealthiest and most notable persons lived on "Girard Row," the group of

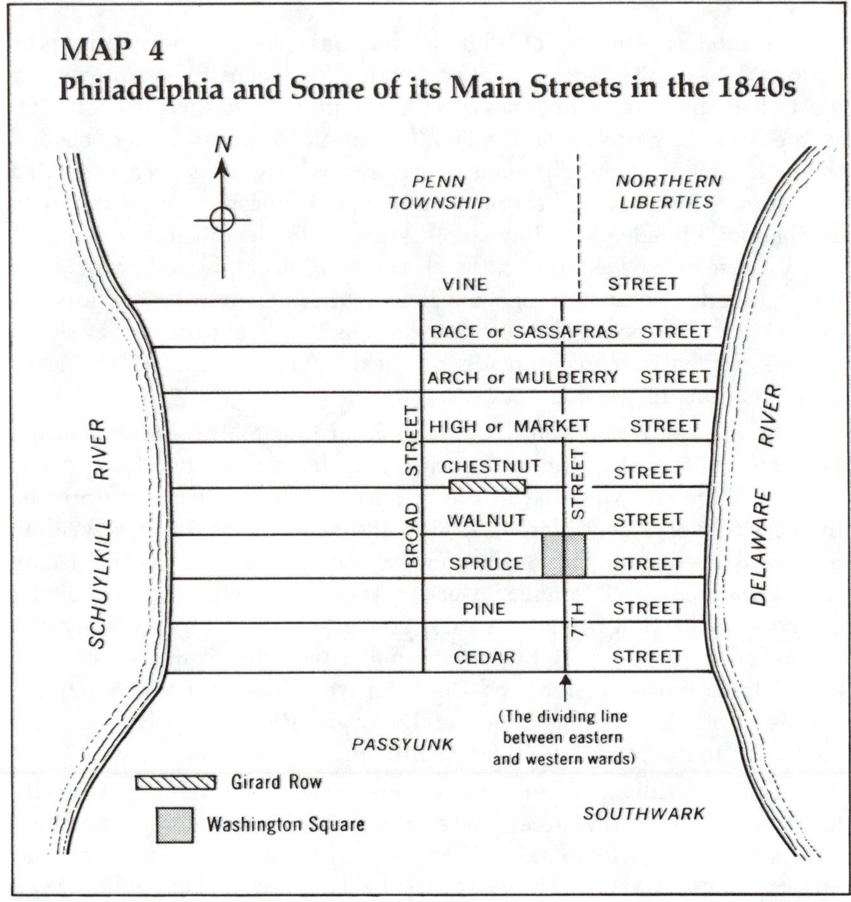

houses on the north side of Chestnut Street between 11th and 12th streets.[23]

In his recent study of residential mobility in antebellum Philadelphia, Stuart Blumin relied on local tax records to determine the wealth of the city's wards and residential districts. He worked out the per capita assessed worth of residents of the different wards by dividing the total assessed value of each ward by the number of its taxable inhabitants for 1820; for 1830 he divided by its total population. Map 5, based on his work, ranks the wealthy wards for these two periods. "A preliminary scanning of the tax register," had indicated to Blumin that, on the one hand, "neighborhoods did in fact exist"—since distinctive areas of the city tended to have houses of comparable assessed value—and, on the other hand, that the outlines of the wards were "a fairly reliable guide to the boundaries of the city's neighborhoods," including the wealthiest ones.[24] In effect, he inferred that before 1840 the residential

MAP 5
The Wealthy Wards of Philadelphia, 1820, 1830 (Numbered in order of wealth)*

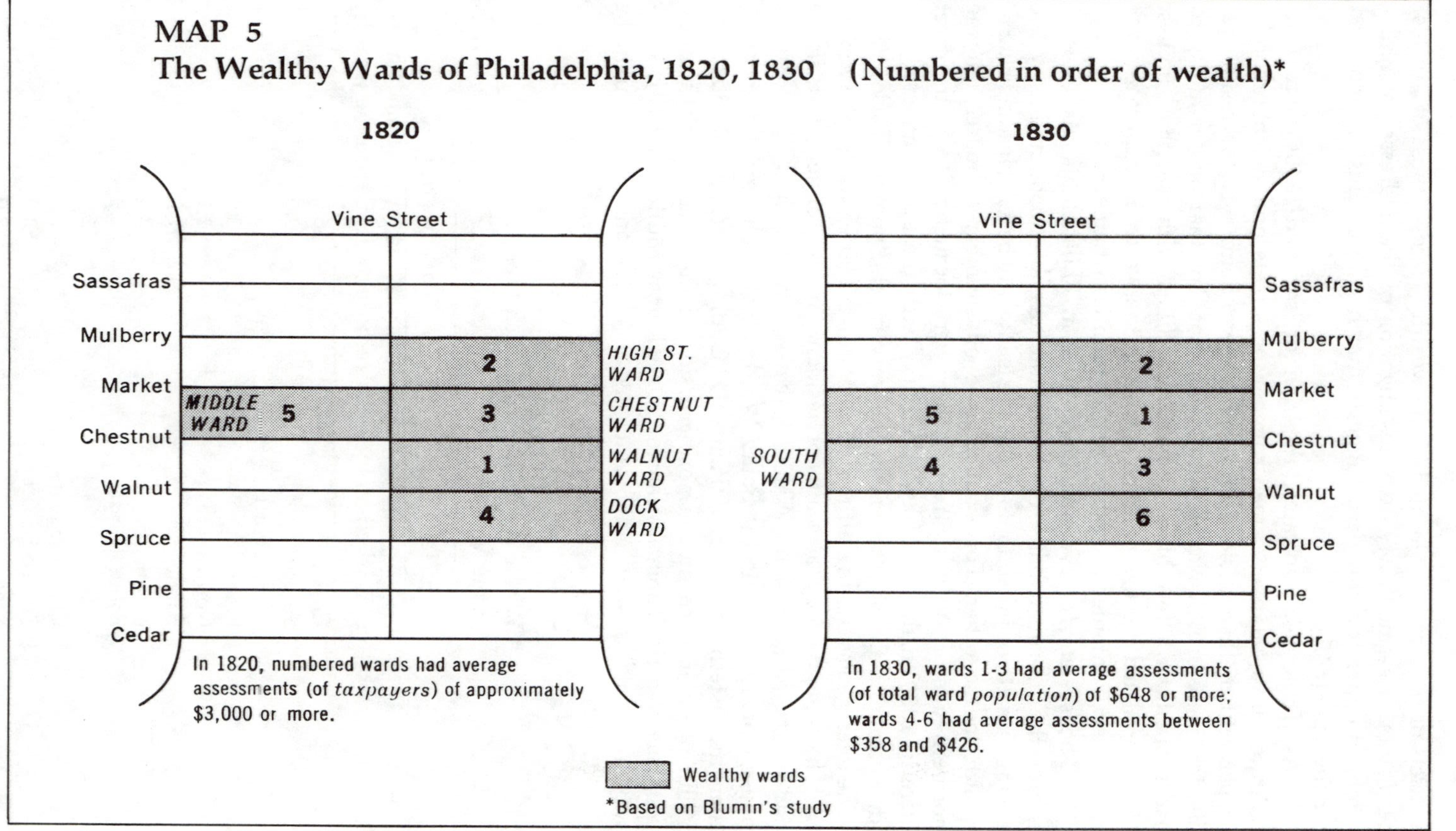

*Based on Blumin's study

districts of the rich were located in the wealthy wards—those of greatest per capita assessment. My own investigation of the addresses of Philadelphia's upper four hundred suggests that his thesis must be modified for the mid-1840s.

As Table 9–3 indicates, the rich of the mid-1840s were concentrated in a relatively small number of streets and neighborhoods; 67 per cent of them resided on seven streets. Some wealthy residential districts were in rich wards, others were not. For that matter, no ward had more than a few blocks which were filled with wealthy families. Most populated blocks and streets, even in the wards of highest *average* assessment, contained no truly wealthy families whatever.

The system for drawing ward lines in Philadelphia makes even clearer the irreconcilability of wards and neighborhoods and why the average wealth of inhabitants in the one is likely to be a misleading clue to wealth in the other. For example, the odd-numbered houses, on the northern side of Walnut Street, if they were located east of 7th Street were in 1830 in the "wealthy" Walnut Ward; the even-numbered residences across the street were in the very much "poorer" Dock Ward. (The average assessed wealth of residents of the latter was slightly more than half the per capita wealth of residents in the former.) But, if the odd-numbered address on Walnut Street was higher than 165, then the house would fall within the South Ward, a ward substantially "poorer" than its eastern neighbor. If Henry D. Gilpin, George M. Dallas, and William Rawle lived on the northern side of the street, Charles Ingersoll, Isaac Norris, Thomas Wharton, Dr. Thomas Mütter, and J. J. Ridgway lived on the south; different sets of Walns and Copes might be

TABLE 9–3.
Where the Philadelphia Rich Lived in the Mid-1840s

Street	*% of city's rich*
Walnut	19.0
Mulberry	16.0
Chestnut	16.0
Spruce	7.0
South Fourth	3.0
Pine	3.0
North Sixth	2.5
South Front	2.0
Sassafras	2.0
South Third	2.0
Market	2.0
Clinton Square	2.0
Portico Square	2.0
Vine	2.0

found on different blocks of Walnut Street, in different wards. It does not appear that residences located in "wealthy" wards on Walnut or other streets housed wealthier men and families than those across the street.[25]

While some eminent Philadelphians occupied splendid mansions in the sparsely settled western areas of the city and in outlying districts not within the city proper—such as the Northern Liberties—the residential concentration of the city's elite appeared to be significantly greater than in New York City. Map 6 offers a graphic block-by-block representation of the Philadelphia pattern.

The evidence almost speaks for itself. In the mid-1840s, each of the great east/west thoroughfares favored by the elite was more heavily occupied west of 7th Street. Although the distribution of Walnut's wealthy residents was fairly evenly divided between the eastern and western wards, on Mulberry and Chestnut streets roughly four out of five rich families lived in the western wards. Of course, the latter were "western" only in a very special sense, for fewer than 3 per cent of the richest citizens actually lived west of Broad (14th) Street. In this context, "western" meant the western part of the eastern half of the city.

Another interesting feature of the residential pattern of Philadelphia's elite is its southern orientation. More than twice as many rich families lived on Chestnut and other streets to the south as on streets to the north of it. Discovering that the wards with high average assessments prior to 1840 were located toward the center of the city's heavily populated area, Blumin reasoned that the center attracted the rich primarily for utilitarian reasons: "the major institutions of the city—the port, the banks, the Merchants' Coffee House, the State, the fashionable and important shops—were all located in its center. Before the omnibus and the streetcar, proximity to these institutions was the first requisite of urban life and, accordingly, the major criterion for judging the desirability of a neighborhood." [26] Clearly, by the mid-1840s the center of Philadelphia's wealthy population was well to the south of the Market Street line that designated the city's north-south center.[27] And yet, no statistically precise explanation is likely to be forthcoming as to why a very large cluster of the rich elected Mulberry (Arch) Street—northwest of the center—or Spruce and Walnut streets—to the south of it. Map 6 suggests that the *outer* fringes of the center appealed increasingly to successful families.

The revolutions in urban transport described by George R. Taylor had by no means bypassed Philadelphia. Still, to judge from the behavior of the city's elite of the mid-1840s, their residential choices were determined, not by the availability of omnibus lines, but by their desire to live on prestigious streets in proximity to families of similar rank and substance. The three streets containing over half of the upper four hundred—Chestnut, Walnut, and Mulberry—were at their most westernmost point of population density no more than half a mile from

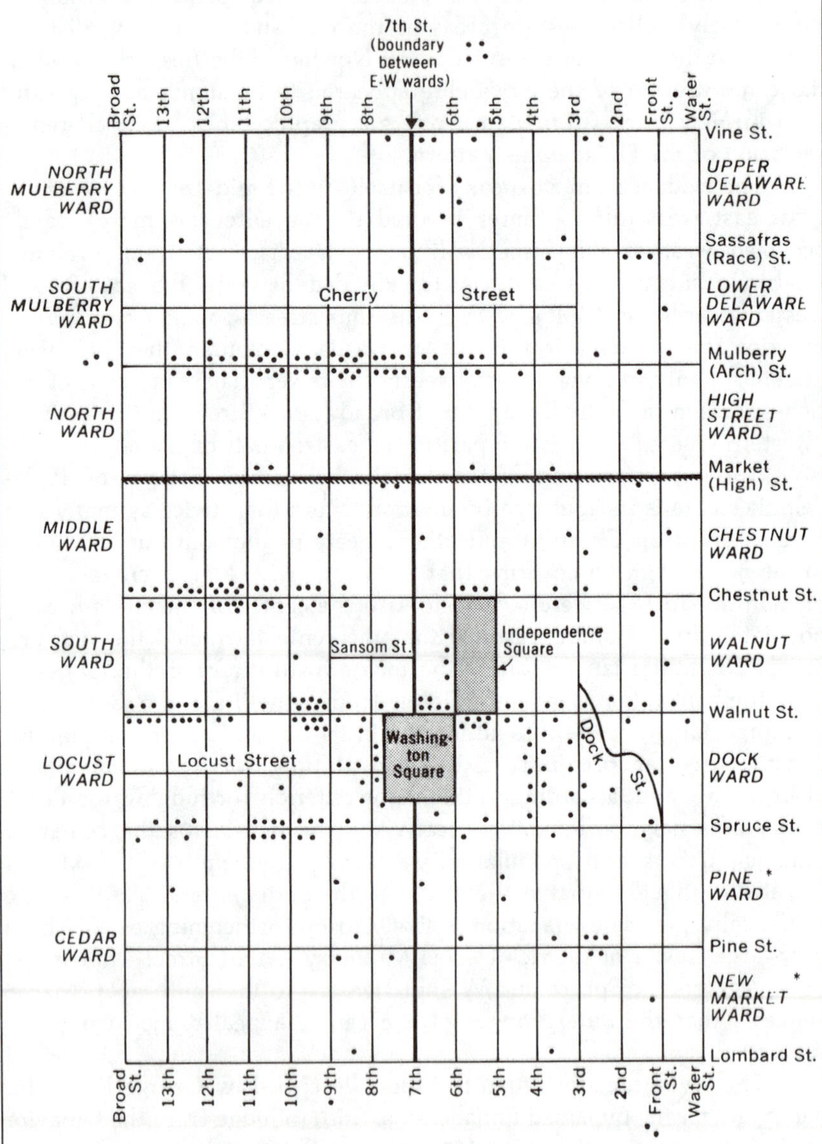
MAP 6
Where the Philadelphia Rich Lived, 1846
7th St. (boundary between E-W wards)
Broad St.
13th
12th
11th
10th
9th
8th
7th
6th
5th
4th
3rd
2nd
Front St.
Water St.
Vine St.
NORTH MULBERRY WARD
UPPER DELAWARE WARD
Sassafras (Race) St.
SOUTH MULBERRY WARD
Cherry
Street
LOWER DELAWARE WARD
Mulberry (Arch) St.
NORTH WARD
HIGH STREET WARD
Market (High) St.
MIDDLE WARD
CHESTNUT WARD
Chestnut St.
SOUTH WARD
Sansom St.
Independence Square
WALNUT WARD
Walnut St.
LOCUST WARD
Locust Street
Washing-ton Square
Dock St.
DOCK WARD
Spruce St.
CEDAR WARD
PINE WARD *
Pine St.
NEW MARKET WARD *
Lombard St.
• Wealthy residence.
* The Pine and New Market wards had earlier been one ward.
Boundary between north and south wards.

the city's commercial district. Chestnut Street had "retained its genteel atmosphere throughout the period" 1820–1840, just as Mulberry and Walnut Streets—centers of "fine residential sections" that had resisted change during the same period—continued to be upper-class enclaves during the next decade.[28] In contrast to New York City's rich, whose movement northward in the 1830s and 1840s placed them beyond the confines of the walking city, the Philadelphia elite's westward movement in the same period covered less ground and, more significantly, was less dependent on transport. The essential similarity of the residential choices made by the upper classes of the two cities was that, in the one as in the other, prestigious locations were sought. Prestige appeared to be conferred largely by tradition or reputation and the presence on a street of some of the city's leading families.

Boston

In the second quarter of the nineteenth century the city of Boston was an area measuring not one mile from east to west and less than two miles north to south (lying north of lightly populated South Boston). Expansion south was slowed by the city's many marshes, mudflats, and other peculiarities of terrain. Within this slender realm, what Dr. Oliver Wendell Holmes once called "the sifted few"—or the Bostonian families of status and wealth—managed to create distinctive residential islands that combined beauty with social gentility, isolating them from lesser mortals. According to a modern student of the city's changing physiognomy, Boston was "a series of contiguous villages, whose villagers rarely cross[ed] the invisible boundaries that separate[d] them from wholly different worlds." [29] It is, of course, impossible to corroborate so broad an assertion about so unmeasurable a phenomenon as the walking habits of Bostonians. Tax records that point to the wealth of the elite, directories that list their addresses, and contemporary local maps that chart the streets where they lived, do make it possible, however, to locate the residential areas favored by Boston's upper orders early and late in the era.[30]

Boston's wealthiest five hundred in the early 1830s lived on about 85 of the city's 325 streets. The actual concentration of the rich was greater than these figures suggest, however, since most of these 85 streets contained only one, two, or three eminent families. As Table 9–4 indicates, half of the city's rich families lived on only eight of its streets.

Impressionistic accounts had noted the disposition of many among Boston's elite, even before the end of the eighteenth century, to desert the North End (the northeastern corner of the city containing the first three wards) in favor of the West End (sixth ward) or the west central area of the city (seventh ward) adjacent to the Boston Common. Wealthy families had responded enthusiastically to the architectural ideas carried

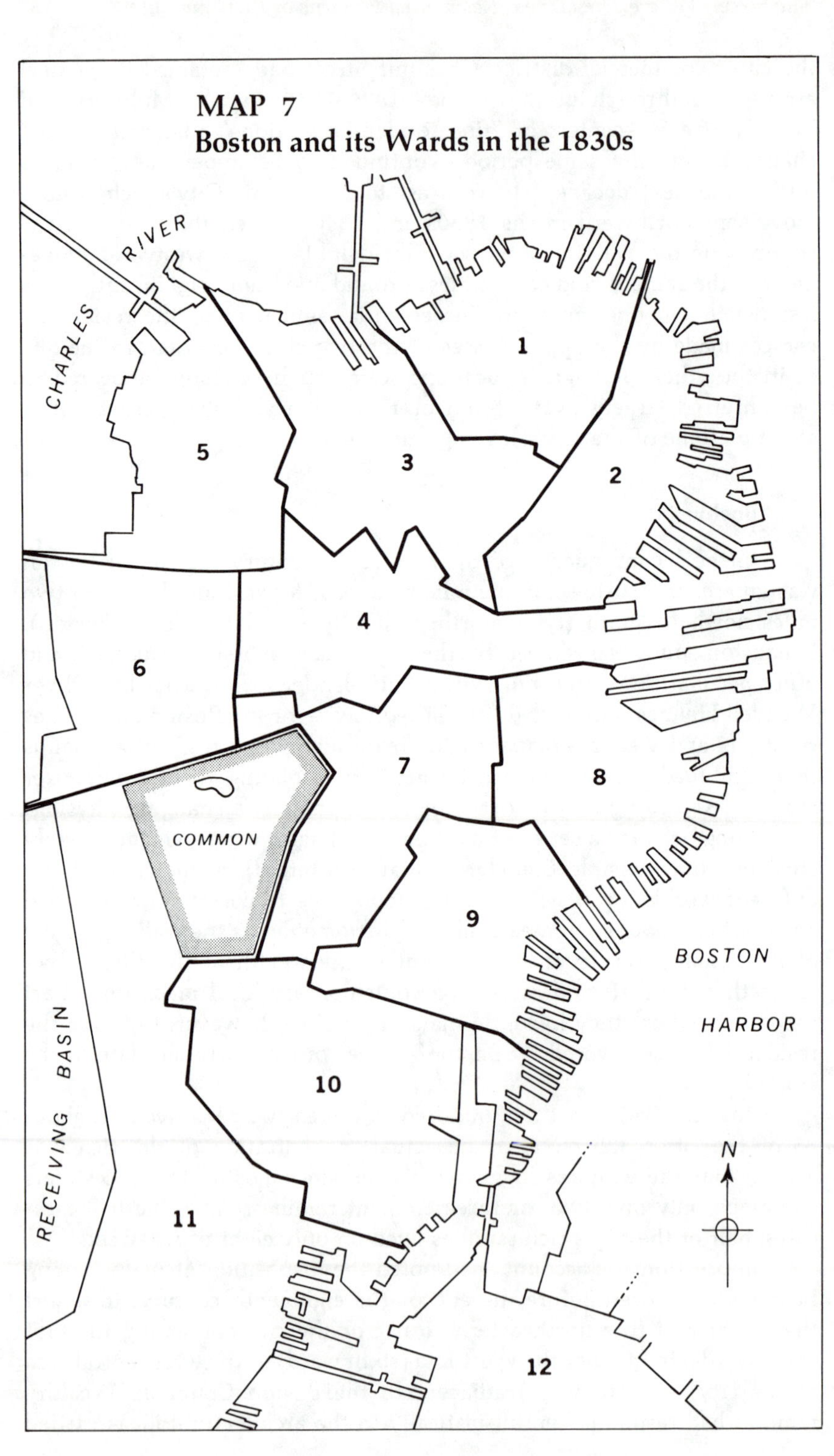
MAP 7
Boston and its Wards in the 1830s
CHARLES RIVER
COMMON
RECEIVING BASIN
BOSTON HARBOR
N
1
2
3
4
5
6
7
8
9
10
11
12

TABLE 9–4.
Where the Boston Rich Lived in the Early 1830s

Street	*% of city's rich*	*Average wealth of rich families*
Beacon St.	10.0	$110,000
Tremont St.	9.0	85,000
Mt. Vernon St.	8.0	75,000
Summer St.	6.0	100,000
Washington St.	5.0	75,000
Bowdoin Square	4.0	115,000
Chesnut St.	4.0	80,000
Franklin Place	4.0	65,000
Pearl St.	4.0	70,000
Park St.	2.5	95,000
Bedford Place	2.5	70,000
Winter St.	2.0	60,000
Otis Place	2.0	70,000
High St.	2.0	45,000
Federal St.	2.5	60,000
Hancock St.	2.5	80,000

back from France to his native city by young Charles Bulfinch, ideas he promptly put into execution with a series of remarkable houses he designed in a small area just to the northwest of the Common—a circle the diameter of which measured perhaps four hundred yards. Bulfinch planned a "noble mansion" for the great merchant Joseph Coolidge; the three-story brick house built in 1792 which stood in "large gardens near Bowdoin Square between Temple and Bowdoin Streets." In 1796 he built a similarly impressive structure for Harrison Gray Otis at the corner of Cambridge and Lynde Streets, in the "increasingly handsome West End region of his [Bulfinch's] birth." Four years later he put up Otis's magnificent structure at 85 Mt. Vernon Street. In 1810–1811 he designed Colonnade Row, two dozen "handsome brick houses" on the southwest corner of West Street overlooking the Common. Marked by columns "supporting a second-story balcony along the front . . . the elegance of their design and their superb situation made [the houses] inviting to families of means; and Colonnade Row was at once admitted to the best society." In 1815 Bulfinch built for Samuel Parkman "the fine pair of double houses of Chelmsford granite that long stood at the end of Bowdoin Square between Cambridge and Green Streets." [31] A quarter of a century ago, Walter Firey described how in the late-eighteenth and early-nineteenth centuries Bulfinch and such elite Bostonians as Harrison Gray Otis and Jonathan Mason had carefully planned a district of fashionable homes and estates along the southern slopes of Beacon Hill,

View of Franklin Street, Boston. This was one of the elegant streets on which fashionable Bostonians lived. *(Woodcut courtesy of the Bostonian Society.)*

taking great pains to minimize the chances for social intercourse between the elegant southern and the always plebeian northern side of the Hill.[32] Class exclusiveness had been very much on their mind.

In deserting the North End that had been the first seat of Boston gentility, the opulent had moved to the attractive areas near the Common —such as Beacon Hill and Pemberton Hill toward the west—and the Fort Hill section below State Street and the business area to the south. In view of the mere several hundred yards separating the one district from the other, and the accessibility of the commercial streets along Long Wharf and Central Wharf to both areas, it seems clear that utility or business considerations were not the sole or necessarily the chief factors determining the residential choices of the elite. In the narrow physical city of that day, the business center was within easy walking reach of all the city's classes. Residents of Pearl Street, such as Elijah Loring, Henderson Inches, Frederick Tudor, Josiah Bradlee, Pliny Cutler, or Sarah Perkins, lived on "generous grounds, with the unencumbered slopes" of Fort Hill above them providing a lovely setting and a "beautiful view of the Harbor." During a stroll on Fort Hill one fine spring day, the great merchant Thomas Handasyd Perkins, accompanied by Harrison Gray Otis, "had the pleasure, after watching a ship in its progress up the harbor, of recognizing it as one of his own, arriving from China" ahead of schedule.[33]

At the beginning of the nineteenth century the sites around Beacon and Cotton Hills just off the northeast corner of the Common were "shaded by great trees . . . and made fragrant by the perfume of roses and honeysuckle." It was in this area that Gardiner Greene had after 1803 "developed behind his house on Tremont Street a hillside garden that was one of the wonders of the first third of the nineteenth century"; it was next to another admirable garden, that of his eminent neighbor Ebenezer Francis. Close by were the "double granite house" built in 1810 by David Hinckley (subsequently occupied by Benjamin W. Crowninshield and John Lowell Gardiner) and the great square brick house at the corner of Park and Beacon Streets, built a few years earlier by Thomas Amory, and "later divided in two and occupied in part by George Ticknor."[34] Families such as John Lothrop Motley's, which lived just off the northwest corner of the Common, could look "down Chesnut Street over the water to the western hills," comforted by the beauty of the view and by the status of their neighbors on Beacon, Mount Vernon, and Park Streets. Such eminences as David Sears, John L. Gardner, Samuel A. Eliot, Edward Tuckerman, Nathaniel P. Russell, Thomas Winthrop, John Bryant, Martin Brimmer, Daniel and Peter Parker, William and Samuel Appleton, and Harrison Gray Otis (who after 1806 had moved once again to an even more imposing house at 45 Beacon Street, facing the Common) lived on Beacon Street. Thomas B. Curtis, William

Lawrence, Charles G. Loring, Abigail Joy, Justice Lemuel Shaw, Benjamin Adams, Nathan Appleton, George W. Lyman, Jonathan Mason, and Samuel C. Gray resided on Mount Vernon, while Edmund Dwight, Josiah Quincy and Josiah Quincy, Jr., and the famous surgeon Dr. John Charles Warren were on Park Street.

Some discerning contemporaries thought that the "oblong quadrangle" enclosed by Washington, Bedford, and Summer Streets—particularly where the latter was intersected by Chauncey Street and Otis and Winthrop Places—was the most charming residential area in the city. Reminiscing at a later time when the area was occupied by "great warehouses and other massive edifices," Dr. Holmes recalled that in the 1830s and 1840s it was still a "most attractive *rus in urbe.* The sunny gardens of the late Judge Charles Jackson and the late Mr. S. P. Gardner opened their flowers and ripened their fruits" there. The intellectual

MAP 8
Streets Favored by the Boston Rich in the Early 1830s

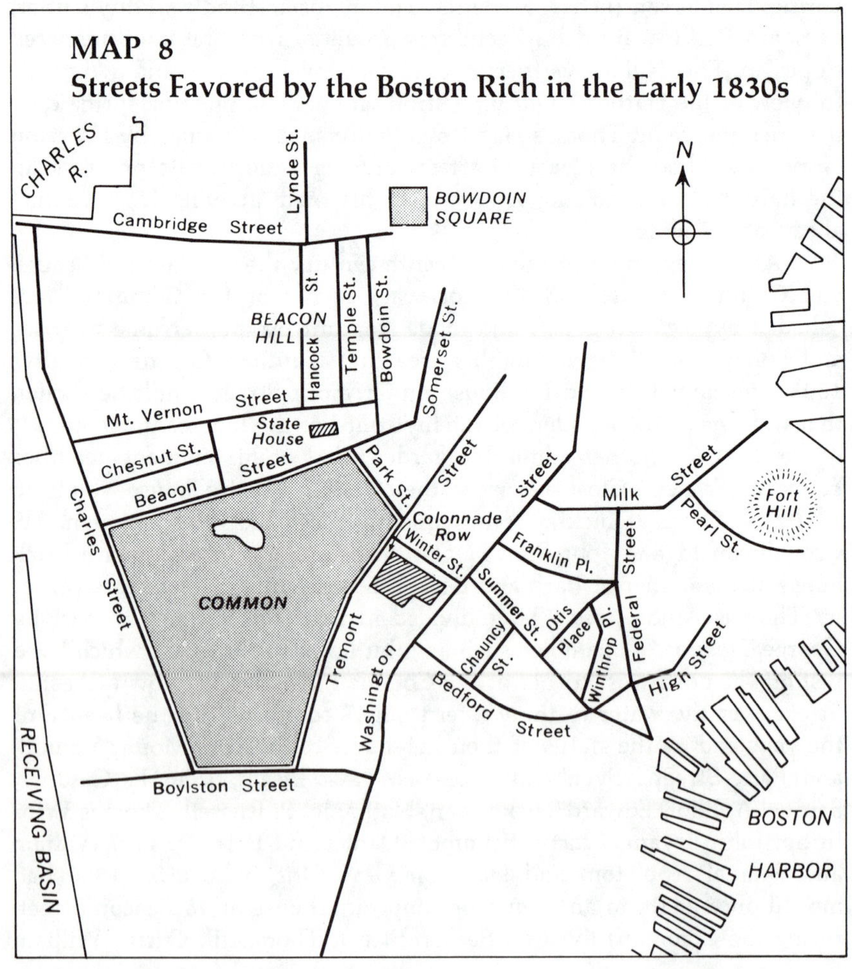

aristocracy of the city "found their natural homes in these sheltered enclosures. The fine old mansion of Judge William Prescott looked out upon these gardens. [Holmes could] well remember the window of [Prescott's] son, the historian's, study, the light from which used every evening to glimmer through the leaves of the pear trees while the 'Conquest of Mexico' was achieving itself under difficulties hardly less formidable than those encountered by Cortes. It was a charmed region, in which Emerson first drew his breath. '[35] E. C. Wines, a Philadelphia visitor to Boston in the 1830s, agreed with Holmes; Wines found one of Boston's most pleasant features "the many green and shady front yards which relieve and refresh the eye," as one wandered through its "winding streets." "More or less of these are met with in every part of the city; but Summer Street, on both sides, is lined with them from one end to the other." According to him, Summer Street was "decidedly the handsomest street in Boston. Town and Country seem here married to each other, and there is no jar between the husband and the wife. It is a harmonious union, and the source of many pleasures."[36] Evidently of the same opinion were Israel Thorndike, Henry Cabot, Nathaniel Goddard, William Sturgis, the Grays (Jonathan, Horace, and Francis C.), and Daniel Webster, who all lived on Summer Street, and Henry Lee, John A. Lowell, Franklin Dexter, Augustus Thorndike, William J. Loring, Nathaniel I. Bowditch, and Thomas H. Perkins, Jr., who in the early 1830s lived alongside it.

Not all wealthy Bostonians lived in fashionable districts. Israel Ames, Jonathan Parker, and James Bartlett lived in the North End, while Hall J. How lived in the relatively poor twelfth ward to the south. But these men were very much the exceptions; in the 1830s, the preponderance of the city's social and economic elite lived in a small number of fashionable streets located in the wealthy seventh, sixth, and eighth wards. A long meandering thoroughfare such as Washington Street traversed the tenth and eleventh wards, as well as the more prosperous northern ones, and some of its richest residents lived in the former wards. Perrin May, Otis Everett, Josiah Vose, Joseph Lovering, John Griggs, Daniel Weld, and the redoubtable John D. Williams occupied a thin upper-crust enclave that cut across the humble streets and quarters of their neighbors in the lowly wards in the southwestern quarter of the city. Since the city's great financial institutions, wherever located, were taxed almost entirely on the limited value of their real property alone, in Boston—unlike New York City and Brooklyn—the per capita wealth of a ward's residents was not significantly altered by the presence of banks or insurance companies. Boston's wealthy wards were indeed the wards containing most of the city's richest families, as Table 9–5 indicates.

Boston's eminent families sought housing not by particular wards, however, but by particular streets and neighborhoods. When wards were

Daniel Webster's House, Boston. The great man resided on Summer Street among Boston's elite of wealth and standing. (*Photograph courtesy of the Print Department, Boston Public Library.*)

TABLE 9–5.
The Distribution of Boston's Wealthiest Families in the City's Wards, 1830, 1835

Ward	*% of city's rich*	*Per capita wealth of the ward, 1830**	*Per capita wealth of the ward, 1835**
1	1	$312	$468
2	1	308	712
3	1	420	430
4	10	1,448	1,236
5	4	474	482
6	12	1,200	1,424
7	28	2,150	2,378
8	14	1,648	1,736
9	10	1,702	1,480
10	10	810	938
11	5	770	736
12	4	420	342

*Computed from Shattuck, *Census of Boston 1845*, pp. 15, 28. Since assessments were made at half the value of property in these years, the figures have been doubled in this table.

realigned in the 1830s and 1840s—with the new fourth ward encroaching on the wealthy seventh—almost all wards were enlarged and extended southward in order to keep up with the city's increasing land and residential area. There was no sudden exodus by wealthy residents from "poorer" wards into "wealthier" ones. Many rich Bostonians moved to new locations during these two decades but the per capita wealth of wards does not appear to have been a consideration in their decisions. The changing average wealth of Boston's wards resulted, not from any internal migrations of the opulent, dictated by new attitudes concerning the desirability of this as against that ward, but rather from political decisions to modify the boundaries of the wards. Streets inhabited by the rich when relocated from the seventh to the fourth ward thus added to the relative wealth of the latter. (See Table 9–6.)

TABLE 9–6.
Changing Wealth of Selected Wealthy Wards from 1833 to 1848

	Early 1830s		**Late 1840s**	
Ward	*per capita wealth of residents*	*% of richest families*	*per capita wealth of residents*	*% of richest families*
4	$1,236	10	$2,328	21
7	2,378	28	3,342	24

The evidence on the addresses of the Boston rich by the middle of the nineteenth century indicates that for all the building up and filling in of land and the increase in population in the southern portions of the city that had marked the 1830s and 1840s, the preferred residential areas of the opulent had changed little.[37] Concentration had increased, however, and half of the rich lived on only six streets.

TABLE 9–7.
Where the Boston Rich Lived in the Late 1840s

Street	*% of city's rich*	*Average wealth of rich families*
Beacon St.	14	$160,000
Mt. Vernon St.	12	125,000
Tremont St.	10	115,000
Summer St.	6	175,000
Pemberton Square	4	135,000
Boylston St.	4	125,000
Bowdoin Square	3	80,000
Washington St.	3	200,000
Chesnut St.	3	100,000
Cambridge St.	3	110,000
Temple St.	3	90,000
Franklin Place	2	175,000
Hancock St.	2	80,000
Park St.	2	300,000
Somerset St.	2	115,000
Winthrop Place	2	110,000

About half of the wealthiest families either remained at the same location over the two decades or, in the case of a few, moved several yards to a new address on the same street. As for the wealthy families that did relocate, their movement hardly constituted a great trek, either to a new section of the city or to a significantly more prestigious area; typically they transplanted themselves from one desirable section to another a few hundred yards away. Varied and unique considerations doubtless explained the restlessness of some successful Bostonians. In contrast to Horace Gray and Henry Gassett, who continued living on Summer Street, Francis C. Gray moved to Park Street, while Nathaniel Goddard moved to Pemberton Square. Judging from the fortunes of these men during the period, wealth as such had little to do with their varied housing choices. Similarly, the successful Samuel Fales and Amos Lawrence stayed on Tremont Street, while Jonathan Phillips moved to Mount Vernon Street and Robert C. Winthrop to Summer Street for reasons that appear unconnected with their changing material fortunes. Whatever the reasons may have been—and they varied from one individual to another—the best we can do is infer them, since men then, no more than now, thought of writing down the precise reasons they decided to move to a new address. Even Philip Hone, who left the most detailed account of one man's private actions and thoughts, tells us when and where he moved during the period, but not why he did so.

Changing tastes and significant economic and demographic changes inevitably resulted in the decline of some streets and the rise of others. The Fort Hill section was abandoned as warehouses and railroad terminals threatened encroachment. Henderson Inches continued to dwell on Pearl Street between Milk and High Streets in the old 9th ward, but most of its other elite residents followed Thomas H. Perkins and removed to the vicinity of Beacon Hill.[38] Boylston Street, running along the southern boundary of the Common, became increasingly popular, as the families of John P. Thorndike and Giles Lodge were joined by Francis Codman, Elias Hasket Derby, George Dexter, and George H. Loring. Winthrop Place near Summer Street; Temple Street, running between and parallel to Hancock and Bowdoin Streets off the northeast corner of the Common; and Somerset Street, on the west side of Pemberton Hill, were other avenues that attracted increasing numbers of eminent families. Pemberton Square grew rapidly in popularity during the 1840s.

Pemberton Square had been developed in the 1830s by the dynamic Patrick Tracy Jackson on land bought from Gardiner Greene with an eye toward speculative profit. The houses and lots of Pemberton Square were situated on what Walter Muir Whitehill has called the "decapitated hill" above Somerset and Tremont Streets. (The top of it had been shaved off and sold by Jackson as landfill.) On this excellent location were constructed "high-ceilinged red brick houses" on sites described by the square's promoters as "not surpassed if equalled by any in the city for elevation, refinement, and proximity to business." Their success in attracting such residents as Robert Bennet Forbes, Nathaniel Goddard, Joseph Coolidge, Amos Lawrence, Nathaniel I. Bowditch, John A. Lowell, James Jackson, Nathaniel and Henry Sturgis, and Henry Sigourney helped transform the promoters' promises into prophesy. The aging Bulfinch decried the new pattern of building as many as five brick houses where previously one "noble mansion" had stood amidst ample gardens. According to the reminiscences of Thomas Wentworth Higginson, Beacon and Park Streets at this time resisted the pressure to turn trees, flowers, and grass into living quarters, and the houses in the "aristocratic region" of Beacon Hill still stood amidst gardens and extensive grounds.[39]

Whether they occupied substantial grounds or small, the wealthiest families of Boston in the 1840s lived somewhat more exclusively than they had done two decades earlier. By mid-nineteenth century the three great aristocratic thoroughfares of Beacon, Tremont, and Mount Vernon Streets housed over one-third of Boston's rich, in contrast to the slightly more than one-quarter of the city's plutocracy they had contained at the beginning of the 1830s. Residing on only one-eighth of the city's streets at the later date—where earlier they had lived on about two-ninths of the streets—the Boston elite appeared to be inspired not at all by egalitarian considerations in choosing housing, but by the desire to live comfortably amidst pleasing surroundings that were relatively accessible to business and, above all, in areas whose great prestige derived from the presence in them of other families of similar wealth and eminence.

The emergence of omnibuses and as many as seven separate railroad lines to the city before 1850 appeared to have little impact on the residential patterns of wealthy Bostonians. Even the exaggerated claims made by railroad spokesmen conceded that only a small minority of the city's merchants commuted from suburbs to the city's business center by mid-century. The immediate impact of the great influx of, above all, poor Irish immigrants into Boston before 1850 should not be exaggerated. Some historians' versions of an alleged elite exodus from "the noise and confusion" of the "core" or "central city" well before mid-century are not borne out by the facts. A recent book, arguing that Boston's antebellum elite remained in the "core" only because they "could escape the central city in the summer, enjoying the residential amenities of the suburbs," hardly suggests the beauty, the charm, and the abundance of amenities of that part of the central city inhabited by the fashionable.[40] That old urban sociologists' abstraction, the core, turns out to have been an area of pleasant tree-lined streets, beautiful homes, and spacious gardens presided over by persons of wealth, distinction, and manners. Theoretical assumptions about its alleged deterioration should not be permitted to distort its actual appearance.

What *should* have been happening to the core was not, in fact, happening to it in Boston. For, as David Ward has noted, upper-class residential enclaves persisted in the central city where certain streets and avenues, such as Beacon Hill, retained their "long established status." Although he believed that the Hill had certain practical advantages of site and location that helped account for the durability of its prestige, Ward also stressed the importance of its symbolic ancestral status and its "advantages of cultural association."[41] Firey had earlier attributed to Beacon Hill a halo effect that was due to factors other than any intrinsic qualities of the "elevated piece of ground." According to him, upper-class families sought to be identified with Beacon Hill for reasons having nothing to do with the emphases in "the empirically rationalistic schemes," but rather because of the Hill's "affective significance" as a "symbol for certain cultural values . . . with respect to family lineage, neighborhood traditions, and local antiquities." Firey inferred this judgment from the "probable states of mind" of elite Bostonians suggested by the "innumerable pamphlets and articles" some of them wrote, in which they reported on their subjective feelings about Beacon Hill.[42] The movement of their feet alone—quite apart from the subjective testimony given by a few of their number—indicates that the wealthiest families in Boston, as in the other great northeastern cities, were influenced significantly by the value of class exclusiveness in choosing the sites of their residences.

As Leo Schnore has pointed out, in postulating his concentric-zones theory Burgess was by no means so obtuse as to be unaware of the role played in urban growth by a variety of factors unlike, if not inimical to, the central impersonal tendencies whose importance he emphasized.[43] The Burgess model is not applicable to antebellum urban spatial relationships, not because it fails to allow for the elements of personal choice guided by subjective and non-rational considerations, but simply because the underlying forces assumed by the theory to promote the particular ecological relationships it posited, did not *in fact* operate as assumed. The facts of history in this instance, as in others, do not bear out the neat generalizations made by thinkers unaware of the perversity and complexity of these facts.

The residential patterns displayed by the rich in the great northeastern cities were not all of a piece. Wealthy Philadelphians appeared to be clustered together on a smaller number of prestigious avenues than their counterparts elsewhere; the explanation may have more to do with the relatively neat spatial organization and small number of east-west thoroughfares in the city than with any unusual sense of class exclusiveness among its elite. New York City's eminent families were more footloose than Boston's and more inclined to move to previously unoccupied sections, doubtless encouraged by the availability of ten times as much landspace as beckoned to their northern neighbors. In contrast to the Bostonians, whose preferred neighborhoods became more concentrated during the second quarter of the nineteenth century, rich New Yorkers became slightly more dispersed. Other variations can be found. The burden of the evidence, however, is the essential similarity shown by the social and economic elites of the great cities in their residential decisions. While a number of wealthy families in each city were dispersed in locations of declining prestige, the great preponderance of the rich and eminent chose locations, the exalted status of which derived primarily from the fact that they were almost exclusively the neighborhoods of the elite rather than of those "common men" after whom the era has been named.

Notes

[1] Walter Firey, *Land Use in Central Boston* (Cambridge, Mass., 1947), p. 3.
[2] Glaab, "The Historian and the American City: A Bibliographic Survey," in Philip M. Hauser and Leo F. Schmore, eds., *The Study of Urbanization* (New York, 1965), p. 58.
[3] Gideon Sjoberg, "Theory and Research in Urban Sociology," in Hauser and Schnore, *The Study of Urbanization*, p. 182.
[4] See the critical discussion in Eric E. Lampard, "American Historians and the Study of Urbanization," *American Historical Review, LXVII* (Oct. 1961), pp. 49–61; Lampard, "Urbanization and Social Change: On Broadening the Scope and Relevance of Urban History," in Oscar Handlin and John Burchard, eds., *The Historian and the City* (Cambridge, 1963); and in Glaab, "The Historian and the American City."
[5] The play on words is drawn from the title of an essay by one of the leading urban historians, Sam Bass Warner, Jr., "If all the World Were Philadelphia: A Scaffolding for Urban History, 1774–1930," *American Historical Review, 74* (Oct. 1968), pp. 26–43.
[6] Kenneth Wheeler, *To Wear a City's Crown: The Beginnings of Urban Growth in Texas, 1836–1865* (Cambridge, 1968), p. 132. Michael Katz reports that "residential segregation by wealth appears minimal" in mid-nineteenth century Hamilton, Ontario. "Patterns of Inequality, Wealth, and Power in a Nineteenth-Century City," pp. 5–6.
[7] Richard C. Wade, *The Urban Frontier* (Chicago, 1959), p. 206.
[8] In addition to Blumin's, "Mobility and Change in Ante-Bellum Philadelphia," see Walter Hugins, *Jacksonian Democracy and the Working Class* (Stanford, 1960), pp. 205–212, Edward Pessen, "Did Labor Support Jackson?: The Boston Story," *Political Science Quarterly, LXIV* (June 1949), pp. 262–74; William A. Sullivan, "Did Labor Support Andrew Jackson?" *ibid., LXII* (Dec. 1947), pp. 569–80; and Dixon Ryan Fox, *The Decline of Aristocracy in the Politics of New York* (New York, 1919), pp. 440–49.
[9] In Boston between 1830 and 1845 the per capita worth of individuals in the wealthiest ward was never more than ten times that of residents in the poorest ward. For Brooklyn in the mid-1840s the ratio was no greater than roughly five to one. In Philadelphia in 1830 the per capita assessed worth of the wealthy Chestnut Ward was seven-and-one-half times as great as the assessed worth of the poorest ward, according to Blumin, "Mobility in a Nineteenth-Century American City," p. 127. The greatest disparity occurred in New York City, where during the mid–1830s the per capita assessed wealth of the first ward was about 27 times that of the thirteenth ward. For the far greater disparities between the wealth of rich and poor *individuals*, see Pessen, "The Egalitarian Myth and the American Social Reality," pp. 1020–25.
[10] The addresses of close to 90 per cent of the five hundred wealthiest New York City families were ascertained, both for 1828 and 1845. City maps in the Municipal Archives and Records Center made it possible to locate these addresses in the different wards of the city.
[11] Charles Astor Bristed, *The Upper Ten Thousand: Sketches of American Society* (New York, 1852), p. 23; Dayton, *Last Days of Knickerbocker Life in New York*, p. 153.
[12] See Ernest W. Burgess, "The Growth of the City" in Robert E. Park, Burgess, Roderick D. McKenzie, eds., *The City* (Chicago, 1925), pp. 47–62. Whether the spatial areas are best described as sectors or not, Hoyt's thesis that preferred residential districts might be found in varying parts of the city, from its core to its periphery, is borne out by the residential habits of the rich. See Hoyt, *The Structure and Growth of Residential Neighborhoods in American Cities* (Washington, D.C., 1939).

The term "walking city" connotes one whose physical size places its business and other important locations within easy walking distance of residents.
[13] On May 25, 1836, Hone wrote: "I can always get an omnibus in a minute or two by going out of the street door and holding up my fingers." Hone Diary, XI:368.
[14] Hone Diary, IX:111; XXIII:359 and XXIV:406.

[15] The New York City tax-assessment rolls listed resident taxpayers and their addresses. Since our data bank includes the assessed wealth of almost all of the city's property owners, it was possible to compare the wealth of neighbors.
[16] Gabriel Furman, "Notes on Brooklyn, New York," p. 337, undated manuscript located in the Long Island Historical Society.
[17] Stiles, *Civil, Political, Professional and Ecclesiastical History . . . of Brooklyn*, I, 364.
[18] Nathaniel Scudder Prime, *A History of Long Island* (New York, 1845), p. 379.
[19] Warner, *The Private City, Philadelphia in Three Periods of Its Growth* (Phila., 1968), p. 50.
[20] Johnston, "The Caste and Class of the Urban Form of Historic Philadelphia," *Journal of the American Institute of Planners*, XXXII (Nov. 1966), pp. 342–47. Johnston sought to determine the degree of "pre-Civil War Philadelphia's class structure as expressed in certain of its churches' members and their spatial segregation." He accorded upper-class membership to members of particular Protestant churches (Episcopalian and Presbyterian) who had high-status occupations. Because he was interested in segregation by color as well as by class, Johnston excluded the Quakers. But, although the white skin color of the Friends did not lend itself to a study of how racial differences among members of a denomination correlated with residential segregation, the great wealth of many Quaker families certainly weakens the force of any study of class segregation that omits the Friends.
[21] Ellis Paxon Oberholtzer, *Philadelphia: A History of the City and Its People* (Philadelphia, n.d.), cited in Blumin, "Mobility and Change in Ante-Bellum Philadelphia," p. 189.
[22] For an excellent discussion of Penn's original plan of layout see Anthony N. B. Garvan, "Proprietary Philadelphia as Artifact," in Handlin and Burchard, *The Historian and the City*, pp. 177–201.
[23] My generalizations are based on John F. Watson, *Annals of Philadelphia in the Olden Time*, Willis P. Hazard, ed. (Philadelphia, 1927), III, p. 247; Carroll Frey, *The Independence Square Neighborhood* (Philadelphia, 1926); McElroy's *Philadelphia Directory* for 1845 and 1846; and William S. Hastings, "Philadelphia Microcosm," *Pennsylvania Magazine of History and Biography, XCI* (April 1967), pp. 164–80.
[24] Blumin, "Mobility and Change in Philadelphia," p. 186.
[25] Information on the block-by-block locations of Philadelphia addresses at mid-century appears in a table, a copy of which was furnished me by John Daly. He advises me that the original document is in the possession of the Philadelphia Historical Commission.
[26] Blumin, "Mobility and Change in Philadelphia," p. 188.
[27] The main difference between the outlines of the area enclosing the rich of 1846 in Map 6 and Johnston's "Generalized Class Ecology; Spatial Analysis, 1838" (his map outlining the area containing upper class residences) is that by the later period Spruce Street west of 7th Street and Pine Street east of 4th Street contained small but significant sprinklings of elite residences. Johnston's ethnic and class map for Philadelphia on the eve of the Civil War, "Caste and Class of the Urban Form of Historic Philadelphia," p. 347, hardly confirms the validity of Warner's references to an alleged chaotic juxtaposition of races and occupational categories in the "core" and "ring" of the city in 1860; "If all the World Were Philadelphia," p. 34.
[28] Hastings, "Philadelphia Microcosm," p. 170. Hastings' generalizations about Philadelphia's streets are based on tax assessments by street for the period 1820–1840.
[29] Walter Muir Whitehill, *Boston: A Topographical History* (Cambridge, 1959), p. xi.
[30] Excellent maps are on the front pages of Charles Stimpson's *Boston Directory* for the early 1830s and in the directories prepared by George Adams and published by Stimpson and James French in the late 1840s.
[31] Whitehill, *Boston*, pp. 51–52, 63–64; and Edwin Munroe Bacon, *Rambles Around Old Boston* (Boston, 1921), pp. 108–109.
[32] Firey, *Land Use in Central Boston*, pp. 43–46. See Bibliography for other valuable studies of Boston streets and neighborhoods.
[33] Whitehill, *Boston*, p. 114.
[34] *Ibid.*, pp. 64, 106–107, 111.
[35] Caroline Ticknor, ed., *Dr. Holmes's Boston* (Boston, 1915), pp. 44–45.

[36] Cited in Whitehill, *Boston*, pp. 113–14.
[37] A comparison of the rich concentrations in the early 1830s with Firey's map of "Residences of Wealthy Persons in Boston, 1846," in *Land Use in Central Boston*, p. 56, shows a remarkable similarity in contour. Firey used the anonymous pamphlet, *"Our First Men": A Calendar of Wealth, Fashion, and Gentility* (Boston, 1846), rather than the printed tax-assessment lists, as the source of his "wealthy persons." Firey's pinpointing of each residence is valuable, although the absence of streets and even wards detracts from the impact and clarity of his map. In view of the silence of the directories about some individuals, I suspect it was not "possible to obtain the addresses of all the persons listed" in *"Our First Men."* George R. Taylor's point that in the 1840s most merchants had deserted Summer Street is not supported by the evidence on the wealthiest of their number. "Beginnings of Mass Transportation in Urban America," *Smithsonian Journal of History*, I (Summer and Autumn, 1966), p. 40.
[38] Firey argues that the decision, first of Perkins and then of a number of his wealthy associates, to relocate on Temple Street constitutes an important example of the role of individuals in determining the shape of spatial expansion within a city, and is thus a refutation of the "impersonal and automatic 'natural trends' " ostensibly postulated in the Hoyt and Burgess theories.
[39] Thomas Wentworth Higginson, "Other Days and Ways in Boston and Cambridge," in Rossiter, *Days and Ways in Old Boston*, pp. 35–36.
[40] Taylor, "Beginnings of Mass Transportation," p. 40; Ward, "Emergence of Central Immigrant Ghettoes: 1840–1920," *Annals of the Association of American Geographers*, 58 (June 1968), p. 343; and Knights, *The Plain People of Boston, 1830–1860*, p. 90, which speaks of an alleged escape from the central city.
[41] Ward, "Emergence of Central Immigrant Ghettoes," pp. 350, 359.
[42] Firey, *Land Use in Central Boston*, pp. 42, 43, 170.
[43] Schnore, "On the Spatial Structure of Cities in the Two Americas," in Hauser and Schnore, *The Study of Urbanization*, p. 352.

10

The Marital Theory and Practice of the Rich and Elite

> I used to think that in your unsophisticated republican country, people married out of pure love, but now it looks as if the fashionables, at least, marry for money as often as we do.
>
> An Englishman to his American friend, in Charles Astor Bristed, *The Upper Ten Thousand*, p. 119

> One of the tests of the "openness" of social structure is the extent of marriages between persons of different social origins.
>
> Jerzy Berent, "Social Mobility and Marriage," in D. V. Glass, ed., *Social Mobility in Britain* (London 1967), p. 321

Reminiscing about social life in New York City during the 1830s, a member of the city's social and economic elite wrote that a "comfortable independence," ostensibly available to most persons, "assured cordial welcome by one class to the other."[1] If his recollection were accurate, antebellum New York would have been, if not a classless society, than an open society in which class had slight effect on the everyday lives of people. For, as modern scholars of class have noted, a class society manifests itself above all in the exclusiveness and the walls of separation it erects around such institutions as marriage, "friendships characterized by mutual entertainment in homes, common memberships in 'social' organizations, and simply mutual visiting." Where, in the esoteric language of sociological scholarship, "an essential characteristic of all known stratification systems is that they employ the kinship system as their agent of transmission of inequities," the folk wisdom would claim more simply that money marries money and people seek their own level.[2] In the following chapters, the marital choices and private lives of the antebellum urban elite will be examined to see whether the facts of upper-class life bear out the cheerful conjecture that a "cordial welcome by one class to the other" characterized American society in the second quarter of the nineteenth century.

Leading sociologists have asserted, with a clarity that is so great perhaps because it is so obvious, that "the less emphasis which a culture places on family background as a criterion for marriage, the more class mobility that can occur, both up and down through marriage." [3] "Cultural emphasis" is devilishly difficult because it is so imprecise a phenomenon to determine. The historian's way of ascertaining the extent to which this unverifiable impersonal force operates on the thinking, feeling, and behavior of living persons is to gather evidence on their actions. As with all factual evidence, the result is imperfect and incomplete, inevitably less precise than the questions it would answer. The data on marriages, for example, rarely suggest, let alone disclose, the motives of the parties or the degree to which one or another partner (or his or her family) may have been consciously responding to the "emphasis of his culture." Their motives must be inferred, and motives that are inferred are certain to be inexact.

The facts, however, do better than determine the motives underlying the marriages made by the rich and the eminent. They disclose the social and economic backgrounds of the couples. Only God can know motives with certainty: the post-Freudian age, even if it remains skeptical about id, ego, or sublimation, can hardly reject the insight that men, even when they honestly describe what they believe to be their motivation, are themselves neither fully aware of it nor capable of explaining it. If "the family is the keystone of the stratification system," and "all members of the conjugal family are at the same social level" or class,[4] then the marital choices of the urban rich provide a matchless insight into Amercian society and the nature and extent of its stratification system during the "age of egalitarianism."

Seventeenth- and Eighteenth-Century Elite Marital Patterns

The patterns revealed by the marital choices of the antebellum rich become more meaningful when juxtaposed with the evidence for other periods. Unfortunately, such evidence is in short supply.[5] Sociologists, being sociologists, have been more concerned with the theoretical implications of intra-class marriage than with mundane evidence on the prevalence or extent of the phenomenon. Historians, not being sociologists, have had different interests, typically preferring to gather data on presidential elections rather than information on the status of partners in obscure marriages. Since some adventurous scholars, fortunately, do not respect the lines dividing one academic specialty from another, a number of historians have invaded the sociologists' preserve to examine both the extent and the role of upper-class intermarriage. The historians' discussion has been largely confined to the colonial era.

The reasons for the emphasis on the seventeenth and eighteenth centuries seem apparent. On the one hand, certain well-known families of great wealth, prestige, and influence—such as the Pages, Byrds, Carters, Harrisons, Berkeleys, and Fairfaxes in Virginia; the Bulls, Draytons, Middletons, Izards, and Pinckneys in Charleston, South Carolina; the Lloyds, Norrises, Prestons, Pembertsons, and Logans in Philadelphia;

and the Van Cortlandts, Van Rensselaers, Bayards, DePeysters, Livingstons, and Beekmans in New York—were known to be "tightly consolidated by intermarriage." On the other hand, the colonial towns and colonies examined by these scholars were believed to be communities dominated by a small upper crust, that "tended to consolidate its privileged position by close matrimonial alliances." [6] In other words, upper-class intermarriages have been investigated, if haphazardly and by focusing on a small number of elite families, for the one period in American history when a class society was believed to prevail.

A closer look at the seventeenth and eighteenth centuries, based on genealogical data on the wealthiest and most eminent families in the northeastern cities, reveals that the ancestors of hundreds of them—many relatively obscure—had contracted marriages with their social equals, precisely as did the few prominent figures. In New York City, such elite Dutch families as the Rapelyes and the Van Nests, and the Roosevelts and the Van Schaicks, maintained particularly intimate relationships, while the Bleeckers, Remsens, Quackenbosses, Bogerts, Wynkoops, Cornells, Motts, and Suydams intermarried among themselves and with leading English, Scottish, Flemish, and Huguenot families. Included in the latter were the Phoenixes, Ingrahams, Gardiners, Kortrights, Gouverneurs, Ogdens, Kembles, Ludlows, Aspinwalls, Haights, a variety of Lawrences, Leggetts, Whites, Lords, Jays, Thorns, Hoffmans, and Cuttings.

Brooklyn's colonial and Revolutionary elite also married within a confined social sphere. The ubiquitous Dutch gentry of Gowanus, Wallabout, Bedford, Cripplebush, and the neighboring villages had become a kind of extended clan, composed of myriad pairings of young Dutch men and women. A genealogical table tying together the old families of Flatbush and "Midwout" with the social ilk of their own and other towns would remind a student of European history of the Hapsburg marital connections. Such families as the Lotts, Van Brunts, Vanderbilts, Martenses, Rapelyes, Cortelyous, Bergens, Barkeloos, Schencks, Cornellisons, Van Sicklens, Ditmases, Van Nuyses, Vanderveers, Van Pelts, Strykers, Bro[u]wers, Bennets, Hegemans, Leffertses, Ryersons, Van Wycks, Bogerts, Gerritsons, Voorheeses, and Polhemuses followed the rule of endogamy.

In addition to the Philadelphia families mentioned earlier, the Walns, Shippens, Whartons, Rawles, Welshes, Mifflins, Balches, Tilghmans, Willings, Cadwaladers, Biddles, Penroses, Bartons, Callendars, Perots, and Morrises single-mindedly married with their own kind in colonial Philadelphia. In his study of a small group of Boston families for the period 1756–1844, Kenneth W. Porter observed that "in the Jackson-Lee-Cabot circle one does not encounter barefooted farm boys." Young merchants tended, not only to come from mercantile families, but "to marry the daughters or sisters of other merchants." [7]

What was true for the Cabots, Jacksons, and Lees was true for many other families in colonial and Revolutionary Boston. If, as was said, "the ramifications of Elizabeth Saltonstall's descendants would fill a book by itself," it was also noted that "no family surpassed the Gardiners in making proper marriages," their alliances embracing the Putnam, Crowninshield, Cabot, Pickering, Lowell, Peabody, and Derby families during the era. The Lowells were aligned with Higginsons, Russells, and Cabots; the Cabots with the Ornes, Putnams, and Higginsons; the Higginsons with the Cottons, Perkinses, and Codmans; the Putnams with the Lorings and Amorys; the Amorys with the Lymans and Coffins; the Lorings with the Curtises, Goddards, and Sigourneys; the Sigourneys with the Dexters and the Brimmers; the Brimmers with the Sohiers, the Greenes, and the Incheses; the Dexters with the Bradfords and the Wards; the Lymans with the Eliots; the Eliots with the Dwights of Springfield and the Ticknors; the Jacksons with the Quincys; the Quincys with the Adamses, Hancocks, and Phillipses; the Phillipses with too many to enumerate; and such esteemed families as the Pickerings, Searses, Swetts, Peabodys, Welleses, Grays, Otises, Masons, Parkmans, Tuckermans, Odins, and Dorrs—to name only a few—were also interwoven among the city's elite of blood. The Winthrops forged ties outside as well as within Boston, intermarrying with such eminences as the Bayards and Stuyvesants of New York City.

Less than exhaustive though it may be, the evidence indicates strongly that in the seventeenth and eighteenth centuries, elite families in the urban northeast sought to marry within their own charmed circle. The great question is whether the pattern changed during the so-called era of the common man. Were the marital choices made by the sons and daughters, the nephews and nieces of the rich, no longer dictated by considerations of wealth and prestige?

Antebellum Marital Patterns

The data on marriages during the "egalitarian era" are, of course, imperfect. A wealthy family that was childless—if treated as part of the statistical population whose marital behavior is scrutinized—would falsely skew the result in the direction of social democracy, since verily none of their (non-existent) offspring married well. A similar problem arises with the children of an elite family who never married. Church and public records, newspaper accounts, genealogies and family papers were examined closely. They disclose a great deal, but they do not account for every marital liaison made by every child of every rich family. Nor do the typically sparse accounts in these sources always reveal the status of a prominent person's spouse; this difficulty is compounded when the latter's surname is a common one and the social standing of his family can only be known through supplementary information which may not be available. All of these problems notwithstanding, it was possible to secure pertinent information on better than 90 per cent of the "richest of the rich"—those several hundred families worth at least $100,000 in the late 1820s and $250,000 two decades later. Data were also secured on more than half of the almost two thousand rich families in the great cities whose wealth fell just below these exalted figures. Since many of the greatest accumulators of the 1830s were old men whose own marriages —entered into in the late-eighteenth or early-nineteenth century—are not indicative of the marital patterns for the later period, attention was given not to their choices but to those of their children and next-generation relatives who married during the antebellum decades. What follows are generalizations and representative examples drawn from evidence on the majority of the wealthy families of antebellum Brooklyn, New York City, Philadelphia, and Boston.

Brooklyn

During the second quarter of the nineteenth century, wealthy families whose members entered into marriage did so almost without exception with partners whose own families possessed wealth or high standing or both. In the "era of the common man," as during the age of deference, the wealthy and eminent of Brooklyn sought marital partners of similar status from within Brooklyn's own elite or—as in the case of Henry Evelyn Pierrepont—from the even-more-prestigious elite of New York City. As befitted the charming son of Brooklyn's wealthiest man, Pierrepont married the granddaughter of the great John Jay. In the nineteenth century, as in the seventeenth and eighteenth centuries, Brooklyn's oldest families continued to act as though eligible marital partners might be found only within their own circle. A partial list of what might be called "Dutch patrician pairings" would include Judge John A. Lott and the daughter of his cousin Jeremiah Lott; Stephen Schenck and Maria Martense; Lucas J. Voorhees and Gertrude Suydam; John Lott Van Pelt and Anna Maria Cortelyou; Garret Co[u]wenhoven and Magdalen Van Nuyse; Theodore V. Bergen and Nettie Co[u]wenhoven; John C. Vanderveer and Elizabeth Van Brunt; Judge Garret L. Martense and Jane Vanderveer; Dr. Adrian Vanderveer and Elizabeth Lott; Rem Hegeman and Helen Wyckoff; Abraham D. Polhemus and Mary C. Gerritson; John Vanderbilt and Gertrude Lefferts; Garret Martense and Jane Ann Ditma[r]s; Teunis G. Bergen and Catherine Lott; Isaac Cornell and Maria Rapelye; Henry Boerum and Susan Rapelye; John Middagh and the sister of Losee Van Nostrand; and Samuel B. Sands and Magdalen Middagh.

Another pattern, in which relatively new wealth married the daughters of old family, is represented by the couplings of Tunis Joralemon's daughters with Samuel Smith, Thomas G. Talmadge—wholesale grocer and mayor of Brooklyn in 1845, whose first marriage had been to a

The "Rose" of Long Island (Julia Gardiner), 1840. A daughter of the wealthy Long Island family is shown modelling in front of a commercial establishment in New York City. (*From a colored lithograph by Alfred E. Baker. Photograph courtesy of the Museum of the City of New York.*)

daughter of Cornelius Van Brunt—and Parmenus Johnson; Joseph Sprague and Maria DeBevoise; Joshua March and Magdalen Middagh (the widow of Samuel B. Sands); William R. Gracie and Miss Middagh; James C. Brevoort and Elizabeth D. Lefferts; and the wealthy distiller James S. Clark and Evalina Hicks.

A pattern that appeared to owe at least as much to considerations of the marketplace as to expectations of romantic bliss paired wealth with wealth. Hezekiah Beers Pierrepont's most important step toward acquiring his large estates in New York State was to marry the daughter of their original owner, William Constable. Pierrepont's own daughters, Emily and Harriet Constable Pierrepont, were in turn coveted and won by the wealthy Joseph A. Perry and Edgar J. Bartow, while another daughter, Julia Evelyn Pierrepont, herself married a Constable. Other examples of marriage that may or may not have been made in heaven involved Henry C. Murphy and Amelia Greenwood; Robert Speir and Hannah Fleet; Benjamin W. Davis and Louisa Philip, daughter of the prosperous William Philip; and Philip's son, Frederick, and Julia Bach, the daughter of the wealthy distiller Robert Bach.

New York City

The onset of political democracy appeared to have no effect on the kind of family partners desired by New York City's oldest and most admired families. In the new era, as in the old, they bound themselves to families of distinction. Young Bayards continued to marry into great families such as the Schermerhorns, Schuylers, Beekmans, Verplancks, Winthrops, DeLanceys, Livingstons, Van Cortlandts, and Van Rensselaers, in addition to Cuttings, Rogerses, Campbells, Pintards, and Jays, whose eminence was more recently come by. Like the Bayards, the numerous Beekman clan maintained its liaisons with families representing old renown—such as the Bayards, DePeysters, Van Cortlandts, Livingstons, Gardiners, and Clintons—and also with the Bedlows, Keteltases, Milledolers, Lorillards, Foulkeses, Fishes, and Coxes—representing new. The family of General Mathew Clarkson continued to combine with members of the Lawrence, DePeyster, Cornell, Crolius, and their own Clarkson families, while also uniting with Jays, Goodhues, Denisons, Rutherfords, and Romaines. The general's own daughter went outside the city to marry John Ralston, an eminent lawyer-capitalist of Philadelphia. DePeysters married Van Cortlandts, Remsens, Clarksons, Beekmans, Livingstons, Wattses, and Schuylers—as they had in the old days—and Fields, Hamersleys, Goodhues, and Stevenses, in the new. Descendants of Lion Gardiner continued to unite with Beekmans and Van Wycks, with Diodatis and Thompsons, as well as with Kissams and Griswolds. The beautiful Julia Gardiner, daughter of David, married the tenth president of the United States, John Tyler, whose family—if not in the very first rank—held no mean place among Virginia's aristocracy.

Now, as before, Crugers married Schuylers, Van Rensselaers, DeLanceys, Kortrights, and Dyckmans, in addition to Churches, Glovers, Bards, Pells, Jaunceys, Whettens, Joneses, and Cuttings. The different branches of the great Lawrence family married Morrises, Suydams, Kips, Clarksons, Kanes, and Brinckerhoffs, as well as Whitneys, Ogdens, McVickars, Bownes, and Schieffelins. The Livingston genealogy became more tangled than ever as descendants of the family renewed old liaisons and created new with Van Rensselaers, De Peysters, Ludlows, Beekmans, Hamersleys, Van Hornes, and Van Wycks—on the one hand—and Sampsons, Rutherfords, McVickars, Cuttings, Delafields, Boggses, Murrays, Depaus, Bronsons, and Thompsons, on the other. The Morrises, great landholders of the Bronx, maintained their ties with Ludlows, Lawrences, Van Cortlandts, Gouverneurs, and Wattses, while developing particularly close bonds with the Rutherfords and Waltons. As befit members of a family which, while old, had achieved its greatest eminence in the new time, Schermerhorns married Suydams, Joneses, Van Cortlandts, and Bayards of the earlier elite, and Astors, Hones, and Costers, of the later. Probably no families surpassed the Van Rensselaers and the Stuyvesants in prestige. The children of the one, like those of the other, contracted marriages in the new style, combining venerable and relatively newer families among their choices. Van Rensselaers chose Schuylers, Kanes, Crugers, Livingstons, and Stuyvesants, as well as Whites, Kings, Rays, and Delafields. Nineteenth-century descendants of the governor of New Netherlands were sought after and won by members of the Livingston, Rutherford, Reade, Winthrop, Morris, and Van Horne families, as well as by Akerleys, Chesebroughs, Barclays, and Mildebergers.

Richly varied genealogical connections were swiftly woven in the new era by families whose great wealth, quite recently accumulated in some cases, made them a new aristocracy of sorts, invincibly attractive to prestigious partners whether of old family or new. William B. Astor, John Jacob's son, had married Margaret Armstrong, the daughter of General John Armstrong and Alida Livingston, while William's daughter Emily married Samuel Ward. Other Astor children during the era married into the Delano, Schermerhorn, Brevoort, Roosevelt, Van Allen, and Drayton families, while Dorothea Astor wed Walter Langdon, of a "prominent New Hampshire family." The Costers, an old family but new to great wealth, entered into liaisons with members of the DeLancey, Schermerhorn, and Cortelyou families, as well as with the Primes, Hosacks, Emmets, Laights, Boardmans, Depaus, Heckschers, and Wilkeses whose wealth and eminence were fresher. The popular John Delafield, who brought great wealth with him from England in the late eighteenth century and went on quickly to make a great deal more, rapidly earned a lofty place in the city's social ranking. Delafields were successfully courted by members of the Van Rensselaer, Livingston, Dubois, King, Prime, Bard, Tallmadge, Parish, and Bard families. Children and grandchildren of the Revolutionary figure, Rufus King, married Van Rensselaers, Joneses, Rogerses, Gracies, Duers, Wilkses, and Rays. Goelets married Kips, Ogdens, and the daughters of Thomas Buchanan, while Hannah Goelet, daughter of Peter P. Goelet, married Thomas Gerry, son of the Founding Father Elbridge Gerry. Relatives of Philip Hone, New York City's great diarist, onetime mayor, retired merchant, public-spirited activist, and social lion, married Heywards, Kneelands, Howlands, Van Schaicks, Anthons, Costers, and Schermerhorns, among others. The Jays, whose social attractiveness in the late eighteenth and early nineteenth centuries matched the distinction achieved by their most famous member, married with the Pierreponts—as has been noted—and with Clarksons, Rutherfords, Van Cortlandts, McVickars, and Kanes. The bride of the similarly named grandson of the great John Jay was Eleanor Kingsland Field described by George Templeton Strong in his diary as "ugly as sin." If this sour comment was accurate, perhaps the high standing of both branches of the bride's family was a compensation.

Great wealth rather than long renown appeared to attract James P. Kernochan, Nathaniel P. Bailey, J. Lawrence Kip, Thomas Ward, and Thomas Ronalds to young women of the Lorillard family, and Captain William A. Spencer—himself of a prestigious old family—first to Catherine and then to Eleanor Lorillard. Sons of the great tobacco merchants married into the families of John David Wolfe, Blazius Moore, Nathaniel Griswold, and the Beekmans and Livingstons. The great merchant Nathaniel Prime had married Cornelia Sands, daughter of the wealthy, esteemed, and venerable Comfort Sands. Primes subsequently aligned with Bards, Hoffmans, Delafields, Setons, Jays, and Costers. Rhinelanders married Joneses, Rogers, Lispenard Stewarts, Renwicks, and Oakleys, while members of the Rogers family paired with Winthrops, Suydams, Van Zandts, Bayards, Pendletons, Livingstons, Hoffmans, Woolseys, Kings, Morrises, Scofields, Wards, and above all, Gracies, in addition to Rhinelanders. Daughters of Alexander L. Stewart and Sarah Lispenard contracted marriages with the publisher James Watson Webb, Herman LeRoy, and John Skillman, while the Stewart sons married Louisa Salles and Mary Rogers Rhinelander, daughters both of extremely wealthy merchants.

Inasmuch as nearly every wealthy New York City family whose members married during the antebellum decades either consolidated or established ties with successful families, perhaps it is wisest to do no more at this point than allude to the fact. The varied prestigious alliances thus far described can be ascribed in part to the attractiveness, in part to the fecundity of the families in question. That the number of elite connections made by other leading families was smaller could have been due, in some cases, to their infertility, and, in others, to the particularly close (and exclusive) ties forged with only one or two families. Ingrahams married Phoenixes. Phoenixes married Rikers. Minturns married Bownes. Morrises married Rutherfords and Waltons. Crommelins married Verplancks. The children of New York City's successful families who married during the "era of the common man," married not at random but rather with their social and economic peers from within and outside the city.

Philadelphia

The evidence for Philadelphia and Boston points in the same direction. During the early decades of the nineteenth century, wealth and eminence married wealth and eminence. In Philadelphia, Dr. Rhea Barton —"a handsome man," we are told—won the daughter of the fabulously wealthy Jacob Ridgway of that city. Dr. William Barton married Esther Rittenhouse Sergeant, daughter of two great Philadelphia lines; while the daughter of Dr. John Rhea Barton married Edward Shippen Willing, bearer of two names even more honorific socially than her own. Emily Borie married Henry Bohlen. Biddles married Cadwaladers, Balches, and Binghams; Clymers, Franceses, Hares, Shippens, and Ralstons all married Willings. Camacs married Markoes. Chancellors married Whartons. Horace Binney's daughter married Judge John I. C. Hare. Sidney George Fisher—whose diary indicates he was socially esteemed if never quite as rich as he desired—married Elizabeth Ingersoll, while Rodney Fisher married a daughter of Thomas Cadwalader's (their child, in its turn, marrying Charles Godfrey Leland). The daughter of Joseph R. Evans married Samuel Welsh. Various Dundases combined with Pratts, Lippincotts, and McKeans, while Gratzes married Eltings and Hayses. Daughters of Alexander Henry married S. A. Alibone and the eminent auctioneer Silas E. Weir. Dr. Samuel G. Morton married Rebecca Pearsall of the prominent Quaker family. Lippincotts married Wetherills and Keenes, while Miss Lippincott wed Benjamin W. Richards, a mayor of Philadelphia during the era. The daughter of the great Dr. Philip Syng Physick married Dr. Jacob Randolph. McKeans united with Bories, Pettits, Ingersolls, and Wistars; Mifflins with Worrells and Whartons; Longstreths wih Parrishes and Prices; Leas with Careys; members of the Meigs family with Forsyths, Meades, and Ingersolls; Thomas Leiper's daughters with Dr. Robert Patterson and with Attorney General John K. Kane; Rawles with Tilghmans; Perots with Sansoms; Sansoms with Callenders, Biddles, Morrises (Philadelphia branch), and Vauxes; Richard Vaux with the daughter of Jacob Waln; Dr. James Rush with a daughter of John Ridgway; and John Welsh with the daughter of William Maris. If these Philadelphia alliances were not always between precise social equals, in no case did they involve a family of less than substantial wealth or prestige.

Boston

In Boston, as in New York City, families whose stay in America had been relatively brief but whose wealth was great, established intimate ties with the city's patriciate. The elite of the era appeared to be composed of families prominent for two centuries with others renowned not half as long, without stigmatizing the latter. When the editor of Boston's *"First Men"* distinguished between the city's select "two-year aristocracy" and its less exalted "yearling aristocracy," the chief difference he noted between the two was not the length of time their families had been here but rather their "relative standing in society" and their quality of refinement.[8] To judge from the manner in which marriages into a number of fairly-recently-arrived families were coveted, standing and refinement were considered to be categories not created by time alone.

The children and relatives of the great merchants and manufacturers William and Nathan Appleton were courted by Emily Warren, Henry Wadsworth Longfellow, the son of Sir James McKintosh, and the daughters of Jonathan Amory and Daniel Webster. Members of the Everett, Frothingham, and *the* Adams family sought out the daughters of Boston's richest man, Peter Chardon Brooks, while Elizabeth Boott and Mary Ann Phillips married his sons. In the new time as in the not-too-distant old, Cabots married Jacksons and Lees, as well as Higginsons and Kirklands (of the Harvard president's family). Jacksons continued to marry Cabots and Lees, Dr. James Jackson even marrying *two* Cabot girls, first Elizabeth and then Sarah. Other Jacksons married into the Lowell, Putnam, Minot, Boott families. The Lawrence family of manufacturing fame also aligned itself with eminences old and new. The "Miss Turnbull" of Baltimore who was wed by Samuel Lawrence during the period, may have been relatively obscure, but according to the discerning Philip Hone, she was "one of the loveliest women [he] ever saw." Other great merchant families whose children sought and were in turn sought after by the city's most prestigious elite were the Perkinses, Parkmans, Russells, Bradlees, Codmans, Coolidges, Searses, Sturgises, Francises, Masons, Grays, Parkers, Greenes, and Boardmans.

If the relatively recently arrived members of the Boston elite married into long established New England and Boston families, the children of the latter appeared to be no more socially democratic in their marital choices. During the "age of egalitarianism," young women of the great Amory family married Lorings, Sohiers, Dexters, Eckleys, Prescotts (Susannah marrying the great historian William Hickling Prescott), Codmans, Lowells, and Appletons, while male Amorys gave their name to wives of the Greene, Sargeant, Codman, and Sears families, with William Amory marrying Anna Sears, daughter of the redoubtable merchant,

David Sears. John Collins Warren married first a Mason and then a Winthrop—vast wealth followed by peerless rank—while other Warrens married Greenes, Appletons, Lymans, and Dwights. One son of Harrison Gray Otis married the wealthy Elizabeth Henderson Boardman; another, if he did not gain so rich a prize, nonetheless did admirably in marrying Emily Marshall, widely regarded as one of the great beauties of the age. George C. Crowninshield married Harriet, another daughter of the mighty David Sears, while Mary Crowninshield united with William Putnam Endicott. Sedgwicks married Dwights, Minots, Ellerys (of Rhode Island), while Codmans won Amorys, Russells, Lymans, and Sturgises. Putnams chose Endicotts, Cabots, Lowells, and Jacksons; while Dexters combined with Prescotts, Amorys, Mays, Apthorps, Parkers, Blakes, Minots, and Parkmans. Eliots married Lymans, Ticknors, Dwights, and Guilds. A daughter of Samuel A. Eliot married John Bray, a wealthy English-born merchant. Lowells aligned with Lowells, but also with Putnams, Russells, Duttons, Jacksons, and Amorys; while Lymans entwined with Pratts, Sturgises, Warrens, and Eliots. Endicotts chose Putnams, Crowninshields, and Gardners. Gardners chose Peabodys, while *Gardiners* won John P. Cushing, Caroline Perkins—daughter of the great merchant Thomas Handasyd Perkins—John Gray, and the daughter of William Tudor. Higginsons continued to marry Cabots as well as Channings and Lowells, while Hunnewells married Welleses and Lamsons.

Interurban Elite Marriages

Marriages uniting great families of different cities illustrate both the force of social considerations in the matrimonial choices made by the era's social and economic elite and the sometimes cosmopolitan character and attitudes of the best families. Lucius Manlius Sargent, one of the adornments of Boston's leisure class, married Mary Binney, a sister of Philadelphia's eminent lawyer and politician, Horace Binney. Joseph Coolidge, heir to a substantial merchant fortune of Boston, married Eleanora Randolph, granddaughter of Thomas Jefferson. Elias Hasket Derby of Boston married Eloise Strong, daughter of an eminent New Yorker and sister to that city's caustic diarist, George Templeton Strong. Mary Henderson, a "great beauty" of New York City, was won by Theodore Lyman the second. Grace A. Sedgwick, daughter of the early-nineteenth-century bearer of the illustrious New England name, Theodore Sedgwick, married the charming, versatile, and eminently suitable grandson of John Jacob Astor, Charles Astor Bristed. The Lawrence fortune made the sons of the great manufacturing family irresistible to young women of wealth and/or beauty from as far apart as New Hampshire and Maryland.

Philadelphia's Thomas Barton married the daughter of Edward Livingston. Robert Morris's son had married the daughter of John Kane—

the Kanes being a great New York family that in the nineteenth century had assumed a leading position in Philadelphia society. William Meredith of the Philadelphia elite wed Gertrude Gouverneur Ogden, whose name alone conveys her status, while Harriet, the daughter of Cadwalader Evans, married Gouverneur Ogden. Dr. Thomas Mütter, one of the Quaker City's most eminent physicians, married Mary Alsop of the distinguished Connecticut family. Another Philadelphia doctor, William Wetherill of the prominent mercantile family, married Mary Bloomfield, of the family of New Jersey's governor. William Ashhurst married Elizabeth Hone of New York City; while, as has been earlier noted, John Ralston, wealthy Philadelphia lawyer, married the daughter of the esteemed General Matthew Clarkson of New York. Other eminent Philadelphians who contracted prestigious marriages with New Yorkers were Horace Binney, Jr., and John Hare Powel.

As is already clear, children of New York City's merchant and professional elite were highly valued as marriage partners by leading families of other communities. In addition to the New York-Boston alliances mentioned above, a number of other ranking marriages were made between New Yorkers and New Englanders. Hannah Goelet married Thomas Gerry. William M. Johnson married Sarah Rice of a leading Boston family; Henry Marquand had chosen Elizabeth Love Allen, said to be of a "prominent Berkshire family;" while Dr. John W. Francis (whose professional standing was approximated in New York City perhaps only by David Hosack and Valentine Mott) had married Maria Cutler of Boston, a member of the family of General Francis Marion. Other New England marriages were made by Rufus Prime, who wed Augusta Palmer of Boston, Courtland Palmer, who won Elizabeth Thurston, daughter of the governor of Connecticut, James W. Gerard, who married Elizabeth Sumner of Boston, and the various New York City eminences who married into the Langdon family of New Hampshire: Dr. Edward Delafield, Benjamin W. Rogers, and Dorothea Astor.

Philip Hamilton, son of the first secretary of the treasury, had married Rebecca McLane, daughter of the eminent political figure, Louis McLane, while James Bogert, Jr. was of that number who also married into a prominent Philadelphia family. John William Hamersley, one of New York City's *ton*, married Catharine Hooker, whose family had vast real estate holdings around Poughkeepsie. Robert Bowne Minturn, in marrying the daughter of Judge John L. Wendell of Albany, was blessed with a young woman "noted for high intellect and personal charm," as well as prominent family. The marriage of Alice Colden of New York to Henry Izard of South Carolina was a North-South alliance of the purest social quality, as were the unions of a pride of Bayards to Fairfaxes and Washingtons in Virginia, Bowdoins and Winthrops in Massachusetts, and Willings in Pennsylvania. Given the reverential attitudes of many American fashionables toward European aristocracy, it is likely that few alliances contracted by New Yorkers evoked greater envy than the marriage of Helen Rutherford Watts to Archibald Russell, a child of the British nobility.

What a great social historian has said about the English peerage of the late Tudor and early Stuart period appears to apply too to the urban rich in antebellum America: "they mostly married among themselves."

Although God alone may know the precise motives of the elite in undertaking marriage, intrepid modern scholars have joined Jane Austen and Balzac in offering explanations. Their interpretations have typically—and sensibly—been quite realistic. According to the leading student of the Elizabethan and early Stuart aristocracy in England, to them, "essentially, marriage was not a personal union for the satisfaction of psychological and physiological needs; it was an institutional device to ensure the perpetuation of the family and its property. The greatest attention was therefore paid to the financial benefits of marriage." [9] By the nineteenth century, the English landed aristocracy continued to be "so linked by intermarriage that they have been likened to tribes." As for the motives of the English contemporaries of the American elite, they evidently had changed little: "social compatibility, adequate provision for children and for the bride should she chance to be widowed, the formation of desirable connections and the advancement of the family's standing were the important purposes served by matchmaking. Those who escaped from the toils and found spouses of humble birth served to emphasize the conventions through the comment which their mésalliances regularly excited." [10]

Modern American scholars have proffered similarly realistic evaluations of the motives of the American elite. To New England merchants, "marriage into another mercantile family was not only natural and advantageous to [their] own business, but also resulted in benefits extending into future generations." Marriage was ostensibly "based either upon previous business connections or membership in the same social or economic group." Another historian holds that in order to resist feared "social change [that] threatened stability," prominent Boston families "utilized an elaborate web of kinship ties which made the family a potent institution that gave them cohesion, continuity and stability so they might perpetuate their power, prominence and way of life." [11]

Whether fear was pervasive in Boston or elsewhere is debatable. Yet articulate contemporaries among the antebellum elite would have agreed that perpetuation of their way of life was indeed on the minds of young men and women of the fashionable set. As in Tudor and Stuart England, money appeared to be a vital consideration. To the aristocratic Englishman's expression of surprise that elegant Americans married for money as often as his own countrymen, John Jacob Astor's grandson had his American reply: "they don't marry for anything else." Commenting on

Lispenard Stewart's marriage to a daughter of Laurent Salles, June 4, 1834, Philip Hone reported that on this day Stewart had "married 2 or $300,000." Julia Gardiner's mother regularly admonished her daughters that unless a young woman had "a fortune in her own right," she should not "marry any man without means." [12]

Ah, but what if the young woman did have a fortune in her own right? To judge from the evidence, great fortunes were no less intent on marrying wealth than were lesser fortunes. The children of the rich, the exclusive, and the prestigious married—and I conclude that they sought to marry, as their relatives and parents sought to have them marry—into families possessed of wealth, eminence, and status fed by generations of renown and achievement. Yet it is also clear that wealthy young men took great pride in the beauty of their wives when in the fortunate position to do so. Remarks by Philip Hone, George Templeton Strong, Sidney George Fisher, as well as comments made by other contemporary chroniclers and genealogists about the marriages made by a number of the elite, indicate that many young people married for love. Sadly, their number can never be measured nor the degree of their passion proved.

Human beings are complicated. God knows what was on the mind of the wealthy New Yorker, Thomas W. Moore, who on the day of his wedding to Alida M. Bibby spent the evening at "the club where he played at whist until 10," to the chagrin of at least one of his friends.[13] My own view is that idiosyncratic factors—romantic love, physical passion, those assorted foolishnesses that compel one person to want another—combined with other, more politic considerations in the thinking and the feeling of the rich about marriage. The precise balance of these ingredients doubtless varied with each individual case. But it would be unrealistic as well as overly mechanical and doctrinaire to discount sentiment and the element of personal desire in these matters. According to a family tradition, Elizabeth Emlen Physick, wife of the great surgeon of Philadelphia, Philip Syng Physick, grew cold to her husband as she became attracted to his nephew, Dr. John Syng Dorsey, "a very handsome man" much younger than her husband. When Francis B. Cutting, in effect, stole the affections and broke up the marriage of Mrs. Hosack and her eminent husband, we can be fairly sure that utilitarianism and financial gain were not solely on his mind and certain that they were not on hers at all.

It is of interest, of course, that the fair game in this pursuit was a woman of eminence as well as beauty. Proper recognition of the roles of youthful independence and the emotions in the marital choices made by the elite hardly refutes the interpretation that swells sought to marry swells. They may have wanted them for a variety of reasons, but want them they did, as the evidence conclusively shows. For if the private and social worlds of the elite were confined almost entirely to their own sort, great ardor, if and when it erupted, would be great ardor felt for social equals. Even in the absence of other evidence, the record of marriages entered into by members of most of the wealthy and eminent families of Boston, Philadelphia, Brooklyn, and New York City indicates that the social world of the antebellum elite was a most exclusive one.

Notes

1 Abram C. Dayton, *Last Days of Knickerbocker Life in New York* (New York, 1882), p. 196.
2 Hodges, *Social Stratification: Class in America*, p. 79; Melvin M. Tumin, "Reply to Kingsley Davis," *American Sociological Review*, *5* (Dec. 1953), pp. 672–73.
3 S. M. Lipset and Hans L. Zetterberg, "A Theory of Social Mobility," in Bendix and Lipset, *Class, Status, and Power*, p. 565.
4 William J. Goode, "Family and Mobility," in *ibid.*, p. 582.
5 Hodges, *Social Stratification: Class in America*, pp. 124–25.
6 Carl Bridenbaugh, *Cities in the Wilderness: The First Centuries of Urban Life in America 1625–1742* (New York, 1938), p. 254; Frederick B. Tolles, *Meeting House and Counting House* (Chapel Hill, 1948), pp. 119-20.
7 Porter, *The Jacksons and the Lees: Two Generations of Massachusetts Merchants, 1765–1844* (Cambridge, Mass., 1937), I, p. 97.
8 *"Our First Men,"* pp. 5–7.
9 Lawrence Stone, *The Crisis of the Aristocracy, 1558–1641* (London, 1965), pp. 58, 613, 627. Working with a group of about a hundred, Stone was able to find out the social standing of every wife married by every peer from 1540 to 1659. The same kind of precision, alas, appears to be impossible for the many thousands of children and young relatives of the two thousand wealthiest families in the urban northeast.

Of course, to speak, as Stone does, of the *essential* purpose of an institution is to leave room for other, not-necessarily-insignificant, purposes.
10 F. M. L. Thompson, *English Landed Society*, pp. 17, 19.
11 Porter, *The Jacksons and the Lees*, I, pp. 95–97; and Paul Goodman, "Ethics and Enterprise: The Values of a Boston Elite, 1800–1860," *American Quarterly*, *XVIII* (Fall 1966), p. 437.
12 Bristed, *The Upper Ten Thousand*, p. 119; Hone Diary, *VIII*:233; Robert Seager, II, *And Tyler Too: A Biography of John and Julia Gardiner Tyler* (New York, 1963), p. 23.
13 Hone Diary, *VI*:166.

11
The Private World and the Social Circle of the Rich and Elite

> The most decisive characteristic of American society is its aristocracy; its downright exclusiveness. We Americans may say what we please, evade it, deny it, modify it, soften it, still it is true in all its force. I know of scarcely any country where the circles of society are more distinctively marked than in the United States, certainly not . . . in the continent of Europe.
>
> Undated manuscript by Nicholas Biddle

> 'Twill be a dance where you will meet just our own set—the most elite.
>
> Invitation sent by Lydia Kane to Philip Hone's son. Hone Diary, XI:241

This chapter traverses a tricky and largely unexplored terrain—the private world of the antebellum urban elite—in order to see who and what type of persons moved within it. Contemporaries had contrasting notions; some people, as we have seen, discerned a "cordial welcome by one class to another," while others detected rigid class barriers that divided the fashionables from their social inferiors. Such visitors as Francis Grund, Charles Murray, James Logan, Godfrey T. Vigne, and Tocqueville—as well as such disparate native observers as John Quincy Adams, Ralph Waldo Emerson, Nicholas Biddle, and James Fenimore Cooper—reported numerous examples of private exclusiveness practiced by the "better sort" in the nation's cities. The evidence, however, is not substantial, typically consisting of nothing more than an anecdote or two reported by an anonymous informant, while the instances recounted of social pretentiousness are often so ludicrous as to suggest that the described exclusiveness was practiced by the more parvenu or ridiculous of the elite rather than by its more sensible and solid members. The discussion that follows is based then on evidence that bears on the behavior, not of the shrill and the more stridently social-climbing, but of the most respected members of the urban social and economic elite.

Such evidence, while ample, is inevitably less than comprehensive. For we are dealing here with private matters. Who recorded and how could later scholars hope to know the number of social calls made by the thousands of members of the several hundred wealthiest or most prominent families in each of the great northeastern cities? Or the persons present and the relative standing of each individual in the judgment of every other individual on these occasions? I fear that the private lives of a social group do not lend themselves to quantitative analysis. For all its incompleteness, however, much valuable contemporary evidence is available, which goes well beyond the random incident that has often served as the basis of earlier discussions of antebellum class and lifestyle. Some individuals kept records; above all Philip Hone.

A monument should be built by social historians to honor that marvelous man, not for his political or economic successes, interesting as these were, but for that unbelievably detailed diary he kept, whose treasures are barely hinted at in the excerpts published to date.[1] Hone gives detailed descriptions of social visits, dinner parties, excursions to the country, summer holidays, winter sleigh rides, fancy balls, weddings, funerals, restaurant meals, fishing trips, boat rides, "cultural evenings," and informal parties. Perhaps better than any other source, the diary reveals not only the lifestyle of the urban elite but precisely which individuals participated in shaping it. Our knowledge of the wealth of these persons—drawn from the manuscript tax assessments—and of their eminence—known from varied genealogical and contemporary data—enables us to determine both the status of the individuals who occupy Hone's universe and the extent to which their more informal activities were apparently guided by ideals of social exclusiveness.

A contemporary sociologist has observed of the social world of our own time that "status considerations play a [very great] part . . . in the formation of informal social ties. Close friends and clique mates are likelier to share equivalent social-class rank than Rotarians or Elks for a basic reason: they are likelier to share common values and mutual experiences which facilitate and encourage social intimacy."[2] The discussion that follows tests the validity of this hypothesis for the "era of the common man." What kind of persons were sought out by the urban rich in their leisure hours? What social values were reflected in their choice of intimates?

Social Clubs

A "rage for association" was widely noted in antebellum America. It has been remarked that, then as later, "Americans were a nation of joiners."[3] Rich or upper-class Americans clearly exhibited this national habit, joining or creating clubs and societies in great numbers. These organizations took two forms. One type of association, concerned with significant public issues and problems, is perhaps most revealing of the influence and values of the elite and will be considered in the next chapter. The other type, organized in newer western cities[4] as well as in older northeastern ones, was typically a social club, offering the well-to-do the opportunity to spend their leisure hours agreeably, while affording the student of their behavior a glimpse into the kind of persons they sought to surround themselves with on what might be called the more formal or organized level of social intercourse.

Philadelphia

E. Digby Baltzell has written a discerning analysis of the significance of social clubs to the upper class families of modern Philadelphia. He concludes unequivocally that "the primary function of the [modern] Philadelphia and Rittenhouse clubs is the ascription of upper-class status." The latter organization was founded in 1875 and thus does not concern us at the moment. The Philadelphia Club, however, was a child of the "egalitarian era" and is described by Baltzell as a "Proper Philadelphia stronghold since its founding in 1834."[5] For purposes of this study, the first dozen years of the Philadelphia Club are of particular interest.

According to its anonymous historian, the club grew out of an informal organization of "a number of gentlemen [who since 1830 had been] in the habit of meeting to play cards" at a coffee house in the elite residential district. On March 21, 1834, members of the Adelphi or Philadelphia Club held the "first recorded meeting for the purpose of organizing and adopting a constitution and by-laws." These documents were drawn up primarily to achieve strict social exclusiveness. Membership was never to exceed five hundred; "entrance money" of $200 and annual dues for the same amount were designed to assure that the select five hundred would be the rich five hundred.

The founders of the Philadelphia Club were such luminaries as Henry Bohlen, Edward Shippen Burd, Henry Chancellor, George Cadwalader, Henry Pratt McKean, Henry Ralston, Joseph Peter Norris, William Camac, Joseph R. Ingersoll, George Mifflin Dallas, and Commodore James Biddle. In 1846 83 per cent of its 160 members could be found in the anonymous listing of wealthy Philadelphians published in that year (exclusive of such eminent members as James Hopkinson, James Markoe, and William Shippen, whose names were missing from the imperfect ranking of the opulent). It seems safe to conclude that the chief purpose of the Philadelphia Club was indeed to ascribe status to its select members. After noting that it finally got around to creating a small library only after the club had been in existence for thirteen years, the club's historian drily reports that at the very same time one of its illustrious members "used to perform the uncommon feat of drinking a glass of madeira while standing on his head."[6] Who but a member of the elite could have been expected to know the proper way to appreciate fine wine?

Smaller and more informal associations also attracted the Philadelphia elite during the period. Samuel Breck's unevenly kept diary records Breck's initiation in 1837 into a "Walking Club," whose thirteen members included three Whartons, John R. Coates, Jacob S. Waln, George Rundle, and Condy Raguet. According to Breck, these were mainly "old codgers, who, to use the French phrase, *se promenant en voiture*—that is to say, take their walks in a carriage." Twice a year the club's members were required to walk two miles to a tavern and to return on foot. That the company they kept was evidently more important to the members than the club's ostensible purpose is suggested by the fact that they took carriages "out and home" on these festive occasions.[7]

In the same period, men of affairs joined Philadelphia's "literary and scientific men" of the Philosophical Society in weekly soirées or Wistar Parties, named after the eminent Dr. Caspar Wistar, the initiator of these evening assemblages. During the 1830s and 1840s, meetings were held at members' houses every Saturday evening from October to April. At these gatherings, "strangers suited for genteel company" were "introduced to most of the leading men in the city." Members represented the great families of the city, including such eminences as William Meredith, John Sergeant, Samuel Breck, Joseph Hopkinson, William Shippen, Chief Justice William Tilghman, Peter Duponceau, Nicholas Biddle, Drs. Benjamin Rush, Robert M. Patterson, Charles Meigs, Franklin Bache, Nathaniel Chapman, Robert Hare, Adam Kuhn, Isaac Lea, Horace Binney, Mathew and Henry Carey, Roberts Vaux, and William Rawle. Invited to partake of the party's sumptuous meals and sparkling conversation were such renowned figures as William Thackeray, Baron Von Humboldt, John Quincy Adams, James Madison, and the admired Dr. John W. Francis of New York City.[8]

Boston

Boston had few social clubs before the Civil War, perhaps because of the unique "reserve [that characterized] the social life of Boston," and "a clannishness of family."[9] Persons of the "highest respectability" did form the Temple Club in 1829, an organization "fashioned closely after the high-grade London clubs, even to the custom of members keeping their hats on." Its earliest presidents included such men as George T. Bigelow and John T. Coolidge. The club persisted, although under a variety of names—becoming the Tremont Club in the 1840s and the Somerset Club before mid-century. The Somerset Club has been described as the "swell" of Boston clubs, "drawing in the young bloods and more mature votaries of fashion." The original 41 founders included such elite members as William, James S., and Thomas C. Amory, Jr., Edward A., Francis B., and George C. Crowninshield, George T. and Joseph Lyman, Jr., John Bryant, Jr., Fred R. and David Sears, Jr., Richard

S. Fay, S. G. Ward, C. J. Higginson, John Lothrop and Edward Motley, Jr. Each member agreed to pay "the sum of one hundred dollars . . . to be invested in furniture and stock for the proposed club." According to the modern historians of the Somerset Club, its founders had no wish that it undertake any loftier objective than providing good food and drink and the pleasure of companionship to "individuals mutually congenial." [10] As the roster of the club's earliest membership indicates, the organizers found the necessary qualities of companionship in themselves and in such others as John T. and Joseph Coolidge, Thomas B. Curtis, John L. Gardner, Samuel Hammond, Horatio H. Hunnewell, Abbott Lawrence, Francis C. Loring, Francis C. Lowell, George F. Parkman, Enoch Train, and William Hickling Prescott, the great historian.

In 1846, Dr. John Collins Warren, a man whose great wealth barely approximated his lofty scientific reputation and social standing, founded the Thursday Evening Club; it was modelled after the Wednesday Evening Club, a prestigious dining club founded in 1777. Consisting only of "congenial gentlemen," the new association combined tasteful suppers, fine wines, and good talk of the most varied nature.

New York

New York City had more social clubs during the era than did its great urban rivals. Some of these associations were dedicated to nothing more than assuring greater exclusivity to their elite memberships in their leisure-hour activities. Other societies, although stressing broad public or artistic or scientific purposes, appeared actually to be more concerned with offering their socially prominent members the twin assurances of exclusiveness and enhanced status. Such a group was the Bread and Cheese Club, founded in 1824; its diverse membership included James Fenimore Cooper, William and John Duer, Gulian C. Verplanck, Charles A. Davis, and Philip Hone. Another was "The Club," a most exclusive organization created a few years later to "bring more frequently into contact" such men as Peter A. Jay, Chancellor James Kent, Jonathan Goodhue, Albert Gallatin, and Professors John McVickar and Clement C. Moore of Columbia College, for good talk and a "light repast" once a week. A similar organization was the Kent Club, a "club of lawyers," which took its name from Chancellor Kent. The group was founded in 1838 by Kent and such other leaders of the bar as Chief Justice Samuel Jones, Francis B. Cutting, Thomas Oakley, Ogden Hoffman, John Anthon, John Duer, and the much-sought-after Peter A. Jay. The club did not confine itself to lawyers, since Hone more than once had a "jovial time" at meetings that included such other prominent non-lawyers as James Watson Webb, Dr. John W. Francis, and Charles King.[11] Larger, better organized, and altogether more imposing were the St. Nicholas Society, organized in 1835, and the Century Club, founded in 1847.

On February 28, 1835, Hone reported that the "new society of St.

Nicholas met this evening at Washington Hall and elected their officers," the crême de la crême of Knickerbocker society. Joining Peter G. Stuyvesant, President, Abraham Bloodgood and Peter Schermerhorn, Vice-presidents, Hamilton Fish, Secretary, and John Oothout, Treasurer, were the major literary lion—Washington Irving—and the minor one—Gulian C. Verplanck—as second and third vice-presidents respectively. William A. Lawrence was chosen assistant secretary, while Drs. John W. Francis, Edward G. Ludlow, and William H. Hobart were appointed physicians. A lofty purpose cited in the society's charter was the collection and preservation of information respecting the "history, settlement, manners and other matters as may relate thereto of [the] city of New York." Another stated purpose of the Society was "to promote social intercourse among [New York City's] natives." It would have been more accurate had the Society promised to promote social intercourse among *some* of the city's natives. As for the very first of the listed purposes—"to afford pecuniary relief to indigent or reduced members and their widows and children"—there was little ground for concern that the treasury would be depleted, in view of the wealth and ranking of the membership.[12] Nor was the emergence of such a membership in any sense uncontrived.

To qualify for one of the five hundred places in the St. Nicholas Society, a man had to be of "respectable standing in society," while he or his family had to have been residents of New York City or New York State prior to 1785. The society's roster prior to 1850 reads like a list of New York City's wealthiest and most eminent families. The slate of officers one decade after its founding included James R. Manley, Peter Schermerhorn, William J. Van Wagenan, Abraham R. Lawrence, Ogden Hoffman, and Frederick DePeyster, a group in no sense the social inferiors of the original executives. Other men who served as officers prior to mid-century included Cornelius Heyer, Samuel Jones, Abel T. Anderson, George Rapelye, James F. DePeyster Ogden, John Alsop King, Hamilton Fish, James H. Kip, F. C. Winthrop, Jacob Harsen, C. Westervelt, Robert and Egbert Benson, John B. Schmelzel, Abraham R. Wyckoff, and Anthony J. Bleecker. Close to one-third of the St. Nicholas Society's membership in 1849 were among the "richest of the rich" New Yorkers and as large a proportion again were of families that either were among the wealthiest one thousand in the city or slightly below in wealth.[13] Across the river, descendants of colonial and early Dutch families organized their own St. Nicholas Society, to "promote social intercourse" among families of distinction in Brooklyn and Long Island. By mid-century this branch included Martenses, Kissams, Sandses, Polhemuses, Leffertses, Van Brunts, Bergens, Suydams, Spaders, Robbinses, Hegemans, Debevoises, Gerritsons, Vanderveers, Strykers, Boerums, Barkeloos, Van Antwerps, Voorheeses, and others who belonged to the upper crust of what was then known as Long Island.

The Century Club was even more restrictive, for its name signified a membership that in 1847—the year of its founding—was less than 100. Meeting at first in the rotunda of the New York Gallery of Fine Arts, this association's twin objects were "the cultivation of a taste for letters and the arts" and the promotion of social intercourse among its members. These were luminaries from the world of arts and letters and the world of commerce and finance. The former were represented by the ubiquitous Verplanck, John G. Chapman, and William Cullen Bryant, among others. Men of affairs included Thomas Addis Emmet, Jonathan Sturgis, Eleazer Parmley, Ogden Haggerty, Charles M. Leupp, David C. Colden, and others whose creativity was less apparent than their wealth.

No matter what formal purposes were adopted by these societies of New York City, it is clear that one of their most significant objectives was to provide men of wealth and distinction a social outlet largely confined to others of similar standing. Another sort of social club was created with no purpose but the latter in mind. Two weeks before he attended the first meeting of the St. Nicholas Society, Hone met with others "with a design to form a regular Knickerbocker society as a sort of setoff against St. Patrick's, St. George's, and more particularly, the New England Society."[14] He anticipated nothing to come of it but a few ceremonial dinners attended by his companions at the first meeting: Rapelyes, Stuyvesants, Laights, Fishes, Irvings, Moores, Renwicks (the latter two representing the Columbia contingent) Wilkeses, Schermerhorns, Brinckerhoffs, Costers, Wyckoffs, and himself.

One of the most exclusive of the city's social clubs was named after the diarist himself: the Hone Club. This loosely structured organization met for the first time on October 22, 1838, at the home of John Ward on Bond Street, where it was agreed that the membership should be confined to an even dozen. The original roster makes clear the cosmopolitanism of the group, since several of the initiators were not native New Yorkers. In addition to Hone and Ward, they included Simeon Draper, Moses H. Grinnell, William G. Ward, John Crumby, Rosewell A. Colt, Edward R. Biddle, Jonathan Prescott Hall, R. M. Blatchford, Charles H. Russell, and James W. Otis. Agreeing to dine every two weeks at one another's homes, each host was "allowed to invite four gentlemen not members." Among the distinguished guests were Daniel Webster, William Seward, Edward Curtis, Paul Spofford, James Watson Webb, and Dr. John W. Francis. Francis spoke at least partial truth when he later described the membership of the Hone Club as representative of the "wealth and intellect of the city." A wrong impression can easily be gotten from Francis's description of the various highminded topics the group discussed or from the comment made by a nineteenth-century historian that "it was a club of Whig tendencies."[15] As we have recently been reminded, the urban rich were almost invariably Whigs.[16] What appeared to inspire the Hone Club was neither national political considerations nor intellectual or moral uplift.

The chief item on the agenda of the Hone Club's first meeting sought an answer to the classic question: what's for supper? A consensus was achieved; meals were to be selected from soup, fish, oysters, four dishes of meat, with desserts of fruit and ice cream. Fine wines were also permissible. In fact, punishment for an unexcused absence was a basket of champagne. And singing, loud if not boisterous, was stipulated. Outsiders might speak of the club's exalted tone. Not Hone. Describing a meeting held almost ten years after the club's formation, Hone reports that after a fine meal the company "had more than the usual quantity of unrestrained gaiety, unalloyed wit, unrepressible noise, and unsurpassable wine." According to a guest, "their festivals were of the highest order of gustatory enjoyment—the appetite could ask no more—and a Devonshire Duke might have been astounded at the amplitude of entertainment." [17] The club ceased to exist when Hone died in 1851, an event that, if it did not mark the end of an era, did mark the passing of a signal presence.

Other informal status-conscious associations also flourished in the 1840s. According to one account, "on the 30th of July [1844] the following gentlemen met on board the schooner *Gimcrack* for the purpose [of forming the New York Yacht Club]: John C. Stevens, Hamilton Wilkes, William Edgar, John C. Jay, George L. Schuyler, Louis A. P. Depau, George B. Rollins, James M. Waterbury, and James Rogers." [18] Most of these men were known to possess great wealth and eminence; it can be assumed that in this instance the relative unknowns also met the stiff test that legend insists J. Pierrepont Morgan later put to all potential yacht owners (if they had to be concerned about the price of a yacht, it was beyond their means). One is surprised not to find Hone on the list since his family met the qualification. Perhaps his failing health accounts for the absence of the dear fellow. He had also evidently convinced himself that he was no club man: how could a sensible man who enjoyed the comforts of a snug home be lured by such attractions? In 1846, nevertheless, Hone is pleased to have "been admitted a member of the Racket Court, and made [his] first appearance . . . in their splendid new clubhouse on Broadway." [19]

The most formal, by far the largest, and probably the most influential and significant of the purely social clubs in New York City during the period was the Union Club. Modelled after the clubs of London, which, in Hone's words, gave a "tone and character to the society of the British metropolis," the Union Club was created by members of New York City's oldest and wealthiest families. On June 30, 1836, a circular letter signed by Samuel Jones, Thomas J. Oakley, William Beach Lawrence, Charles King, G. M. Wilkins, Frederick Sheldon, J. DePeyster Ogden, Ogden Hoffman, and, of course, Philip Hone, among others, was sent to "gentlemen of social distinction, inviting them to become members." Seeking 250 members at first and no more than 400 thereafter, the club's early failure to attract even 200 encouraged prophets of gloom, who ridiculed the high prices of its fare and predicted the failure of an organization ostensibly anithetical to the character of so "joyous, natural, independent a city as New York."[20] The skeptics underestimated the force and durability of the elite's desire for new ways of demonstrating status. And what ways were more admirable than the ways of England's older and more prestigious urban aristocracy?

The original charter put on no airs about the club's essential purpose. It was to "promote social intercourse among its [elite] members," by affording them "the convenience and advantages of a well-kept hotel . . . combining elegance and comfort." An entrance fee of $100 was designed to assure that the United States citizens or longtime residents who qualified for membership were persons of the proper social complexion. The headquarters of the club were in a fashionable part of town, outfitted with expensive furniture, servants, and a "*recherché chef de cuisine*," capable of preparing peerless meals. Bachelors, out-of-town visitors, "men about town," could sleep in the club's ample quarters. In addition, the club offered chess, whist, billiards, two annual meetings, and above all the status derived from membership in its 400. A list of its officers and members prior to Hone's death was a roll of New York City's social and economic leadership. Families eminent in Peter Stuyvesant's day combined with wealth and renown more recently come by to provide what a nineteenth-century historian described as "great social coherence and more of that distinction which is peculiar to the leading London associations" than any other club in the country.[21] The Union Club was the social organization of Livingstons, Crugers, *the* Long Island Joneses, Schuylers, Lawrences, Kortrights, Lows, Coldens, LeRoys, Pendletons, Chaunceys, Deforests, Constables, Cuttings, DeRhams, Emmets, Grinnells, Hamersleys, Hamiltons, Hoffmans, Howlands, Hoyts, Kanes, Laights, Masons, Ludlows, Schermerhorns, Primes, Ogdens, Van Wagenans, Suydams, Strongs, Stuyvesants, and dozens of others who belonged to the New York City elite.

Neither the size of the memberships nor the significance of the social clubs should be overestimated. Most rich men appeared *not* to belong to them. Their activities were few, confined largely to providing a limited number of tangible benefits and harder-to-evaluate intangible or spiritual benefits to their members. They are nevertheless of great interest to students of social history, if less for what they did than for what they signify. Their not insubstantial elite memberships indicate that many men of eminence were eager to proclaim their status, to identify it to peers and inferiors as dramatically as possible. Organized gourmet dining and dilettante discussions confined to men of "social distinction" represented an interesting attempt by successful men of affairs to create the lifestyle of an aristocracy in a society that lacked such a group in a formal or official sense. New York City's flourishing club life was interpreted by some contemporaries, particularly caustic Bostonians, as indirect testimony to the parvenu character of the Knickerbocker elite. The latter allegedly sought status in alliances with their peers, lacking as they were in the self-assurance that was said to characterize the leading men of the New England city. And yet, many New York clubmen were of prestigious seventeenth-century families; it seems likely that gregariousness rather than insecurity explained their participation. What appears to be least in doubt is that social clubs, consisting as they did almost entirely of the social and economic elite of the great northeastern cities, provided their members a recognizable status in a society lacking in official emblems of social hierarchy.

Informal Social Relationships

An even more significant clue to the social mind of the rich, if much harder to trace than club memberships, were their intimate social relationships. For not everyone belonged to clubs; yet all but the most misanthropic persons had social intercourse with others. The great difficulty is in identifying the vast number of private associations and the wealth or standing of the parties to them. A comprehensive or perfect performance of this task is manifestly impossible. Who on earth would record each social contact he made? If someone did, how can we discover the relative ranking of each member of his social universe? And if the latter feat were somehow possible, by what unique calculus would we determine the relative rank of persons of dissimilar status in the minds of their beholders? Although Philip Hone's diary, amazingly enough, permits partial responses to these unanswerable questions, it was, after all, the record of one atypical man. But no other individual was more typical of his class. Hone's account, as well as those of other private journals, disclose the social character of the persons who moved within the private world of the keepers of the journals. They also provide revealing, sometimes rather full, glimpses into the range of contacts maintained by hundreds of other individuals who were close to the diarist and therefore of great interest to him, subjects of his detailed reports. When these accounts are supplemented by impressionistic or random contemporary reports, a solid, if imperfect, basis is created for determining the extent to which considerations of class or social status influenced the private lives of the urban elite during the antebellum period.

According to Sidney George Fisher, writing in 1837, the "best Philadelphia society" contained "few whose families [had] not held the same station for several generations." Fortunate consequences of this continuity were "an air of refinement, of gaiety, and simplicity of manner," ostensibly lacking in New York City, and also a "great degree of intimacy among the different families who comprise[d] our [Philadelphia] society, as their fathers and grandfathers knew each other and associated together in former years and they themselves have probably been playmates and gone to the same school." Fisher could speak with authority as his own family moved in a circle that enclosed many of Philadelphia's leading lineages. His own life provided ample documentation that intimacy begun in childhood continued as elite Philadelphians came of age in the 1830s. He was no doubt right too in asserting that wealth was not the only passport to the best Philadelphia society, "nor want of it a reason for exclusion." And yet the brilliant array whose company he kept, whose homes he visited, whose presence added luster to the balls and parties he attended, typically combined matchless social standing with inordinate wealth.[22]

Over the course of only two months, December 1836, and January 1837, Fisher attended a number of parties in Philadelphia, recording the names of hosts and guests. The list was composed of Biddles, Walns, Willings, Pettits, Dallases, Kuhns, Ingersolls, Reades, Hares, Gilpins, Harrisons, Whartons, Cadwaladers, Norrises, Ridgways, Logans, Rushes, Cassatts, Camacs, Binneys, Chapmans, Markoes, Mifflins, Mütters, Coxes, Eyres, Wistars, Sergeants, Hopkinsons, and Merediths—the upper stratum of Philadelphia society, and wealth. Through his pages run the names of his regular companions, Pierce Butler, and members of the Bache, Clymer, Middleton, Chapman, Burd, Roberts, and Meredith families. According to an informed contemporary, the wealthy Philadelphia merchant, John Jordan, had a small circle of "intimate associates"; prominent among them were Paul Beck, Jacob Ridgway, John Welsh, Stephen Girard, the Willings, and the Latimers, "nearly all of whom were regular visitors to Jordan's house or store." A fellow merchant, Alexander Emslie, was similarly the center of a small social circle confined to men prominent in mercantile affairs. Even this fragmentary data on social exclusiveness explains why Sir Henry Singer Keating, an English visitor to Philadelphia during the era, believed that "a strong aristocratic feeling pervade[d] the wealthy part of the community." [23] They displayed it by traveling in a prescribed social orbit.

Boston's elite sought out one another in a number of prestigious private homes. To the residence of Thomas Handasyd Perkins, Jr., for example, came Harrison Gray Otis, Samuel Appleton, Thomas L. Winthrop, Daniel Webster, Nathaniel Amory, Francis Codman, Augustus Thorndike, Major Jonathan Russell, Edward Everett, Lothrop Motley, and others of like renown from in and out of the city. Mrs. George Ticknor was likely to attract, in addition to Boston's mercantile elite, "the nobility and scholars of Europe," as well as American artists, scientists, and men of letters.[24]

The pages of Hone's diary are filled with references to the exclusiveness of New York City's elite. They spent their summers at expensive resorts and regularly traveled to Europe with parties of social

Fancy Dress Ball in Philadelphia, 1850. This type of event was often attended by Philadelphia's elite. (*Lithograph by C. Harnisch courtesy of the Historical Society of Pennsylvania.*)

equals, secure that such vacations were beyond the means of lesser folk. Daytime activities consisted of nothing more elaborate than "a fishing excursion on a schooner from Jamaica Bay," which would typically be taken by small parties that might include Hone, his sons John and Robert, David S. Jones, one or another Schermerhorn, and young women of the Bayard, Ray, Glover, Lockwood, or Kane families.[25] Elite society glowed even more brightly by night.

Soirées were all the rage in the 1830s. These were musical evenings to which a Dr. John Cheesman, a Mrs. Bored, a Harriet Douglas—"the American Madame de Stael," according to Hone—would invite a "small circle of friends" to their home. Social unknowns do not appear to have cracked these charmed circles. Hone regularly invited sixty to eighty of his friends to his ample home on Broadway near City Hall Park for his *tableaux vivants.* On these uplifting evenings, "beautiful ladies" and eminent men would costume themselves against elaborate backdrops and settings as a "highland chief," or "Madonna," or "Lady Jane Grey," while groups would represent a "scene from *Waverley*," "the dull lecture," or "Cato's death." A late supper, breaking off at midnight, would follow. Present at these rituals would be the William A. Duers, the Abraham Ogdens, the Edward R. Joneses, the John G. Costers, various Schermerhorns, Washington Irving, Dr. David Hosack, and others like them. Hosack himself presided over regular Saturday evening salons that were regarded by many contemporaries as the city's chief intellectual as well as social adornment.

Elaborate parties and balls added zest to the social season. Although usually called for the evening hours, occasionally a truly splendid affair would commence early in the day and continue until after dark. Such was the "*fête champêtre*" held at Thomas W. Ludlow's villa at Phillipsburg, on the Hudson, to which perhaps several hundred members of New York City's business, professional, and artistic elite came by private steamer for a day of eating, drinking, dancing, and general merriment. Doubtless adding to the charm of the affair was the satisfying knowledge that its delights were shared exclusively by the fashionables.

The same restrictive rule appeared to govern evening balls and parties, whether large or small, formal or informal. At a "fancy ball" in August 1830, the "large and brilliant party" given by the Waddingtons in November 1830, or the ball at the DeRhams, the following February, Hone rubbed shoulders with the same individuals or social types. The first of these occasions was graced by Mrs. Isaac Jones, the daughters of Lyman Denison and John Mason, Sarah Livingston, Harriet Kane, "Mr. Van Zandt," Myndert Van Schaick, John Mason, William Whetton, John C. Hamilton, Mr. and Mrs. John Coster, and Hone himself. An invitation to Mrs. Gouverneur to attend a dance sponsored by the New York Assembly in 1841 was signed by the twelve "managers": Abraham Schermerhorn, Edward Pendleton, James W.

Otis, William Douglas, Henry Delafield, Henry W. Hicks, J. Swift Livingston, Jacob R. LeRoy, Thomas W. Ludlow, Charles McEver, Jr., William S. Miller, and Charles C. King, younger members all of the city's economic and social elite. The "Boz Ball," held in honor of Charles Dickens that same year, was arranged by such gentlemen as Hone, Dr. Valentine Mott, Dr. John W. Francis, Dr. John Cheesman, Hamilton Fish, Henry Brevoort, Moses H. Grinnell, Churchill C. Cambreleng, William H. Appleton, and David C. Colden. Ticket purchasers were "strictly scrutinized" to assure that "the company might be perfectly select and unexceptionable." Evidently, the elite had no difficulty in recognizing one another or in recognizing the proper qualities in strangers. The masked ball given by Henry Brevoort the year before was an affair of such extravagant opulence and exclusiveness that even some swells were embarrassed by it. The round of elaborate parties triggered by the marriage of Charles Augustus Heckscher to the daughter of John G. Coster in 1834 had dismayed even Hone, an inveterate partygoer, by their costliness. The diarist, like the highminded John Pintard a few years earlier, bemoaned the excess of champagne, of fine foods, and of vulgar entertainments and people at these affairs. Hone's idea, however, was not to put an end to these rarified gatherings but only to organize them more intelligently, so that elderly folk and the middle-aged might breathe more freely at what were in danger of becoming "heterogeneous assemblages."[26]

Dinner Parties

The dinner party emerges from the pages of Philip Hone's diary as one of the most fascinating of elite institutions. While the old gentleman had a great zest for fine cuisine, he had at least as much interest in the companions he shared it with. I have elsewhere noted that many contemporaries—natives and foreign visitors alike—ridiculed American table habits and were offended, above all, by the coarse quality of the admittedly ample portions that were acceptable here, the speed with which Americans "pitchforked" their food down, and the absence of any semblance of charm or small talk at meals—if indeed an American ever ate with social companions.[27] Hone's circle was guiltless of these charges, believing, as did the ancients, that one could *dine* only in the company of pleasant companions.

Hone was intensely concerned with the attractiveness and amiability of his table mates, in part, at least, because good food, fine wine, and enjoyable dining meant a great deal to him. He was delighted that after first experiencing disappointment with the fare at the highly touted Delmonico's, a return visit in 1837 rewarded him with a "capital dinner of cuisine." He was by no means an uncritical gourmet. Dining out later that year with a large party at a club known for its *haute cuisine,* he reports: "the dinner was execrable, for a French *artiste de cuisine* knows nothing about turtle." Fortunately, the punch and wine were good, if not superb. On March 2, 1839, he invited Robert Ray, Dr. Hugh McLean, Charles March, James DePeyster Ogden, Jacob Giraud, Hamilton Wilkes, and Moses H. Grinnell—elite New Yorkers all—to a dinner called primarily "to taste some wine which was sent by Col. Hunter of Savannah as a sample of the fine madeira of Georgia." The bottle was disappointing, but happily one of the host's own stock saved the day, a sequence Hone "didn't wonder at." If the edibles were satisfactory, his enthusiasm could be boundless. At a small dinner he attended in the company of Dr. Wainwright, John Alsop King, and his friend Richard Ray, he exulted, "we drank some of the finest wine in America," while he regularly praised the "sumptuous dinners" presented by the great merchant Nathaniel Prime. Yet his interest extended beyond the table, his assessment of the relative success of a dinner depending as much on its social as on its gastronomic ingredients.

"A great variety of [Jacob] Giraud's fine wine," helped make a dinner party at Hone's old friend's a success on the night of May 9, 1834, but so did the "good talk" and a conviviality that induced the guests to stay till midnight. On another occasion, his friend Dominick Lynch, social and cultural lion, provided "an exceedingly pleasant dinner party, a great deal of good talking, some fine songs from Lynch, a pretty liberal consumption of wine, and nearly the whole of the party sat until half past twelve." The "party" contained no unknowns, but rather Charles King, Drs. Francis and Hosack, John Delafield, John C. Hamilton, and their like. Conversation that took an unusual turn also helped fashion a "splendid dinner party," such as one given for 24 guests—"all highly respectable persons"—by the eccentric George Rapelye on February 4, 1835. While the "dinner was well arranged and very good," if not of the very highest order, the evening's interest derived from the host, who "was somewhat of a curiosity . . . [who talked] loudly at table and swears like a trooper and his conversation is enlivened with many queer anecdotes of what he has seen in foreign parts." In a manner so infectious that I cannot forebear quoting perhaps more than adherence to a stricter sociological canon would permit, Hone recounts what turned out inadvertently to be an all-day affair: "I went this morning," he writes on Saturday, January 16, 1836, "to dine with John C. Stevens at his place on Long Island. . . . Charles King, General Fleming, and Cornelius Ludlow went with me on my sleigh. We arrived at Stevens' about 3 o'clock, had a most capital dinner, fine wine, good fires, and plenty of laughter, jokes, and joviality. We found on our arrival John A. King, Commodore Ridge" and several other eminent fellows. Since the sleigh carrying the visitors back to the city overturned, back to Stevens's went the party, this time for supper, more good wine and good talk, and then all "were well accommodated with [the] good beds of [their] hospitable host."

Dinner invitations appeared to be fraught with great significance to Hone and no doubt to others as well. From time to time he tries to give an impression that these affairs are a bit *de trop*, as in the case of the excellent dinners given by Alexander E. Hosack: "very handsome and very expensive, [yet] too much so as all dinners are nowadays." (This was 1834, when he had almost 17 years of fine dining still stretching out before him.) To hear Hone tell it, it would be good to retreat to "mutton soup and Adams ale." But only "now and then"! The numerous invitations made to this attractive man created the physiological problem of too much of too many good things and the psychological and social problems of a not dissimilar kind. On February 11, 1833, he writes in mock despair: "this is a severe week in the dinner way. I am engaged every day after today [Monday], and on Thursday I have four invitations, namely Mr. George Jones, George Griswold, Peter G. Stuyvesant, and Mr. Maury, the first of which I have accepted. I sometimes think it would be better to give it all up . . . but the experiment might not succeed. The habit becomes confirmed, and the respect of our friends, which is indicated by those attentions, is not without its value." One wonders how Hone construed "value." Actually Hone remained so zealous about responding to these invitations that he somehow managed later in the week to dine out also with three gentlemen he had not even mentioned—Isaac Carow, Francis Olmstead, and Henry Cary—while the next week he drank quantities of champagne with his great friends Captain Rogers and Commodore Chauncey.

Dinner invitations created some tension because they obviously had much significance. Hone was mortified one January night in 1835 to run into Harrison Gray Otis at a dinner party at Peter Schermerhorn's. Otis had earlier pleaded indisposition in refusing Hone's own invitation and had promised that Hone's would be the first house he would visit if his condition permitted him to visit anyone during this sojourn in New York City. Otis went to some pains immediately thereafter to assure Hone that his was one of the very few homes he enjoyed visiting. Otis threw himself "on the mercy of the court," while Hone "summoned" the celebrated Bostonian "to appear," as the two men strove manfully to deal with the matter in a light tone and gentlemanly spirit that does not obscure at all the significance of the possible affront that compelled them to the exchange in the first place.[28]

Hone's diary contains many single entries such as the one for February 26, 1846: "I declined an invitation to dine with Sidney Brooks." One wonders, why? And why were such things so important to Hone? Picking and choosing from among competing social offers was clearly a touchy matter. Invited to dine with his friend, the great merchant

Samuel Howland, Hone writes he "was compelled to decline this for a less agreeable party." How would Samuel Glover, the alternate, have felt had he known his guest's private feelings? Obviously punctilio was involved here. It was evidently *de rigueur* to accept the prior invitation. My own impression is that Hone's words can be taken literally: the distinction between one host and another was not their relative wealth or social standing but their personal "agreeableness."

Such a standard would appear to point to a socially democratic rule for private preferences and friendships but for one thing. The choice, whether made by Hone or by his friends, was between persons who were almost all members of the elite of wealth and status. Just as elite marital preferences might be attributable to passion, so informal friendships and the choice of dinner companions could be due to sentimental or emotional considerations; but in the one case as in the other, the potential objects of ardor or affection came from the same selective circle.

The amazing pains Hone took to record hosts, guests at his own home, and fellow guests at other's homes, make possible a "quantitative analysis" of the social standing and wealth of his dinner companions, friends, and acquaintances. Better than 80 per cent of the more than five hundred New York City residents who dined or socialized with Hone during the 25-year period in which he recorded such data (1826 to 1851) were among the wealthiest 1 per cent of the city.[29] Most of the other New Yorkers who moved in his orbit were either quite rich or prominent. Many entries in Hone's not-always-accurate spelling are cited without Christian names, are otherwise unclear, or simply not known to me. In view of the cosmopolitan character of Hone's social list, it is quite possible that a number of the latter were from outside of New York City and that the percentage of Hone's friends from the city who were wealthy or prominent was in fact close to a hundred.

Hone entertained or was entertained by many dozens of persons from outside his home city. Many of these were persons of international eminence and were no doubt accounted for by the fact that Hone had, after all, been the mayor of New York City. Ambassadors, *chargés d'affaires*, earls, barons, chevaliers, were often present at parties given or attended by Hone. When the analysis is confined to the substantial number of Boston and Philadelphia families with whom he mingled socially, just about every single one of them, so far as I can determine, was among the wealthiest or most eminent persons in their cities. Hone's social contacts in the great northeastern cities neighboring New York were not with ordinary persons but with Pierreponts, Willings, Merediths, Amorys, Brookses, Adamses, Quincys, Lymans, Cabots, Peabodys, Lawrences, Derbys, Appletons, Brimmers, Coolidges, Codmans, Grays, Otises, Forbeses, Searses, Sturgises, Shaws, Welleses, and Thorndikes.

Since most wealthy persons were Whigs rather than Democrats,

Pleasure Railway at John Stevens' Hoboken Resort, "Elysian Fields." Stevens was an intimate of Philip Hone and a member of New York City's elite. *(From a colored lithograph by D. W. Kellogg & Company courtesy of the Museum of the City of New York.)*

Hone's friends favored the former party over the latter. But there is no evidence that wealthy or eminent persons who somehow aligned themselves with the Jacksonians lost their standing or their places in the social circle of the elite as a result of such political aberration. Hone's dislike of the politics of James A. Hamilton, Stephen Allen, Walter Bowne, John L. Morgan, Jonathan Coddington, James Buchanan, William Marcy, Azariah Flagg, or Churchill C. Cambreleng did not interfere with his friendly relations with these and many other men who shared their views. He invited them to his home, joined them at parties, attended funerals of mutual friends with them.[30] The social set of Philip Hone and his friends appeared to be concerned not with the national party preferences but with the eminence and standing of the persons who sought entry into it.

Hone did not refer to great wealth as a required characteristic of those with whom he would be intimate. But as a very wealthy man himself, he—like other rich men—was part of a social world inhabited primarily by those who had been similarly fortunate in worldly accumulation. Those persons who belonged to families that intermarried with Hone's or whose many contacts with him over a quarter of a century clearly established their special elite status were, almost without exception, very rich. The members of this most exalted group, persons who *regularly* mingled socially with Philip Hone, were John Jacob Astor and his son, William B. Astor, Harrison Gray Otis, Nathaniel and Edward Prime, George Griswold, Henry Brevoort and Henry Brevoort, Jr., James Brown, Walter Bowne, Isaac Carow, Cadwallader and David C. Colden, Gerard and John G. Coster, Edward and George Curtis, the Delafield family, Dr. John W. Francis, Jacob P. Giraud, William A. Duer, President of Columbia College, Jacob Harvey, Dr. David Hosack, Ogden Hoffman, Gardiner Greene Howland and his brother Samuel, Gould Hoyt, Judges John T. Irving, Edward R. Jones, Thomas Oakley, and Chancellor Kent, Charles and James Gore King, Chancellor Samuel Jones, David S. Kennedy, Edward and Maturin Livingston, General Morgan Lewis, Thomas W. Ludlow, Dominick Lynch, Robert Bowne Minturn, Abraham Ogden, Henry Parish, Edmund H. Pendleton, Robert Ray, Charles H. Russell, Commodore Chauncey of the Brooklyn Navy Yard (whose quarters Hone loved to visit), Abraham and Peter Schermerhorn, John C. Stevens, Peter G. Stuyvesant, Herman Thorn, Benjamin L. Swan, Gulian C. Verplanck, Myndert Van Schaick, and Stephen Whitney. These were not the sixty richest men in New York City. Hone did not choose his friends on the basis of a dollars-and-cents calculus. But what is of great interest is the fact that most of the group indeed belonged on such a list, while the few who were not actually in the upper sixty were also wealthy or eminent.

There is no evidence that poor or common men—no matter how impeccable their party preferences or their social ideology—were in the social circle of the urban elite. Men of letters there were, such as Washington Irving, William Hickling Prescott, or James Fenimore Cooper; but typically they too belonged to families that were both wealthy and eminent.

Elite Funerals

The funerals of elite personages also afford an insight into the social quality of their intimates. Hone dutifully recorded the names of pallbearers of departed friends and acquaintances. Since the social horizons of the elite characteristically extended beyond their own city, occasionally a pallbearer would be an outsider, geographically if not socially. At the funeral of Jonathan H. Lawrence even Hone found that one of the pallbearers was "a gentleman [he] did not know." In almost every other case, however, the mourners were identifiable.

On these sad occasions families were likely to choose pallbearers from among the close friends, the business associates, and occasionally the relatives of the deceased, confining the choices essentially to intimates.[31] These sober groupings of eight were precisely the persons who had comprised the very closest social circle of the eminent persons they attended. The evidence is clear; the elite were borne to their final resting place by the elite.

The breadth and diversity of Hone's own social relationships is suggested by the great number of leading families who called on him as pallbearer. He served at the funerals of the richest of the rich, such as John Jacob Astor, Hezekiah Beers Pierrepont, Isaac Lawrence, Mrs. Peter Goelet, and his great friend, John G. Coster; for such eminent professional figures as Chancellor James Kent, David S. Jones, David B. Ogden, and Dr. Alexander Hosack; for such old Knickerbockers as Mrs. Robert Benson (the mother of Egbert Benson), Gabriel Furman, Mrs. Peter Schenck, and Catherine and John Schermerhorn; for such New York eminences as Cadwallader Colden, General Lewis, Benjamin Strong, and Oliver Kane; for such great merchants as Isaac Carow, Henry Brevoort, Allison Post, George Richards, Peter A. Mesier, and David Lydig; and for the deceased wives of the city's leaders such as Harriet Kane (Mrs. William Wood), Mrs. Joshua Jones, Mrs. Jacob Morton, and Mrs. John C. Stevens; as well as for dozens of other departed luminaries. Only one month before his own death, the pain-ridden man was a pallbearer for Elizabeth Manning, the daughter of Thomas Storms.[32]

Another man whose numerous performances as pallbearer testified to the scope and the intimacy of his contacts with the elite of New York City was Hone's friend Edward W. Laight. Laight was present with Hone at the funerals of Schermerhorns and Ogdens, Mrs. Morton and Mrs. Jones, John Coster, Mr. Mesier, Mr. Lydig, Dr. Hosack, and John Morgan, as well as the funerals of Herman LeRoy, Mrs. Hobart, and

Jonathan Lawrence. Others who were called on regularly as pallbearers were Joshua Waddington, William Bard, Henry Beekman, Peter Schermerhorn, Peter G. Stuyvesant, Benjamin L. Swan, William A. Duer, Jonathan Goodhue, Judge Oakley, David B. Ogden, John Oothout, Gardiner Howland, Gould Hoyt, Chancellor Jones, Washington Irving, Peter A. Jay, General Lewis, Professor Clement C. Moore, Chancellor Kent, and James Gore King—eminences and friends of Philip Hone, every one of them.

The burden of the diverse evidence on the formal and the informal associations, the lighter and the darker side, of the private lives of the urban elites is that their social circle was a most exclusive one. Far from mingling on easy or equal terms with social inferiors or commoners, the rich and renowned sought out the company of their own kind. Their cosmopolitanism consisted, not in the maintenance of ties with individuals of diverse social rank within their own cities, but rather in occasionally going outside their own cities, invariably, however, to persons of status similar to their own.

One of the pallbearers at the funeral of Philip Hone's nephew, John Hone, was a member of the Boston Dorrs. Amorys and Apthorps were among the Boston elite who were transported to a "general fête" at Samuel Breck's Philadelphia residence on April 29, 1829, in the carriage of Thomas M. Willing. Aspinwalls and Kortrights of New York joined Bradfords of Massachusetts at the elite Philadelphia parties attended by Sidney George Fisher, while Bayards, Rhinelanders, and Van Rensselaers of New York City mingled with Lymans and Perkinses of Boston as guests of the Philadelphia Club. And as has been indicated, Hone and his family exchanged social calls with the leading families of New York City's chief urban rivals.

One is not surprised that in the "Federalist Era" immediately following the Revolution, the "Dinner and Supper List" of so prominent a social figure as Mrs. John Jay was confined exclusively to the elite of New York City. This circle consisted of persons prominent in law, such as Egbert Benson, Richard Varick, Alexander Hamilton, Robert Livingston, Gouverneur Morris, James Kent, or Josiah Ogden Hoffman; or in medicine and the ministry, such as Drs. John Rodgers, Benjamin Moore, Samuel Bard, Benjamin Kissam, or Nicholas Romaine; or of families that had long been prominent landholders and merchants, such as the Verplancks, Van Cortlandts, Wattses, Beekmans, Crugers, DePeysters, and Bayards.[33] That earlier era had made no claims to social leveling. What is more striking is that matters had changed so little by a half century later during the "age of egalitarianism." The elite—or in Warnerian terms the upper-upper class—of the great cities had grown, encompassing not simply a greater *number* of families but families such as the Astors and Hones, whose great wealth and prestige were of relatively recent origin.

The new elite, impervious to the alleged "spirit of the age," maintained a lifestyle as exclusive as the one managed by its predecessor two generations earlier. If anything, the barriers dividing the upper orders from those below were more impenetrable during the 1830s and 1840s than they had ever been before. For in the "era of the common man," clubs and other formal associations had been created as a supplement to the more informal means that had earlier been used and now continued to be used in screening inappropriate persons out of the world of the social elite.

A cautionary note must be sounded. The impossibility of securing anything like full evidence on the private circles and the range of social contacts maintained by most of the urban rich obviously detracts from the universality of generalizations based on the behavior of several of their number. There may be very complete evidence that Philip Hone mingled with most of the wealthiest New Yorkers who lived during the second quarter of the nineteenth century and with their equals from other cities and countries; it may be that he confined his social set to such persons alone. As a matter of simple logic, however, it does not follow that the persons on his social list similarly restricted their own private lives. Detailed evidence is still needed to prove the point, evidence that is, alas, non-existent. Yet, many signs do point to the typicality of Hone's behavior.

Who Were The Elite?

In a sense, the social exclusiveness described in this chapter might be ascribed not to the urban rich as a whole but rather to that ineffable group, the "elite." Nelson Polsby has obviously described the author of this book, as well as other scholars, in noting that users of the term seldom define it. In view of the variety of meanings that have been given to the word "elite" and the real danger that any attempt to prepare a strict definition will produce a rigid definition that limits the usefulness of a term that is both vivid and evocative, there may be wisdom either in eschewing formal definition or in sticking with the simple Websterian usage that the elite are the choice, the elect, or the socially superior. When scholars—Polsby included—do attempt to define the term, they often do so by referring to a small number of discrete, arbitrary criteria: the "elite characteristics" thus set forth turn out to be criteria for which relevant data are available.[34] Such an elite is indeed clearly defined and workable, but it is a bookish thing, a scholar's tool; moreover, it is not the elite that contemporaries had in mind when they used the term. It is this living elite, or the elite as understood by contemporaries, that, I would suggest, was preoccupied with exclusiveness.

In common with scholars and other sensible people of our own time, antebellum personages (including those who considered themselves members of the elite), did not try to define the term. To Miss Kane, whose invitation to John Hone is inscribed at the head of this chapter, the elite were those who belonged to her and to young Hone's set. That "set" was never formally listed. Its membership is impossible to know accurately, not least because of shifts (no matter how slight) in the personnel who composed it from one year to another. For that matter, the nature, as well as the membership of this set, doubtless was differently perceived by the individuals who were regarded as belonging to it. Certainly the members of the prestigious social clubs and those persons who were regularly invited to the gatherings of such eminences as the Winthrops, Warrens, Otises, Brecks, Wistars, Hosacks, and Hones have strong claims to inclusion in the charmed circle. Suggestive of the intractability of the problem, however, is the fact that some recluses also commanded great prestige, despite their nonparticipation in socially honorific gatherings.

All approaches to the problem are necessarily imperfect. Perhaps the most sensible means of treating it is not to seek out the names of the individuals who composed the elite—a hopeless task—but rather to focus on the discernible characteristics shared by eminent personages who were almost universally accorded high status. This method is, of course, no more foolproof than others. The observable ingredients or "discernible characteristics" of elite members were neither rigidly fixed nor of unchanging weight, socially. The method does not allow for the part played by intuitive or nonrational factors in ascribing high standing to individuals. And yet, if imperfect, the method has much to recommend it; not least, the greater degree of correspondence between its integrated definition and contemporary usage than can be achieved by using "political elites," "economic elites," "status elites," and other arbitrary and artificial conceptions of scholars.

To qualify for elite status, a family need not have been marked by all or even most of the characteristics associated with that status. Long renown dating back several generations in this country was, for example, a significant criterion. But it was not an absolutely imperative criterion. A family or an individual who achieved very great success in one or another appropriate way—John Jacob Astor, the Bories, John Delafield, Philip Hone himself come immediately to mind—could earn membership in the social elect despite relatively brief careers there. As for the required "renown," it could be gained in a variety of ways but ways—such as landholding, commerce, finance, officeholding, military rank, law, and medicine—that were socially acceptable. The arts *per se* did not always measure up: Irving, Prescott, Motley, Parkman, Lea, were after all men of *family* as well as men of genius. True, the "Boz Ball" was not thrown for an upper-class swell; but Dickens was an Englishman, a foreign celebrity, and therefore subject to special rules. Attendance at the great universities was useful, but it did not gain one automatic entry. Let the graduate be of respected family, make the Grand Tour, have cultivated manners, dress like a gentleman, as a host give splendid affairs in his own home and as a guest be an adornment to the homes he visited, and matters were different. In a word, let him be a man of means.

Elite status was an intangible, but it rested heavily on possession of that most tangible thing, wealth. All families are old families. The valued term, Old Family, signified a family long successful and usually long wealthy or well-to-do. Americans, as has been shown, were fond of proclaiming their allegedly humble origins, and they appear to have found it genteel to assert the subordination of money to more spiritual phenomena in their scale of values. Lawrence Stone has shown that the Tudor aristocracy were not so squeamish. Those sixteenth-century peers who could "no longer maintain status because of poverty were quietly dropped from the list. . . . If and when wealth once more came their way, however, they again took their rightful place." By and large, during the sixteenth and seventeenth centuries in England, "the hierarchy of ranks corresponded . . . roughly to categories of income." In Stone's judgment the first criterion of membership in what he calls the "gentry élite and the titular peerage" was wealth: "As a result of this wealth [the élite] lived in a more opulent style than their neighbors, with more servants, more horses, more coaches, and a more open table. They occupied a larger house than . . . those of lesser means. They were often educated by private tutors . . . and they rounded off their adolescence with the Grand Tour."[35] The early-nineteenth-century United States had an informal rather than a true aristocracy, but, as in England two centuries earlier, one needed inordinate wealth in order to afford the way of life that accompanied membership in the most exalted class. A family's level of wealth was no sure key to the place it occupied in the American social hierarchy; yet it was surely no accident that almost all families of high status were among the rich of their cities. Nor was the correlation between standing and wealth confined to the northeast alone. In Natchez, Mississippi during the era, the "nabobs" or aristocrats were found to be a "privileged class [that] was separated from the masses primarily by distinctions of property and economic power."[36] The elite were overwhelmingly Protestant: Episcopalians, Presbyterians, Quakers, Unitarians, rather than Methodists, Baptists, or pietists. Yet Catholics who qualified on other counts were not excluded, while membership in the prestigious denominations was insufficient in itself when other attributes were lacking.

It is, in a sense, circular reasoning to hold that residence—whether judged by quality or by location—marital ties, club memberships, or social circle defined elite status. The question is rather what kind of traits earned neighbors, spouses, social intimates of lofty standing? The requisite attractiveness was a blending of diverse ingredients, all of them substantial, having to do with place and eminence in the affairs of men, and with the material abundance that flowed from success in commerce, landholding, and other pursuits.

The evidence of this chapter suggests that in antebellum cities, persons of admired status—the elite—went to great pains to spend their leisure with, and to lead lives likely to be inhabited by, their own set alone. As men of affairs they unavoidably mingled with other social types, in the process charming observers-on-the-run with so amazing a display of social egalitarianism. *The pursuit of wealth and power compelled the upper orders to do business with the lower.* But in their private affairs, where they were free to indulge their personal desires and social values, the antebellum elite rejected egalitarianism for class exclusiveness.

Notes

[1] The published excerpts emphasize national political issues and incidents of obvious interest and dramatic character. See Bayard Tuckerman, ed., *The Diary of Philip Hone*, 2 vols. (New York, 1889); and Allan Nevins, ed., *The Diary of Philip Hone, 1828–1851*, 2 vols. (New York, 1927).

[2] Hodges, *Social Stratification: Class in America*, pp. 115–16.

[3] The phrase "nation of joiners" was popularized by the elder Arthur M. Schlesinger in his *Paths to the Present* (New York, 1949), pp. 23–50. On the American penchant for association see Tocqueville, *Democracy in America*, I, chap. 12.

[4] According to Richard C. Wade, the "main function" of the "quasi-academic" clubs popular with fashionable young men in western cities in the early nineteenth century, "was to maintain class ties." *The Urban Frontier*, p. 209.

[5] Baltzell, *Philadelphia Gentlemen: The Making of a National Upper Class* (New York, 1958), pp. 345, 347, 353. He writes that "an inspection of the names of the 2,101 members of the club between 1834 and 1940 reads like an economic and social history of Philadelphia."

[6] *The Philadelphia Club, 1834–1934, Being a Brief History of the Club for the First 100 Years of its Existence, together with Its Roll of Officers and Members to 1934, with a Foreword by Owen Wister* (Philadelphia, 1934), pp. 186–87.

[7] *Recollections of Samuel Breck, with Passages from His Note-Books, 1771–1862*, H. E. Scudder, ed. (Philadelphia, 1877), pp. 288–89.

[8] Russell M. Posner, "Philadelphia in 1830: An English View (excerpts from the diary of Sir Henry Singer Keating)," *Pennsylvania Magazine of History and Biography, XCV* (April 1971), p. 242; *Recollections of Samuel Breck*, p. 288; Horace Mather Lippincott, *Early Philadelphia, Its People, Life, and Progress* (Phila. 1917), pp. 295–98; John Russell Young, ed., *Memorial History of the City of Philadelphia* (New York, 1898), II, p. 121.

[9] Albert Langtry, ed., *Metropolitan Boston, A Modern History* (New York, 1929), III, p. 1030.

[10] Hugh Whitney and Walter Muir Whitehill, "The Somerset Club," in *The Somerset Club 1851–1951* (Boston, 1951), pp. 7–35, 44–119; Alexander W. Williams, *A Social History of the Greater Boston Clubs* (Barre, Mass., 1970), p. 4; Edwin Munroe Bacon, *The Book of Boston: Fifty Years' Recollections of the New England Metropolis* (Boston, 1916), p. 120; Langtry, *Metropolitan Boston*, III, pp. 1030–31.

[11] John W. Francis, *Old New York, Reminiscences of the Past Sixty Years* (New York, 1858), p. 291; William Cullen Bryant, II, "Poetry and Painting: A Love Affair of Long Ago," *American Quarterly, XXII* (Winter 1970), p. 803; *Memorials of Peter A. Jay* (privately printed in Arnheim, Holland, 1929), pp. 134–35; and Francis Gerry Fairfield, *The Clubs of New York: an Essay on New York Club-Life* (New York, 1873), p. 8.

[12] *Charter, Constitution, and By-Laws of the St. Nicholas Society* (New York, 1842, 1850), pp. 1, 5.

[13] Estimated from the list of New York City's wealthiest residents in Edward Pessen, "The Wealthiest New Yorkers of the Jacksonian Era: A New List," *New-York Historical Society Quarterly, LIV* (April 1970), pp. 145–172.

[14] Hone Diary, Feb. 14, 1835, IX:261–62.

[15] *Ibid.*, Oct. 22, 1838, XIV:411–12; Francis, *Old New York*, p. 295.

[16] Frank Otto Gatell, "Money and Party in Jacksonian America: A Quantitative Look at New York City's Men of Quality," *Political Science Quarterly, LXXXII* (June 1967), pp. 235–52; Robert Rich, "'A Wilderness of Whigs': The Wealthy Men of Boston," *Journal of Social History*, 4 (Spring 1971), pp. 263–76.

[17] Francis, *Old New York*, 295; Hone Diary, March 12, 1846, XXIII:391.

[18] Lossing, *History of New York City*, II, p. 595.

[19] Hone Diary, Jan. 24, 1846, XXIII:333.

[20] Reginald T. Townsend, *Mother of Clubs, Being the History of the 1st Hundred Years of the Union Club of New York 1836–1936* (New York, 1936), pp. 16–19; Lossing, *History of New York City*, II, p. 434; Wilson, *Memorial History of the City of New York*, IV, p. 236.

[21] Fairfield, *The Clubs of New York*, p. 66.

[22] Diary of Sidney George Fisher, Feb. 9, 1837; located in the Historical Society of Pennsylvania.

[23] Stephen N. Winslow, *Biographies of Successful Merchants* (Philadelphia, 1864), pp. 28, 58; Posner, "Philadelphia in 1830: An English View," pp. 239–43.

[24] Mary Caroline Crawford, *Romantic Days in Old Boston* (Boston, 1910), pp. 317–18.

[25] Hone Diary, Aug., 1834, VIII:338–39; IX:11.

[26] Hone Diary, Dec. 16, 1834, IX:125.

[27] Pessen, *Jacksonian America: Society, Personality, and Politics*, pp. 25–27.

[28] Hone Diary, IX:164–67.

[29] Their names appear on the lists of wealthiest for 1828 and 1845. See Appendix C. For two years before he began to keep his detailed diary in 1828, Hone recorded the names of persons with whom he dined and socialized.

[30] Hone Diary, May 1842, XIX:229ff. Compare Rich, "A Wilderness of Whigs," p. 268. According to Rich, Bostonians lost their elect status on becoming Democrats. His documentation for this assertion is a libel suit brought against George Bancroft by Daniel Webster and a later reminiscence by Henry Cabot Lodge, written almost a hundred years after the fact. Actually, bearers of Boston names of greater repute than Bancroft's managed to retain both their unusual Democratic affiliations and the elite status earned by their families before them.

[31] I infer this point from the known closeness of the relationships linking the hundreds of pallbearers mentioned by Hone to the deceased persons they attended. This too is the information given me by spokesmen for the elite New York City funeral parlors, The Abbey and Frank E. Campbell, and by Trinity Church of New York City.

[32] I have tried, thus far without success, to discover who were the pallbearers at Hone's own funeral. His old friend Charles King "pronounced a very eloquent eulogy," and moved memorial resolutions before an assemblage that included all the members of the Mercantile Society as well as members of the New-York Historical Society. Dr. John W. Francis also spoke at the funeral ceremony on May 7, 1851, two days after Hone's death. The *New York Daily Tribune*, May 8, 1851.

[33] Wilson, *Memorial History of the City of New York*, III, pp. 87–101; and Kulikoff, "The Progress of Inequality in Revolutionary Boston," p. 387.

[34] Polsby, *Community Power and Political Theory* (New Haven, 1963), p. 85. Polsby's own usage of the term is not particularly instructive. He distinguishes between an

"economic elite" and a "status elite," defining the latter group in mid-twentieth-century New Haven as the families of the "Cotillion Set," who subscribed to the Assembly of the Lawn Club. In fairness to Polsby, it is clear that he regarded these categories less as ultimate definitions than as useful if arbitrary starting points for his research on the political behavior that most interested him.

[35] Stone, *The Crisis of the Aristocracy*, pp. 52–53, 56–58.

[36] D. Clayton James, *Antebellum Natchez*, p. 136.

PART IV
Influence and Power

On Influence and Power

The following chapters are concerned with the influence and power of the antebellum urban rich. The expression "money talks," popular long before Karl Marx was born, conveys the old truth that men of great wealth command great power. The question, particularly for a period long reputed to have been dominated by ordinary men of modest means, is: "how much power?"

Influence and power are manifested in various ways. Great wealth, for example, gave its possessors great economic power within the community. Masters of capital, finance, and real estate determined the price and availability of credit, the scale of employment and unemployment, the wages of labor, the price of housing. In discussing power, historians typically examine political institutions and the kind of men who administer them. The good sense of such analysis is too obvious to require comment. Certainly the part played by the rich in the governments of their cities throws great light on the original question. But, as a number of political scientists and sociologists have recently reminded us, influence and power are demonstrated in non-political bodies as well.[1]

One of the more provocative studies goes so far as to suggest that in the city of the mid-twentieth century, power is to be sought not primarily in formal structures of any sort, whether political or non-political, but rather in covert elites whose domination derives primarily from their great wealth.[2] Not the least of the problems associated with such a thesis is the difficulty in finding facts to establish it. Covert elites after all "work in the dark"; by their very nature they will not leave evidence of their power around. As I shall try to show, there is little evidence for such a thesis in the antebellum decades. The following chapters will rather consider the overt and explicit relationships rich men had with the agencies of power. Agencies of power include, not only government, but also the army of voluntary associations of significant public purpose.

Although the latter organizations were a striking and significant phenomenon of the period, they have, to date, received little consideration by scholars. The great national reform movements—such as abolitionism, women's rights organizations, and religious associations—have, of course, been subjected to intensive analysis. But urban groups of a more pedestrian nature, seeking the attainment of less sweeping objectives, have been largely neglected.[3] The significance of the latter associations is in no wise diminished by their modesty of purpose or their sobriety. In a sense, therefore, the discussion of the part played in such groups by the rich and the eminent may be a contribution to a fuller understanding of a type of organization long believed to be one of the most unique and attractive features of American life. Above all, evidence on the participation of the elite in diverse urban institutions and in local government helps answer the question: "Was the power and influence of the antebellum urban rich commensurate with their great wealth and status?"

Notes

[1] Norton E. Long, "Political Science and the City, " in Leo F. Schnore, ed., *Social Science and the City: A Survey of Urban Research* (New York, 1968); Charles M. Bonjean and David M. Olson, "Community Leadership," in Roland L. Warren, ed., *Perspectives on the American Community* (Chicago, 1966); Floyd Hunter, *Community Power Structure: A Study of Decision Makers* (Chapel Hill, N.C., 1953); Robert A. Dahl, *Who Governs? Democracy and Power in an American City* (New Haven, 1961); and Edward C. Banfield, *Political Influence* (New York, 1961).

[2] Hunter, *Community Power Structure.* For a criticism of Hunter's thesis see Dahl, "A Critique of the Ruling Elite Model," *American Political Science Review*, 52 (1958), pp. 463–69; and *Polsby, Community Power and Political Theory.*

[3] Arthur M. Schlesinger, Sr., *Paths to the Present*, pp. 23–50, is one of the few fairly comprehensive treatments of nineteenth-century voluntary assocations. Schlesinger confines his discussion essentially to *national* organizations of sizable membership, reasonably long duration, and fairly large territorial extent.

12

The Role of the Rich and Elite in Local Voluntary Associations

> Among democratic [in contrast to aristocratic societies] . . . all the citizens are independent and feeble; they can do hardly anything by themselves. . . . They all, therefore, become powerless if they do not learn voluntarily to help one another.
>
> Tocqueville, *Democracy in America,* II:115

> In response to these new conditions [of 1830–1860] all Philadelphians, of every class and background, reacted in the same way to the loss of the old patterns of sociability and informal community. They rushed into clubs and associations.
>
> Sam Bass Warner, Jr., *The Private City: Philadelphia in Three Periods of Its Growth* (Philadelphia, 1968), p. 61

> The Colonization Society of New York has been recently instituted. I was elected vice president but declined. I have more already of engagements of that kind than I can attend to.
>
> Hone Diary, Jan. 29, 1831, III:271

The American people have long been known as a "nation of joiners." Tocqueville found one of the most amazing features of life in the United States to be "the immense assemblage of associations in that country" during the period of his visit; organizations created and composed of "Americans of all ages, all conditions, and all dispositions." In an influential essay written a quarter century ago, Arthur Schlesinger, Sr., likewise found that the membership of voluntary associations embraced Americans of "all classes." A modern historian of Philadelphia agrees that persons of "every class and background" participated in the voluntary associations that proliferated in that city during the antebellum decades.[1] Actually, it is not at all clear, let alone proven, that the constituencies of most of the early nineteenth-century associations were socially heterogeneous.

The burden of modern sociological studies of volunteer organizations in the twentieth century is that their membership "is not characteristic of the majority of Americans, and that membership is directly related to socio-economic status . . . the higher the status, the greater the membership."[2] Eminent men were enormously active and influential in hundreds of the voluntary associations that flourished in the nation's cities during the second quarter of the nineteenth century. My purpose is to explore the extent and assess the significance of that activity. Our interest in this chapter is not in the social organizations—such as New York City's Union Club, Boston's Somerset Club, or the Philadelphia Club—that reflected primarily their members' desire for exclusivity and status, but rather in the associations dedicated to broad public, moral, cultural, and humanitarian purposes.

Such organizations are never lacking either in interest or importance. In view of the limited scope of responsibilities borne by urban governments and an alleged breakdown of municipal authority in the face of the unprecedented problems confronting it in the 1830s and 1840s, the role of volunteer associations during the period was a particularly crucial one. At a time when, according to modern scholars, "established institutions no longer served to integrate and regulate the growing community," voluntary associations dealing, for example, with poverty and its amelioration "filled an important social need in nineteenth-century American cities." According to Sam Bass Warner, a major function of the associations in Philadelphia at mid-nineteenth century was to help "preserve the mental health of the joiners," by providing a replacement for the social homogeneity that had ostensibly characterized the earlier "street, shop, and neighborhood life" of the city.[3] The precise needs filled by voluntary associations may be open to varied interpretation, but there can be no doubt that in an age characterized by weak municipal government of niggardly budgets and limited scope, the voluntary associations of the early nineteenth century indeed filled a void. Moreover, they appeared to do a great deal more than serve as an outlet for the diverse needs of their members or provide them with emotionally rewarding uses of leisure.

Antebellum volunteer associations dealt with a variety of urban issues. Poverty, illness (physical and mental), the plight of ethnic minorities, illiteracy and ignorance, vice, immorality, crime and prison conditions, the meager cultural resources available to most families, deficient public-health facilities, the inadequate and stigmatized "pauper schools" available to the poor, skimpy municipal amenities, and the causes and cures of these maladies were among the themes that engaged social activists. It is hardly an exaggeration to state that matters of such moment complemented, if they did not surpass in importance, the limited tasks assumed by mayors, recorders, city councils and boards of aldermen before mid-century.

Elite Involvement in Voluntary Associations

In view of the number of urban organizations and their complexity of backgrounds, no attempt will be made here to write even short summaries of their activities. Substantial volumes would be required for such a task. The more limited task of evaluating the role played by the rich and eminent in voluntary associations should throw some further light —even if less than full light—on a phenomenon that, for all its importance, has been amazingly neglected since Tocqueville wrote his remarkable description of it. The discussion that follows may also help answer a number of interesting questions. How valid is the Tocquevillean concept that the associations were in a sense created by the weak, who allegedly sought a strength in numbers that they lacked as individuals? What of Arnold Rose's recent judgment that voluntary associations are both mechanisms for social change and safeguards against concentration of power? [4] The evidence also makes possible an assessment of the comparative highmindedness of social activists in different cities. Appraisals popular then and later, to the effect that New York City's leading men were more profit-minded and less altruistic than those of its great commercial rivals, have rested on impressions drawn from a few incidents rather than from a factual investigation. Above all, the discussion may provoke further enquiry into these important organizations. Much attention has properly been paid in recent years to the great national reform associations concerned with abolition, pacifism, the establishment of "backwoods utopias," and matters of like interest. Although more parochial, and certainly more prosaic than were these dramatic national movements, the bewildering array of ephemeral local voluntary associations soberly confronting the central urban problems of the antebellum decades offers no less illuminating or revealing a glimpse into the character of Americans and American society.

Boston

On June 29, 1833, Philip Hone recorded in his diary his great admiration for the charitableness and public-spiritedness of Boston's leading men. Hone was much impressed by the great merchant Thomas Handasyd Perkins's donation to the New England Institute for the Blind of a house and lot said to be worth more than $30,000, on condition that the grant would be matched by gifts from other sources. Hone noted that $51,117 was swiftly contributed by others. Earlier, under the administration of Dr. Samuel Gridley Howe, the gifted New Englander who had launched his career as reformer with this enterprise, the "Thomas Perkins Institution and Massachusetts School for the Blind" had been created in 1829 by some of Boston's most eminent and wealthy citizens. Joining Perkins as founders were Theodore Sedgwick, William Appleton, Samuel A. Eliot, Amos and Abbott Lawrence, Robert Rantoul, William Hickling Prescott, and John Lowell, Jr. Helping to raise funds to "ensure the perpetuity of the institution" was the city's "undisputed society leader," Mrs. Harrison Gray Otis.[5] As was to be expected of a city that reserved its highest praise for wealth beneficently spent, Boston's social and economic elite included many, in addition to Perkins, who contributed financially and in other ways to the welfare of the larger community. Amos Lawrence was said to have given more than $600,000 to worthy causes during the second quarter of the nineteenth century. According to a modern scholar, if other merchants too "gave liberally to a galaxy of causes, educating the blind, succoring the poor and rescuing the orphan . . . they often gave quietly and anonymously [since] public display that one had done one's duty cheapened the spirit of liberality and substituted greed for fame for love of money."[6] Of course, social duty could be done through the gift of time and energy as well as money. In view of the impossibility and doubtful propriety of masking these kinds of contributions, it is unlikely that public knowledge of them detracted from the grace stored up by the men who made them. Some of the most eminent figures in Boston's commercial, public, and professional life were as esteemed as they were precisely because of their known commitments to non-utilitarian enterprises.

In addition to being the city's best-known doctor and surgeon, John Collins Warren was professor of anatomy and surgery at Harvard Medical School, the counsellor for the Suffolk Medical Society, and a founder of the Massachusetts General Hospital. He had also been a founder of the Anthology Society early in the nineteenth century and later served as president of both the Massachusetts Society for Suppressing Intemperance and the Boston Society of Natural History. In the decade after 1821 Warren was first a trustee, then a first and later a second vice-president of the Humane Society of Massachusetts.[7] The character of these organizations that occupied Warren and other members of the urban elites will be considered in the following section. For the moment, the titles alone give a clue to the nature of these enterprises.

The famous attorney and mayor of Boston for the period just before midcentury, the second Josiah Quincy, Jr.—like a number of the mayors in other cities—was a man of diverse affiliations. A member of the Massachusetts Historical Society after 1813, he had also been a trustee of the Massachusetts General Hospital, treasurer of the Boston Athenaeum, and a president of the Massachusetts Peace Society. Jonathan Phillips combined lavish financial contributions with the expenditure of great effort for a variety of wholesome causes. He divided close to $100,000 between a special fund for adorning streets and public grounds, the Boston Public Library, and the Society of Natural History. He also served as a trustee of the city library society, manager of its dispensary, vice-president of the Peace Society, and president of the Institute for the Education of the Blind. The rich merchant Robert Gould Shaw joined many of his peers in the Somerset Club, a haven for the elite, but he was also a leader in the humane society, the colonization society, and the Massachusetts Charitable Eye and Ear Infirmary. Men such as these typified the combination of lofty standing, great wealth, and participation in public affairs that had earned for Boston's elite the respect, if not the envy, of citizens in other cities.

Philadelphia

Mathew Carey, wealthy publisher and famous philanthropist of Philadelphia, in making a diary notation about a fellow humanitarian in his city, wrote that it had been "suggested that the name of Roberts Vaux was too cheap by being too often before the public." [8] Evidently even altruists were not above voicing suspicion of the motives of their colleagues. Such was the price paid for being perhaps the most public-spirited individual among the entire notheastern elite, a man without peer in the number and range of his involvements. Roberts Vaux was not merely a member, but he was active or an officer in more than fifty humanitarian, educational, scientific, and artistic or cultural organizations! Of a prosperous and admired Quaker family, young Vaux early renounced the countinghouse in order to serve the Magdalen Society, the Vaccine Society, the House of Refuge, the Academy of Natural Science, the Linnaean Society, the Philadelphia Society (for alleviating the miseries of public prisons), the Philadelphia Dispensary, the Infant School Society, and several dozen others. Perhaps a fairer assessment than Carey's was uttered by another of Philadelphia's most eminent personages. According to Thomas I. Wharton: "Mr. Vaux possessed a large fortune, and expended it like a man who felt that he was merely a trustee, appointed by Divine Providence, and accountable hereafter not only for its use, but for its non-use." [9] If none could match the record of this outstanding joiner, many other wealthy and eminent Philadelphians could display impressive backgrounds of public service, in no sense inferior to the benevolent careers of their counterparts in Boston.

Praise from Thomas Wharton was not cheap, coming as it did from a man esteemed both for the lofty status of his family and for his own impressive and versatile contribution to the city's welfare. A highly successful lawyer, Wharton's attachments represented a nice blending of aristocratic exclusiveness and *noblesse oblige.* Active in the business affairs of the Historical Society of Pennsylvania and a contributor to its publications, Wharton was a trustee of the University of Pennsylvania, treasurer of the Law Library Company, and a director of the Philadelphia Athenaeum. He was also a steady participant in "Wistar parties," a manager of the cotillion, and a member of Samuel Breck's exclusive walking club—high-status private social pursuits all.

That Samuel Breck's family had only recently arrived in Philadelphia (*ca.* 1792), detracted not at all from its standing, in view of the great eminence and commercial distinction it had achieved in Boston subsequent to its arrival in Massachusetts at the beginning of the seventeenth century. If Breck had attended the Royal College in Languedoc, it was because his father, a leading Boston merchant, had served as maritime agent for Louis XVI. Like Thomas Wharton, Breck sought to balance private exclusiveness with social purposefulness in his uses of leisure. Dining with men of like standing in what he admitted was only ostensibly a "walking club," managing a splendid ball for Lafayette, adorning Wistar parties—weekly social evenings devoted to good talk with the elite of in and out of Philadelphia—was complemented by service in the institution for the blind, the University of Pennsylvania, the historical societies both of Pennsylvania and New England, the Philosophical Society, and the Athenaeum. Undoubtedly, Breck's most significant public contribution was made as a member of the state legislature where, as leader of a committee on education, he earned the reputation as "father of the public school law" of 1834.[10]

Numerous other Philadelphia elite families contributed heroes of philanthropy and social activism. Rebecca Gratz worked indefatigably in such organizations as the Female Association for the Relief of Women and Children in Reduced Circumstances, the Philadelphia Orphan Society—which she served as secretary from 1819 to 1859—and the Hebrew Sunday School Union, which she founded in 1838. Jacob and Joseph Gratz were charter members of the board of directors of the Philadelphia Institute for the Deaf and Dumb, while Hyman, the most prominent member of this redoubtable family, was the treasurer and later the president of the Philadelphia Academy of Fine Arts and a founder of the Jewish Publications Society. Joseph R. Ingersoll was trustee of the University of Pennsylvania and held high office in the historical society, the colonization society, the academy of fine arts, and the house of refuge. John K. Kane, in addition to attending Wistar parties and managing arrangements for the Lafayette Ball, was a director both of the academy of fine arts and the musical fund society, secretary and later president of the Philosophical Society, a trustee of Girard College and of the general assembly of the Presbyterian church, and vice-president of the institution for the blind. A representative, but by no means complete, list of Philadelphians who stood out for the number and diversity of their memberships in voluntary societies would include the revered Peter Duponceau, William M. Meredith, Alexander Henry, Paul Beck, Jr., Thomas Pym Cope, Mayor Benjamin W. Richards, William Rawle, Robert Ralston, John Sergeant, Alexander Emslie, and Thomas Ridgway, the nephew of Philadelphia's second-richest man. As for Stephen Girard, the wealthiest Philadelphian of them all, his will clearly demonstrated his readiness to set aside huge sums in support of charitable and educational purposes.

New York City

A modern scholar has written that in the 1820s, "with the exception of a small group of civic leaders, the mercantile community [of New

York City] literally abandoned the city in the quest for private profit. They successfully surmounted problems related to commerce, manufacturing, and transportation but ignored until too late the human needs of the city." [11] This judgment echoes the contemporary plaint voiced by Philip Hone and John Pintard that their fellow New Yorkers were not as public spirited as were wealthy merchants in the other great northeastern cities. At the beginning of the 1820s, Pintard complained that his city did not abound in "citizens of independent circumstances who have talents or inclinations to attend to the multiplied demands on humanity and benevolence." Such duties fell "oppressively heavy on a few public-spirited citizens," such as himself. "In this respect, Philadelphia [was] more fortunate." A decade later, he was still bemoaning the fact that while he was of that small number who were "engaged in doing all the good [they could before their] final departure," others were "attending splendid balls, concerts, and oratorios." [12] Active in a multiplicity of causes, it is understandable that Pintard found the altruism of other men wanting when measured against his own.

Prior to his death in 1844, the range of social commitments of this highminded octogenarian rivalled in general scope, if it did not equal in number, the affiliations of Roberts Vaux. A typical week found Pintard putting aside only Sunday for rest and prayer, devoting the other days to meetings of the Society for the Prevention of Pauperism, a committee for a savings bank, the New-York Historical Society, American Academy for Fine Arts, American Bible Society, New York Society library, trustees of the free school society, literary and philosophical society, and the inevitable engagements attendant on being, as he was, a "zealous Episcopalian" and long-time vestryman of his Huguenot church. While John Pintard was a most unusual man, a substantial number of the wealthiest New Yorkers had records of social and cultural involvement which, if they did not quite match his own, nevertheless compared favorably with the careers in benevolence of rich men elsewhere.

The life of Philip Hone illustrates the principle that there was no necessary conflict between devotion to the good life and dedication to diverse forms of moral and community uplift. Hone was an enthusiastic bon vivant and gourmet, a pillar of a number of exclusive private clubs, a dedicated partygoer, an adornment of the sparkling balls, fêtes, and excursions that enlivened the social life of his own and other cities. His residence—whether on fashionable Broadway or in the Rockaways, where he spent his summers—was long regarded as "one of the most colorful and active social centers in the city." Convinced that New York City was "deplorably lacking in cultural activities," Hone labored manfully to correct the alleged deficiency, after an early retirement made possible by his great business success. A diary notation of June 8, 1828, records not merely memberships but the following offices which Hone at the time held: president of the German Society; vice-president of the savings bank; vice-president of the American Seaman's Fund Society; governor of the New York Hospital and of the Asylum Committee; trustee of Columbia College; manager of the asylum for the deaf and dumb; vestryman of Trinity Church; vice-president of the New-York Historical Society; manager of the literary and philosophical society; vice-president of the free savings society; trustee of the Merchant Exchange Company (and a number of business directorships); chairman of the board of managers of the Mechanical and Scientific Institute; and trustee of the Clinton Hall Association. Nor was this list exhaustive, omitting as it did his very real activity in the Horticultural Society and several associations concerned with disseminating art to a broad public. It is easy to sympathize with Hone's complaint that these offices occupied "too much of [his] time." On a fairly typical day, he might surround social visits to Commodore Chauncey at the Brooklyn Navy Yard and to John Coster's for a dinner party with an afternoon meeting of the trustees of Columbia College, an early evening meeting of the vestry of Trinity, and a brief visit to the evening meeting of the Common Council. He evidently did not find it easy to divest himself of these allegedly excessive commitments. At age 69, two years before his death, the old man is still repeating his theme of two decades before: "I am willing to work but I have too many irons in the fire. I must withdraw some of the unprofitable ones." [13] By "unprofitable" he did not have in mind the dollars-and-cents matters that denigrators of New York City assumed alone occupied the minds of the city's merchant elite.

Over a hundred of the wealthiest New Yorkers of the second quarter of the nineteenth century—more than 15 per cent of the city's richest men—belonged to or were active in five or more cultural and benevolent associations, religious and secular. The likelihood is that this figure underrepresents the number of wealthy social activists.[14] New York City's socially involved wealthy stalwarts represented every stratum of the city's great wealthholders: the "richest of the rich," such as John Jacob Astor and his son William B. Astor, James Boorman, George Griswold, Stephen Allen, John Haggerty, Edward R. Jones and John I. Jones, James Lenox, or Peter Schermerhorn; the more moderately rich such as James Beekman, James Harper, John Treat Irving, David S. Jones, Eleazer Parmley, George Bruce, and Richard Riker; the "old rich," such as Stephen Van Rensselaer, Peter Gerard Stuyvesant, Frederick DePeyster, Henry Rutgers, Hubert Van Wagenan, Peter Remsen, and William B. Crosby; and the newer rich, such as John Delafield, William E. Dodge, Isaac Hone, Anson G. Phelps, Samuel B. Ruggles, Arthur Tappan, and William Colgate; the mercantile or landed rich, such as James Brown, Jonathan Goodhue, James Gore King, Samuel Ward, Robert Ray, Jacob LeRoy, Isaac Carow, and Robert Minturn; and the "professional rich," such as Valentine Mott, Thomas Addis Emmet, John W. Francis, Samuel

Arlington House, Brooklyn. The owner, James Bennett, who described himself as "sole architect of his own house and of his own fortune," was not among Brooklyn's upper crust. *(From a colored lithograph, 1839, by J. H. Bufford from the Edward W. C. Arnold Collection of the Metropolitan Museum of Art. Photograph courtesy of the Museum of the City of New York.)*

Boyd, Peter A. Jay, Hugh Maxwell, Samuel Akerley, Gulian C. Verplanck, and above all David Hosack.

The elite of New York City, like their counterparts in Brooklyn, Boston, Philadelphia had a per capita representation in their era's voluntary associations that was greater by far than that of more moderately situated persons. (As the following section will make clear, the urban rich, who comprised less than 1 per cent of their cities' populations, were a substantial component of both the leadership and the membership of the voluntary societies.)

A few additional accounts of the activities of benevolent New Yorkers convey better than statistical generalizations the quality of their participation. The famed Dr. Hosack's record is remarkably similar to Hone's, for all the disparity in their means of earning income and in their interests. If Hone's home was a lively social center, Hosack's, according to his eminent colleague John W. Francis, was the "resort of the learned and enlightened from every part of the world,"[15] its atmosphere enhanced by its valuable paintings and its large and costly library. For all his intellectualism and scientific curiosity, Hosack appeared to enjoy the amenities of good living no less than the great diarist. Like Hone, Hosack's affiliations were most impressive. He was an important worker for the American Academy of Fine Arts; a founder and the fourth president of the New-York Historical Society; vice-president of the literary and philosophical society; president of Rutgers Medical College; a founder of Bellevue Hospital; with Hone, a governor of New York Hospital; founder of the Elgin Botanic Garden; active in the Humane Society; president of the temperance society of Hyde Park; and publisher and contributor to scientific journals and associations. Hosack embodied as well as any man the ideal of *noblesse oblige* that appears to have had so large an influence on so many of the rich men of his time and place.

Dr. John Wakefield Francis succeeded Hosack, not only as New York City's most eminent medical figure, but also as one of the city's most sought-after social lions. Like Hosack, Francis adhered to a variety of artistic, scientific, literary, and charitable organizations. That a cultured physician such as Valentine Mott, a man of refinement such as Gulian Crommelin Verplanck, a hero of piety such as Arthur Tappan, a publisher such as James Harper, or a scholar and religious eminence such as the Reverend John McVickar were active in secular benevolence was in a sense fitting, in view of the affinity between their backgrounds or occupations, on the one hand, and the good works they undertook, on the other. What is surprising, particularly in the case of a city whose elite had so great a reputation for crassness, is the extent to which the *commercial* rich were socially active. In addition to giving "princely dinners" to those fortunate enough to be his guests, John Jacob Astor supported a home for aged ladies, an orphan asylum, the New York Dispensary, and the library movement. The merchant-banker James Brown was "deeply interested in religious, educational, and philanthropic enterprises," serving for many years as president of the Society for Improving the Condition of the Poor. The merchant and banker James Gore King combined leadership in the Chamber of Commerce, exclusive social clubs, and artistic and educational enterprises. James Lenox and the rich shipping merchant Robert Bowne Minturn had similarly diverse affiliations. The wealthy John David Wolfe, longtime vestryman of Trinity Church and senior warden of Grace Church, helped found schools for poor girls, a house for crippled and destitute children, presided over the Working Women's Protective Union and the American Museum of Natural History. Such successful merchants as Samuel Ward, William E. Dodge, and Anson Phelps were leading figures in what has been called the "benevolent empire"—men devoted to religious principles at least as much as to material accumulation. Of particular interest is the great number of wealthy New Yorkers with no reputation for benevolence who, in fact, were engaged in one or another voluntary association.

Brooklyn

Brooklyn, of course, had far fewer rich men than its giant neighbor, but the proportion of the socially active was similar on both sides of the East River, As in Manhattan, so in Brooklyn, it mattered not whether wealthholders were mercantile or professional, old settlers or new, descended of seventeenth-century Dutch families or more recently arrived New Englanders; all backgrounds produced vigorous humanitarians. Furmans, Hegemans, Leffertses, Van Sinderens, Vanderveers, and Van Nostrands, were active in the city's churches, its bible and missionary societies, its orphan asylum and its dispensary, its libraries and its lyceum, its savings bank, and its Society for Promoting Agriculture and Manufacturing. Astor's onetime partner, Cornelius Heeney, was a bulwark of Catholic charities throughout the early nineteenth century. The outstanding lawyer, Democratic leader, and man of culture, Henry C. Murphy, helped found literary associations and libraries, the city's historical society, and its Association for Improving the Condition of the Poor. Henry Evelyn Pierrepont, son of Brooklyn's richest man and son-in-law of Peter A. Jay, largely owed his reputation as perhaps Brooklyn's most refined citizen to his activities in behalf of the city's library, its leading cemetery, its hospital, its historical society, and its Academy of Music. Joseph Sprague, Cyrus Porter Smith, and George Hall, each of them a mayor of Brooklyn during the era, were also active in the city's churches and religious benevolent enterprises, apprentice libraries, Mechanic's Bank, city hospital, temperance society, dispensary, Association for Improving the Condition of the Poor, and diverse cultural and educational institutions.

The wealthy Brooklynites, New Yorkers, Philadelphians, and Bostonians whose leadership in voluntary associations has been described constituted only a small segment of the elite social activists of their cities. They have been singled out, not because their careers were unusual, but rather because they were representative. A quantitative study of the diverse social involvements of the rich of Brooklyn and of New York City discloses that more than half of the persons who were among the richest 1 per cent in the 1830s and 1840s participated in at least one public-spirited voluntary association. One out of five of New York City's rich of 1828 and of the Brooklyn rich of the early 1840s were active in five or more such organizations, while two out of five belonged to two or more associations. The rule prevailed: the richer the individual, the more likely he was to be a member of a socially purposeful organization. For the "richest of the rich"—the 30 Brooklynites assessed for at least $100,000 in 1841; the 60 New Yorkers assessed for $100,000 or more in 1828, and the 55 assessed for $250,000 or more in 1845—the rate of participation was greater than for the rich as a whole. Of Brooklyn's super rich, 75 per cent were involved, most of them in three or more organizations. About 70 per cent of New York City's wealthiest were similarly occupied. Not only were the rich inordinately socially conscious when compared with other classes in the older northeastern cities; their altruism compares favorably with that of upper-class benevolents in the new cities of the west as well.[16]

Elite Leadership in Voluntary Associations

That most rich men appear to have been joiners of non-utilitarian societies is interesting information, not least for the light it throws on the values of the socioeconomic elite. Yet such information does not reveal the extent to which these associations consisted of or were led by men of wealth. The rich were so few in number that conceivably they could have been only a small minority in the organizations that attracted them, for all the enthusiasm with which they seemed to join. The way to discover the comparative role played by wealthholding elites in the important social, cultural, and artistic associations of the antebellum era is to examine evidence on the activities and above all the memberships of these groups. This section attempts to do precisely that, drawing on several hundred randomly selected voluntary associations in the great northeastern cities. The characteristic purposes and policies of the organizations have also been examined, in order to throw greater light on the causes as well as the extent of elite social involvement.

The historian of the "benevolent empire" has shown, if impressionistically, the important role played in northeastern bible, mission, tract, Sunday school, temperance, and Christian educational societies by wealthy laymen.[17] With the national offices of three benevolent organizations located within its midst, New York City was the national "center of trusteeship," and constitutional provision required that 24 of the 36 managers of the American Bible Society be New Yorkers. Eleven of the 24 were members of the city's wealthy families. Of the life membership of the New York Bible Society, a branch of the national organization, 70 per cent were among the upper 2 per cent of the city's taxpayers. The American Tract Society, also based in New York City, was also composed of the city's richest men; 40 per cent of the life directors were of the rich (a term standing for membership in the upper 1 per cent of a city's wealthholders, unless otherwise indicated), as were a majority of the group's vice-presidents and lay directors. Drawing on leaders from a number of northern cities, the American Board of Commissioners for Foreign Missions, located in New York City, had as officers such wealthy men as Samuel T. Armstrong of Boston and Stephen Van Rensselaer, besides men of great eminence in the legal profession. Seven of ten leaders of the City Mission Society of the Episcopal Church were of rich New York families, as were ten out of fifteen of the Society for Promoting Religion and Learning in New York State.[18]

Evidence from the other cities points in the same direction. The wealthy Armstrong was also the president of the Massachusetts Sabbath School Society in Boston, Dr. John Collins Warren was president of the Society for Suppressing Intemperance, John Tappan was the vice-president of the American Education Society, and Francis Parkman was the corresponding secretary of the Massachusetts Bible Society; each of these gentlemen belonged to that exalted group who comprised the richest one-tenth of 1 per cent of Boston's population in the late 1840s. In Philadelphia too every one of the religious benevolent societies in the mid-1840s had one or more of the city's social and economic elite among its small number of leaders. Alexander Henry was president of the American Sunday School Union located in Philadelphia, with Silas E. Weir and Paul Beck, Jr., as vice-presidents; all were very wealthy men, as were 30 per cent of the organization's managers. Other historians have shown that the stock in trade of the "benevolent empire" was the glory of the Protestant faith and conservative social doctrine.

In the face of sharp inflation, a financial panic followed by a depression lasting the better part of a decade, unprecedented immigration of the poor of western Europe, and a widening gulf between the rich—who owned a greater share of urban wealth than ever—and the mass of men—who owned less—the plight of the poor was perhaps the most pressing issue facing urban society in the second quarter of the nineteenth century. Urban governments hardly faced up to the problem. They allocated large proportions of their budgets for the purpose, true, but the actual sums were piddling because of the paltry treasuries of the time. In view of the inadequacy of municipal government, dozens of voluntary associations sprang up to supplement organizations founded earlier, in order to deal with different facets of the problem, whether poverty in general or the plight of particular groups. In New York City, one of the most influential of these organizations was the Humane Society. Established shortly after the Revolution, its long experience and prestige earned for it a primary role in alleviating the manifestations of poverty and want that troubled the early nineteenth century.

The Humane Society of New York City has been described recently as a "model reform group, widely imitated in organization and technique." [19] Founded originally to relieve the plight of imprisoned debtors and to secure the release of those imprisoned for small sums, the society had expanded its activities over the course of time. By the nineteenth century, it sought (and largely achieved) better fare for prisoners, "soup houses" to provide them with special meals, broad penal and judicial reforms, abolition of imprisonment for debt; the society had led the fight to outlaw the dangerous occupation of chimney sweep. The Boston [or Massachusetts] and the Philadelphia societies were at first concerned with restoring life to those saved from drowning, but subsequently turned to the health needs of the poor and conditions of confinement of debtors. The Brooklyn Humane Society early in the nineteenth century distributed hundreds of daily rations to the poor. The reason given by its officers for putting an end to the Brooklyn group's existence is instructive. They were "convinced by painful experience that institutions of this nature have a direct tendency to beget, among a large portion of their fellow citizens, habits of imprudence, indolence, dissipation, and consequent pauperism." If humane society leaders elsewhere did not go so far as their Brooklyn brethren and actually close up shop, they doubtless understood well the fears of the Brooklynites, since they appeared to share a common ideology. In Philadelphia, for example, the guardians of the poor (who were the unpaid municipal officers in charge of poor relief), warned repeatedly that outdoor or home relief, which gave assistance to the poor outside of almshouses and workhouses, was calculated "to blunt and ultimately destroy the noble pride of independence." Instead, it created a "dependence on the bounty of others," producing "idleness and not infrequently crimes." [20] Soup, fuel, clothing, when distributed to the poor were often accompanied by broadsides purveying the wholesome teaching that the poor were the authors of their own misery.

These were not large membership organizations. New York City's society for example consisted of two dozen managers. From the outset "composed of men of influence and position in the community," Raymond Mohl's previous study disclosed that 73 per cent of 102 identifiable managers of the New York Humane Society between 1787 and 1831 were businessmen and attorneys, while another 20 per cent were physicians and ministers. Most of these men were also members of the New York City rich. While it lasted, the Brooklyn society was led by the wealthy (or persons whose families were among the Brooklyn rich in 1841, almost a quarter century after the society's demise). In the 1830s and 1840s at least a third of the officers of the Philadelphia society and more than two-thirds of the leaders of the Boston Humane Society were of the wealthy families of their cities. Nor were these patterns atypical.

A sampling of the officers, managers, and directors of the Provident Society for Employing the Poor, the House of Refuge, and the Infirmary for the Relief of Poor Persons Laboring under Hernia or Rupture, in Philadelphia, discloses that wealth was also heavily represented in these organizations. Two-thirds of the officers and more than 50 per cent of the directors and managers were members of the city's rich families. The wealth of officers and managers of such Boston associations as the Asylum and Farm School for Indigent Boys, the Howard Benevolent Society, the Charitable Mechanic Association, the Charitable Fire Society, the Children's Friend Society, the Female Orphan Asylum, and the Young Men's Benevolent Society has been examined. Approximately two-thirds of the leadership of these groups belonged to the city's wealthiest families. Brooklyn's Association for Improving the Condition of the Poor was created in the 1840s, not to assist the "permanent poor" or those of "vicious or indolent habits," but those persons deemed likely to benefit from *advice* and moral improvement as well as from relief of their "immediate necessities." Two-thirds of the officers and elected members came of the city's economic upper crust. The Brooklyn Benevolent Society dispensed free fuel to the city's poor during the winter, shoes, stockings, and other "necessary articles of clothing" to poor schoolchildren, and the salaries of teachers for "said poor children." This society, founded by the wealthy Cornelius Heeney and financed by a portion of the rents he collected on property in Brooklyn Heights, was supervised by trustees such as James Friel, Henry Patchen, Noel Becar, and Francis Cooper, wealthy and eminent Brooklynites all.

The New York Association for Improving the Condition of the Poor is interesting as much for the motives as for the activities of its founders. It was established in 1843, "for the purpose of controlling the evils growing out of almsgiving, which often encouraged idleness and led to crime." At a time when there were almost forty separate societies to help the poor in New York City, it was hoped that the new association would erase the evils attendant on the chaotic and "injudicious" almsgiving believed to result from this proliferation. Determined to put an end to street begging and vagrancy, the association sent visitors to the dwellings of the poor, in order to determine need and "through friendly intercourse" to inculcate "habits of frugality, temperance, industry, and self-dependence." It dispensed food, clothing, and fuel—never money—to those deemed worthy, where the gift of these necessities was compatible with the main objectives of the society. According to the first annual report of the Association, its purpose was "the elevation of [both] the moral and physical condition of the indigent." Moral elevation required understanding of the great truth that failure was due to individual fault, as success was due to individual merit. Roy Lubove has shown that most of the association's leaders were businessmen and professionals.[21] New York City's assessment rolls disclose that the first president, every one of the five vice-presidents, and the treasurer of this organization were of New York City's elite of wealth, as were half the elected members of the board of managers.

The New York Society for the Reformation of Juvenile Delinquents, which supervised the House of Refuge, sought to help youthful offenders by teaching them skills, finding them work in the country, and by inculcating "habits of industry" and the "social and moral obligations of citizens." According to its modern historian, the New York House of Refuge was managed by men of great wealth, who constituted a "self-perpetuating group [who] chose their replacements from others of like backgrounds," almost none of whom had ever experienced want.[22] At the time of its founding, at the beginning of our period, 8 of its 10 officers were members of New York City's richest 500, as were 15 of its 26 managers. Two-thirds of this society's 70 managers over the years from 1824 to 1850 were members of wealthy families.

The Society for the Reformation of Juvenile Delinquents had grown out of the New York Society for the Prevention of Pauperism. The latter group was formed in 1817 in order to ascertain the causes of poverty. Characteristically, these causes were identified by the NYSPP as ignorance, idleness, and intemperance. In the fashion of the time, the society sought to toughen the state's poor laws, "so that public relief would only be granted after thorough investigation, to aged, sick, or othewise helpless and unemployable individuals." Raymond Mohl has found that more than 80 per cent of the society's 89 leaders were merchants or professionals.[23] Its first president General Matthew Clarkson, and Brockholst Livingston, John Murray, Jr., William Few, and Nicholas Fish, vice-presidents, were all members of New York's social and economic elite, as were all but one of its officers at the time it transformed itself into the Society for the Reformation of Juvenile Delinquents. The sole exception was the Quaker humanitarian Thomas Eddy. Most of the managers were of families that were among the richest 2 per cent of the city's taxpayers.

Dozens of dispensaries and hospitals primarily serving the needy, orphanages, savings banks for the poor, societies for the encouragement of faithful domestic servants, and the like, supplemented the humane societies, the societies for the prevention of pauperism or alleviation of the condition of the poor in general. These associations gave practical help to the deserving poor, accompanied by moral preachments designed to balance material assistance with proper social and moral attitudes. The rich in every city played inordinately large roles in these groups. The first dispensaries had been established after the Revolution, the first in Philadelphia in 1786, the others shortly thereafter; their purpose was, typically, that of "relieving such sick, poor, and indigent persons as are unable to procure medical aid." In every city the majority of dispensary managers and directors were members of elite families. Philadelphia was represented by Norrises, Whartons, Perots; Boston by Frothinghams, Cutlers, Bradlees, Parkmans, Fosters, Grays; Brooklyn by Sandses, Van Sinderens, Thornes, Willoughbys, Hoyts, Nostrands. In New York City in 1838 8 of the 10 trustees of the New York Dispensary were rich, as were slightly more than two-thirds of 139 life members of the organization. More than half of the 45 trustees of the Eastern Dispensary, set up in the 1840s in response to the overflow of ailing indigent poor, were among the city's richest men.

That the officers and trustees of the Massachusetts General Hospital in Boston were almost exclusively from the city's elite of wealth is not surprising in view of the origins of the institution. The circular letter signed by the wealthy James Jackson and John Collins Warren was addressed to Boston's wealthiest and most influential citizens, reminding them that "the wealthy inhabitants of . . . Boston have always evinced that they consider themselves as 'treasurers of God's bounty' and in Christian countries . . . it must always be considered the first of duties to heal the sick." [24] During the 1830s and 1840s the famous hospital was under the leadership of such men as Ebenezer Francis, Nathaniel P. Russell, Henry Codman, Josiah Quincy, Jr., William Appleton, Theodore Lyman, Francis C. Gray, and others of equal eminence. The Massachusetts Charitable Eye and Ear Infirmary had as its president the great merchant Robert Gould Shaw, while the Boston Lying-In Hospital had as president and vice-president the large wealthholders James Savage and Thomas B. Wales, and as non-physician trustees members of the Amory, Parkman, Lowell, Andrews, and Inches families. The State's mental hospital "was conceived and [the project] carried through by the members of the Boston elite." [25]

The New York Hospital was controlled by New York City's elite of the period. Philip Hone's diary indicates that he gave a great deal of thought and time to the hospital, regularly visiting it in order that he might see at first hand its operations. Its officers were almost entirely of the upper crust of wealth, as were more than 80 per cent of its governors in 1833 and its trustees in 1848. In Brooklyn, where local government was unable to provide the necessary funds, Augustus Graham and such other wealthy citizens as Henry E. Pierrepont, Cyrus P. Smith, E. D. Hurlbut, George S. Howland, John Greenwood, Edgar Hicks, and Abiel A. Low stepped into the breach, founding and then running the Brooklyn City Hospital during the mid-1840s.

Orphans, fallen women, "indigent females," victims of tragic physical afflictions, all were the objects of benevolence. Whether the orphanage looked after white or colored children, the staffs of officers and advisers were typically composed of some of their cities' "best men"—and women. For example, in the case of the Association for the Benefit of Colored Orphans, established in New York City in 1836, its officers and chief workers were the wives and daughters of the elite such as Martha Codwise, Sara C. Hauxhurst, Anna H. Shotwell, and Mary Murray. Institutions for the blind in Philadelphia and New York City, as in Boston, were managed primarily by the wealthiest men of their communities. Duponceaus, Vauxes, Lippincotts, Richardses, Baches, Meigses, and Dallases served in the one city; Stuyvesants, Wards, Ackerlys, Crosbys, and Staggs in the other. The lunatic asylum, like New York City's institution for the instruction of the deaf and dumb, was governed by a special committee of the New York Hospital; two-thirds of the managers belonged to the elite of status and wealth. Magdalen societies, created to "reclaim" repentant prostitutes primarily through religious instruction and the inculcation of moral and industrious habits, inevitably were led by zealots of religious benevolence, such as Arthur Tappan in New York and Robert Ralston in Philadelphia. These men, like slightly less than half of the other leaders of these associations, combined religious zeal with great wealth.

Savings banks for the poor during the "era of the common man" were directed mainly by those uncommon men who belonged to the wealthiest 1 per cent in the community. Designed primarily to encourage habits of thrift and sobriety among the laboring poor, while also setting aside for them their own hardearned sums to cushion the shock of unemployment or illness, these institutions held out additional promise to the wealthy. For, as one of the sponsors had written in support of the creation of a savings bank in New York City, by removing "one of the causes of mendicity [such a bank would] thereby lessen the burthens on the more favored class of citizens in supporting paupers."[26] An even clearer appeal to the self-interest of large property owners can be detected in the language used by the founders of the Society for Encouragement of Faithful Domestic Servants in 1826. Dividing its leadership between the rich and the highminded—Arthur Tappan and the altruist John Griscom, on the one hand, John Haggerty and Moses Allen, on the other—this group sought to counteract the pride and arrogance (particularly in foreign servants), that threatened "if not to destroy, at least to mar much of the calm happiness of domestic life," by distributing prizes "for long and faithful service." The awards took the form of Bibles and "parchment certificates" testifying to faithful service.[27]

Few urban associations of the 1830s matched in importance those concerned with education or, more specifically, with the quality of education available to the great bulk of urban residents who could not afford private schools. Public education was a crucial issue at a time when small sums were budgeted by municipal governments for the purpose, and public schools were stigmatized as charity schools because of the pauper's oath requirement. During the first half of the nineteenth century, public education in New York City was in fact under the control and management of a voluntary association, the Free School Society, which after 1825 was known as the Public School Society of New York. Recently subjected to an intensive study, this society "for almost half a century dominated the educational scene in the city, enrolling thousands of pupils in a system which grew to 74 schools." [28] For most of the period it actually received state funds for schools in New York City; this power was conferred after 1825 with the intent of closing off funds to denominational schools. Although state funds were denied the society after 1841, it continued to be influential through the following decade. It used the common school fund to provide free schooling for children of "all classes," parents paying "such compensation as [might] be within their pecuniary ability." The Public School Society's objectives, stated in a number of reports over the years, were to "prepare for usefulness a large portion" of the population, "who might otherwise grow up in idleness, remain a burden on the community, and become victims of every species of vice and profligacy incident to extensive and populous cities." The society's efforts would instill "feelings of independence, which [were] highly important to cultivate, and be promoted among [the] poor and laboring classes." [29] William W. Cutler reports that the society "attracted the services of many wealthy men," noting that for the periods 1820–1837 and 1838–1853 approximately two-thirds of its several hundred trustees were merchants, financiers, and manufacturers, while an additional one-fifth were physicians and attorneys. I have discovered that four of the society's six presidents were rich men. A random check reveals that slightly less than two-thirds of the 65 trustees in 1828 were of New York City's wealthiest families, as were three-fifths of the trustees in 1841. Inasmuch as the tax assessments that are the basis of my determinations of wealth were notoriously incomplete, it is possible and indeed likely that a number of the merchant and professional trustees assessed for little wealth were actually men of some personal property. Altogether, it is clear that the society was controlled by men of great wealth.

Refuting what he calls the "warm and pleasant myth" that educational reform in the nineteenth century was largely a product of democratic and humanitarian forces, a modern student of such reform in Massachusetts notes the important role played by "social leaders" in the coalition that achieved the desired changes.[30]

Certainly wealthy Philadelphians were instrumental in transforming the public school system of Pennsylvania from a restricted, poorly-financed one, "in which the poorer children were forced publicly to make a show of their poverty," into a broadbased system free of stigma. Students of the Pennsylvania reform have stressed the importance of the Public School Law of 1834 and the vital role played in its passage by leading men in the community. On the political level, the wealthy Samuel Breck introduced the legislation of 1834 in a special report he prepared for the state legislature's joint committee on education. Breck was also a member of the Pennsylvania Society for the Promotion of Public Schools, a voluntary organization created in 1827 which probably had more to do with common-school reform in the state than any other group. Led by Roberts Vaux, this society had a membership of slightly less than a hundred. Joseph McCadden's study disclosed, that while most of the leaders were young men whose fame was yet to come, they hardly represented a cross section either of Philadelphia society or the city's occupations. They were chiefly lawyers, merchants, doctors, publishers, with a sprinkling of highminded members of the "cultured leisure class." If the latter "spent their time in promoting benevolent and intellectual interests, scorning the pursuit of further wealth," they could do so only because they had much wealth to begin with. Breck's report affords an interesting glimpse into the social mind of the benevolent rich. To their minds, equal primary education for rich and poor alike would mean that "all start[ed] with equal advantage, leaving no discrimination, then or thereafter, but such as study shall produce." Since common schools would foster among "the rich, the comparatively rich, and the destitute" a similar feeling of "perfect equality," it was "the duty of the State to promote and foster such establishments."[31]

The law of 1834 reformed and broadened the public school system of Pennsylvania, but a law of 1818 had established the system. The earlier enactment, like the later one, was due primarily to the work of a voluntary association led, of course, by Roberts Vaux—the Philadelphia Society for the Promotion of Public Economy. The society's public-school committee in 1818 "proposed and brought about the passage of the school law." The committee was composed primarily of "substantial citizens of Philadelphia," dedicated to preserving the morals of the people through industry, temperance, economy, and public education.

Wealthy men also provided the leadership in associations that sought to expand higher educational opportunities. New York University ultimately emerged out of a meeting called in New York City in 1830 to consider "the expediency and the means of establishing a university in the city." The assemblage voted to create a university "on a liberal foundation," with a student body composed primarily of "respectable but not wealthy citizens" (mainly mechanics and tradesmen), supplemented by a few rich young men whose parents did not wish to send them abroad. Six of the nine signers of the letter of January 4, 1830 calling for the meeting to consider the creation of the new university, were among the richest men in the city, friends of Philip Hone all. The men who composed the councils subsequently elected to run the new institution were also predominantly wealthy.[32] That wealth was inordinately represented in the councils of the trustees and overseers who managed the great higher educational institutions of the northeastern cities is perhaps too obvious to warrant anything more than a mention. Similarly, every single one of the lay members of the standing committee which governed the General Theological Seminary in New York City for randomly selected years in the 1830s was of a rich and eminent family.[33]

Supplementing the urban movement to increase and improve public school facilities were numerous associations concerned with uplifting the cultural lives of the mass of urban residents. Each city had lyceums, athenaeums, "mercantile," apprentice, or other library associations, and institutes of one sort or another designed to offer commoners the opportunity to hear lecturers of repute. Seeking to counteract the widespread impression that New York City was derelict in supporting literature and learning, leading citizens in 1824 founded the Athenaeum. Its purpose was to sponsor "public discourses" and a library containing "the whole of the works, periodicals, or standards, that hourly issue from the presses of America and Europe." The Athenaeum, the New York Society Library, the Stuyvesant Institute (organized in 1834 "for the diffusion of knowledge, by means of popular lectures," and which also offered a library and reading room housed in its "granite building of the most substantial style"), and the Clinton Hall Association (which administered a mercantile library in order to accomplish the "moral and intellectual improvement of the merchants' clerks") were led by men of similar socioeconomic status. Roughly three-quarters of the officers, trustees, managers, and directors of these associations were members of the city's wealthiest and most eminent families.

In Brooklyn the Apprentices Library, the Brooklyn City Library, the Hamilton Literary Association, the Athenaeum, the Lyceum, and the Brooklyn Institute had purposes and activities quite similar to those inspiring their Manhattan counterparts. They were also led by men of equivalent status. A check of random years in the period 1820–1850 discloses that the leadership of Philadelphia's Athenaeum, Apprentices Library, Mercantile Library Association, and the Library Company of the city was also composed primarily of the city's elite. Such men as William Rawle, Horace Binney, John Sergeant, Joseph P. Norris, Robert Waln, Dr. James Mease, Thomas Wharton, William Tilghman, Jacob Gratz, Clement or Thomas or Nicholas Biddle, George M. Dallas, and the inevitable Roberts Vaux were omnipresent. The Lowell Institute—founded by John Lowell, Jr.—the Boston Library Society, and the Boston Athenaeum were likewise governed by the elite; two-thirds of the officers and subscribers to such organizations typically came from the city's wealthy families.

While critics bemoaned the poverty of cultural life in their cities, a variety of voluntary associations devoted to learning and the arts managed to flourish during the second quarter of the nineteenth century. Of course, the character and effectiveness of these organizations differed from one city to another. Naysaying detractors may well have had a point in asserting the small achievements and the small memberships of such groups. The purpose of this brief discussion, however, is not to explore in depth the history of these associations, but to ascertain the extent to which the upper class was involved in their activities.

Much importance was attributed to cultural matters by leading men—if for diverse reasons. Where a moralistic zealot like Pintard believed that "theatres, operas, academies of arts, museums," could be the means to "prevent the growth of vice and immorality" within the city,[34] other men of means were charmed by the down-to-earth benefits likely to accrue from the flourishing of "culture." The historian of antebellum Cincinnati notes that the city's reputation for being "the intellectual as well as the hog center of the middle West" in 1838, "enhanced the wealth and power of the city," in the judgment of its leaders. Academies and museums "symbolized elegance and refinement," which helped bring "needed capital into the city." The positive practical benefits likely to result from cultural development were also discerned by some of its champions in the great northeastern cities.[35]

Whatever their motives—and there is little doubt they were as varied and complex as the motives of men usually are—many of Boston's "first men" participated in the city's richly diverse cultural associations. The wealthy piano manufacturer Jonas Chickering was, quite properly, president of the Handel and Hayden Society, founded for the purpose of "cultivating and improving a correct taste in the performance of sacred music"; Samuel A. Eliot was the first president of the city's Academy of Music. The beneficiary of sizable bequests by John Phillips and Benjamin D. Greene, the Boston Society of Natural History was headed during the era by Greene and by such luminaries as Drs. John Collins Warren and Amos Binney, Patrick Tracy Jackson, and Thomas Bulfinch. The Boston Anthology Society, devoted to "elevating the literary standard of the time," from its founding in 1805 to mid-century was composed of Gardiners, Shaws, Tuckermans, Tudors, Thachers, Grays, Welleses, Warrens, and Jacksons. The leaders and the several hundred members of the Massachusetts Historical Society and the New England Historical and Genealogical Society appeared to be identical with the leaders of Boston's social and economic life. About two-thirds of the genealogical society's membership for the period 1844 to 1850 were among the wealthy taxpayers of the city.

The first volume of memoirs of the Pennsylvania Historical Society in 1825 contained articles on the "Great Treaty of William Penn in 1682," the boundary controversy between Penn and Lord Baltimore, and the "Provincial Literature of Pennsylvania,"—the latter title, of course, referring to a chronological period rather than to any narrowness of outlook. The articles were the work of Roberts Vaux and Thomas I. Wharton, among others. Leading nineteenth-century historians of Pennsylvania were filled with admiration at the fact, writing: "when it is considered that the gentlemen who prepared those papers were men of business, whose minds were constantly engaged with weighty affairs, it must be admitted that their enthusiasm was shown to be warm by the care they had taken and the time which they had spent in preparation of their papers."[36] The presidents of the society, from its founding in 1825 to the outbreak of the Civil War, were William Rawle, Peter Duponceau, Judge Thomas Sergeant, and Dr. George W. Norris—eminences all. Most of the other Philadelphians represented on the council of the organization during various years selected at random in the 1830s and 1840s were of comparable social and economic status; and three-quarters of the historical society's membership in the year of its establishment were among Philadelphia's elite.

During the same era, the American Philosophical Society, which had been an adornment of the city since Franklin's time, was led by men —often the same men who ran the historical society—of similarly lofty status. Presided over without exception by one of Philadelphia's crême de la crême, the philosophical society's vice-presidents, secretaries, counsellors, and curators, were also primarily wealthy and prestigious citizens, as were the officers of the Academy of Natural Sciences. In the 1820s, artists and professors of art were unhappy with the policy of the Pennsylvania Academy of Fine Arts, the nation's oldest, for refusing to give them greater authority over professional matters. Founded by well-to-do lawyers at the beginning of the nineteenth century, the academy later continued to be run by successful men of affairs, determined "to improve and refine the public taste in works of art." Toward this worthy end, "elegant and approved specimens" of our "native genius" were to be made available to schools for instruction. Presidents of the academy included such figures as Joseph Hopkinson, Joseph R. Ingersoll, Henry D. Gilpin, Caleb Cope, and Edward H. Coates.

As has been indicated earlier, New York City's wealthiest and most fashionable citizens were widely denigrated as allegedly caring for "wealth and the pomp which wealth can purchase, more than virtue, genius, or beauty." The kind of judgment given by a contemporary musical scholar, who had happily forsaken London for New York City, that "many excellent institutions existed, and good music, good acting, and a variety of good, valuable, and artistic things were known and thoroughly enjoyed by the people of New York," was not generally accepted.[37] Yet the city did possess a great array of artistic, literary, scientific, historical, and other cultural organizations during the period 1825–1850.

An interesting example of the involvement of New York City's elite in the arts is afforded by the American Academy of Fine Arts. Created at the beginning of the nineteenth century, when it was called the New York Academy, this society lasted until 1839. It was "done in" by a combination of declining public interest in the art works made available by its wealthy sponsors, its unpopularity with working American artists, and, above all, by the limited artistic ideals of its administrators; the latter failing was doubtless largely responsible for the other two. Characterized by the contemporary art historian William Dunlap as an organization of "gentlemen of every profession but that of an artist," a modern critic finds that the academy "had little concern for the practicing artist, but prompted by civic pride, it was an endeavor to bring together men of social distinction and affluence in cultivating an interest in the 'Polite Arts.' "[38] Its activities never strayed far, certainly not in spirit, from those conceived at its founding, when its hundred wealthy members each paid $50 per share, in addition to annual dues, to be turned over to Robert R. Livingston, Ambassador to France. Livingston was to purchase casts made in France for subsequent viewing without charge by New Yorkers in an exhibition room made available by the wealthy patrons. The academy was regarded by John Pintard as an effective means of opposing vice, since according to him, "gross dissipation always prevail[ed] where refinement [was] not cultivated." Edward Livingston spoke for the founders when he expressed the hope that the academy's efforts would result in the planting of "a germ of those arts so highly cultivated in Europe, but not yet planted here."[39] The academy's reputation for relying upon the protection of "the rich and the great," is well-founded. Although no membership list was ever compiled, its officers and patrons are listed in a number of sources. The officers and directors in the early years were such eminences as Chancellor Livingston, DeWitt Clinton, Cadwallader D. Colden, Robert Fulton, William Cutting, John R. Murray, and Dr. David Hosack. Men of this sort continued at the controls; approximately 75 per cent of its 217 non-artist patrons were members of New York City's social and economic elite, of prestigious families old and new.

Out of the ashes of the Academy of Fine Arts, friends to art in 1839 organized the Apollo Association for the Promotion of the Fine Arts. Trying to profit from the mistakes made by the academy, the Apollo Association was "particularly devoted to the native living artist." Smaller sums were sought, subscribers paying only $5.00 each to the new association for the purchase of "native works of art." The works were exhibited and at the end of the year they were distributed to the subscribers through a lottery, in the hope of accomplishing a "diffusion of improved taste." The hoped for diffusion unfortunately did not occur, for the society went into a swift decline. During its brief career, it was led by men of status similar to those who had governed the academy. The president of the Apollo Association was Dr. John W. Francis, while Philip Hone, George Bruce, William Kemble, James W. Gerard, and the publisher James Watson Webb were among the "merchant amateurs" who monopolized the places on its board of managers.[40] In 1844, the Apollo Association became the American Art Union. Prior to its collapse in 1852—when it was declared an illegal lottery—the American Art Union did enjoy great success in bringing art to the people. Collecting $5.00 from each of 2,000 subscribers, 80 per cent of whom were not residents of the city, the union, in the enthusiastic words of Lydia Maria Child, was a "most excellent institution." Its objects were "to scatter abroad works of native art among the masses of people, who [were] not able to pay such high prices as the rich [could] afford," and to encourage American artists of merit. Although founded by New Yorkers, it was an organization of national scope. The committee of managers of the art union typically were leading merchants, half of whom came from the city's leading families. Included were Philip Hone, William H. Johnson, David C. Colden, Charles H. Russell, William Duer, Evert A. Duyckinck, and Moses H. Grinnell.

As for the New York Gallery of Fine Arts which emerged late in the era, it began with the collection left by the wealthy merchant Luman Reed. Reed had constructed a gallery over the top floor of his home on Greenwich Street and initiated "one of the first private collections of American painting." Reed's son-in-law, the wealthy Jonathan Sturges, became the president of the gallery, with other leading merchants predominant on its executive committee. Of its not quite 50 trustees in 1844, 57 per cent were among New York City's wealthiest taxpayers, while another 33 per cent were of well-known, if not the very richest families.[41]

Philip Hone's most intimate circle were also devotees of music. They were particularly fond of Italian opera, described by Miss Lydia Maria Child as the "most patrician" of New York amusements. Hone's good friend Edmund A. Laight was first vice-president, James I. Jones was secretary, and John Delafield was the treasurer of the city's Philharmonic Society, which was formed in the mid-1820s; the list of governors was filled with "the names of many New York men, prominent both in business and society."[42]

New York City's leading men were also concerned with stimulating an appreciation of literature and learning. In 1814 the Literary and Philosophical Society had been founded, to "cultivate the most useful branches of knowledge" and to "stimulate into activity the literature and talents of the community." Whether it did these things is questionable. There can be no doubt however that over the following quarter of a century it provided yet another outlet for civic-minded and successful men. At its birth it was led by DeWitt Clinton, James Kent, David Hosack, John Mason, and a dozen other uniformly famous or wealthy men. A Hone diary entry on February 15, 1829, records the society's officers for that year. With the exception of the few men whose eminence derived from their clerical titles and their membership on the Columbia College faculty, the others were the wealthy merchants and professionals who moved in Hone's social orbit. A decade later, the society was still governed by Duers, Van Rensselaers, Francises, DePeysters, Motts, Hosacks, and the ubiquitous Hone. The same social types provided leadership to the Lyceum of Natural History from its founding, under Dr. Samuel L. Mitchell in 1817, through the middle of the century.

Probably the most active and perhaps the most important of the city's learned associations was the New-York Historical Society. For the half century after its founding in 1804, this society was led by the patriciate of the city: Egbert Benson, Gouverneur Morris, DeWitt Clinton, David Hosack, James Kent, Morgan Lewis, Peter G. Stuyvesant, Peter A. Jay, and Albert Gallatin. Hone and his circle of friends made up a substantial segment of the society's membership during the second quarter of the nineteenth century. A check of the wealth and status of the society's more than 500 members in 1846 discloses that about 60 per cent of them were of the city's wealthiest families. Their devotion to history suggests that in the antebellum era those most interested in preserving the record of the past were those who best thrived in the present.[43]

No attempt has been made here to deal comprehensively with every type of urban association. National societies such as St. Andrews, the German Society, St. George's Society, have been excluded because of their small impact on the lives of cities, while professional societies have been omitted because of their inevitable domination by wealthy and successful men. Chambers of commerce and business associations come under a similar ban. There were associations that the rich did not join: trade unions, for example. Mutual-aid groups, such as the Boston Benefit Society, whose $2.00 initiation fee enabled members when sick to receive a weekly sum of $5.00 or widows to receive small sums, were led by the men of little property who composed them. The great preponderance of associations however do appear to have attracted the rich and the eminent.

The evidence assembled here is admittedly thin, and throws little light on the quality of participation of most wealthy "activists." This discussion is merely a beginning. Incomplete though the evidence may be, it compares favorably, in one respect, with the modern sample surveys that inquire into the affiliations of city dwellers. For where the contemporary respondent is prone to distort, giving imaginative versions both of his status and his affiliations,[44] ancient rosters of voluntary association memberships and old tax-assessment lists disclose quite reliably the names and the wealth of antebellum joiners.

The evidence suggests that certain old ideas about voluntary associations may have to be revised, at least for the second quarter of the nineteenth century. Most urban organizations do not appear to have been composed of Americans of "all conditions" and "every class." Rather, they consisted largely of Americans of the upper class. The citizens who participated in urban societies were not primarily "powerless" persons who "could do hardly anything by themselves." They appear rather to have been successful persons who had accomplished a great deal by themselves. They united not out of weakness, in order to extract a bare minimum from society, but out of strength, in order to help maintain the great advantages that as individuals they had carved out. They sought not "strength in numbers," for they could not have been unaware that the organizations they dominated had minuscule memberships for the most part. The elite joined as vigorously as they did neither out of weakness nor desperation but out of a complex of motives in which feelings of stewardship or social responsibility toward society's unfortunates, morality, religious zeal, pride, and self-interest played varying parts. (A modern scholar suggests that the rivalry dividing the orthodox from the Unitarian "aristocracy" in Boston spurred both groups on to great feats of philanthropy.[45]) The idea that voluntary associations provide a safeguard against concentration of power—resting as it does on the inaccurate premise that such organizations were controlled by a cross section of the population—also appears to be refuted by the evidence for the antebellum era. If anything, their domination of these most influential organizations only accentuated and buttressed the power and influence urban elites had already achieved over the economy and society of their cities.

It is conceivable that, inordinate though their representation in voluntary associations was, the rich sought no special benefit from the fact. However, the evidence on the actions and, above all, on the purposes of the societies does not bear out such a hypothesis. The preponderance of the upper crust in antebellum organizations was not a chance occurrence. Great wealth gave its possessors the leisure necessary for truly vigorous participation. It enabled them to make the contributions or the gifts social activity often entailed. It gave them that stake in society —or perhaps more importantly, the sense of a stake in society—that led men to undertake the responsible and purposive social action likely to protect both their shares and the way of life that those shares had conferred on them. Perhaps the best indications that the rich and eminent had great influence as well as great numbers in the voluntary associations were the policies and practices of the groups. Whether their purposes were educational reform, aid to the poor, or cultural uplift, the hand of large property owners was apparent.

This is not to impugn the sincerity of the wealthy men who devoted themselves to social benevolence. In advising the poor that individual social failure was caused by vice, intemperance, sloth, and ignorance, or that an "equal education" would give every child an equal opportunity to make good, wealthy altruists said what they truly believed. In my judgment, they voiced their deepest convictions. The notion popular with some contemporary radicals, that economic and social institutions, particularly private property, were the causes of poverty or that society would have to be redone to ensure social justice, appeared literally to be unthinkable to most men who had thrived under existing arrangements. In any case, the issue is not the rightness or the good sense or even, primarily, the sincerity of the viewpoints of the elite but the influence they held. If influence, as Edward Banfield has written, is the "ability to get others to act, think, or feel as one intends," [46] then the urban rich had great influence indeed within the societies they joined during the antebellum decades. For it was by no means inevitable that agencies dealing with poverty would eschew criticism of contemporary institutions; that they did in fact avoid such criticism points to the great control property owners exercised. If the goals of most of the voluntary associations were modest and their methods characteristically sedate, it was precisely because their eminent leaders would have it so. Control over the plentitude of organizations created to deal seemingly with every aspect, every problem of urban life, when combined with control over the economic life of the great northeastern cities, gave to the urban rich a vast influence during the second quarter of the nineteenth century. That the period has long had a contrary reputation suggests that we may have been looking in the wrong places for evidence of power during the years ironically labeled the "era of the common man."

Notes

[1] Sam Bass Warner, Jr., *The Private City: Philadelphia in Three Periods of its Growth* (Philadelphia, 1968), p. 61; Schlesinger, *Paths to the Present*, p. 50; Alexis de Tocqueville, *Democracy in America* (New York, 1954), II:114.

[2] Charles R. Wright and Herbert H. Hyman, "Voluntary Association Memberships of American Adults: Evidence from National Sample Surveys," *American Sociological Review, XXIII* (June 1958), pp. 286–94. See also David L. Sills, *The Volunteers: Means and Ends in a National Organization* (Glencoe, 1957); and Murray Hausknecht, *The Joiners* (New York, 1962), pp. 57–59, 89, 114, 122.

[3] James F. Richardson, *The New York Police: Colonial Times to 1901* (New York, 1970), 16; Warner, *Private City*, pp. 60–62.

[4] Arnold Rose, *Theory and Method in the Social Sciences* (Minneapolis, 1954), p. 50; cited in Hausknecht, *The Joiners*, p. 9.

[5] For a detailed discussion of the institution and of Perkins's contribution to it see Harold Schwartz, *Samuel Gridley Howe: Social Reformer 1801–1876* (Cambridge, 1956), pp. 50–53.

[6] Paul Goodman, "Ethics and Enterprise: The Values of a Boston Elite, 1800–1860," *American Quarterly, XVIII*, p. 446.

[7] On Warren's affiliations, see Justin Winsor, ed., *Memorial History of Boston* (Boston, 1884), IV, p. 266; Mark A. DeWolfe Howe, *The Humane Society of the Commonwealth of Massachusetts: An Historical Review, 1785–1916* (Cambridge, 1918), pp. 31, 284, 286; Lucius M. Sargent. *An Address Delivered Before the Massachusetts Society for Suppressing Intemperance*, May 27, 1833 (Boston, 1833), p. 36; Nathaniel I. Bowditch, *A History of the Massachusetts General Hospital* (Cambridge, 1872), p. 4; *Acts of Incorporation and Acts Regulating the Practice of Physic and Surgery with the By-Laws and Orders of the Massachusetts Medical Society* (Boston, 1826), p. 79; and Josiah Quincy, *Figures of the Past From the Leaves of Old Journals* (Boston, 1883), p. 4. To avoid excessive footnotes in this chapter, the chief sources on the affiliations of hundreds of other elite individuals are discussed in the Bibliography.

[8] Cited in Joseph J. McCadden, "Roberts Vaux and His Associates in the Pennsylvania Society for the Promotion of Public Schools," *Pennsylvania History, III* (Jan., 1936), p. 11. For an example of Carey's social ideas, see Mathew Carey, *Appeal to the Wealthy of the Land* (Philadelphia, 1833).

[9] Thomas I. Wharton, *Address Delivered at the Opening of the New Hall of the Athenaeum of Philadelphia, October 19, 1847* (Philadelphia, 1847), p. 20.
[10] Warren F. Hewitt, "Samuel Breck and the Pennsylvania School Law of 1834," *Pennsylvania History, I* (April 1934), pp. 63, 70–71.
[11] Raymond Mohl, *Poverty in New York, 1783-1825* (New York, 1971), pp. 12–13.
[12] John Pintard, *Letters from John Pintard to his Daughter Eliza Noel Pintard Davidson* (New York, 1940), I, pp. 155–56, II, p. 333.
[13] Hone Diary, I:95; III:149–50, 184–85, 319; VIII:29; XXVII:213.
[14] The wealthy are taken from the lists of wealthy taxpayers in Appendix C. The evidence I have relied on most heavily is public evidence, material disseminated by the associations. This material has gaps in it for various years and is typically incomplete: some of the short-lived organizations left no useful records; in other cases the records have disappeared. The probable effect is to detract from the actual extent of the elite's participation in voluntary associations.
[15] Francis, *Old New York* (New York, 1866), p. 85.
[16] See Daniel Aaron, "Cincinnati, 1818–1838: A Study of Attitudes in the Urban West" (Harvard University Doctoral Dissertation, 1942), Appendix. A recent study of Cincinnati's voluntary associations for the period 1839–1842 finds that they were run by a "relatively small and atypical[ly wealthy] group of men." Walter S. Glazer, "Participation and Power: Voluntary Associations and the Functional Organization of Cincinnati in 1840," *Historical Methods Newsletter*, 5 (Sept. 1972), pp. 151–68.
[17] Clifford S. Griffin, *Their Brothers' Keepers: Moral Stewardship in the United States, 1800–1865* (New Brunswick, 1960); see also Charles I. Foster, *An Errand of Mercy: The Evangelical United Front, 1790–1837* (Chapel Hill, 1960).
[18] The extent to which rich men or members of elite families participated in benevolent and other associations is obtained by juxtaposing lists of society officers and members against the tax lists for New York City, Boston, and Brooklyn, and a list I have drawn up of Philadelphia's wealthy and socially prominent persons. The lists of organization personnel come from a variety of sources: reports published by the organizations, reminiscences by leaders, contemporary histories of the organizations, city directories, local histories and memorial histories, and the private papers of activists.
[19] Mohl, *Poverty in New York*, p. 136.
[20] Benjamin J. Klebaner, "The Home Relief Controversy in Philadelphia, 1782–1861," *Pennsylvania Magazine, LXXVIII* (Oct. 1954), p. 417.
[21] *First Annual Report of the New York Association for Improving the Condition of the Poor* (New York, 1843), pp. 5–17; Lubove, *The Professional Altruist: The Emergence of Social Work as a Career, 1880–1930* (Cambridge, 1965), pp. 313–14; and Lubove, "The New York Association for Improving the Condition of the Poor," *New-York Historical Society Quarterly, XLIII* (July 1959), pp. 307–27.
[22] Robert S. Pickett, *House of Refuge: Origins of Juvenile Reform in New York State, 1815–1857* (Syracuse, 1969), pp. 44, 76, 112–26.
[23] Mohl, *Poverty in New York*, p. 303 n. Mohl's statement that the managers "came almost exclusively from the middle-class," assumes a definition of the latter class that may be more suitable for European society of the eighteenth century than for the United States in the nineteenth. In terms of wealth and status as well as occupation, these men were of the American upper class rather than the middle.
[24] Bowditch, *History of the Massachusetts General Hospital*, pp. 4, 9.
[25] Gerald N. Grob, *The State and the Mentally Ill: A History of Worcester State Hospital in Massachusetts, 1830–1920* (Chapel Hill, N.C., 1966), p. 19.
[26] *Letters of John Pintard*, I, p. 38.
[27] *First Annual Report of the Society for the Encouragement of Faithful Domestic Servants in New York* (New York, 1826); and *Third Annual Report . . .* (New York, 1828), pp. 2, 8.
[28] William W. Cutler, III, "Status, Values, and the Education of the Poor: The Trustees of the New York Public School Society, 1805–1853," *American Quarterly, XXIV* (March 1972), pp. 69–85. See also *Memorial and Remonstrance of the Trustees of the Public School Society of the City of New York to the Senate of New York*. Document No. 97, Senate New York, May 22, 1841.
[29] *Report of Committee of Trustees of the Free School Society on Distribution of the Common School Fund* (New York, 1825); *An Address of the Trustees of the Public*

School Society in the City of New York to their Fellow Citizens Respecting the Extension of their Public Schools (New York, 1828), *passim.*
[30] Michael B. Katz, *The Irony of Early School Reform: Educational Innovation in Mid-Nineteenth Century Massachusetts* (Cambridge, 1968).
[31] Joseph J. McCadden, "Roberts Vaux and His Associates in the Pennsylvania Society for the Promotion of Public Schools," *Pennsylvania History, III* (Jan. 1936), pp. 1–17; Warren F. Hewitt, "Samuel Breck and the Public School Law of 1834," *ibid., I* (April 1934), pp. 63–75.
[32] *Considerations upon the Expediency and the Means of Establishing a University in the City of New York* (New York, 1830); and Joshua L. Chamberlain, ed., *New York University, Its History, Influence, Equipment, and Characteristics* (Boston, 1901).
[33] *Proceedings Relating to the Organization of the General Theological Seminary of the Protestant Episcopal Church, Together with Proceedings of the Board of Trustees 1821–1838* (New York, 1854).
[34] *Letters of John Pintard,* I, p. 25.
[35] Aaron, "Cincinnati, 1818–1838," pp. 345–46; Sam Bass Warner, *The Private City,* pp. 81, 104–107, contains an interesting discussion of the awareness of Thomas Pym Cope and other wealthy Philadelphians of the role of self-interest in the city's cultural development.
[36] J. Thomas Scharf and Thompson Westcott, *History of Philadelphia, 1609–1884* (Philadelphia, 1884), II, p. 1220.
[37] Anne Marie Dolan, "The Literary Salon in New York 1830–1860," (Columbia Univ. Doctoral Dissertation, 1957), p. 142. Rufus Osgood Mason, ed., *Sketches and Impressions Musical, Theatrical, and Social, 1799–1885, From the After-Dinner Talk of Thomas Godwin* (New York, 1887), pp. 153–54.
[38] Dunlap's comment quoted in William Cullen Bryant II, "Poetry and Painting: A Love Affair of Long Ago," *American Quarterly, XXII* (Winter 1970), p. 861; Eliot Clark, *History of the National Academy of Design 1825–1953* (New York, 1954), p. 5.
[39] Mary Bartlett Cowdrey, ed., *American Academy of Fine Arts and American Art Union* (New York, 1953), II, 95.
[40] *Ibid.,* pp. 60, 102–103, 237; Francis, *Old New York,* p. 280; Bryant, "Poetry and Painting," p. 866.
[41] Lossing, *History of New York City,* II, p. 616. The one-third of the trustees who were "rich and renowned" (although not among the most heavily assessed one thousand), were either members of the families of the latter or prominent persons who were taxed for substantial wealth just below the amounts assessed against the richest thousand.
[42] Mason, *Sketches and Impressions Musical, Theatrical and Social,* pp. 159–60.
[43] For a history of the society see R. G. Vail, *Knickerbocker Birthday: A Sesquicentennial History of the New-York Historical Society 1804–1954* (New York, 1954).
[44] See Hausknecht, *The Joiners,* pp. 15–16, for a discussion of the unreliable features of sample surveys.
[45] Grob, *The State and the Mentally Ill,* p. 16.
[46] Banfield, *Political Influence* (New York, 1961), p. 3.

13

Who Governed the Nation's Cities in the "Era of the Common Man?"

> Those who possess property and carry on the business of the country, can look forward only to living under a government over which they have no influence.
>
> Sidney George Fisher, Diary of Sidney George Fisher, Dec. 1, 1839

> The more affluent classes of society are . . . directly removed from the direction of political affairs in the United States.
>
> Tocqueville, *Democracy in America,* I:192

If the second quarter of the nineteenth century has long been known as the "era of the common man," it is largely because of the great political power supposedly commanded by persons of little or no property. The respected French visitor, Michel Chevalier, observing that poor men in most states had the right to vote, concluded that in the United States the propertyless masses "rule[d] the capitalists, merchants, and manufacturers." [1] It was widely assumed both here and abroad that the democratization of the suffrage had made rich men in America politically impotent. This chapter tests the accuracy of that assumption against the evidence. The wealth and standing of officeholders in New York City, Brooklyn, Philadelphia, and Boston are considered, as well as the policies of governments in these cities. The political patterns of the great northeastern cities are compared with those of small cities and towns in other parts of the country and with earlier eras, in order to place the politics of the second quarter of the nineteenth century in clearer perspective.

To determine the power of a select number of political actors over government bodies, political actions must also be examined; for it is conceivable that a small group—such as the rich—had disproportionate representation in government and yet little influence over it. The obverse is also possible: great influence could have been wielded by a small clique barely, if at all, represented. An influential modern theory holds, in fact, that the American city at mid-twentieth century is ruled by covert elites *external* to government.[2] Evidence on the character of governmental actions as well as on the status of governmental officials should indicate the extent of plutocratic influence on politics in the antebellum period.

From the vantage point of the late-twentieth century, the assumption of the political powerlessness of the wealthy appears excessive, even prior to assembling evidence to the contrary. We have gone to school, if not with Karl Marx, then with any number of other realists: the very facts of life seem to us to cry out "money talks!" But, of course, the facts of life do not speak for themselves; they are interpreted differently by men of varying persuasion or predilection. Certain eras, characterized by what intellectual historians describe as distinctive frames of reference, evoked unique explanations of political and social phenomena. In the second quarter of the nineteenth century, observers were prone to interpret American politics and society in egalitarian terms. European visitors, amazed at a democratic system so unlike their own and quick to relate popular suffrage to the mediocre standards and lack of aristocratic glitter they detected in American life, concluded that the latter were caused by the former. The masses were believed to prevail in politics as in manners. Americans too were prone to believe—or say they believed—that Tom, Dick, and Harry were king here. Scheming politicians and shrewd yeasayers no doubt propagated these comforting pleasantries which they considered useful to their purposes; and yet, many sensible Americans appeared sincerely convinced that the common man ruled here. The weight of evidence for this notion did not, however, match the depth of conviction of the men who held to it.

A leading urban historian has recently complained that "historians of the Jacksonian era have yet to undertake the kind of systematic quantitative studies of urban [political] leadership" that would carry the modern discussion beyond impressionism.[3] Actually, modern scholars have investigated the backgrounds and occupations of officials in a number of towns and small cities in different geographical sections.[4] The discussion that follows on four northeastern cities of great wealth and population complements those earlier studies and should help bring us closer to a coherent overview of urban politics and power in the antebellum decades.

Occupation, Wealth, and Status of City Officials, 1825–1850

In his well-known study of New Haven, Robert A. Dahl asked the question, who governs? and answered: the commercial and professional patriciate before 1842 and a new class of industrial entrepreneurs for the rest of the nineteenth century. Dahl's generalizations were based primarily on the occupations of the mayors and the family backgrounds of several of them. I have investigated, not mayors alone, but also recorders, trustees, aldermen, assistant aldermen, selectmen, and common councilmen for the period 1825–1850. The wealth and status, as well as the occupations, of officeholders have been considered. Occupation can be, as we have seen, a most misleading designation. Wealth *and* occupation provide surer clues to economic standing than occupation alone.

That elusive intangible, status, has also been singled out. Every one of the great cities had an elite, a group of notables distinct from—if containing many members of—the rich, with whom they are so often bracketed. The elite of a city typically numbered several hundred families of great prestige; many of them had been eminent since the seventeenth century, but a surprising number were renowned only since the middle of or late in the eighteenth. These families moved in a restricted social orbit, maintaining exclusive relationships both on a formal and informal level, attending the same dinner parties and balls, active in the same clubs and voluntary associations, living in residential enclaves populated by their own sort, marrying by a rule of social endogamy, and usually—although not invariably—possessing great wealth. The question is to what extent such socioeconomic elites met Dahl's definition of a ruling elite: "a minority of individuals whose preferences regularly prevail in cases of difference . . . on key political issues." [5]

In order to permit a clearer evaluation of changing trends, the second quarter of the nineteenth century has been divided into two parts, with 1837 the middle year. Since the data were available, the tables on occupations record average percentages based on almost every year from 1825 to 1850—rather than randomly selected years—thus reducing the risk that generalizations about an era might be based on an unrepresentative or atypical sample.

No trends are discernible in the kind of men who sat in the mayor's office. Throughout the period, mayors were almost invariably merchants or lawyers: Philadelphians rarely chose other than attorneys; New York City favored merchants; Brooklyn and Boston preferred first the one, then the other. These were unusually wealthy men of relatively high status. In the early 1830s, a "master builder," Charles A. Wells, managed to be chosen mayor of Boston, sandwiched in between such eminences as Harrison Gray Otis and Theodore Lyman, Jr. Wells was no ordinary mechanic, however; his assessed wealth placed him among the richest 1 per cent of taxpayers, the lofty plateau of wealth occupied by most mayors during the period.

Elite representation varied in the four cities. The wealthy Philadelphians who occupied the mayor's office were for the most part *not* of the city's greatest families; George M. Dallas, mayor in the late 1820s, was very much the exception. Boston was another story. In the first part of the period, Josiah Quincy, Harrison Gray Otis, and Theodore Lyman, Jr., eminences all, were mayors, while between them, Quincy's son and Samuel A. Eliot held the title for half of the second period. Brooklyn's diverse elite of old Dutch families and later migrants from New England

TABLE 13–1.
Occupations of Mayors, 1825–1850* (by percentage)

Occupation	*NYC*	*Brooklyn†*	*Boston*	*Philadelphia*
merchants	72	50	60	5–10
merchant/manufacturers	—	10	—	—
lawyers	20	20	32	90–95
officials	—	15	—	—
publishers	4	—	—	—
wholesale grocers	—	5	—	—
artisans-manufacturers	4	—	8	—

*In this and in the tables that follow, repeaters or men re-elected in the annual municipal elections that were the norm, are treated as new officeholders for each subsequent term. Treating a man elected a number of times as though he were one officeholder is misleading: men of high-status occupation typically were re-elected more often than those of less prestige.
†Includes the years prior to 1834 when Brooklyn was a village whose chief officer was the "president."

and elsewhere were represented by the very rich General Jeremiah Johnson in the late 1830s and the highly successful lawyers and men of affairs, Henry C. Murphy and Edward Copland in the 1840s. New York City had a distinctive pattern. For most of the period before 1837 mayors came of such revered families as the Bownes and Lawrences, two great Long Island lines that had long intermarried with one another. Philip Hone, mayor in 1826, was a nice example of the new elite, wealthy, active in a great variety of organizations both exclusive and socially purposive, and near the center of a social world inhabited by great figures in commerce and the professions. In the 1840s, such mayors as James Harper, the publisher, William F. Havemeyer, the sugar merchant, and Caleb Woodhull, the attorney, represented the prestige of relatively recent achievement rather than distinguished family.

The backgrounds of municipal legislators were, inevitably, more diverse. During the period 1825–1837, the occupational distribution for each city was unique. Lawyers made up 25 per cent of Philadelphia's select council, for example, while they were only 10 per cent of the trustees of Brooklyn Village and of the chartered city of Brooklyn. In very few cases was an occupation represented by precisely the same proportion of officeholders in more than one city; and yet, the overall configurations were not markedly dissimilar. Merchants, corporate and financial officials, and varied types of businessman comprised more than half the governing bodies—when Philadelphia's "gentlemen" category is treated as the retired merchants so many of them in fact were. Lawyers comprised 20 per cent of New York City's aldermen and not quite 15 per cent of the two houses of Boston's legislature. Manufacturers typically

TABLE 13–2.
Occupations of City Councils and Boards of Aldermen, 1825–1837* (by percentage)

			Boston		*Philadelphia*	
Occupation	*NYC*	*Brooklyn*	Aldermen	Council	Select Council	Common Council
Merchants	28	34	43	32	26	28
"Gentlemen"	—	—	—	—	16	9
Bankers, insur. co. executives, brokers	2	—	6	4	6	—
Businessmen, publishers	13	2	17	14	4	5
Owners of yards, bldgs., wharves, bldrs., shipbuilders	4	10	4	6	—	4
Manufacturers	3	13	3	4	10	4
Attorneys	20	10	11	15	25	11
Physicians	3	—	3	2	—	5
Officials, military and naval officers, ship captains	1	2	3	3	1	3
Engineers, accountants, printers	1	2	—	1	—	—
Grocers, distillers, butchers, bakers, druggists, retailers	14	16	3	6	7	13
Artisan-entrepreneurs	6	—	1	7	1	7
Artisans, mechanics	6	8	3	7	3	10
Farmers	—	2	—	—	—	—

*To 1840 for Philadelphia. Since fractions were not included, totals do not always sum to 100%.

hovered around the 5 per cent mark, while retail storekeepers, some of them quite wealthy, ranged from 5 per cent of Boston's officeholders to almost 15 per cent of New York City's. Craftsmen or artisans made up 10 per cent of the Philadelphia Common Council and closer to 5 per cent in the other cities. Unskilled laborers, who together with journeymen mechanics constituted roughly three-fifths of urban populations, were not to be found in office. The occupations of common men were barely visible in local government during the first part of the era named after them.

Wealth was inordinately represented in office in the years before 1838. Mayors, almost without exception, belonged to the rich or the upper 1 per cent of taxpayers for the entire quarter century. In the years before 1838, 75 per cent of Brooklyn's identifiable trustees and aldermen were of rich family. For the other cities, the rate of wealthy representation was not as great, and in two of them it declined significantly (if not drastically) between 1825 and 1838. The rich remained at slightly more than 50 per cent of Boston's aldermen, a body of eight, in the 1830s as in the 1820s; but in the Common Council, a more plebeian body six times as large, their percentage dropped from 42 to 33. In Philadelphia, however, three out of four select councilmen were rich men, whether at the beginning or the end of the 1830s; the proportion actually rose in the Common Council, going from about one-third to three-fifths in the decade. But where rich men had comprised two-thirds of New York City's aldermen in 1826, the proportion fell to one-half for 1831 and to about three-eighths in 1837.

The *elite* were also represented in local legislatures but not as heavily. Notables evidently had other interests. Several great names of commerce sat in the Philadelphia Council: Eyres, Masseys, and Wetherills, next to Duanes, Bories, Lippincotts, Rawles, and Merediths, whose status was perhaps higher. New York City had Motts, Schieffelins, Nevinses, Roosevelts, Bensons, Van Schaicks; Brooklyn had Van Nostrands, Thornes, Furmans, Hickses, Hegemans, Polhemuses, and Bergens; and Boston had Lorings, Grays, Lowells, Everetts, Shaws, Reveres, Winthrops, Prescotts, and Peabodys. In the second part of the period, ending at mid-century, elite representation held fairly firm in Boston as in Brooklyn: Crowninshields, Bigelows, Coolidges, Gardners, Cushings, and Frothinghams stepped in to serve the New England city, while Ryersons, Boerums, Leffertses, and Van Voorhises took office in Brooklyn. There was a slight falling off in Philadelphia, despite the appearance in councils of Gilpins, Brecks, Bartons, Binneys, and the great merchant Thomas Pym Cope. In New York City, Caleb Woodhull and Gouverneur Ogden alone stepped forward to replace the eminences who had departed the Board of Aldermen and assistant aldermen in the 1840s.

The occupations of councilmen shifted during the 1840s in a noticeably plebeian direction. The pattern was not entirely consistent, however. Although merchant and lawyer representation fell sharply in New York and slightly in Boston, the proportion rose in Philadelphia and Brooklyn. While manufacturers became more evident, the "entrepreneurial pattern" of New Haven was hardly matched in the great northeastern cities; nowhere did the group comprise more than roughly one-tenth of elected officials. The most significant change was the increase in artisans. By 1850, skilled workers made up more than one-tenth the aldermen of New York City and of the "lower houses" of Boston and Philadelphia. These changes, while significant, did not quite add up to the proletarianization of city government; the occupations of officeholders at mid-century remained unrepresentative of how most city

TABLE 13–3.
Occupations of City Councils and Boards of Aldermen, 1838–1850* (by percentage)

			Boston		*Philadelphia*	
Occupation	*NYC*	*Brooklyn*	Aldermen	Council	Select Council	Common Council
Merchants	15.0	42	28	29.0	42	37
"Gentlemen"	—	—	—	—	4	4
Bankers, insur. co. executives, brokers	3	—	1	6.5	—	1
Businessmen, publishers	18	4	21	16.0	5	1
Owners of yards, bldgs., wharves, bldrs., shipbuilders	6	14	4	6.0	—	—
Manufacturers	9	7	7	3.0	3	13
Attorneys	11	13	13	5.5	28	13
Physicians	1	—	1	1.5	—	2
Officials, military and naval officers, ship captains	4	—	3	4.0	—	3
Engineers, accountants, printers	1	—	—	4.0	—	—
Grocers, distillers, butchers, bakers, druggists, retailers	14	18	1	6.5	16	15
Artisan-entrepreneurs	7.5	1	13	8.0	2	2
Artisans, mechanics	10	1	18	10.0	1	9
Laborers, farmers	—	—	—	—	—	—

* 1840–1850 for Philadelphia. Totals do not always sum to 100%.

residents earned their living. The distortion between governors and governed had lessened, however.

The proportion of rich men on urban councils also declined during the 1840s. Where in 1846, 83 per cent of Philadelphia's Select Council and 60 per cent of the Common Council were members of wealthy families, by 1850 only half of the former body and 15 per cent of the latter were of rich families. At five-year intervals between 1838 and 1848, the rich men in Boston's Common Council declined from 29 per cent to 25 and, finally, to 17 per cent. The falling off in New York City between 1838 and 1850 was from 38 per cent to 25. Brooklyn too became less of a plutocracy during the decade, although at 1850 half of her identifiable aldermen remained among the richest men in the community. While the extent of their representation diminished significantly during the 1840s, rich men at mid-century continued to have inordinate representation in urban government.

Causes of Overrepresentation of the Rich and Elite

What accounted for the disproportionate involvement of wealthy men in antebellum government, on the one hand, and the perceptible diminution of this involvement with the passage of time, on the other? An answer to this question must be complex, taking note of a variety of factors. It must also be imprecise, because among the factors to be considered are the moods and values of men—phenomena that, unlike either the occupations or the wealth of officeholders, do not lend themselves to objective measurement. Quantification can take us only so far.

One of the negative explanations for the undue representation of the well-to-do in antebellum urban government is the amazing extent of geographical mobility among the poor. In addition to barring them from political participation because of their violation of residence requirements, the inordinate footlooseness of the poor appears to have produced in them a mood of non-concern for community affairs most unlike the feelings held by more stable and substantial elements in the community. We know these things about the unusual "shiftlessness" of the poor from a number of quantitative studies that have recently been done.[6] Yet, nothing said in these studies can provide the historian with a slide rule formula for allocating an appropriate weight to the factor of lower-class physical mobility in accounting for the roles of different socio-economic groups in urban government. The sorting out of the diverse elements for this—or for any other—historical interpretation is not an automatic process that follows somehow from the configurations of the data. Rather it is an intellectual process in which choices are made by the historian. Each historian is likely to make a unique combination of choices that reflects his mentality and social ideology. If these reflections are construed as an apologetic introduction to a subjective analysis of objective evidence, so be it.

Neither particular electoral reforms, such as the broadening of the suffrage, nor general changes in the provisions of city charters appear to have had very much to do either with the undue representation of rich men in city councils throughout the era or the falling off of their direct participation in the 1840s. Councilmen in Philadelphia before 1854 were chosen in general elections that made possible the selection of men concentrated in high-value residential districts. In Boston, New York City, and Brooklyn, on the other hand, councilmen were elected in separate ward elections.[7] Most of these wards were inhabited primarily by men of little property. Nonetheless, the social and economic standing of elected officials was quite similar—whether they were elected from a

Mr. and Mrs. Ernest Fiedler and Children, New York. The Fiedlers, shown here in the drawing room of their house at 38 Bond Street in 1850, were not among the truly wealthy of the city. *(Painting by F. Heinrich owned by Mrs. William Lothrop Rich. Photograph courtesy of the Museum of the City of New York.)*

general ticket as in Philadelphia, or in a series of separate contests, as in the other cities.

Poor men of little property had won the right to vote *before* the beginning of our period. By 1822, male New York City residents who were "five dollar taxpayers" were eligible to vote for councilmen. After its incorporation as a city, the same year, Boston granted the vote to all taxpayers. While this system did bar transients and men of no property whatever, it nevertheless enfranchised a voting population composed predominantly of poor men. By the late 1830s all white Philadelphia males of 21 and over were granted the vote in local elections; the taxpayer qualification that had prevailed earlier, based on the charter of 1790, has been appraised by scholars as approximating universal manhood suffrage. The inordinately well-to-do men elected to office in the late 1820s and 1830s were therefore elected by relatively poor voters. The diminution in the wealth of councilmen that occurred in the 1840s was due to other causes than a change in the socioeconomic composition of the electorates. What D. Clayton James has said of antebellum Natchez became increasingly true of antebellum New York City, Brooklyn, Philadelphia, and Boston: "the situation was not that rich men tried for office and were defeated: very few of them even offered as candidates." [8] The rich who did offer were rarely of the group I have elsewhere called the "richest of the rich." Thomas Pym Cope and Robert Gould Shaw were exceptions among this exalted group.

The election of the mayor had been transferred in the 1830s from the council to the people in Philadelphia, Brooklyn, and New York City. And yet, as we have seen, mayors elected by the people were as high status and wealthy as mayors elected by the councils. Of course, the mayor's office, in contrast to the councils, carried with it a salary that ranged from $2,000 to $3,000 per annum and perquisites worth several times as much. Philip Hone's description of New York City's council applied equally to the councils of the other cities: "the common council —where there is much to do and no pay." [9] The comparatively good salary of the one office and the non-existent salary of the other appear to explain but little about the standing of candidates. According to the argument made in that era by the British Chartists—a variation on a critique that dated back to Roman antiquity—offices without salary would invariably be filled by the rich, who alone could afford to hold them. Yet richer men stood for the well-paying mayoralty than for the non-paying council. As a matter of fact, antebellum city councils were available means of political involvement to poor men, as they seldom met, typically holding from one to four meetings a month; even more important, they held their meetings at night, after working hours. Poor men did not hold office not because it was impossible for them to attend but because they were not nominated.

The diminishing representation of the rich and the eminent suggests that municipal office exerted no irresistible pull on the greatest accumulators or on men of lofty status. The mayoralty was fairly appealing because, combined with the greater prestige accruing to the position, was a potential power that, for all the weaknesses built into the office, permitted a man of force and stature such as Josiah Quincy to place his own imprint on it. But what attraction could the city council or board of aldermen have for great figures, in view of the small part played by any one member in the performance of its tasks and the limited and prosaic nature of these tasks?

After he completed his term as mayor, Philip Hone showed no interest in sitting on the council. When a crisis arose in the winter of 1828–1829, however, Hone agreed to preside over a meeting of the third ward on February 27, 1829, "to adopt measures to relieve the distress of the poor in the present inclement season." [10] Let an issue of critical importance arise and the very rich and the eminent displayed a lively interest in political participation. In 1829 perhaps half of New York City's 28 aldermen were rich men, with only 3 of them worth at least the $100,000 that placed them in the "super rich." Possibly seven or eight were among the city's socioeconomic elite. Yet when meetings were called and delegates elected that spring to attend a convention that would consider the vitally important matter of changes in the city charter, Hone and a large number of other notables participated. Despite the fact that delegates to a planning meeting were elected in separate ward elections, 60 per cent of the persons elected were wealthy, most of them of prominent family. The rich and the eminent comprised 80 per cent of the 70 delegates elected on June 9, five from each ward. Lambert Suydam, Evert Bancker, Peter Augustus Jay, Garret Storm, Robert Bogardus, Effingham Schieffelin, John Hone, Stephen Allen, John Bradhurst, Cornelius Schuyler, M. M. Quackenboss, Hone, and dozens of other men of lofty status were elected. According to Hone's diary entry, what moved him to action was not the prospect of public activity: he had had more than enough of such diversions. Rather, he had "an apprehension that the mistaken zeal of some persons concerned might lead to violent and indiscreet measures." [11]

Not that the duties of urban government were unimportant. Modern historians may find it hard to write dramatic accounts of police and fire protection, water supply, public health, garbage disposal, poor relief, regulation of markets, street maintenance and lighting, harbors and wharves, building codes, tax assessments, and tax collection. These were nonetheless significant responsibilities. No doubt the ineffable blandness of much urban history derives from the routine and neutral quality of so much of what municipal government did, useful as it was to persons of whatever status, devoid of conflict, and seemingly an obligatory consequence of the problems posed by the crowded, "artificial" urban environment. And yet, for all the routine character of these themes, the particular manner of treating them could and did reflect conflicts of interest. Whether harbors were to be improved or working-class districts kept clean was an example of the kind of choice that indicates whether inordinate influence as well as representation was possessed by the urban rich and business classes. For, as was noted at the outset, influence and power are manifested above all in the *actions* of government.

Policies of Antebellum Urban Governments

Detailed and comprehensive modern studies of municipal governments' policies and enactments in the antebellum period remain to be done. The evidence to date, however, is not insubstantial, and its burden is fairly clear. Antebellum governments were governed largely by the propertied for the propertied. Typically, expenditures were made and ordinances administered as the business and professional classes would have wished them to be. Municipal budgets were minuscule, largely because wealthy taxpayers were known to be unwilling. Wealth was notoriously underassessed because rich men insisted that it be.[12] Public outdoor and indoor relief was administered by well-to-do guardians, its limited scope explained by the parsimony of the great taxpayers, its dissemination of conservative social doctrine reflective of their values. On June 23, 1837, Samuel A. Eliot, Mayor of Boston, wrote a private letter to his fellow mayors in the great cities, urging a joint memorial to Congress protesting the "great evils arising from the influx of paupers among us."[13] The things government did not do were as instructive as their positive actions: detailed itemizations of municipal expenditures reveal much. Social services received comparatively little. Social inequities and pervasive misery were not simply dealt with in a niggardly way: they were treated as the wages of sin and of individual fault. In Boston, far more money was spent on street repairs and sewers. Street improvements were a matter of broad public interest, to be sure, yet most contemporaries agreed that prosperous districts got the first, the most, and the best attention.

The history of each city contains numerous examples of the special sensitivity municipal governments showed their wealthier constituents. In New York City, valuable real estate in the form of wharves and "water grants" was leased on easy terms or sold cheap to members of the Astor, Lorillard, Lenox, Schermerhorn, Havemeyer, Roosevelt, Colden, Bowne, and Goelet families. And aldermen subsequently granted special rights solicited by wealthy owners or lessees.[14] In Brooklyn, merchant opposition to the special assessment necessary to finance a proposed sewer system on a major thoroughfare, succeeded in blocking the project until mid-century. Mayor Henry C. Murphy, a highminded member of Brooklyn's elite, complained in the 1840s that the city's legislators were indifferent to health problems in poor sections.[15] Unhappy with a situation in which their city's per capita public expenditures on poor relief in the mid-1820s were almost double the New York City rate, Philadelphia's leaders succeeded, in part by a "more careful screening of applicants," in reducing total costs over the next two decades despite a doubling in the city's population. During the same period, the city's businessmen and politicians lobbied for and helped finance the transportation improvements likely to promote their business prospects.[16] In Boston, men like Harrison Gray Otis cut back expenditures for a proposed expansion of the sewer system, since, "living on well-drained Beacon Hill," they saw little purpose in it. As mayor, Josiah Quincy was more public spirited and gets higher marks than Otis from a modern historian of Boston. Yet to both mayors, the city was "primarily a place of business, a port, a market and financial capital." [17] In Boston as in New York City, police expenditures were minimal and service pitifully incompetent when men of substance felt no need for better. The professionalization of police services and the high costs it entailed were delayed until lower-class ethnic riots and disorders posed a threat to the life and property of the privileged.[18]

Rich men and their interests did not invariably prevail. For one thing the rich were not a monolithic class of single mind. Nor did they conceive of themselves in such terms. The wealthy had diverse interests —no matter whether the latter term is construed in a realistic or idealistic sense. The opposition of many property owners to an expensive improvement of Faneuil Hall, for example, did not stop Quincy from going ahead with it. Otis was compelled by "public demand" to maintain streetcleaning operations he wanted to cut back. What is of interest is how often rich men won. A contemporary New Yorker explained their success in realistic terms: "nearly every alderman has in some degree owed his success to the personal efforts and influence of 'backers,' who must be recompensed for their services. This recompense sometimes consists in a return of political assistance." [19] It is more likely that the relatively substantial men who predominated in city government dealt with issues from the viewpoint of the property owners they themselves were. Until demonstrated otherwise, it appears more sensible to view them as men honestly acting out their conviction that the prosperity of the city depended on the prosperity of its most successful residents than as political corruptionists.

Whatever the reasons, wealthy men appear to have had great power in urban government, their influence over local affairs far transcending their small numbers. While the super rich rarely sought office during the era, the presence in city councils and mayors' offices of substantial numbers of large property owners meant that the viewpoints and socioeconomic interests of wealth would have direct representation in government. That such representation declined in the 1840s is no sure sign that the influence of the rich suffered a similar diminution. Men of status, as Robert Zemsky has shown for colonial Massachusetts, need not be in a majority to dominate.[20] Certainly the pattern of municipal legislation and policy does not suggest that the plebeian interests were any more vigorously promoted in the later part of the period.

There is no way of proving whether covert elites dominated antebellum cities in the way that Floyd Hunter has suggested they control the modern American city. For, even if we stumbled across evidence the equivalent of Hunter's—in which very influential men stated flatly that a given number of named individuals "ran the city"—what ground would there be to accept as authoritative such a subjective assertion? Robert Dahl has argued that, whatever the merits of Hunter's thesis—and Dahl grants it few—it had no applicability to antebellum New Haven, in view of the overt control a commercial and professional patriciate ostensibly had over that city. Where would the covert leaders have come from "if not from among the patricians themselves?"[21] New York City, Brooklyn, Boston, and Philadelphia were hardly governed by a "patriciate" in the decades before 1850. Instead the elite of the great northeastern cities governed the hundreds of voluntary associations that complemented, and in some cases surpassed, in importance the work done by municipal political bodies. Politics were left to men of wealth, but not the greatest wealth, and to a sprinkling of elite family representatives. The latter combination appeared sufficient to assure men of substance—whether of the social elite or not—that local governments would not only pose no threat but would be sympathetic to their interests as well.

The Major National Parties and the Urban Elite

Discussions of politics in what historians continue to call the Jacksonian Era usually assign a central role to the major parties. Certainly Democrats and Whigs competed vigorously for local offices. Occasionally contests between them became so hot that Whig and Democratic voters cracked one another's heads, most notably in New York City's local elections of 1834. Councilmen representing the one party or the other were not indifferent to the fact. At one point Brooklyn Democrats voted against the continuation of the comptroller's office because Whigs had created the post.[22] Since rich men appear to have overwhelmingly preferred the Whigs to the Democrats, it might seem that the wealthy men influential in local government could be equally well understood if treated as Whigs in local-government contexts. A recent study of antebellum Boston does precisely that, reporting that "the Common Council, Board of Aldermen, and other city posts were often filled by [wealthy] Whigs."[23] Assuredly, wealthy Whigs often filled municipal posts in the other cities as well. But the question is: does the Whiggery or the wealth and standing of such men better explain their behavior as municipal officeholders?

The issues confronting Whig and Democratic councilmen bore little relation to the matters agitating Martin Van Buren and Daniel Webster in Washington, or David Henshaw and William H. Seward in state capitals. A feature of the political history of antebellum Natchez also appears to apply to the great northeastern cities: "national party alignments figured little in city politics."[24] Many of the rich men who sat in local legislatures were Democrats. While Whigs were great winners in Boston elections during the 1830s and 1840s, in New York City they were more often losers. Yet the socioeconomic composition of New York City's legislature was no more plebeian than the other city's. In Philadelphia, leading Democratic officeholders and political figures such as Benjamin Richards, Richard Vaux, George Wharton, Henry D. Gilpin, were men of wealth. In Brooklyn, Democratic candidates for council "were in the main local merchants and large property holders," as for that matter they were in a number of other cities.[25] There is a dearth of evidence to show that the national party preferences of wealthy Democrats in municipal office led them to support policies and expenditures that were either distinctive or inimical to the interests of large property owners.

Leaders of the urban elite appear to have approached local politics in terms of class and standing rather than party affiliation. Philip Hone so detested the Democrats that from the 1830s on he would not call the party by its rightful name; yet he maintained close personal relations and often cooperated politically with such elitest "locofocos" as John Treat Irving, Stephen Allen, Walter Bowne, and Jonathan Coddington. Evidence of similar cooperation in the other cities suggests that class attachments counted for more than party differences in determining the political—as the social—behavior of rich men.[26]

Elite Urban Politics in the Colonial and Revolutionary Periods

Early-nineteenth century urban politics can be placed in clearer perspective when contrasted with the politics that went before. In a letter he sent on April 1, 1793, William Bingham, the fabled accumulator of Philadelphia, wrote that "the interests of commerce, as connected with politics, are so striking, that it is difficult to separate one from the other." Given the strategic importance of politics, it followed, as an early eighteenth century author had written, that political leaders should come from "families of distinction, education, and substance."[27] Practice, whether early or late in the colonial era, lived up to theory. Modern studies of such towns as Salem, Massachusetts and Kent, Connecticut reveal that both in the seventeenth and eighteenth centuries political leadership correlated with wealth. There were perhaps one-seventh the number of Salem merchants as artisans; but the merchants outnumbered the artisans in government by five to one, as "political power fell in disproportionate share to men of wealth." As for Kent, the rule was clear: the higher the position, the wealthier its occupant. If the mass of officeholders were an economic cut above non-officeholders, the town leaders "tend[ed] to be among the wealthiest men" of the community. In colonial Connecticut as a whole, "poor men were outcasts in their own society."[28]

The earlier patterns in the four northeastern cities that have been considered in this essay are of particular interest. In his classic study of colonial urban society, Carl Bridenbaugh found that "the commercial, political, and social leadership of [all] the towns was in [the] hands" of a small commercial aristocracy. Detailed investigations both impressionistic and "quantitative" of each of the great northeastern cities tend to confirm the validity of Bridenbaugh's generalizations about all of them. A small, wealthy, largely Quaker oligarchy controlled the government of colonial Philadelphia. In the words of one student, "political hegemony went hand in hand with economic wealth." An important explanation of the political dominance of wealth before 1776 were property requirements that confined the vote to the wealthiest 2 per cent of the population. Yet the liberalization of the suffrage that followed the Revolution produced no great change in the social quality of local officeholders. According to Sam Bass Warner, at the end of the eighteenth century "the wealthy presided over a municipal regime of little government" whose power was confined to "the management of the markets and the holding of the Recorder's Court." Bridenbaugh had noted that such power was not insignificant in the mind of the wealthy merchants who controlled it, since it enabled them to "throttle economic competition from below."[29] Regardless of the breadth of their voting constituencies or the scope of their powers, the men who sat in the mayor's office, the board of aldermen, or the common council early and late in the eighteenth century were predominantly of the great families of Philadelphia. Before and after 1750 the city was ruled by Willings, Shippens, Biddles, Mifflins, Morrises, Hopkinsons, Chews, Cadwaladers, Binghams, Duchés, Powels, Emlens, and Tilghmans.[30]

The politics of colonial Boston have not been as thoroughly examined by modern researchers as the politics of its two great commercial rivals. However, recent studies of related themes do nothing to weaken Bridenbaugh's conclusion that Boston, like the other great cities, was dominated by a commercial aristocracy. After the Revolution as before, "the [Boston] economic elite dominated the most important town offices."[31] Brooklyn in the eighteenth century was a rural village, as for that matter it continued to be in the early decades of the nineteenth century; its population was less than 5,000 in a landspace that did not yet include such areas as Williamsburgh, Bushwick, and Flatbush. Lists of officers of the later community, from the early eighteenth century to the nineteenth, reveal that the old Dutch families of the early time also ruled in the later. Lotts, Boerums, Vanderveers, Wyckoffs, Couwenhovens, Rapelyes, Strykers, Hegemans, Leffertses, and Gerritsons were the supervisors, treasurers, and chief clerks of the town.

Two recent detailed studies of the socioeconomic status of New York City councilmen and other officials cover the period from 1689 to 1815. "It is clear that at all times during the colonial period, men from the upper occupational strata ["merchants, lawyers, large landowners"] held a disproportionate share of the seats of the council," reports one author. When the period 1689–1800 is broken down into smaller parts, more precise patterns emerge. In the period 1689–1733, 44 per cent of the identifiable councilmen were of the occupational elite, while the remaining 56 per cent were "members of the city's middle occupational range ['carpenters, bolters, bakers, innkeepers . . . virtually the entire spectrum of crafts and trades practiced in New York City']." Between 1733 and the outbreak of the Revolution, the proportion of councilmen of elite occupations rose to slightly more than 50 per cent. For the prestigious Board of Aldermen, the percentage in elite occupations went from 56 per cent in the earlier period to 74 per cent in the later. The status of officeholders, as measured by religious affiliations, occupations, and previous offices held by their fathers, also became loftier than they had been earlier. Skipping over the war years, when the city was controlled by the British, to 1784–1800, slight changes occurred in occupations and status of officeholders. 47 per cent of the council were of upper occupational groups, as were 57 per cent of the aldermen. In the generation or one-third of a century after the Revolution, "mechanics" made up one half of the city's elected officials, with merchants and lawyers equally dividing the other half. These mechanics were not ordinary working men, however, since their median wealth almost matched that of the merchants, and a significant portion of them were bank and insurance company directors. As for status, measured by a variety of criteria, New York City's officeholders definitely "constituted an elite." [32] As in Philadelphia, property restrictions on voting doubtless played an important part in accounting for the disproportionate representation of upper-class New Yorkers in colonial city government. Yet even after the post-Revolutionary suffrage liberalization, only a tiny fragment of the eligible voting population cast ballots in the "charter elections" of the late eighteenth and early nineteenth centuries.[33]

The role of tradition should not be discounted in attempting to explain the socioeconomic standing of nineteenth-century urban officeholders. The earlier "habit" of electing merchants and lawyers of high status and "mechanics" whose wealth and backgrounds indicated they were better classified as entrepreneurs than as workingmen, continued to be followed in the nineteenth century as in the eighteenth. The enlarged, increasingly plebeian electorate of the later time continued to look for leadership from among men of substance, as election returns from poor wards often indicated. The occupational backgrounds and relative wealth levels of New York City's councilmen for 1825–1837 hardly differ from the pattern of the previous half century. Important changes did occur in that city during the 1840s, as the less prestigious occupations and men of little property and status gained at the expense of the rich and the eminent. But, as has been noted, the actions of local government suggest that the declining representation of the patrician types was not accompanied by a decline in the influence of large property. Rich men appear to have gained what they needed from municipal government without exercising direct influence over it.[34]

Urban Politics Elsewhere

The great political influence exercised by substantial property owners in the second quarter of the nineteenth century was evidently not a phenomenon confined to the great cities of the northeastern seaboard. Small towns elsewhere in the northeast, in the south, and in the west had similar patterns. Along the "urban frontier," "the mercantile class presided over urban affairs" in the youthful cities. In Cincinnati, after the democratization of the suffrage in 1827, as before, wealthy "bankers, merchants, and lawyers" controlled government in a city marked by an "indisputable connection between the policies of the City Council and the interests of the wealthier inhabitants." Natchez's selectmen "usually came of two bourgeois categories, young lawyers . . . and the 'rising entrepreneurs.'" Despite its democratic suffrage, the Mississippi city was dominated by a small upper crust. In the small town of Hamilton, Ontario, "the wealthy monopolized local political offices" at mid-century; "the connection between wealth and political power was clear." In Springfield, Massachusetts, in 1850 aldermen were primarily lawyers, bankers, businessmen and merchants, manufacturers and builders. Artisans and workmen, who constituted slightly more than 30 per cent of the total representation shrank to 6 per cent over the next two decades, as the town's economic development brought it closer to the character of its great neighbors in the antebellum period.[35]

In contrast to the beliefs expressed by Chevalier, Tocqueville, and Sidney George Fisher, the more affluent classes and "those who carried on the business of the country" had a great deal of influence over the government of the nation's cities during the second quarter of the nineteenth century. The political scientist Norton E. Long has written that American government "places its fundamental politics out of the reach of its formal politics." [36] Men of property had so direct a control over the government of the antebellum community as to place the "fundamental politics" well within the reach of the formal politics. In view of the power and influence they commanded over the economic, social, and political life of antebellum cities, the rich appear to have been a true "governing class." [37] Despite his possession of the suffrage, the common man had little influence, let alone power, in the nation's cities during the era named in his honor.

Notes

1 Chevalier, *Society, Manners, and Politics in the United States* (Boston, 1839).

2 Floyd Hunter, *Community Power Structure.*

3 Sam Bass Warner, *The Private City*, p. 80.

4 Dahl, *Who Governs?*; James, *Antebellum Natchez*; Wheeler, *To Wear a City's Crown*; Michael H. Frisch, "The Community Elite and the Emergence of Urban Politics: Springfield, Massachusetts, 1840–1880," in Thernstrom and Sennett, eds., *Nineteenth-Century Cities*, pp. 277–96; Michael Fitzgibbon Holt, *Forging a Majority: The Formation of the Republican Party in Pittsburgh, 1848–1860* (New Haven, 1969), chap. 1; Katz, "Patterns of Inequality, Wealth, and Power"; and Aaron, "Cincinnati, 1818–1838."

5 Dahl, *Who Governs?*

6 See Bibliography.

7 For the electoral provisions of city charters see Edward P. Allinson and Boies Penrose, *Philadelphia 1681–1887: A History of Municipal Development* (Philadelphia, 1887); Eli K. Price, *The History of the Consolidation of the City of Philadelphia* (Philadelphia, 1873); James McKellar Bugbee, "Boston Under the Mayors, 1822–1880," in Justin Winsor, ed., *The Memorial History of Boston* (Boston, 1881), III, pp. 217–92; C. W. Ernst, *The Constitutional History of Boston* (Boston, 1894); Josiah Quincy, *A Municipal History of the Town and City of Boston* (Boston, 1852); Henry H. Sprague, *City Government in Boston, Its Rise and Development* (Boston, 1890); Arthur W. MacMahon, *The Statutory Sources of New York City Government* (New York, 1923); Sidney I. Pomerantz, *New York, An American City, 1783–1803: A Study Of Urban Life* (New York, 1938); Frederick Shaw, *History of the New York City Legislature* (New York, 1954); and Ralph Foster Weld, *Brooklyn Village, 1816–1834* (New York, 1938).

8 James, *Antebellum Natchez*, p. 91.

9 Martha Lamb and Mrs. Burton Harrison, *History of the City of New York*, III, p. 471; Hone Diary, XX:419.

10 Hone Diary, I:240.

11 *Ibid.*, II:27, 31, 66–67.

12 The charge was made by several contemporary publishers and municipal committees. See, for example, William H. Boyd, comp., *Boyd's New York City Tax-Book . . . 1856 and '57* (New York, 1857), p. iv; and John F. Whitney, introductory remarks in William A. Darling, *List of Persons, Copartnerships and Corporations, Who Were Taxed on $17,500 and Upwards, in the City of New York in the year 1850* (New York, 1851), pp. iii, ix, and Chap. 2.

13 Letter of Samuel A. Eliot to the mayors of New York City, Philadelphia, and Baltimore, New York City Board of Aldermen, City Clerk Filed Papers, Location 2990.

[14] *List of Real Estate Belonging to the Corporation of the City of New York* (New York, 1838); *Proceedings of the Board of Aldermen, 1832–1833,* IV, pp. 416–18; Gustavus Myers, *History of the Great American Fortunes* (Chicago, 1909), I, pp. 148–50.
[15] Jacob Judd, "The History of Brooklyn, 1834–1855: Political and Administrative Aspects" (Ph.D. diss., New York University, 1959), p. 128.
[16] Klebaner, "The Home Relief Controversy in Philadelphia," pp. 405, 420–21; Warner, *The Private City,* p. 79.
[17] Lane, *Policing the City,* pp. 26-27.
[18] James F. Richardson, "The Struggle to Establish a London-Style Police Force for New York City," *New-York Historical Society Quarterly, XLIX* (April 1965), pp. 175–98; Lane, *Policing the City;* and Jacob Judd, "Policing the City of Brooklyn in the 1840s and 1850s," *Journal of Long Island History, VI* (Spring 1966), pp. 13–22.
[19] [William A. Brewer] *A Few Thoughts for Tax Payers and Voters* (New York, 1853), p. 74.
[20] Zemsky, "Power, Influence, and Status: Leadership Patterns in the Massachusetts Assembly, 1740–1755," *William and Mary Quarterly, XXVI* (Oct. 1969), pp. 502–20.
[21] Dahl, *Who Governs?,* pp. 62–66, 117.
[22] Judd, "History of Brooklyn, 1834–1855."
[23] Frank Otto Gatell, "Money and Party in Jacksonian America: A Quantitative Look at New York City's Men of Quality," *Political Science Quarterly, LXXXI* (June 1967), pp. 235–52; Robert Rich, " 'A Wilderness of Whigs': The Wealthy Men of Boston," *Journal of Social History,* 4 (Spring 1971), p. 266.
[24] James, *Antebellum Natchez,* p. 94.
[25] Judd, "History of Brooklyn, 1834–1855," p. 81; Warner, *Private City,* pp. 82, 92; Joseph J. McCadden, "Roberts Vaux and His Associates," p. 10; Dahl, *Who Governs?,* pp. 12, 18–19; John V. Mering, *The Whig Party in Missouri* (Columbia, 1967), pp. 72, 83–84; *New England Historical and Genealogical Register, XL* (April 1888), p. 141; Ralph D. Gray, "Henry D. Gilpin, A Pennsylvania Jacksonian," *Pennsylvania History, XXXVII* (Oct. 1970), pp. 340–51.
[26] However, according to Rich, eminent Bostonians who became Democrats lost their elect status. His documentation for this assertion, as I have noted earlier, is a libel suit brought against the Democratic publicist George Bancroft by Daniel Webster and a later twentieth-century reminiscence. " 'A Wilderness of Whigs'," p. 268. Actually, bearers of Boston names of greater repute than Bancroft's managed to retain both their unusual Democratic affiliation and the elite status earned by their families before them.
[27] Bingham to W. and J. Willink, cited in Margaret L. Brown, "William Bingham, Eighteenth Century Magnate," *Pennsylvania Magazine of History and Biography, LXI* (Oct. 1937), p. 388; Samuel Fisk, *The Character of the Candidate for Civil Government* (Boston, 1731), p. 40, cited in Zemsky, "Power, Influence, and Status," p. 520.
[28] Donald Warner Koch, "Income Distribution and Political Structure in Seventeenth-Century Salem, Massachusetts," Essex Institute *Historical Collections, CV* (Jan. 1969), pp. 60–66; Charles S. Grant, *Democracy in the Connecticut Frontier Town of Kent* (New York, 1961), pp. 150–51; and Richard L. Bushman, *From Puritan to Yankee: Character and the Social Order in Connecticut, 1690–1765* (Cambridge, Mass., 1967), p. 52.
[29] Carl Bridenbaugh, *Cities in the Wilderness: The First Century of Urban Life in America* (New York, 1938), pp. 478–79; Frederic B. Tolles, *Meeting House and Counting House: The Quaker Merchants of Colonial Philadelphia, 1682–1763* (Chapel Hill, N.C., 1948), p. 117; Warner, *Private City,* p. 9; Carl and Jessica Bridenbaugh, *Rebels and Gentlemen: Philadelphia in the Age of Franklin* (New York, 1942), p. 13.
[30] *The Minutes of the Common Council of the City of Philadelphia, 1704 to 1776* (Philadelphia, 1847).
[31] Bridenbaugh, *Cities in the Wilderness,* p. 479; Henretta, "Economic Development and Social Structure in Colonial Boston," pp. 79–92; and Kulikoff, "The Progress of Inequality in Revolutionary Boston," pp. 390–92.
[32] Bruce M. Wilkenfeld, "The New York City Common Council, 1689–1800," *New York History, LII* (July 1971), pp. 249–74, passim, examines the occupations and a few indices of "status"; Edmund Willis, "Social Origins of Political Leadership in

New York City from the Revolution to 1815" (Ph.D. diss., University of California, 1967), is an extraordinarily broad-gauged quantitative study that considers ten significant criteria.

33 Pomerantz, *New York: An American City, 1783–1803*, is masterful on changing voting requirements.

34 Professor Ira M. Leonard, who is engaged in a study of New York City politics at mid-century, advises me that the elite tried to reassert in the 1850s the kind of direct influence they had exercised in the 1820s and 1830s.

35 Richard C. Wade, *The Urban Frontier* (Chicago, 1959), p. 247; Aaron, "Cincinnati, 1818–1838," p. 113; James, *Antebellum Natchez*, pp. 92–94; Katz, "Patterns of Inequality, Wealth, and Power in a Nineteenth-Century City," p. 9; and Frisch, "The Community Elite and the Emergence of Urban Politics: Springfield, Massachusetts, 1840–1880," pp. 282, 284–85.

36 Norton E. Long, "Political Science and the City," in Leo F. Schnore, ed., *Social Science and the City: A Survey of Urban Research* (New York, 1968), p. 247.

37 William Domhoff defines a "governing class" as a "social upper class which owns a disproportionate amount of a country's wealth, receives a disproportionate amount of a country's yearly income, and contributes a disproportionate number of its members to the controlling institutions and key decision-making groups of the country." *Who Rules America?* (New York, 1967), p. 5. Domhoff's definition is unsatisfactory, since what is disproportionate is not necessarily substantial or decisive. A more precise, and at the same time, bolder definition is required, one that indicates more clearly the kind or amount of disproportionate influence a governing class will exercise.

14

Conclusion

Much work remains to be done before we can lay claim to having a comprehensive grasp of antebellum society or even of those aspects of it considered in this book. Although substantial evidence has been assembled in this discussion, it is evidence, after all, that bears primarily on a small number of atypical persons who lived in four hardly representative cities. New York City, Brooklyn, Boston, and Philadelphia were not the nation. Urban and rural communities in all sections of the country remain to be studied in depth. Other forms of social mobility than those examined here need to be investigated. Data on the subsequent careers of workingmen and the lower-middle class and on the social and economic fate of their children would be invaluable. Detailed exploration of the social mind of the rich would add another important dimension to our knowledge of the era, as would close examination of the policies and actions of particular voluntary associations and urban governments. Although it would require massive research in the papers of political figures and men of affairs, an intensive study of national politics to uncover indications of the direct or indirect influence of the rich would be rewarding, rounding out our understanding of the power they wielded in the larger community. The purpose of this book is not to close the discussion, but to open it.

Quantitative data on the origins, the wealth, the careers and the varied roles of the rich obviously throw a great deal of new light on that often-neglected group. To an amazing extent, this evidence also illuminates related, more general issues that are central to an understanding of American civilization in the second quarter of the nineteenth century. It is curious that the situation of so few appears to be so informative about the situation of so many. The puzzle is explained by the *inordinate* share of diverse important things controlled by the rich. For if the portion of material goods, status, and influence commanded by the wealthy was disproportionately great, the share held by all other men was extraordinarily small. And, for all their atypicality, New York City, Brooklyn, Boston, and Philadelphia were not altogether unrepresentative; a number of recent studies of other, smaller communities indicate that while the size and wealth of the great northeastern cities were unique, their social and economic patterns were not. Elsewhere in the Northeast, in the South, and in the West wealth was distributed, opportunity was available, and status and power allocated very much as they were in the great centers of commerce. For Natchez, Pittsburgh, Cincinnati, and Springfield, Massachusetts, the evidence points in the same general direction as it does for New York City, Brooklyn, Boston, and Philadelphia.

All of the chief assumptions underlying the egalitarian thesis appear to be undermined by the evidence for 1825–1850. Great fortunes did exist in this country, and many hundreds of American families lived opulently even by European standards. An inequality that was marked at the beginning of the era became even more glaring at its end, as the share owned by the wealthiest 1 per cent rose from roughly one-quarter to one-half. Nor was opportunity more equal than material condition. Although legend claimed they were mostly self-made men born to poverty, the rich with few exceptions had been born to wealth and comfort, owing their worldly success mostly to inheritance and family support. Instead of rising and falling at a mercurial rate, fortunes usually remained in the hands of their accumulators, whether in the long run or the short. The great financial panics of the late 1830s appear to have strengthened rather than destroyed great wealthholders, even while they wiped out modest property owners. Antebellum urban society was very much a class society. Surface manifestations of easy mingling among diverse social orders may have given European visitors the impression that class barriers were easily breached. In fact, the several hundred most eminent of the wealthy families in each of the great cities sought marital partners, neighbors, dinner companions, formal and informal social relationships, almost exclusively from among their own sort. And, far from lacking direct representation in or influence over the agencies that ran their communities, the wealthy and eminent were inordinately present and powerful in such bodies. They dominated and shaped the policies of the army of voluntary associations that complemented municipal government during the era, while retaining the sufficient if diminishing membership needed to ensure their substantial control over city councils. During the "era of the common man," rich men had power and influence in the affairs of urban communities that appeared to be commensurate with their great wealth and lofty status.

Incomplete though it may be, the evidence indicates the need to reevaluate the second quarter of the nineteenth century and to rethink some of our fondest conceptions of the period. In the light of the evidence, what happens to the allegedly vast differences between Old World society and New? Until detailed studies are completed on social mobility and the distribution of wealth and influence in early nineteenth-century western Europe, it will remain impossible to make precise comparisons of the civilizations on the two sides of the Atlantic. Peter Stearns and Seymour Martin Lipset have recently suggested that society on the Continent was not as rigid as had been supposed. Certainly the American evidence reduces the disparities so long believed to have prevailed between the two continents. European visitors, discovering the absence here of the formal aristocracy that still glittered there, and startled by manifestations of social democracy on the streets and in the public places of America, leaped to the conclusion that the two societies were worlds as well as oceans apart. Honest men often mistake appearances for reality, particularly when the appearances are strange to them. Native Americans had no difficulty in accepting a view of things equally comforting to inveterate yeasayers, boastful nationalists, and sour snobs. The one was blind to evidences of inequality, the other convinced of American superiority in these as in other things, while the last appeared perversely to relish gloomy dicta proclaiming the rule of vulgarity and mediocrity in this land.

In view of the new data, what happens to the "heroic battles" waged by Andrew Jackson and his cohorts in behalf of the common man? Bank policy, internal improvements, corporation laws, and the other matters that divided the major parties were hardly insignificant. But their resolution, one way or the other, did not touch the condition, the opportunities, the status, or the influence of the poor. Democratic control over city hall —a commonplace in all of the cities except Boston—affected ordinary citizens no differently than did Whig control.

What happens to Tocqueville's famous "tyranny of the majority?" If the concept has any validity at all—and I think it does—it must be accompanied by the question: "tyranny over what?" Manners? The style and rhetoric of political discourse? The tone and content of newspaper columns? For with regard to wealth, status, and power, the notion of popular tyranny appears to be some kind of a joke, its widespread acceptance testimony to the naïveté of its author, the gullibility of the masses, the cleverness of the classes.

And, above all, what happens to the romantic glorification of the common man? Amid all of the hullabaloo about his alleged dominance in the era, the common man appears to have gotten very little of whatever it was that counted for much. Flattery he received in abundance from politicians, genre painters, poets, and essayists. But apart from the boost such public praise doubtless gave to his ego, there is some question as to how it affected the poor fellow's life.

Any notion that the Jacksonian era was a kind of socially democratic interim between the aristocratic characteristics of earlier generations and the admittedly great inequalities of the industrial era of the late-nineteenth century, is largely undermined by the evidence. The political representation of poorer men increased in the latter part of the period. But the portion of wealth they held, the standing they commanded, the actual opportunities to rise that were available to them, marked no break with but rather a continuation or even a worsening of inegalitarian tendencies that had commenced in the colonial era.

Contemporary naysayers such as Seth Luther and Thomas Skidmore come off better and appear to have been more discerning than they have been given credit for. In an earlier study of the era's labor radicals, I had suggested that the social portrait they drew, featuring drastic inequality, the poverty, low status and political impotence of the masses, and the great power of the rich over all aspects of American life, testified above all to the state of *mind* of men who could hold such a "one-sided" view. The evidence suggests that their portrait testified rather to the actual state of *things*.

The data do not wholly negate the significance of appearances or of what people believed. Part of the "reality" of the period was a surface equality that dazzled contemporaries. The reality of an era also includes what contemporaries thought about it, whether such impressions were accurate or not. A famous historian once said that what people think is so is more important than what in fact is so, presumably because only God can know the actuality. In this instance, however, we mere mortals have come into possession of a portion of the actuality that was earlier hidden from view. Without detracting from the importance of earlier beliefs in equality, in swift and easy movement up the social ladder, and in popular power, the new evidence indicates that such notions were largely illusions. Since they afford insight into the mind of those who cling to them, illusions would be dismissed as unimportant to history only by the insensitive; but only the insensible would prefer illusions about measurable phenomena to factual evidence.

The social portrait drawn in these pages has rested on "quantitative data," much of which could have been run through computers. There are historians, most respected ones, who scoff at the quantitative method and the impression conveyed by some of its practitioners that theirs is the road to scientific precision. I would agree with the critics that no such guarantee exists. A small point does not become larger because it is made through an elaborate methodology. The quantitative method will not make unimaginative history any the brighter, although in several instances it may have made potentially lively subject matter deadly dull. I have argued elsewhere that in many cases the wrong things have been counted by quantifiers and that there may be questions resistant to the approach. It is no wiser, however, to be doctrinaire about method than about other things. Some questions can be answered best by evidence, detailed and comprehensive. The questions posed by the egalitarian thesis are precisely of this sort. To amass large amounts of data in trying to answer these questions betrays not a fascination for the quantitative method but rather an awareness of the patient effort needed to transform undocumented assertions into tenable conclusions.

Before there were quantitative historians there were historians. The ancient practitioners of the craft also gathered evidence, and in some cases a great weight of the indispensable stuff. If I have at some points appeared to be concerned with amassing a benumbing quantity of data, it is because he who purports by reference to factual evidence to test the accuracy of a theory so durable and prestigious as Tocqueville's is well advised to gather a great deal of such evidence.

The evidence indicates that the egalitarian version of antebellum American society should be discarded. That charming notion of equality of condition and opportunity has catered too well to our inclination to believe the best about our past, however, for it to be easily dislodged from our historical consciousness. Comforting illusions are understandably more attractive than harsh truths. But, since we value truth, there appears to be no alternative to replacing the egalitarian interpretation with one that corresponds better to the reality of the pre–Civil War decades. Whatever it was, the antebellum period was neither the "era of the common man" nor the "age of egalitarianism." Since ancient historical rubrics confirmed by long usage are powerfully resistant to scholarly attempts to discard them, historians might spend their time more fruitfully in rethinking their estimates of the period in the light of the new evidence than in trying to replace old labels with new. Truer captions will follow on the heels of truer explanations of the nature of the era.

Appendix A
Some Reflections on the Values of the Rich

When George Lorillard died at age 66 in September 1832, Philip Hone took note of the fact in his diary with the brief comment that the departed was "an old batchelor [sic]" who "lost an immense sum of money by dying."[1] How heartless and materialistic a comment! How contradictory of Hone's public expressions that great wealth was a lesser good! Yet one more example of the gulf between expressed values and actual. For in the privacy of his diary, Hone appears to have recorded what he truly felt rather than what was politic to say. The diary was a long one, however; Hone revealed different values in other instances.

In recording the death of the wealthy Isaac Jones a few years later, Hone notes that if Jones was "a very rich man," he "deserved to be," adding sarcastically, "he [Jones] has thought of nothing for the last 40 years of his life but the accumulation of wealth, and did not trifle with the object of his solicitude by idly squandering it in works of benevolence, taste, or public spirit," works to which Hone himself had devoted much of his life. And earlier, on the death of the wealthy Gerardus Post, Hone had described him as "a man who has worshipped money all his life and whose only talent was the amassing of it. What a pity it is that he cannot take it with him."[2]

What are we to make of these contradictory attitudes toward money? Which is the real Hone? Some skeptics might interpret Hone's first comment as an unguarded indication of his true scale of values, in contrast to the more self-conscious comparisons of his values with those of Jones and Post—invidious appraisals that Hone may have tinctured slightly with sour grapes because of the immensity of their fortunes by comparison with his own. It is more likely that Hone's private utterances reflect the complexity of men and the ambivalence that often characterizes their feelings.

Rich men are as complicated as any other. When dealt with as a socioeconomic class, the wealthy can be said to have had common interests. The accumulation of wealth was a consuming goal. When the rich are dealt with in terms of their inner feelings and values, however, they become unique individuals. One of them, Robert Watts of New York City, renounces an opportunity to receive a great additional fortune, because he will not give up his surname for that of his would-be benefactor; in contrast, a rich young Philadelphian under similar circumstances behaved in a totally opposite way. Not only are no two of them alike; the convictions of no one of the rich can be fully understood, certainly not by reference to so few of his public writings as may be available. I have read all of Hone's available private writings and do not fully understand him—nor would any one else, no matter how closely he examined Hone's diary. An investigation of the expressed or stated social beliefs of the eminent and successful, as the historian Paul Goodman has noted in his study of the social values of the antebellum Boston elite, would "define [their] aspiration," above all.[3] Goodman concedes that "how well men integrated ideals and behavior is another matter."

Professed ideals, even when they are contradicted by behavior, are by no means devoid of value: by their deeds *and* by their professions shall we know men. Even when public statements are transparently mouthings, designed above all to disguise true intent, they are of interest, throwing light on the public image desired by their authors. To students of the total man, nothing about him—not even the style of his hypocrisy—is irrelevant. I find fascinating that Hone can in the same paragraph express his delight that men of affairs are forming a musical club to combat his city's indifference toward culture and his dread that the club might become too popular. He who leaped to the conclusion that Hone was, therefore, a snob would have to reconcile this judgment with Hone's delight at Miss Mowat's play, *Fashion*, an uncompromising lampoon of fashionable snobbishness.[4]

Since this book is about the actual situation of the rich and the light this situation throws on "long accepted views of the era," it has focused on the measurable actions of the rich rather than their unfathomable psyches. Its attention is confined to actual rather than expressed values. The operative values of the antebellum rich were revealed in their actions. This, of course, is as true for great thinkers as for ordinary men. We study in detail the ideas of influential writings not to discover the actual values of their authors, but to understand as fully as possible beliefs of great originality or intellectual merit or consequence. Rousseau's values are better obtained from the frank revelations of his *Confessions* than from his *Social Contract*. We read the *Social Contract* as carefully as we do because it is a great and influential book; but the antebellum rich were hardly great or original thinkers. John Jacob Astor's attack on speculation interests us, not for the insight it affords into the phenomenon he attacks, but for the insight into the mentality of a man who had invested great sums so diversely and so remorselessly and yet could utter such words.

The aspirations of the rich, as defined by their public statements, are a matter of some interest—but one which lies outside the scope and purpose of this book. Detailed consideration of the values of particular individuals and of the tensions generated by their conflicting impulses or by the gulf between their theory and their practice will have to await another, different kind of study.

The operative values of wealthy men as a group have been suggested, if implicitly, by the discussion of their actions. They appear to have regarded the accumulation and the perpetuation of wealth as great goods. They valued highly the diverse and comfortable material life made possible by riches. Life was made more attractive when enriched by art and music. While some of the rich professed enthusiasm for a democratic mingling of unlike social orders, the behavior of most of them indicated their preference for exclusiveness. The elite evidently admired and wished to play the part of an aristocracy. They placed great store in broad social service, as a manifestation of *noblesse oblige,* as a means of enhancing the quality and significance of their lives, and for adding to their own influence within the community. And they believed it fitting and proper that men of great material substance should have an overall power commensurate with their wealth.

Of course, when the wealthy class is broken down into the individuals who comprised it, all coherence disappears from the discussion of their values, actual or professed. I suspect that Philip Hone was no more complex than most of his wealthy contemporaries, only more helpful in revealing the inner springs of his behavior. The detailed recording of his thoughts reveals a man of complicated moods and impulses. And, when we focus on the 'movement of his feet' rather than his words, the courses he followed at times resembled a zigzag rather than a straight path. The convictions underlying his "deeds" are not at all transparent or simple to grasp. When Hone makes a sudden trip to New York in the summer of 1832, leaving the safety of the Rockaways for the cholera-infested city, his words and his action indicate his beliefs that business must be pursued at all costs; that a family man must be courageous; and that personal safety must be subordinated to the needs of the community—at one and the same time. But there must be a limit to all things. The investigation of the motives and values of the antebellum rich is the stuff of another volume.

Notes

[1] Hone Diary, Sept. 25, 1832, V:330.
[2] *Ibid.,* Dec. 1, 1835, XI:65; Oct. 22, 1833, VII:252.
[3] Paul Goodman, "Ethics and Enterprise: The Values of a Boston Elite, 1800–1860," *American Quarterly, XVIII* (Fall 1966), p. 451.
[4] Hone Diary, Dec. 15, 1831, IV:317–18; April 5, 1845, XXII:460.

Appendix B
Moses Beach Revisited: A Critical Examination of His Wealthy Citizens Pamphlets*

A curious literary genre flourished in the United States during the 1840s. In each of the major cities of the Northeast, publications appeared that listed the purportedly wealthiest 500 or 1,000 persons in the community. Typically, these monuments to American dollar worship also included estimates of the wealth owned by each individual named, as well as short biographical sketches that promised to be both useful to businessmen and interesting to the general public. The pioneer compendium was *Wealth and Biography of the Wealthy Citizens of New York City,* first published early in 1842 by Moses Y. Beach, the editor and publisher of the New York *Sun.* Its success stimulated imitators in Philadelphia, Brooklyn, Boston, and many towns in Massachusetts.[1] Since the assessors' department in New York City, unlike its counterpart in Boston, printed no official lists of tax assessments, scholars in need of data on wealth and how it was earned in the metropolis have had to seek other evidence. From Gustavus Myers to Lee Benson and Frank Otto Gatell, they have turned to Beach's *Wealthy Citizens.*

Most of the historians who have relied on Beach's list have been aware that in doing so they were in a sense engaging in an act of faith. They have expressed doubts concerning Beach's silence as to his principle of selection, his omission of some men of great wealth, and his undervaluation of the riches of others, as well as the authenticity of his biographical sketches. As Gatell noted, "the principal recommendation for the use of Beach's list is its availability." In view of the "lifetime of research in the city directories and tax lists" that was believed to be involved in drawing up a more accurate list than Beach's, scholars have acted as though they had no realistic alternative but to use the *Wealthy Citizens* list.[2] An alternative is now available.

A new list of New York City's wealthiest persons during the Jacksonian era has recently been published. Based on the evidence of the city's manuscript assessment rolls for 1828 and 1845, it discloses that most of the "wealthy citizens" of Beach's sixth edition (1845) were not in fact among the wealthiest 1,000 persons in New York City.[3]

The evidence of New York City's tax assessments for 1845 indicates that the sixth edition of Beach's listing grossly exaggerated the wealth

*This essay makes clear why contemporary published listings of New York City's wealthiest persons could not be relied on. It was published originally in the *Journal of American History,* LVIII (Sept. 1971). Some of the original footnotes are deleted.

of most of the individuals it cited. Fewer than 300 persons were assessed for the magic $100,000 that earned one a place in *Wealthy Citizens*. The tax data, imperfect and incomplete, tend always to underestimate personal estate drastically. But if the wealth of most of the Beach list's "membership" was undervalued by the assessment figures, so was the wealth of almost everyone else. Interestingly, for all the exaggeration in the amounts attributed to most persons named in Beach's sixth edition, the tax records also show that dozens of persons were worth substantially more than the *Wealthy Citizens* list indicated.

If the sixth edition omits most of the 1,000 wealthiest New Yorkers of 1845, its record is far better for "the richest of the rich." It does contain the names—if it exaggerates the wealth—of 80 per cent of the 50 persons each taxed on an estate of $250,000 or higher, and about 56 per cent of the 230 persons whose wealth was assessed at between $100,000 and $250,000. That no great expertise may have been needed to know that John Jacob Astor, Isaac Bronson, Harmon Hendricks, Peter G. Stuyvesant, and William C. Rhinelander were very wealthy, does not detract from Beach's relative accuracy on this score. His pamphlet, however, omitted the names of several hundred persons each taxed on estates of close to $100,000 or more.

For all the questions raised by *Wealthy Citizens*, its record of apparently regular publication from 1842 through 1855 seems to suggest that it was accepted by the New York City mercantile community as a useful contribution. The good contemporary reputation evidently enjoyed by *Wealthy Citizens* would appear to justify the respect shown it by scholars, for all the pamphlet's imperfections. In reality, however, the overall publishing career of *Wealthy Citizens* is not reassuring. That thirteen (actually twelve) editions were printed between 1842 and 1855 was not a sign that Beach's publication was an annual one, as some historians have assumed. The first four editions came out between April 16 and June 4, 1842. A fifth edition appeared at the end of 1844, the sixth through the eleventh editions in 1845 and 1846. After a lapse of almost a decade, the twelfth and thirteenth editions were published in 1855. Annual publication in itself would have demonstrated nothing vitally significant about the quality of the listings, but the erratic pattern actually followed in the printing of the pamphlets raises questions about the publisher's stability of purpose, as it does about the nature of the audience.

If the checkered publication career of *Wealthy Citizens* and the inaccuracy of most of Beach's estimates for 1845 do not necessarily invalidate other aspects of the ratings, they hardly strengthen belief in their reliability. It therefore seemed advisable to examine contemporary evidence and all of the extant editions of *Wealthy Citizens* in order to subject them to close scrutiny. This essay attempts to answer a number of questions about Beach's listings, including the most interesting question: should scholars have relied on Beach's list in light of the evidence that was available to them?

Why did Beach decide to publish *Wealthy Citizens*? Beach's explanations of his motives were contradictory. In the preface to the third edition (1842), he said that his aim was "to define the true position of sundry individuals . . . , and to tell the whole truth and nothing but the truth." [4] By 1845 he was ready to settle for less than the whole truth. Contributors were advised by Beach that he sought only "such sketches of their history and present possessions as they may deem proper to be given to the world." In one mood he promised to cater to "the public's" presumed curiosity concerning "those whose fortunes have been acquired in a [n] . . . equivocal manner." More typically he sought to convey the wholesome teaching that great wealth was the reward of virtue and honest effort, within the reach of all. For, as he advised readers of the New York *Sun*, in this country the "humble mechanic" had available to him "all the facilities in business and every means of gaining independence which are extended only to rich monopolists in England." Beach seemingly regarded his pamphlets as a means of inculcating sound social doctrine among the poor.[5]

Beach also claimed that one of the important purposes of *Wealthy Citizens* was to provide the business community with a credit rating. But the evidence of the biographical sketches in almost all the editions of *Wealthy Citizens* indicates that their publisher was considerably more interested in "render[ing] his publication more interesting to the general reader." Such an interest, of course, could be achieved by means that had little to do with the requirements of a sound credit rating.

A modern critic has surmised that Beach's "motive perhaps was to advertise that he was worth $300,000 [in 1846] whereas his powerful rival James Gordon Bennett of the *Herald* was set down for only $100,000." [6] Without doubt, Beach sought to gratify his own ego through his publication; readers of the sixth edition were advised that "Beach, M. Y. . . . $250,000," did an "unparalleled business." He also appeared to regard *Wealthy Citizens* as a means of attracting publicity, increasing the circulation of the New York *Sun*, making additional profit, and catering to public curiosity about the rich—not necessarily in that order. Even had Beach's motives been of the purest, only to prepare a document as accurate as it was humanly possible to make it, there would have been no assurance that his performance would match his promises. But his motives were not so philanthropic. *Wealthy Citizens* was published by a man clearly less interested in its accuracy than in the profit—broadly construed—it might bring.[7]

More important than the motives of the publisher are the actual circumstances or method of publication of a credit rating. How did Beach typically assemble his editions? According to Henry W. Lanier, whose

1922 book on the banking history of New York reprinted the entire sixth edition of *Wealthy Citizens*, Beach served merely as a conduit, publishing a list put together by businessmen themselves. Lanier wrote:[8] "In the year 1840, a number of leading New York merchants "in the course of calculations connected with business," made a joint list of the available capital employed by the men they knew. . . . [This subsequently] led to the pooling of the information on which this unique memorandum was based. As the list was added to, it grew to such size and was referred to so frequently that its authors decided to print enough copies for the original contributors, and it was placed for this purpose in charge of Moses Beach, Editor of the *Sun*." Detracting from the force of Lanier's account is the fact that it was nothing more than a reproduction of the explanation of the list's origins that appeared in the preface to the twelfth edition of *Wealthy Citizens* (1855).

Beach first advanced the claim that his lists had originated with "our eminent business men," in the preface to the tenth edition (1846). When their calculations were completed, he wrote, "they communicated the idea to the publisher of the New York *Sun*, by whom it was at once taken up and a bare list, some 7 or 8 pages long [actually five pages long] in coarse type was made out." Could Beach's memory have been misbehaving, as it did when he evidently forgot that the "third" edition was really the second? The publisher of the New York *Sun* was a shrewd businessman who must have known that this account, if accepted, would establish the *bona fides* of his rating. Why had he not offered it earlier when his pamphlet was seeking recognition? The prefaces to the earlier editions said nothing about origination other than that their biographical notices had been "procured from various authentic sources." According to the New York *Sun*, March 6, 1842, the pamphlet "shortly to be published by this office" had been prepared by persons who were not themselves necessarily businessmen: the paper claimed that they were "persons who have for more than thirty years been thoroughly acquainted with the business and businessmen of our great metropolis." Actually, the main point made in the preface to the first edition (April 1842) [9] was that most of the information supplied by the "many sources" was inevitably contradictory.

For all his boasting about his extensive business operations, Beach appears not to have moved in the circles of the city's business elite.[10] He was a newcomer to New York, owing whatever reputation he had to his association with a newspaper that was notorious for its vulgarity, its cheap price, and its mass audience—as well as the hoaxes it was fond of perpetrating on them. It strains credibility that the city's men of affairs would have entrusted so important an enterprise as the publishing of a credit rating to such a man. Before the emergence of Lewis Tappan's Mercantile Agency, businessmen in need of information about their colleagues would have been better advised to have consulted a private credit rating such as the one kept by the White family.[11] In any case, there is no evidence that Beach's list held any standing in the judgment of leaders of the business community.

The circumstances surrounding the publication of the much-cited sixth edition of *Wealthy Citizens* hardly bear out Beach's later claims as to the repute of his compilers or the care with which he prepared their handiwork for publication. According to the New York *Sun,* which publicized the forthcoming edition earlier and more heavily than it had done for earlier editions, the pamphlet was due to be published on January 14, 1845. Yet as late as two days before this scheduled publication date, Beach was soliciting readers of his newspaper for material and "confidential communications." Nor were his requests confined to those who had firsthand knowledge. The day before the printing he was still seeking information, which he promised to receive "in the strictest confidence," from relatives and "friends." Obviously, no time was set aside for checking the accuracy of these last-minute nuggets. It is surprising that the publisher of a ranking of the wealthy, ostensibly put together by the rich themselves, should have appealed publicly to readers of his penny press for authentic information.

Beach's claim that he sold every copy of every edition printed of *Wealthy Citizens* would attest, if true, to a high degree of interest in the pamphlet, despite the absence of information on the number of copies printed for any edition. To those concerned more with the reliability than the popularity of Beach's lists, however, the question is not how many, but what kinds of people read and used them. What is of interest is the contemporary reputation of *Wealthy Citizens,* particularly among the men of affairs the publisher claimed to serve.

Leaders of New York City's business community appear to have been indifferent to *Wealthy Citizens* lists. A number of eminent families did secure copies, although it is not clear just when. The fact could betoken nothing more than curiosity.[12] The papers and correspondence of numerous eminent businessmen failed to turn up a single reference to Beach or his publication. Here was a credit rating published in the nation's commercial center and based on information allegedly supplied by the city's business leaders. One would expect to find some signs of response to a publication that should have caused at least a modest ripple of interest if not a minor sensation. New York City's newspapers during the era paid close attention to what their competitors were doing, and, if quicker to attack than to praise, were in any case not inhibited about commenting on the actions of their fellow publishers. A close look at the news and editorial columns of New York's leading papers during the periods when most of *Wealthy Citizens* editions were published yields not a single comment. That there was some kind of conspiracy of silence is doubtful, since even Greeley, who had no respect for Beach, ran ads for Beach's pamphlets in the *Tribune*[13] The private papers and correspondence of New York City's leading newspapermen are similarly devoid of comment, at least about Beach's pamphlets. Several of Bennett's correspondents did refer to the publisher of the *Sun*, but only to attack him for his alleged antipathy to the Irish, to Catholicism, and to religion in general.

The ultimate question concerns the quality of Beach's pamphlets. The most exasperating feature of the *Wealthy Citizens'* lists was less the evidence of error, contradiction, inconsistency, and omission, than their publisher's indifference to these lapses. First names were regularly—and unnecessarily—omitted. All names starting with a certain initial would be unaccountably missing. The alphabet was regularly violated. The spelling of names was quixotic. Poor spelling was a characteristic of many men in that era, but one would have thought that the editor of a credit rating would have consulted either a directory or the *Proceedings of the Board of Aldermen*, particularly since he himself did not appear to know the individuals in question.[14] A close check of the tenth and eleventh editions shows that evident attempts at revision were abruptly called off for three and a fraction pages. The page makeup for most of the names starting with the letter *J*, all with the letter *K*, and many with the letter *L*, is exactly the same in the one edition as in the other.

The printing of sums was done cavalierly. The drastic changes in the wealth attributed to certain individuals from one edition, the tenth, to the next edition, published only weeks later, induce wonder as to the accuracy of either estimate. Was Jonathan Goodhue supposed to be worth the $500,000 attributed to him by the tenth edition or the $100,000 by the eleventh? John C. Hamilton $200,000 or $100,000? The estate of Thomas Leggett $800,000 or $500,000? Henry Remsen $500,000 or $800,000? Peter Schermerhorn $2,500,000 or $1,250,000? Samuel A. Willoughby $100,000 or $150,000? Stephen Whitney $5,000,000 or $3,500,000? Alexander T. Stewart $800,000 or $500,000? Did Spencer go from $100,000 in the earlier edition to $500,000 in the later, because he was promoted from "Lieutenant" in the one to "Captain" in the other? (His actual promotion had occurred years earlier.) Nor does absence of any explanatory comment encourage one to believe that these instances represented corrections.

Beach's carelessness also extended to his treatment of the short biographies. Depending on which edition was used by the reader, Robert Buloid was either a grocer or a commission merchant; Robert Cheesebrough, a dry-goods merchant or lawyer; F. B. Cutting, a lawyer or something else; Henry DeRham, a German or Dutch or Swiss; James Fellows and William B. Moffat, born rich or poor; Peter Embury, a grocer or merchant; Theodosius Fowler, a stock importer or grocer; George Lovett's wealth derived from lumber or from something else; Moses Taylor, a grocer or a shipping merchant; A. T. Stewart married either Miss Mitchell or Miss Clinch; and Henry A. Coit and E. K. Collins married wealthy women or they had not. Mrs. Fisher's father died "some twenty years since," both in 1845 and 1855. The biography of Henry Brevoort, Jr., in an early edition becomes the life of his father in a later one, a transposition that was also the case for Eugene and William K. Kettletas, Eleazer and Jehial Parmley, and J. I. and T. B. Coddington.

While most of Beach's biographical vignettes were not marred by obvious error, they were hardly impressive. One learns that Barnet Andariese was "an excellent tailor and a very amiable man"; that Henry Laverty was "a very polished man" whose "parlor is hung with very excellent paintings, the production of his accomplished sister's pencil [sic]"; that William Bard was "a son of Dr. Samuel Bard, and fully retains the reputation of an honorable sire"; and that J. W. Bleecker was "of an ancient New York family."

According to Beach, care had "been taken in writing out the memoirs, not to invade the sanctity of private life or wound the sensibilities of any." The promise was not honored, for there was more than a hint of gossip in the life histories. Thus David D. Field "is an illustration of what Lord Coke says—that lawyers are peculiarly susceptible of the tender impressions." The editor fervently hopes that George Laurie is not "too advanced into the *yellow leaf* to forswear and become a Benedict . . . [he was] only to say the word in these hard times and Hymen stands ready to light his altar torch, and cupid to let fly from his quiver one of his most barbed arrows, that not even the tough texture of a bachelor's heart could resist." Jacob Little, "one of the rich 'Jacobs' of Wall Street . . . has some brains as well as money, and people say that his wife is pretty. She has a fondness for opera," while her husband's "ways are past finding out." Edward Minturn is "a fast driver . . . and still is a vigorous bachelor in the green days of his prime. He sips his wine with moderation, and loves with ardour the idols of his attachment." John Mortimer, Jr., was "for many years the 'Stewart' among the ladies." Thatcher T. Payne "lives in snuff 'perforce' of a most capital speculation he made in marrying the rich young blooming widow of Mr. Baily, a rich merchant, deceased, that left a plumb nearly to her, and we hope Thatcher, who is a lucky rogue, don't [sic] forget his poor relations if he has any." These tidbits have the ring of petty truth.

If the sketches were long on trivia, they were deficient in hard data. For over 400 of the not quite 1,000 persons listed in 1845, not even an occupation was offered. The most disquieting thing about these omissions is that they could have been taken care of easily had Beach merely consulted general or business directories.

Readers of *Wealthy Citizens* were assured that the "edition had been carefully revised, and almost every biographical notice entirely rewritten, so as to remove whatever errors and objectionable remarks had crept into the former editions." [15] In some cases, the corrections were of very slight weight. In 1845 the last sentence in the sketch of Richard F. Carman stated: "No man is more respected." Ten years later it was changed to: "His carnation cheek and merry laugh will keep him young for many a year." Some "corrections" took the form of one line, giving occupation, to replace a previously blank entry.

A detailed comparison of the sixth and twelfth editions of *Wealthy Citizens* does not substantiate the claim that the later version was "a careful revision of all previous ones." Over 500 names are common to both pamphlets, well over half the total of each. New biographies were written for only 65 of these persons, of which 11 were essentially gossip. The earlier biographical sketches for 194 persons were simply excluded from the later edition. For 295 persons the earlier sketch—or lack of one—was repeated, with slight but insignificant changes for 72 of these, and word-for-word repetition for all the others.

Another error regularly committed by Beach was his habit of dropping from a later edition hundreds of persons who actually remained among the wealthiest 1,000 in the city. That a number of these men would subsequently reappear in a later edition seemed to be as fortuitous as their disappearance in the first place.

The ignorance of Beach and his informants concerning the actual worth of wealthy New Yorkers made a joke of the characteristic assertion in the preface to *Wealthy Citizens* that it was "more correct than any edition preceding." Every attempt at "improvement" made in subsequent editions usually only increased the rate of error. Thus, if 44 per cent of Beach's 1845 list belonged on a true list of the wealthiest citizens, only 34 per cent of his entries for 1855 were eligible. Almost one-third of the 312 persons on the 1845 list who were dropped from the edition of one decade later were in fact worth the $50,000 or more in the later period that placed them in the upper 1,000. Yet only about 30 per cent of the close to 500 persons added to the 1855 rating truly belonged to the elite.

Ratings based on a comparison of other adjacent editions of *Wealthy Citizens* similarly disclose the existence of this perverse pattern: Beach's replacement of some names with others invariably reduced the level of accuracy of the later edition. If 36 per cent of the slightly more than 200 names added to the sixth edition truly belonged to the upper 1,000, only 22 per cent of the more than 100 newcomers to the tenth edition truly qualified; as did no more than 30 per cent of the three dozen additions to the eleventh edition. But 35 per cent of those excised from the latter edition should not have been. The thirteenth edition (1855), contains 71 names not listed in its immediate predecessor. Only 32 per cent of these were in the upper 1,000. Once again the perverse tendency manifested itself: 45 per cent of the 40 persons dropped from the twelfth edition should have been retained.

The evidence indicates that Beach's pamphlets cannot be accepted as authentic rankings and accounts of New York City's wealthiest citizens. In addition to the errors in Beach's lists, the cavalier quality of their preparation, the carelessness attending their publication, and the indifference that marked their reception disqualify them as serious credit ratings. There would be little point in damning Beach himself for not having adhered to more precise standards. He was what he was, not a scholar sifting evidence carefully in order to assure its reliability, but a business man eager to sell large quantities of his product and not fastidious as to how it was made nor overly concerned about its accuracy. That is precisely why scholars cannot credit—and should not have credited—those remarkable pamphlets, whose deficiencies were so transparent. Paradoxically, the value of Beach's monuments to materialism derives not from their measurement of worldly accumulation, which they did so badly, but from their reflection of the spirit of the age.

Notes

1 The full title of the best known edition, the sixth, is *Wealth and Biography of the Wealthy Citizens of New York City, Comprising an Alphabetical Arrangement of Persons Estimated to be Worth $100,000 and Upwards, with the Sums Appended to Each Name: Being Useful to Banks, Merchants, and Others* (New York, 1845). Moses Y. Beach published twelve editions in all; there is a thirteenth edition, but as is noted below, Beach evidently forgot that he had not published a second edition, mislabelling all editions after the first. The number used for an edition in this essay, however, is the number Beach assigned it. The Genealogical Division of the New York Public Library and the New-York Historical Society Library have in their possession nine of these editions. The first, a simple five-page listing of names and the sums they were estimated to be worth, was entitled *Wealth and Wealthy Citizens. . . .* Since the following edition was said to be "enlarged to ten times the original matter and now containing brief historical and geneological [sic] notices," it was entitled *Wealth and Pedigree of the Wealthy Citizens.* Thereafter the title was changed to *Wealth and Biography of the Wealthy Citizens.*

2 Gatell, "Money and Party in Jacksonian America," pp. 240, 241.

3 Edward Pessen, "The Wealthiest New Yorkers of the Jacksonian Era: A New List," *New-York Historical Society Quarterly, LIV* (April 1970), pp. 145–72. Beach did not state expressly that all persons estimated to be worth $100,000 were included in his pamphlets. The lists were said to comprise "an alphabetical arrangement of persons estimated to be worth $100,000 and upwards." The prefaces and Beach's editorials in the New York *Sun* show, however, that he did regard the lists to be comprehensive rather than selective. In the former he wrote that if "any names of wealthy individuals over $100,000 have been omitted, we beg that they may be communicated." As for the figure of 1,000 for the total number of persons listed in one of his editions, it is based on the number included in the sixth and extant later editions. The sixth edition had 963 names; the tenth edition, 1025; the eleventh, 1018; the twelfth, 1061; and the thirteenth, 1087 names.

4 The New York *Sun*, May 14, 1842, reports that "the demand for the pamphlet has been so great that a 2nd edition has been issued greatly enlarged and improved."

That is the only reference to the pamphlet in the *Sun* for that month, and until June 14, 1842, when the newspaper spoke of a fourth edition. Yet the publication date of the third edition, as indicated in its "Prefatory Notice," was May 14, 1842. In other words, the "third" edition was probably the second.

[5] New York *Sun* (weekend edition), Jan. 8, 1845, New York *Sun*, Jan. 11, 13, 18, 1845; Preface, *Wealthy Citizens*, May 1842. It is interesting to note that Beach was delighted when Congress in 1845 rejected Robert Owen's request for permission to deliver lectures on socialism. New York *Sun*, Jan. 18, 1845.

[6] R. G. Albion, "Commercial Fortunes in New York," p. 159.

[7] Beach wrote in the Preface to the third edition of *Wealthy Citizens* that this was "a country where *money* and not *title* is the standard by which merit is appreciated." Discovering that the market would bear it, Beach doubled the original price of 12½ cents for subsequent editions.

[8] Henry Wysham Lanier, *A Century of Banking in New York: 1822–1922* (New York, 1922), pp. 75, 151–84. Benson used Henry Wysham Lanier's reprint of Beach's sixth edition. Lanier cites no source for another interesting compilation that he reprinted, mislabelled by him as "The Rich Men of 1822" (pp. 92–142). For a critical discussion of this list, see Pessen, "The Wealthiest New Yorkers of the Jacksonian Era," p. 148n.

[9] Frank M. O'Brien, "Moses Yale Beach," Allen Johnson and Dumas Malone, eds., *Dictionary of American Biography* (20 vols., New York, 1928–1936), II, p. 84, gives the year as 1841.

[10] Philip Hone's diary for 1828–1851 refers to many hundreds of men who were important in the worlds of finance, trade, and industry, even if they were not on intimate terms with the diarist. Beach does not appear among them.

[11] Attributed to Robert White, this manuscript notebook gave a credit rating to over 500 firms in News York City in 1835, primarily merchants, grocers, drygoods dealers, and druggists. Men were categorized as worthy of "unlimited credit"; "undoubted credit"; "good credit (5 to $10,000)"; "fair credit (2 to $4,000)"; "slender credit ($1,000 or less)"; or requiring an endorser. Robert White Papers, New-York Historical Society.

[12] Some of the editions in the possession of the New York Public Library and the New-York Historical Society were contributed by the families of Amos R. Eno, William E. Dodge, Frederick Sheldon, and Isaac J. Greenwood.

[13] Horace Greeley referred to the New York *Sun* as the "slimy and venomous instrument of Locofocoism, Jesuitical and deadly in politics and grovelling in morals." O'Brien, "Moses Yale Beach," p. 84.

[14] Among his misspellings were "Thomas Tilerton," "G. Repilye," "Mrs. Banger," "I. I. Drake," "John Robins," "William P. Furmiss," and "Henry Eldard."

[15] From the prefaces to the third, sixth, tenth, and twelfth editions of *Wealthy Citizens.*

Appendix C
The Wealthiest Persons in the Great Northeastern Cities During the Second Quarter of the Nineteenth Century

These data are drawn from the tax-assessment rolls for New York City, Brooklyn, and Boston. The Philadelphia list consists of persons whose wealth was estimated at $100,000 or more in *Memoirs and Auto-Biography of Some of the Wealthy Citizens of Philadelphia* (Philadelphia, 1846). While the Philadelphia list, as I have shown, appears to be reliable in a number of respects, it was not possible to check the accuracy of its estimates of wealth against Philadelphia's assessments of the value of property. Assessors in that city did not distinguish between owners and users of real property. It should be kept in mind that assessments grossly undervalued the actual wealth of the rich.

New York City's Wealthiest Two Hundred in 1828

Wealth Assessed at $100,000 and Over

Astor, Henry
Astor, John Jacob*
Bronson, Isaac†
Coster, John G.*
Douglass, Mrs. Margaret
Eckford, Henry
Flack, John
Gilbert, William W.
Glover, John (estate)
Hart, Eli
Hendricks, Harmon
Hicks, Whitehead
Hone, John
Hone, Philip
Hosack, Dr. David
Ireland, John
Janeway, George†
Jauncey, William
Jones, Isaac C.
Jones, Joshua
Lawrence, Isaac†
Leggett, Thomas H.
Lenox, Robert
Lewis, Morgan
Livingston, John R.
Lord, Rufus L.
Lorillard, George†
Lorillard, Jacob
Lorillard, Peter†
Mason, John
Morse, John
Murray, John R.
Pearson, Isaac G.
Pell, Alfred S.
Post, Gerardus
Post, Joel
Post, William
Prime, Nathaniel†
Rapelye, George
Reed, Luman
Remsen, Peter
Rhinelander, William
Rhinelander, William C.
Rogers, David
Roosevelt, James
Salles, Laurent
Sandford, Charles W.
Schermerhorn, Peter L.

Smith, Thomas H.
Storm, Garret (sometimes spelled Storms)
Stuyvesant, Nicholas W.†
Stuyvesant, Peter G.†
Van Rensselaer, Stephen†
Varick, Richard
Wallace, William
Watts, John
Whitney, Stephen
Whittemore, Samuel
Woodruff, Thomas T.

Wealth Assessed at Between $50,000 and $100,000

Abeel, Garret B.
Allaire, James P.
Allen, Stephen
Alley, Saul
Amos, Richard
Anderson, James
Anderson, John
Appley, Jacob
Arden, Abijah
Austen, David (sometimes spelled Austin)
Ballard, William C.
Bancker, Evert A.
Barclay, Henry
Barnes, Robert (estate)
Barretto, Francis (estate)
Bayard, Henry
Beekman, John K.
Birdsall, Benjamin
Blake, Anson
Bloomfield, Smith
Boardman, Daniel
Bogardus, Robert
Boggs, James
Bool, Henry W.
Boyd, Samuel
Brevoort, Henry
Brooks, David
Bruen, Matthias
Buloid, Robert
Bunker, William I.
Catlin, Lynde
Clarkson, Lavinus
Coddington, Isaac and J.
Colden, Cadwallader D.
Coles, John B.
Contoit, John H.
Crary, Peter
Deane, John
Delaplaine, John F.
Depau, Francis
De Rham, Henry C.
Dominick, James W.
Donaldson, Robert
Edgar, William (estate)
Emmet, Thomas Addis
Few, William
Fickett, Samuel
Fish, Nicholas
Gibbons, William
Glover, the widow
Goelet, Peter
Goodhue, Jonathan
Gouverneur, Samuel
Graham, John L.
Griswold, George
Haggerty, John
Haight, B. and H.
Haight, David L.
Hall, Charles H.
Halsted, Mrs. Mary
Hamilton, Alexander
Hamilton, John C.
Hamersley, Lewis C.
Harmony, Peter
Harsen, Jacob
Hicks, Samuel
Hicks, Silas
Howland, Gardiner G.
Howland, Samuel S.

*assessed at over $500,000.
†assessed at over $250,000.

Hoyt, Gould
Jaques, Isaac S. (sometimes spelled Jacques)
Jay, Peter A.
Jennings, Chester
Jennings, Richard
Johnson, William
Jones, David S.
Jones, William
Kip, Luke
Laverty, Henry
Lawrence, Augustus
Lawrence, John L.
Lovett, George
Low, Nicholas (estate)
Marchant, Frederick
Marshall, Benjamin
McCarthy, Den[n]is
Mienell, James
Minturn, heirs of (sometimes spelled Minthurn)
Moore, Clement C.
Morrison, John C.
Mott, Dr. Valentine
Mowatt, John
Munn, Stephen B.
Munro, Peter Jay (sometimes spelled Monroe)
Murray, Mrs. Hannah
Murray, James B.
Nevins, Peter J. (sometimes spelled Nevius)
Norsworthy, Samuel
Oakley, Charles
Ogilvie, Peter (variously spelled: Oglevie, Ogleby, etc.)
Oothout, John
Overing, Henry
Paulding, William, Jr.
Pearsall, Thomas
Pell, Ferris
Pell, John (estate)
Phyfe, Duncan
Price, Thom[p]son
Pye, John
Quick, Tunis
Rankin, Henry
Reed, Collins
Remsen, Henry
Rogers, John
Rohr, John G.
Romaine, Benjamin
Ross, Azariah
Ross, William (estate)
Rutgers, Henry
Schiff, Wart M.
Seaman, Edward
Shaw, William
Smith, G. W. (estate)
Stagg, Abraham
Steenbach, Anthony
Stephens, Benjamin (sometimes spelled Stevens)
Stewart, Alexander
Suydam, John
Tappan, Arthur
Taylor, John
Thompson, Francis W.
Thompson, Samuel
Thompson, William (estate)
Tillotson, Robert
Underwood, Joseph
Valentine, Abraham
Van Nest, Abraham (sometimes spelled Van Ness)
Wagstaff, David
Ward, Samuel
Warren, John G.
Wells, James N.
Weyman, William
Whetten, John
White, Eli
Wilkes, Charles
Willett, Marinus
Willson, A.
Wright, Grove
Wright, Isaac
Wright, Jordan
Wyckoff, Henry J.
Youle, George

New York City's Wealthiest Three Hundred in 1845

Wealth Assessed at $250,000 and Over

Allen, Stephen
Astor, John Jacob*
Astor, William B.†
Barclay, Henry (estate)
Bininger, I. (estate)
Boorman, James
Brevoort, Henry
Bronson, Isaac (estate)
Coster, John G.†
Depau, F.†
Douglass, William
Furniss, William P.
Gardiner, Thomas (sometimes spelled Gardner)
Gilbert, Clinton
Goelet, Peter†
Griswold, George
Haggerty, John
Hendricks, Harmon (estate)
Hendricks, Mrs. H.
Higgins, Timothy
Hoyt, Gould (estate)
Janeway, Jacob J.
Johnston, John
Jones, Edward R.
Jones, Isaac C.
Jones, James I.
King, James Gore†
Lenox, James (sometimes spelled Lennox)†
Lord, Rufus L.
Lorillard, Catherine
Lorillard, Jacob (estate)
Lorillard, Peter, Jr.†
Low, Nicholas (estate)
Mason, John (estate)
Moore, Clement C.
Morse, John
Munn, Stephen B.
Niblo, William
Phalen, James
Phelps, Anson G.
Post, William (estate)
Prime, Nathaniel (estate)
Remsen, Peter (estate)
Rhinelander, William (estate)
Rhinelander, William C.
Robbins, John (sometimes spelled Robins)
Ronalds, Maria D. L.
Roosevelt, Cornelius V. S.
Salles, Laurent (estate)†
Schermerhorn, Peter (estate)
Stewart, Alexander T.
Stuyvesant, Peter G.*
Suydam, John (estate)
Whitney, Stephen†
Wolfe, John D.

Wealth Assessed at Between $100,000 and $250,000

Adams, John
Alley, Saul
Alvord, Alonzo A.
Anderson, James (estate)
Anderson, Smith W.
Austen, David (sometimes spelled Austin)
Aymar, Benjamin
Barclay, Anthony
Bartlett, Caleb
Bartlett, Edwin
Bartow, Robert
Beach, Moses Y.
Beekman, James W.

*assessed at over $1,000,000.
†assessed at over $500,000.

Beekman, John
Bertine, James T.
Bishop, Japhet
Bishop, Joseph
Bogert, Cornelius
Bowne, Walter
Bradhurst, John M.
Bridge, Lewis K.
Brooks, David
Brown, George W.
Brown, James
Brown, Silas
Bruce, George
Bruen, Matthias
Brush, Joshua
Buchanan, Thomas (estate)
Campbell, Duncan P.
Carman, Richard F.
Cary, Henry (sometimes spelled Carey)
Chesterman, James
Clendenen, Peter
Coddington, Jonathan I.
Cogswell, Nathaniel (estate)
Colgate, William
Contoit, John H.
Cowman, A. T.
Cox, Abraham B.
Cram, Jacob
Cruger, Harriet D.
Cruger, John C.
Cushman, Don Alonzo
Dean, Nicholas
Delaplaine, John F.
DePeyster, Frederick
De Rham, Henry C.
Dickie, Patrick (sometimes spelled Dickey)
Dominick, James W.
Douglass, George
Dubois, Cornelius
Eckford, Henry
Edgar, William
Ellsworth, Henry
Emmet, Thomas Addis
Emmet, Mrs. Thomas A.
Field, Hickson W.
Field, Moses (estate)
Foster, Andrew
Foster, James
Gassner, Peter
Gibbons, William
Gihon, John
Gilbert, Nicholas
Giraud, Jacob (sometimes spelled Girand)
Goodhue, Jonathan
Green, John C.
Greenwood, Isaac
Grinnell, James
Grosvenor, Jasper
Haight, David L.
Halstead, Caleb O. (sometimes spelled Halsted)
Hamilton, John C.
Harmony, Peter
Harrison, James
Harsen, Jacob (estate)
Hart, Eli
Hendricks, M. M.
Hicks, Samuel (estate)
Hitchcock, William R.
Holbrook, Ephraim
Hone, James
Hone, John (estate)
Hone, Philip
Howard, William (estate)
Howland, Gardiner G.
Howland, John H.
Hunt, Jonathan
Hunt, Thomas
Irving, John T.
Jennings, Richard
Johnson, William M.
Jones, David S.
Jones, George
Jones, John C.
Jones, John Q.

Jones, Robert
Jones, William (estate)
Judd, Samuel
Kearny, Philip R. (sometimes spelled Kearney)
Kennedy, Robert
Kernochan, Joseph
Kettletas, Eugene
Kingsland, Daniel C.
Kneeland, Charles
Kortright, N. Gouverneur
Lafarge, John
Laing, Edgar H.
Laverty, Henry
Lawrence, August H.
Lawrence, Dominick L.
Lawrence, Isaac (estate)
Lawrence, John B.
Lawrence, Thomas
Lee, David
Leggett, Samuel
Leggett, Thomas H.
Leggett, William F.
Lewis, Morgan (estate)
Livingston, John R.
Lorillard, George (estate)
Lorillard, Peter (estate)
Loubat, Alphonse
Lovett, George
Ludlum, Nicholas
Manton, Thomas (estate)
McBride, James
Meinell, James
Mesier, Edward S.
Mildeberger, Christopher
Morgan, Matthew
Mortimer, Richard
Mott, Dr. Valentine
Munroe, James (sometimes spelled Monroe)
Murray, James B.
Murray, John R.
Murray, Mary
Nevins, Peter J.
Norsworthy, Samuel (estate)
Ogilvie, William
Olmstead, Francis (sometimes spelled (Olmsted)
Oothout, Catherine
Oothout, John
Palmer, Courtland
Parish, Daniel
Parish, Henry
Parmley, Eleaser
Paulding, William
Peck, Elisha
Peet, Stephen B.
Pendleton, Edmund H.
Phillips, E.
Phyfe, Duncan
Pickersgill, John
Pickersgill, William C.
Pinckney, Peter
Post, Allison
Post, George D.
Post, Gerardus
Post, Waldron B.
Price, Thompson
Prime, Edward
Rapelye, George (estate)
Ray, Richard
Ray, Robert
Ridabock, Frederick (variously spelled)
Ridgeway, James
Rogers, George P.
Rogers, Mary Ann
Roosevelt, James H.
Ross, William (estate)
Ruggles, Samuel B.
Sampson, John (estate)
Sampson, Joseph
Schenck, Cornelius
Schermerhorn, Abraham
Schermerhorn, John (estate)
Schermerhorn, P. A.
Schuchardt, Frederick
Scott, William B.

Smedburg, Charles G.
Smith, Cornelius
Spencer, William A.
Spingler, H. (estate; sometimes spelled Spengler, Springler)
Stephens, Benjamin K.
Steward, John
Stewart, Robert (estate)
Stillwell, Samuel
Storm, Garret
Storm, Isaac T.
Strong, James (estate)
Suckley, George
Suffern, Thomas
Sutton, George
Suydam, Lambert
Swan, Benjamin L.
Talbot, Charles
Targee, John
Taylor, Moses B.
Thompson, J., grandchildren of
Thompson, Samuel M.
Thorne, Col. H.
Tileston, Thomas
Titus, William H.
Tonnele, John
Townsend, Elihu
Treadwell, Adam
Troup, Robert (estate)
Tucker, Gideon (estate)
Van Antwerp, James
Van Nest, Abraham
Van Rensselaer, C. P.
Van Schaick, Myndert
Verplanck, Gulian C.
Wagstaff, Alfred
Wallace, William
Ward, August H.
Ward, Samuel (estate)
Warren, J. (estate)
Watt, Archibald (sometimes spelled Watts)
Weed, Harvey
Weed, Nathaniel
Wells, James N.
Wells, Richard J.
Wendell, John D.
Wetmore, William S.
Weyman, William (estate)
White, Eli
Wilkins, G. M.
Wilson, John
Wolfe, Christopher
Wood, John
Woodruff, Thomas T.
Wright, Grove
Wright, John D.
Wyckoff, Henry J. (estate)
Yates, Henry
Zabriskie, Andrew C.

The Wealthiest Taxpayers in Brooklyn, 1841*

Assessed for $100,000 or More

Bach, Robert
Bergen, Jacob†
Cornell, Simon
Gerritson, Samuel T. (also spelled Gerretson)
Hall, Valentine G.
Heeney, Cornelius
Hicks, Jacob M.
Howland, George S.
Hoyt, Charles†
Jackson, Hamilton H.
Johnson, Rev. Evan M.
Johnson, Gen, Jeremiah
Joralemon, Tunis†
Kelsey, Charles
Lawrence, Susan
Lefferts, Leffert
Luqueer, Nicholas
Manley, Robert F.
Martin, Mulford
Perry, Joseph A.
Pierrepont, Hezekiah B.‡

Powers, Mary
Prince, Anna
Sands, Oliver H.
Schermerhorn, Abraham and Peter
Trotter, Jonathan
Willoughby, Samuel A.

Assessed for Between $60,000 and $100,000

Birkbeck, Alexander
Boerum, Abraham and Henry
Bowne, Rodman
Bowne, Samuel
Bruen, Matthias
Clark, James S.
Cornell, Sarah
Couwenhoven, John
DeBevoise, James and Robert
Denton, Nehemiah
Dikeman, John
Embury, Daniel
Fleet, Samuel
Gracie, William R.
Greenfield, John J.
Hall, George
Jackson, Cornelia
Jackson, John
Johnson, Parmenus
Johnson, William L.
Kellogg, Edward
Lefferts, Rem
March, Joshua
Martense, Helen
Moon, John
Nevins, David and Russell H.
Patchen, George
Patchen, Henry
Philip, William
Polhemus, Theodore
Prentice, John H.
St. Felix, John R.
Sands, Austin L.
Skillman, John
Smith, Samuel
Spader, widow of Jeremiah
Tappan, Arthur
Treadwell, Adam
Treadwell, John
Underhill, James E.
Waring, Henry P.
Wood, George A.
Wood, George S.
Young, Henry

Reputedly Wealthiest Philadelphians in 1846

Wealth Estimated at $1,000,000 or More

Barton, J. Rhea
Beck, Paul, Jr.
Bohlen, John
Girard, Stephen (estate)
Pepper, George (estate)
Pratt, Henry
Ridgway, Jacob (estate)
Ridgway, John J.
Rogers, Evans
Rush, Dr. James
Sibbald, Charles F.

Wealth Estimated at Between $250,000 and $1,000,000

Archer, Joseph (estate)
Ashhurst, Richard
Binney, Horace
Brown, David S.

*includes non-residents.
†over $200,000.
‡over $500,000.

Brown, John A.
Burd, Edmund S.
Butler, Thomas (estate)
Carey, E. L.
Carpenter, George W.
Chauncey, Charles
Coleman, Obed
Cope, Caleb
Cope, Thomas Pym
Dugan, Joseph (estate)
Dundas, James
Evans, Griffith (estate)
Evans, Joseph R.
Everly, Adam
Fassitt, James
Fassitt, Thomas (estate)
Florence, Jacob I.
Fleming, Robert (estate)
Hare, Dr. Robert
Harrison, George (estate)
Henry, Alexander
Justice, Jacob (estate)
Kohne, Mrs. E.
Kuhn, Hartman
McKean, H. Pratt
Messchert, H.
Molony, James
Moss, John
Neilson, Robert
Norris, Isaac
Physick, Dr. P. S.
Powel, John Hare
Ralston, Robert (estate)
Ripka, Joseph
Rogers, William E. (estate)
Rostain, Fournier (estate)
Sheaff, George
Shields, Robert (estate)
Steinmetz, Jacob
Stockton, Robert F.
Swaim, William
Vansyckel, Elijah
Wetherill, John Price
Wistar, Richard
Yarnall family

Wealth Estimated at Between $100,000 and $250,000

Abbott, Timothy (estate)
Alsop, Amy
Alsop, Richard (estate)
Amer, William
Asbury, Samuel
Ashhurst, John
Ashhurst, Lewis R.
Ashhurst, William H.
Atwood, James
Atwood, John M.
Backus, E. F.
Baker, Charles H.
Baker, George N.
Baker, John R. (estate)
Baker, Michael
Barclay, Andrew C.
Barcroft, Stacy B.
Barton, Thomas P.
Bauersachs, J. N.
Beck, Charles F.
Beck, Henry Paul
Beckett, Henry
Bettle, Samuel
Bevan, Matthew L.
Biddle, Thomas A.
Binney, Horace, Jr.
Bird, Charles
Bohlen, Henry
Boker, Charles S.
Borie, Adolph E.
Borie, Charles L.
Borie, J. J.
Bouvier, Michael
Bowen, William E.
Brandreth, Benjamin
Bray, Daniel
Breck, Samuel
Brown, Joseph
Brown, Joseph D.
Brown, Lewis

Burd, Mrs. S.
Burgess, Robert (estate)
Burt, Nathaniel
Burton, Robert
Bury, John
Butler, Elizabeth
Butler, John
Buxby, Hezekiah
Cadwalader, George
Cadwalader, John
Cadwalader, Thomas C.
Caldcleugh, Robert A.
Camac (estate)
Camac, Mrs. William
Chancellor, Hannah
Chapman, Dr. N.
Chauncey, Elihu
Coburn, Robert
Comegys, Cornelius (estate)
Conner, David
Conrad, Matthew
Cope, Israel
Cope, Jasper
Coxe, Daniel W.
Craige, Seth
Crawford, Stephen R.
Cresson, Caleb (estate)
Cresson, Elliott
Cresson, Mrs. M.
Cresson, Sarah C.
Crossman, Dr. T. J.
Culp, Jacob
Dallett, John
David, Jacob
Davidson, Nathan
Davis, Isaac
Davis, William
Dickson, John
Dillingham, William H.
Duhring, Henry
Dulles, Joseph H.
Dunn, Nathan (estate)
Duponceau, Peter S. (estate)
Duval, James S. (estate)
Earp, Robert
Evans, Cadwalader (estate)
Evans, Dr. Charles
Farnum, Joseph
Fassitt, T. S. R.
Fellowes, C.
Firth, Thomas
Fisher, Mrs. Mary P.
Fisher, Mrs. Sarah
Florence, William
Forrest, Edwin
Fotterall, Mrs. S.
Fotterall, Stephen G.
Fotterall, William F.
Frazer, John F.
Gilbert, Frederick (estate)
Gowen, James
Graff, Charles (estate)
Grant, Samuel
Gratz family
Greenfield, Mrs. Elizabeth (estate)
Grover, Thomas D.
Gumbes, Mrs. Rebecca
Hacker, Isaac
Hacker, Isaiah
Hacker, Jeremiah
Hacker, William E.
Harding, John Jr.
Harland, John
Hart, A.
Hart, Thomas
Hart, William H.
Hartshorne, Dr. Joseph
Harvey, Isaac
Haseltine, John
Hazlehurst, Samuel
Henrion, S.
Hewson, Dr. T. M.
Heyl, John
Hildeburn, Samuel
Hillborn, Cyrus
Holme, Thomas
Holmes, John (estate)
Horstmann, William H.
Ingersoll, Charles
Ingersoll, Charles J.
Ingersoll, Joseph R.
Jones, Samuel W.

Justice, G. M.
Kelly, Thomas
Kerr, James
King, Francis
Klett, Frederick
Korckhaus, A.
Kuhl, Henry
Kuhn, Charles
Kuhn, Hartman, Jr.
Lapsley, David
Lapsley, Joseph B.
Latour, John
Laws, George and James
Lehman, William E.
Leiper, Thomas (estate)
Lennig, Frederick
Lennig, N. (estate)
Lentz, Henry (estate)
Lewis, John F.
Lewis, Robert M.
Lippincott, Aaron S.
Livezey, John
Longstreth, Joshua
Longstreth, Morris
Lovering, J. S.
Lowber, Edward
Lynch, William
Macalester, Mrs. Ann
Macalester, Charles
McAllister, John
McCloskey, Michael
McCredy, Bernard
McLanahan, Johnston
Mallery, Garrick
Mann, Daniel
Martin, James S.
Martin, Dr. Joseph
Mayland, Jacob
Meigs, Dr. C. D. and Dr. John F.
Mellon, Thomas
Mellor, Thomas
Meredith, William M.
Miller, Joseph
Mitchell, James
Morris, Samuel B.
Myers, John B.
Naglee, John
Newkirk, Matthew
Newman, John B.
Norris, Mrs. E. H.
Norris, Isaac W.
Paul, Comegys
Paul, Joseph
Paleske, Captain T. W.
Patterson, Robert
Peace, Joseph (estate)
Peters, Jacob
Phillips, William (estate)
Physick, Emlen
Platt, George
Platt, William
Pleasonton, A. J.
Preston, Dr. Jones (estate)
Price, Chandler (estate)
Pritchell, T. B.
Ralston, Henry
Randolph, Dr. Jacob
Randolph, Richard
Rea, John
Reese, Jacob
Richardson, William
Riggs, Romulus
Roberts, George
Roberts, Joseph
Rockhill, Thomas C.
Ronaldson, James (estate)
Ronaldson, Richard
Rosengarten, G. D.
Savage, John
Sayen, George (estate)
Sergeant, Mary
Sharp, John
Sheaff, John D.
Short, William
Shields, Thomas (estate)
Simmons, Stephen (estate)
Siter, John
Smith, Charles W.
Smith, Edward
Smith, Jacob R.
Smith, Samuel F.
Smith, Stephen

Smith, William H.
Snyder, Joseph
Spencer, James S.
Stiles, Benjamin
Stiles, Henry
Stille, Dr. Alfred
Stoecker, John Clement (estate)
Stone, Dexter
Stott, Mrs.
Stuart, Thomas
Sulger, Jacob
Symington, Alexander
Tams, Sampson
Taylor, Amos (estate)
Taylor, E. W. and L. B.
Taylor, Levi
Tete, Francis
Tevis, Benjamin
Thomas, George
Tierman, Francis
Toland, Robert
Trotter, Nathan
Vanderkemp, J. J.
Vaux, George (estate)
Vezin, Charles
Wallace, Mrs.
Waln, Jacob S.
Warner, William
Weir, Silas E. (estate)
Welsh, Henry
Welsh, John
Welsh, S. and W.
Wetherill, George D.
Wetherill, Mrs. R. (estate)
Wetherill, Samuel P.
Wetherill, Dr. William
Wharton, Charles (estate)
Wheeler, Enoch (estate)
White, Ambrose
White, Henry R.
Wicht, John H.
Wickoff, Henry
Wilcox, Benjamin C. (estate)
Willing, Richard
Wistar, Thomas
Wood, Dr. George B.
Wood, Richard D.
Worrell, John R.
Worrell, William
Yohe, Mrs. (estate)

Boston's Wealthiest One Hundred in 1833

I have doubled the assessment figures for 1833 since, according to the most authoritative contemporary source, before 1842 "the valuation was entered on the assessors' records at half the real value, and the taxes assessed on that amount." Lemuel Shattuck, *Report to the Committee of the City Council Appointed to Obtain the Census of Boston for the Year 1845* (Boston, 1846), Appendix, p. 59.

Assessed at $250,000 or More

Brooks, Peter C.
Cushing, John P.
Greene, Gardner (estate)*
Lloyd, James (estate)†
Lyman, Theodore
Otis, Harrison Gray
Perkins, James
Phillips, Jonathan
Sears, David
Shaw, Robert Gould
Welles, John
Williams, John D. and Moses

†assessed at $500,000.
*assessed at more than $1,000,000.

Assessed at $100,000 to $250,000

Amory, Francis
Andrews, Ebenezer T.
Appleton, Nathan
Appleton, Samuel
Appleton, William
Baxter, Daniel
Binney, Amos (administrator)
Blake, Sarah
Blanchard, Edward
Boott, Mary
Bo[a]rdman, William
Borland, John
Bradlee, Thomas D.
Bray, Mrs. F. (estate)
Brimmer, Andrew
Brimmer, Martin (heirs)
Bryant, John
Bussey, Benjamin
Clark, Benjamin C.
Codman, Charles R.
Codman, Henry
Coolidge, Joseph
Crowninshield, Benjamin W.
Cruft, Edward
Cutler, Pliny
Dorr, John
Dwight, Edmund
Eckley family
Eliot, Samuel A.
Ellis, David
Fales, Samuel
Francis, Ebenezer
French, Arthur
Goddard, Nathaniel
Gray, Francis C.
Gray, Horace
Greene, Gardner (heirs)
Greenough, David
Hammond, Samuel
Homer, Benjamin P.
Hubbard, John
Inches family
Jones, Elizabeth (executrix)
Joy, Benjamin (heirs)
Lawrence, Abbott
Lawrence, Amos
Lee, Thomas
Loring, Charles G.
Lovering, Joseph
Lowell family
Lyman, George W.
Mason, Jonathan (heirs)
May, Perrin
Munson, Israel
Parker, Daniel P.
Parker, John
Parkman, Francis
Parkman, George
Parkman, Sarah
Parsons, William
Payne, Mary
Perkins, Thomas
Perkins, Thomas H.
Perkins, Thomas H., Jr.
Quincy family
Robbins, Edward H.
Russell, Nathaniel P.
Sargent, Lucius M.
Shattuck, George C.
Sigourney, Henry
Smith, Ebenezer
Sturgis family
Sumner, William H. (with "others")
Tappan, John
Thompson, Thomas
Thorndike, Augustus
Thorndike, John P.
Thorndike, Israel
Thorndike, Israel (heirs)
Ticknor, George
Torrey, Samuel and John G.
Trull family
Tuckerman, Edward
Upham, Phineas
Wales, Thomas B.
Ward family
Welch, John
Wigglesworth, Thomas
Winthrop, Thomas L.

Boston's Wealthiest Two Hundred in 1848

Assessed at $250,000 or More

Andrews, Ebenezer T.
Appleton, Nathan
Appleton, Samuel
Appleton, William‡
Baker, Eliphalet
Borland, John (with "others")‡
Bradlee, John W.
Bradlee, Josiah
Brimmer, Martin (heirs)
Brooks, Peter C.*
Bryant, John‡
Codman, Charles R.
Codman, Henry
Crowninshield, Benjamin W.
Gardner, John L.
Gerrish, George W.
Gray, John C.
Hancock, John
How, Hall J.
Humphrey, Benjamin
Hunnewell, H. H.
Lawrence, Abbott‡
Lawrence, Amos
Lawrence, William‡
Lovering, Joseph
Lowell, John A.
Minot, William
Otis, Harrison Gray
Parker, James
Parker, Peter
Parkman, George
Perkins, Thomas H.
Phillips, Jonathan‡
Quincy, Josiah, Jr.‡
Robbins, Edward H.
Russell, Nathaniel P.
Sanford, Samuel
Sears, David‡
Shattuck, George C.
Shaw, Robert Gould‡
Shimmin, Mrs. William (estate)
Thompson, Thomas
Wales, Thomas B.
Welles, John‡
Wigglesworth, Thomas‡
Williams, John D.‡
Williams, Moses
Winchester, William P.

Assessed at $100,000 to $250,000

Adams, Benjamin
Adams, Laban
Alger, Cyrus
Allen, Samuel P.
Amory, Francis (heirs)
Amory, Thomas C.
Apthorp, John T.
Armstrong, Samuel T.
Ashton, Elisha V.
Atkins, Thomas G.
Austin, Samuel
Baldwin, Aaron
Ballard, John
Ballard, Joseph
Bangs, Benjamin
Beebe, James M.
Belknap, John
Bennett, Joshua
Binney, Amos (heirs)
Blake, Edward
Blanchard, Edward
Bo[a]rdman, William H.
Bradlee, J. Bowdoin
Bradlee, Samuel
Brewer, Gardner
Brewer, Thomas
Brooks, Edward
Bumstead family

*assessed at more than $1,000,000.
‡assessed at more than $500,000.

Burgess, Benjamin
Bussey, Benjamin (heirs)
Carney, Andrew
Chadwick, Ebenezer
Chapman, Jonathan
Chickering, Jonas
Child family
Codman, Francis
Colby, Gardner
Cooke, Josiah P.
Coolidge, Joseph
Cruft, Edward
Cunningham, James
Curtis, Samuel
Curtis, Thomas B.
Cushing family
Dall, William (heirs)
Davis, James
Dexter family
Dixon, Thomas and Mrs.
Donnison, William (heirs)
Dorr, John
Dowley, Levi A.
Drake, Tisdale
Dwight, Edmund
Earle, John, Jr.
Eliot, Samuel A.
Fales, Samuel
Faxon, Nathaniel
Foster, James H.
Francis, Ebenezer
Gardner, Henry
Gassett, Henry
Goddard family
Goodwin, Ozias
Gray, Francis C.
Gray, Horace
Gray, John
Greene family
Greenough, David (heirs)
Greenwood, William P.
Hallett, George (heirs)
Haskins, Ralph
Haven, Franklin
Hayward, Joseph H.
Hemenway, Augustus
Hinckley family
Holbrook, Henry M.
Homer family
Howe, George
Howe, Jabez C.
Howe, Thomas
Inches, Elizabeth
Inches, Henderson
Jackson, Charles
Jarvis, Deming
Johnson, James
Johnson, Samuel
Joy family
Kimball, David
Knight, William H.
Lamb, Thomas
Lamson, Benjamin
Leeds, Timothy C.
Lincoln, Noah
Lobdell, Thomas J.
Lodge, Giles
Lombard, Ammi C.
Lord, Melvin
Loring, Abigail and Abby
Loring, Benjamin
Loring, Caleb
Loring, Charles G.
Loring, Josiah Q. and George H.
Lyman family
Mason, William P.
May, George
May, Samuel
Moseley, David C. (heirs)
Muzzey, Benjamin B.
Odin, George
Oxnard, Charlotte
Paige, James W.
Parker, Anna
Parker, Charles
Parker, Daniel P.
Parkman, Francis
Perkins, Anna D.
Phillips, Edward B.
Pratt, George

Pratt, William (heirs)
Prescott, William H.
Raymond, Edward A.
Redman, John (heirs)
Revere, Joseph W.
Richards, Reuben
Richardson, Jeffery
Ritchie, Uriah
Roberts, Joseph D.
Salisbury family
Sargent, Henry (heirs)
Sargent, Ignatius
Savage, James
Sawyer, Matthias P.
Sayles family
Shattuck, George C., Jr.
Shaw, Lemuel
Shelton, Mrs. (estate)
Sigourney, Henry
Simmons, John
Skinner, Francis
Smith, Abiel (heirs)
Smith, Ebenezer
Sprague, Phineas
Sturgis family
Swett, Eliz. B.
Swift, John J.
Tappan, John
Templeton, John
Thaxter, Adam W.
Thayer, John E.
Thorndike, John P.
Ticknor, George
Tilden, Joseph
Tisdale, Mace
Torrey family
Trull, Ezra
Trull, John W.
Tuckerman, Edward (heirs)
Tudor, Frederick
Upham, Phineas
Vose, Josiah
Walker, William J.
Ward, Thomas W.
Warren, John C.
Waterston, Robert
Welch, Francis
Welch, John
Weld, Daniel
Welles, Benjamin
White, William S.
Weston family
Whitney, Jonathan (heirs)
Whitney, William P.
Wiggin, Benjamin
Wildes, Solomon
Williams, Samuel K.
Willis, Benjamin
Wolcott, J. Huntington

Bibliography

The sources consulted for this book numbered in the thousands: merely to list them would fill more than a hundred pages. The following discussion focuses, therefore, on sources that were found to be particularly valuable and that are likely to be interesting or useful to the reader. In the interests of space, many sources cited in the footnotes are not repeated here.

General Sources on Wealthy and Successful Families

Private Papers and Unpublished Correspondence

Diverse sources provided information on the backgrounds of the urban rich and prestigious. The unpublished papers of hundreds of individuals and families were examined. Among these were the papers of the Stuyvesants, Fishes, Hones, Grosvenors, Beekmans, Hendrickses, Lorillards, Suydams, Schermerhorns, Tillotsons, Bennetts, Kips, Strongs, Van Rensselaers, Greenwoods, Brinckerhoffs, Astors, Hallocks, Allens, Noahs, Kings, Livingstons, Griswolds, Brevoorts, Dodges, Phelpses, Enos, Whitneys, Aspinwalls, Furmans, Irvings, Cortelyous, Hoyts, Gerritsons, Couwenhovens, Martenses, Rapelyses, Remsens, Hickses, Willoughbys, Emmets, Bories, Fishers, Careys, Hammonds, Brimmers, Appletons, Shaws, Winthrops, Searses, Parkers, Lawrences, Forbeses, Brookses, and Everetts. Although the correspondence and private papers of such families are invaluable for many purposes, typically they yield less valuable information on the family status of wealthy individuals than do other sources that focus more directly on the matter. In many cases, the collections located at the historical societies are sparse for a particular family.

Genealogies

Hundreds of family genealogies were examined. While genealogies are indispensable, they are of varying value. Many of them are devoid of any material of a social nature, content to present elaborate family trees of amazing intricacy. For a pointed criticism of the tendency of too many genealogists to prefer thin biographical to social data, see Edward P. Cheyney, "Thomas Cheyney, a Chester County Squire: His Lesson for Genealogists," *Pennsylvania Magazine of History and Biography* [hereafter *Pa. Magazine*], *LX* (July 1936), pp. 209–28. In other cases, allusions to the wealth or standing of the subjects are undocumented. The habit of some genealogists to attribute a too-exalted status to families of their subjects is counterbalanced somewhat by the disposition to attribute humble origins to substantial men. For comment on the latter tendency, see Benjamin D. Silliman, "Personal Reminiscences of Sixty Years at the New York Bar," in David McAdam *et al*, eds., *History of the Bench and Bar of New York*, 2 vols. (New York, 1897), I, pp. 226–43; and John F. Watson, *Annals of Philadelphia in the Olden Time*, 3 vols. (Philadelphia, 1842), I, p. 530. Other informative criticisms of genealogies are Roy F. Nichols, "The Genealogist and the Historian," *Publications of the Genealogical Society of Pennsylvania* [hereafter *PGSP*], *XIV* (Oct. 1942), pp. 1–2; and Zera S. Fink, "Some Genealogical Absurdities," *New York Genealogical and Biographical Record* [hereafter *NYGBR], LII* (Oct. 1921), pp. 295–96. A useful appraisal written from a different point of view is John F. Lewis, "Some Genealogical Obstacles Considered," *PGSP, III* (1906), pp. 81–104.

Genealogical and Historical Journals

Rich genealogical data were also obtained from the thousands of articles in the *NYGBR*, the *New England Historical and Genealogical Register, the PGSP* and the *Pa. Magazine*, the journal of the Historical Society of Pennsylvania. Every single issue of these journals was scrutinized for useful leads, commencing with the first issue of the New England journal in January, 1847. One reason it was found necessary to read every issue was the fact that biographical statements made in a given issue would sometimes be modified drastically in later issues. The willingness to admit and correct error is only one of the reliable features of these excellent journals, whose authors and editors in many cases knew personally the subjects of their accounts. John Latting, early editor of the *NYGBR*, had studied law under the eminent Francis B. Cutting and worked with Caleb S. Woodhull. Latting's perfectionism in authenticating the most minute items, as he rummaged through probate records and published and unpublished documents or sought out survivors, is assurance of his reliability. Examples of the comforting finickiness of this man, who was widely respected and sought after by contemporary historians and genealogists, can be found in the correspondence between Latting and the historian of Long Island, Henry Onderdonk, Jr., in the Onderdonk Papers at the Long Island Historical Society. In view of the fact that several hundred articles from these great genealogical and historical journals had valuable information on leading contemporaries, most of these articles are not listed separately here.

Contemporary Diaries

Contemporary diaries were invaluable. The twenty-eight folio volumes containing Philip Hone's diary, like the manuscript diaries of George Templeton Strong (for the brave soul who can manage Strong's handwriting) and Edward Neufville Tailer, all in the New-York Historical Society, the diary of Sidney George Fisher in the Historical Society of Pennsylvania, the *Recollections of Samuel Breck, with Passages from His Note-Books [1771-1862]*, ed. by H. E. Scudder (Philadelphia, 1877), or the journals of Gabriel Furman and John Baxter, in the Long Island Historical Society, are filled with intimate glimpses into the backgrounds of the urban elite by men who knew them because they were of them.

Biographical Encyclopaediae

Unless their data were confirmed by reliable contemporaries, little stock was placed on the evidence of the famous biographical encyclopaediae, primarily for its thinness but also for its unreliability. Allan Nevins, *The Gateway to History* (Boston, 1938) [especially page 202 of the reprint of a portion of the Nevins essay in Robin W. Winks, ed., *The Historian as Detective: Essays in Evidence* (New York, 1969)], contains a discussion of the actual invention of material in Appleton's *Cyclopaedia of American Biography.* Nicholas B. Wainwright, ed., *A Philadelphia Perspective: The Diary of Sidney George Fisher Covering the Years 1834–1871* (Philadelphia, 1967), p. iii, discusses an inaccuracy in the *Dictionary of American Biography.* The problem with the latter estimable source for our purposes is that so many of its contributors had little interest in the parental status of their subjects. Daniel Scott Smith, "Cyclical, Secular, and Structural Change in American Elite Composition," *Perspectives in American History, IV* (1970), p. 370, discusses some of the inadequacies of the *DAB* material.

Miscellaneous Material on Elite Families

Hundreds of pamphlets, short memoirs, published speeches, epitaphs, short histories of professional and other organizations, descriptions of streets, neighborhoods and residences, and a diverse miscellany of publications also yielded useful evidence on families, if much of it snippets.

Unusually Good—and Bad—Sources. The value of a number of memoirs and local histories published in the nineteenth century by contemporaries of the rich and eminent is enhanced by the standing of their authors. That Henry Simpson, mid-nineteenth century biographer of Philadelphia's elite, was assisted in his research by such eminences as Horace Binney, Samuel Breck, Henry W. Gilpin, Charles J. Biddle, and Thomas Balch, adds to the credibility of his *Lives of Eminent Philadelphians* (Philadelphia, 1859). John F. Watson's personal encounters with some of the elite whose family histories he sketched in 1842 similarly induce respect for the portrayals in his *Annals of Philadelphia in the Olden Time.* Abraham Ritter's charming and anecdotal account of

Philadelphia and Her Merchants (Philadelphia, 1860), is strengthened by the evidence that dozens of the merchants he discusses respected his judgments. Of course, even the best of contemporary biographers were not free of foibles.

Freeman Hunt's *Lives of American Merchants,* 3 vols. (New York, 1857), is an enthusiastic celebration of the lives of successful businessmen by a responsible and essentially reliable investigator. A great believer in the rags-to-riches theme, Hunt sometimes misreads his own evidence, however. *Hunt's Merchants Magazine* is a fine source.

Thompson Westcott was an indefatigable researcher and an invaluable source on all things Philadelphian. No municipal history is fuller or more valuable than his and J. Thomas Scharf's *History of Philadelphia, 1609–1884,* 3 vols. (Philadelphia, 1884). Yet I have discovered that some of Westcott's biographical vignettes either ignored or omitted pertinent data and in a few cases simply repeated unverified versions written by predecessors. See Westcott, comp. *Biographies of Philadelphians* (Philadelphia, 1861), and Westcott's four-volume "Historical Scrap Book concerning the City of Philadelphia," collected 1848–1852, which is at the Historical Society of Pennsylvania. Westcott is nevertheless a most trustworthy source.

The same cannot be said for Joseph Scoville, who under the pseudonym, "Walter Barrett," wrote *The Old Merchants of New York,* 5 vols. (New York, 1862–1863). I agree with the editor of the authoritative *NYGBR* that "the character of this entertaining, gossipy work is not such as to entitle it to any weight," for all its author's ability and experience; *NYGBR, III* (1872), p. 180. Specific Scoville errors are pointed out in *ibid., LXI* (1930), pp. 342–43.

Miscellany on New York City Families. For New York City the city clerk's misnamed "filed papers," located in the Municipal Archives and Records Center, contain unpublished petitions, applications, requests, resolutions, letters, ordinances, and committee reports that compensate for their chaotic arrangement by their occasional nuggets of information.

Horace Lyman Weeks, *Prominent Families of New York,* 2 vols. (New York, 1897), is an excellent collective biography. Margherita A. Hamm, *Famous Families of New York,* 2 vols. (New York, 1901), is of much more limited usefulness. For testimony on the reliability of Weeks (and the municipal historians Martha Lamb and Benson J. Lossing, whose books are discussed below) see the *NYGBR, XXIV* (1893), p. 92, and *XXIX* (1898), p. 182, and John T. Cunningham, "Historian on the Double [Lossing]," *American Heritage, XIX* (June 1968), pp. 54–64, 78–81.

Also useful for background information on New York City families are *Letters of Stephen Allen [Nov. 1825–Nov. 1828]* (bound by New-York Historical Society, 1957); *Letters of Henry Brevoort to Washington*

Irving (New York, 1916); Alexander J. Patten, *Lives of the Clergy of New York and Brooklyn* (New York, 1874); John Shrady, ed., *The College of Physicians and Surgeons* 2 vols. (New York, n.d.); Philip Van Ingen, *The New York Academy of Medicine* (New York, 1949); J. M. Mathews, *Recollections of Persons and Events* (New York, 1865); *Memorials of Peter A. Jay Compiled for His Descendants* (Holland, 1927); *Memoir of Thomas Addis Emmet* (New York, 1829); *Letters From John Pintard to His Daughter [1816–1827]*, 4 vols. (New York, 1940); Charles King, *Progress of the City of New York During the Last Fifty Years* (New York, 1852); and James A. Hamilton, *Reminiscences* (New York, 1869).

Miscellany on Brooklyn Families. In contrast to the unreliable Scoville is Henry R. Stiles, the founder and first librarian of the Long Island Historical Society and the first president of the New York Genealogical and Biographical Society. For Brooklyn nothing compares with Stiles' monumental *Civil, Political, Professional and Ecclesiastical History and Commercial and Industrial Record of the County of Kings and the City of Brooklyn New York from 1683 to 1884*, 3 vols. (New York, 1884), a sprawling, detailed account filled with family vignettes written by this reliable insider. Useful material is also contained in Teunis G. Bergen, *Early Settlers of Kings County, From Its First Settlement by Europeans to 1700* (New York, 1881). Indispensable for Brooklyn are the 160 scrapbooks at the Long Island Historical Society, a treasurehouse filled with much trivia side by side with invaluable manuscripts and other data on elite families.

Miscellany on Philadelphia Families. Indispensable collective biographies are Frank Willing Leach, *Old Philadelphia Families*, 3 vols. (Philadelphia, 1907–1913); Charles Morris, *Makers of Philadelphia* (Philadelphia, 1894); Stephen N. Winslow, *Biographies of Successful Philadelphia Merchants* (Philadelphia, 1864); Moses King, *Philadelphia and Notable Philadelphians* (New York, 1902); in addition to the works earlier mentioned by Henry Simpson, John F. Watson, Abraham Ritter, J. Thomas Scharf, and Thompson Westcott.

A sampling of other publications that offer revealing glimpses into people and facets of early-nineteenth century Philadelphia are William Tilghman, *An Eulogium in Commemoration of Dr. Caspar Wistar* (Philadelphia, 1818); Thomas I. Wharton, *Address Delivered At the Opening of the New Hall of the Athenaeum of Philadelphia* (Philadelphia, 1847); Stephen Simpson, *Biography of Stephen Girard* (Philadelphia, 1832); Horace Binney, *The Leaders of the Old Bar of Philadelphia* (Philadelphia, 1859); David Ritchie, *Eulogy on the Life and Character of the Hon. Richard Biddle* (Pittsburgh, 1847); James J. Levick, *The Early Physicians of Philadelphia and Its Vicinity* (Philadelphia, 1886); Edward W. Smith, *Narrative of Joseph Wharton* (Philadelphia, 1938); Charles N. Buck, *Memoirs of Charles Buck, 1791–1841* (Philadelphia, 1941); William Otis Sawtelle, "William Bingham of Philadelphia and His Maine

Lands," *PGSP, IX* (March 1926), pp. 207–226; Jonathan Wharton Lippincott, *Biographical Memoranda concerning Joseph Wharton* (Philadelphia, 1909); David Philipson, ed., *Letters of Rebecca Gratz* (Philadelphia, 1929); M. M. Kerr, "Elisha Kent Kane," *Annals of Medical History, VI* (New York, 1924), pp. 71–125; L. L. Van Sant, ed., *The Royal Road to Wealth: An Illustrated History of the Successful Business Houses of Philadelphia* (Philadelphia, n.d.); Charles Winslow Dulles, *Sketch of the Life of Dr. Thomas Cadwalader* (Philadelphia, 1903); Hampton L. Carson, *A Sketch of Horace Binney* (Philadelphia, 1907); Edgar F. Smith, "Robert Hare: An Early American Chemist [1781–1858]," *Archon, VIII* (Rome, 1927), pp. 331–35; and Ralph D. Gray, "Henry D. Gilpin, A Pennsylvania Jacksonian," *Pennsylvania History, XXXVII* (Oct. 1970), pp. 340–51.

Miscellany on Boston Families. Particularly good are William R. Cutter, *Genealogical and Personal Memoirs Relating to Families of Boston and Eastern Massachusetts,* 4 vols. (New York, 1908); and Mary Caroline Crawford, *Famous Families of Massachusetts,* 2 vols. (Boston, 1930). Other valuable treatments include James Spear Loring, *Hundred Boston Orators* (Boston, 1852); Charles G. Loring, *Memoir of the Hon. William Sturgis* (Boston, 1864); S. J. May, *Memoir* (Boston, 1873); Edward Everett, *A Memoir of John Lowell, Jr.* (Boston, 1879); Robert Bennet Forbes, *Personal Reminiscences (Boston, 1882); Josiah Quincy, Figures of the Past From the Leaves of Old Journals* (Boston, 1883); *A Tribute to the Memory of Thomas B. Wales* (Boston, 1853); Henry A. Coit, *A Sermon in Memory of the Late George C. Shattuck* (Boston, 1893); Oliver W. Holmes, *A Biographical Sketch of Dr. George Parkman* (Boston, 1850); *Memoirs of Edward Tuckerman* (Boston, 1887); Theodore Lyman, *Memoir of Theodore Lyman, Jr.* (Boston, 1881); *Memoir of the Late Thomas L. Winthrop* (Boston, 1854); N. L. Frothingham, *A Sermon on the Death of Joseph P. Bradlee* (Boston, 1838); Samuel Adams Drake, *Old Landmarks and Historic Personages of Boston* (Boston, 1873); Thomas Bridgman, *The Pilgrims of Boston and Their Descendants* (Boston, 1856); Robert C. Winthrop, *Memoir of the Hon. Nathan Appleton* (Boston, 1861); John Langdon Sibley, *Biographical Sketches of Graduates of Harvard University,* 3 vols. (Cambridge, 1881); Clifford K. Shipton, *Biographical Sketches of Those Who Attended Harvard College in the Classes 1690–1700* (Cambridge, 1933); and Henry G. Parson, "Frederick Tudor, Ice King," *Proceedings* of the Massachusetts Historical Society, *LXV* (Oct. 1932–May 1936).

Modern Biographies

Biographies have been written in the twentieth century about a number of the more eminent antebellum figures and families. Particularly good are Philip L. White, *The Beekmans of New York in Politics and Commerce, 1647–1877* (New York, 1956), thorough and fact-filled;

Elva Tooker, *Nathan Trotter, Philadelphia Merchant, 1787–1853* (Cambridge, 1955), outstanding for its informative treatment of the economic life of a merchant capitalist; D. G. Brinton Thompson, *Ruggles of New York: A Life of Samuel B. Ruggles* (New York, 1946); Harry Emerson Wildes, *Lonely Midas: The Story of Stephen Girard* (New York, 1943), which is useful for refuting myths about the early life of the great merchant; Christine Chapman Robbins, *David Hosack, Citizen of New York* (Philadelphia, 1964); James A. Rawley, *Edwin D. Morgan, 1811–1883: Merchant in Politics* (New York: 1955); Kenneth W. Porter, *John Jacob Astor, Business Man*, 2 vols. (Cambridge, 1931), amazingly full on the varied economic enterprises of the "fur merchant"; Porter, *The Jacksons and the Lees: Two Generations of Massachusetts Merchants, 1765–1844*, 2 vols. (Cambridge, 1937), excellent on the ties that bound merchant families to one another; Richard Lowitt, *A Merchant Prince of the Nineteenth Century: William E. Dodge* (New York, 1954), evocative of commercial life in antebellum New York City; Burton Alva Konkle, *Thomas Willing and the First American Financial System* (New York, 1937); Irving Katz, *August Belmont* (New York, 1968); Clinton Harvey Gardiner, *William Hickling Prescott: A Biography* (Austin, 1969); Robert C. Alberts, *The Golden Voyage: The Life and Times of William Bingham, 1752–1804* (Boston, 1969); Robert W. July, *The Essential New Yorker: Gulian Crommelin Verplanck* (Durham, 1957); William T. Baxter, *The House of Hancock: Business in Boston, 1724–1775* (Cambridge, 1945); and Bertram Wyatt-Brown, *Lewis Tappan and the Evangelical War Against Slavery* (Cleveland, 1969).

Such popular books as Cleveland Amory's *Who Killed Society?* (New York, 1960), and Nathaniel Burt's *First Families: The Making of an American Aristocracy* (Boston, 1970), offer an interesting glimpse into the present standing of a number of the earlier elite families, as does E. Digby Baltzell's more scholarly *Philadelphia Gentlemen: The Making of a National Upper Class* (New York, 1958) and his *The Protestant Establishment: Aristocracy and Caste in America* (London, 1965).

The Social Background

New York City Social Background

Providing a rich historical background as well as occasional vignettes of New York City's antebellum eminences are James Grant Wilson, ed., *The Memorial History of the City of New York*, 5 vols. (New York, 1892–1893); Mary Louise Booth, *History of the City of New York* (New York, 1859); Martha Lamb and Mrs. Burton Harrison, *History of the City of New York*, 3 vols. (New York, 1877-1896); John William Leonard, *History of the City of New York, 1609–1909*, 2 vols. (New York,

1910); Benson J. Lossing, *History of New York City*, 2 vols. (New York, 1884); and I. N. Phelps Stokes, *Iconography of Manhattan Island*, 6 vols. (New York, 1916–1928), a fascinating if sprawling and uneven work.

Valuable, if less comprehensive, are David Thomas Valentine, *History of the City of New York* (New York, 1853); Samuel I. Prime, *Life in New York* (New York, 1847); Grant Thorburn, *Fifty Years' Reminiscences of New York* (New York, 1845); Rev. Horace Halley, "A Glimpse of Social Life in New York City [1818]," in the papers of Martha J. Lamb, located in the New-York Historical Society; Asa Greene, *A Glance at New York* (New York, 1837); Thomas F. Gordon, *Gazeteer of the State of New York* (New York, 1836); two invaluable reminiscences by John W. Francis, *Old New York During the Last Half Century* (New York, 1857), and *Old New York or Reminiscences of the Past Sixty Years* (New York, 1866); William A. Duer, *Reminiscences of an Old New Yorker* (New York, 1867); William E. Dodge, *Old New York* (New York, 1880); J. Disturnell, *New-York As It Is in 1837* (New York, 1837); Charles Astor Bristed, *The Upper Ten Thousand: Sketches of American Society* (New York, 1852), a satirical treatment of elite mores from the inside; E. Porter Belden, *New York: Past, Present, and Future* (New York, 1849); Levi Beardsley, *Reminiscences* (New York, 1852); David McAdam *et al*, *History of the Bench and Bar of New York*, 2 vols. (New York, 1897); *Valentine's Manuals* (New York, 1841–1842); Stephen Girard, *The Merchants' Sketch Book and Guide to New York City* (New York, 1844); Abram C. Dayton, *Last Days of Knickerbocker Life in New York* (New York, 1897); Robert G. Albion, *The Rise of New York Port, 1815–1850* (New York, 1939); David M. Ellis, "The Yankee Invasion of New York, 1783–1850," *New York History*, *XXXII* (Jan. 1951), pp. 3–17; and Douglas T. Miller, *Jacksonian Aristocracy: Class and Democracy in New York, 1830–1860* (New York, 1967), a lively but impressionistic examination of the effect of "industrialization" on the allegedly egalitarian society of the 1820s.

Brooklyn Social Background

Prior to the publication of his monumental *Civil, Political, Professional and Ecclesiastical History of Brooklyn*, Stiles wrote *A History of the City of Brooklyn: Including the Old Town and Village of Brooklyn, The Town of Bushwick, and the Village and City of Williamsburgh*, 3 vols. (Brooklyn, 1867–1870), which is also excellent. Other good books on early Brooklyn are Nathaniel Scudder Prime, *A History of Long Island from Its First Settlement by Europeans to the Year 1845* (New York, 1845); Stephen M. Ostrander, *A History of the City of Brooklyn and Kings County* [ed. by Alexander Black], 2 vols. (Brooklyn, 1894); Henry Onderdonk, Jr., *Suffolk and Kings Counties in Olden Times* (Jamaica, L.I., 1866); Benjamin F. Thompson, *History of Long Island from Its Discovery and Settlement to the Present Time,* 4 vols., rev. ed., (New York, 1918); and Henry Isham Hazleton, *The Boroughs of Brooklyn and Queens, Counties of Nassau and Suffolk, Long Island,* 5 vols. (New York, 1925).

Other publications that contain useful information on Brooklyn in the early nineteenth century include Gertrude Lefferts Vanderbilt, *The Social History of Flatbush* (Brooklyn, 1909); Charles Andrews Ditmas, *Historic Homesteads of Kings County* (Brooklyn, 1909); Thomas F. Devoe, *Reminiscences of "Old Brooklyn"* (Morrisania, 1867); James H. Callender, *Yesterdays on Brooklyn Heights* (New York, 1927); *Historical Sketches of Brooklyn, Long Island* (Brooklyn, n.d.); Teunis G. Bergen, *Historical Address* (Brooklyn, 1877); *History of the Medical Society of Kings County* (Brooklyn, 1899); J. T. Bailey, *An Historical Sketch of the City of Brooklyn* (New York, 1840); Charlotte Rebecca Bleecker Bangs, *Reminiscences of Old New Utrecht and Gowanus* (Brooklyn, 1912); a series of studies by Jacob Judd: "A City's Streets: A Case Study of Brooklyn, 1834–1855," *Journal of Long Island History, IX* (Winter-Spring, 1969), pp. 32–43; "Policing the City of Brooklyn in the 1840s and 1850s," *ibid., VI* (Spring, 1966), pp. 13–22; and "Brooklyn's Health and Sanitation, 1834–1855," *ibid., VII* (Winter-Spring, 1967), pp. 40–52; and Ralph Foster Weld, *Brooklyn Village, 1816–1834* (New York, 1938).

Philadelphia Social Background

Indispensable for Philadelphia are Emil Paxon Oberholtzer, *Philadelphia, A History of the City and Its People,* 4 vols. (Philadelphia, n.d.); Oberholtzer, *Literary History of Philadelphia* (Philadelphia, 1906); Horace Mather Lippincott, *Early Philadelphia, Its People, Life, and Progress* (Philadelphia, 1917; and John Russell Young, *Memorial History of the City of Philadelphia,* 2 vols. (New York, 1895, 1898).

Also useful are Charles Wetherill, *History of the Religious Society of Friends in the City of Philadelphia* (Philadelphia, 1894); Lord B——— ["Formerly of England, Now a Naturalized Citizen and Resident of Philadelphia"], *A Moral Picture of Philadelphia: The Virtues and Frauds and Follies of the City Delineated* (Philadelphia, 1845); Daniel Bowen, ed., *A History of Philadelphia* (Philadelphia, 1839); Henry Samuel Morais, *The Jews of Philadelphia: Their History From the Earliest Settlements to the Present Time* (Philadelphia, 1894); Charles Godfrey Leland, *Memoirs* (New York, 1893); Thomas Willing Balch, *The Philadelphia Assemblies* (Philadelphia, 1916); and Sam Bass Warner, Jr., *The Private City: Philadelphia in Three Periods of Its Growth* (Cambridge, 1968).

Boston Social Background

Justin Winsor, ed., *Memorial History of Boston,* 4 vols. (Boston, 1894), is indispensable, as are John F. Trow, ed., *Boston Past and*

Present (Boston 1874); Mark Anthony DeWolfe Howe, *Boston: The Place and the People* (New York, 1907); and Albert P. Langtry, ed., *Metropolitan Boston, A Modern History,* 3 vols. (New York, 1929). Altogether unique and fascinating for its statistical data on matters that continue to interest twentieth-century readers is Lemuel Shattuck, *Report to the Committee of the City Council Appointed to Obtain the Census of Boston for the Year 1845* (Boston, 1846). For an appreciative modern appraisal of Shattuck as a statistician, see Walter F. Willcox, "Lemuel Shattuck, Statist, Founder of the American Statistical Association," *Journal of the American Statistical Association, 35* (1940), pp. 224–35.

Other useful studies include Robert H. Lord, John E. Sexton, and Edward T. Harrington, *History of the Archdiocese of Boston* (New York, 1944); *Professional and Industrial History of Suffolk County, Massachusetts,* 2 vols. (Boston, 1894); Isaac Smith Homans, *Sketches of Boston, Past and Present* (Boston, 1851); Caroline Ticknor, ed., *Dr. Holmes' Boston [1809–1894]* (Boston, 1915); John Tracy Morse, Jr., "Recollections of Boston and Harvard Before the Civil War," *Proceedings* of the Massachusetts Historical Society, *LXV* (Oct. 1932–May 1936); William S. Rossiter, *Days and Ways in Old Boston* (Boston, 1915); William Endicott, *Reminiscences of Seventy-Five Years* (Boston, 1913); Mary Caroline Crawford, *Romantic Days in Old Boston* (Boston, 1910); N. I. Bowditch, *"Gleaner" Articles* (Boston, 1855); George H. Blelock, *Boston Past and Present* (Cambridge, 1874); Roland N. Stromberg, "Boston in the 1820's and 1830's," *History Today, XI* (Sept. 1961), pp. 591–98; and Roger Lane, *Policing the City: Boston 1822–1885* (Cambridge, 1967).

Relevant Studies of Other Cities

A number of recent studies afford valuable insights into particular cities or into cities in general. Richard C. Wade, *The Urban Frontier: The Rise of Western Cities, 1790–1830* (Cambridge, 1959), is an important comprehensive if impressionistic examination of such cities as Cincinnati, St. Louis, Chicago, Pittsburgh, and Lexington, that discloses social patterns in the west not markedly unlike those on the Atlantic Seaboard. Also useful are D. Clayton James, *Antebellum Natchez* (Baton Rouge, 1968); Kenneth W. Wheeler, *To Wear a City's Crown: The Beginnings of Urban Growth in Texas, 1836–1865* (Cambridge, 1968); and Michael H. Frisch, *Town Into City: Springfield, Massachusetts, and the Meaning of Community, 1840–1880* (Cambridge, 1972).

General Urban Developments

Historians have been joined by urban sociologists and other social scientists in considering general issues arising out of nineteenth-century urban development. Particularly useful are Jeffrey G. Williamson, "Antebellum Urbanization in the American Northeast," *Journal of Economic*

History, XXV (Dec. 1965), pp. 592–608; Williamson and Joseph A. Swanson, "The Growth of Cities in the American Northeast, 1820–1870," *Explorations in Entrepreneurial History, 4* (Supplement, 1966), pp. 1–101; Sam Bass Warner, Jr., "If All the World Were Philadelphia: A Scaffolding for Urban History, 1774–1930," *American Historical Review, LXXIV* (Oct. 1968), pp. 26–43; Wade, "An Agenda for Urban History," in Herbert J. Bass, ed., *The State of American History* (Chicago, 1970); Oscar Handlin and John Burchard, eds., *The Historian and the City* (Cambridge, 1963), particularly the essay by Eric E. Lampard, "Urbanization and Social Change: On Broadening the Scope and Relevance of Urban History;" Lampard, "American Historians and the Study of Urbanization," *Amer. Hist. Rev., LXVII* (Oct. 1961), pp. 49–61; Philip M. Hauser and Leo F. Schnore, eds., *The Study of Urbanization* (New York, 1965), particularly Charles N. Glaab, "The Historian and the American City: A Bibliographic Survey;" Schnore, ed., *Social Science and the City: A Survey of Urban Research* (New York, 1968); Schnore, *The Urban Scene: Human Ecology and Demography* (New York, 1965); Roland L. Warren, ed., *Perspectives on the American Community* (Chicago, 1966); Harold Dyos, ed., *The Study of Urban History* (London, 1968); and Stephan Thernstrom and Richard Sennett, eds., *Nineteenth-Century Cities: Essays in the New Urban History* (New Haven, 1969), a collection that is informed by its pathbreaking approach to the historical study of American cities and cities elsewhere in the world and the conviction exuded by its contributors that they are participating in a pioneering venture.

Foreign Travelers

Sharp-eyed foreign visitors who took nothing for granted about the American social scene have left fascinating accounts of their observations. The bibliographical essay in my *Jacksonian America: Society, Personality, and Politics* (Homewood, 1969), lists the several dozen most impressive travelers' accounts and the best of the critical literature on the strengths and weaknesses of these observers. Particularly rewarding are Michael Chevalier, *Society, Manners and Politics in the United States* (Boston, 1839); Charles Dickens, *American Notes* (London, 1842); J. S. Buckingham, *America,* 3 vols. (London, 1841); Francis Grund, *Aristocracy in America* (London, 1839); Thomas Hamilton, *Men and Manners in America* (Philadelphia, 1833); Francis Lieber, *The Stranger in America,* 2 vols. (London, 1835); Harriet Martineau, *Society in America,* 2 vols. (New York, 1837); Frances Trollope, *Domestic Manners of the Americans,* 2 vols. (London, 1832); and Godfrey T. Vigne, *Six Months in America* (Philadelphia, 1833). The most valuable, interesting, and provocative account by far was Alexis de Tocqueville, *Democracy in America,* 2 vols. (New York, 1954). The first part of *Democracy* was published in 1835, the second in 1840.

Tocqueville was of course the chief architect of the "egalitarian myth" that is critically examined in this book. Interesting critical appraisals of Tocqueville's flaws as an observer of the American social scene are Seymour Drescher, "Tocqueville's Two *Démocraties*," *Journal of the History of Ideas, 25* (April-June 1964), pp. 201–16; Lynn L. Marshall and Drescher, "American Historians and Tocqueville's *Democracy*," *Journal of American History, LV* (Dec. 1968), p. 517; Edward T. Gargan, "Some Problems in Tocqueville Scholarship," *Mid-America, 41* (Jan. 1959), pp. 3–26; Gargan, "Tocqueville and the Problem of Historical Prognosis," *American Historical Review, LXVIII* (Jan. 1963), pp. 332–45; Marvin Zetterbaum, *Tocqueville and the Problem of Democracy* (Stanford, 1966); George W. Pierson, *Tocqueville and Beaumont in America* (New York, 1938); and Jack Lively, *The Social and Political Thought of Alexis de Tocqueville* (Oxford, 1962).

Wealth

Contemporary Published Sources

A striking phenomenon of the 1840s was the appearance in a number of northeastern cities of pamphlets, each purporting to list the several hundred wealthiest citizens of the city and the amount of his fortune. For the unreliability of the most popular of these, the rankings published by Moses Y. Beach in New York City, see Appendix B. Among the other listings were "A Member of the Philadelphia Barr," *Wealth and Biography of the Wealthy Citizens of Philadelphia* (Philadelphia, 1845); "A Merchant of Philadelphia," *Memoirs and Auto-Biography of Some of the Wealthy Citizens of Philadelphia* (Philadelphia, 1846); John Lomas and Alfred S. Peace, *The Wealthy Men and Women of Brooklyn and Williamsburgh* (Brooklyn, 1847); William Armstrong, *The Aristocracy of New York: Who They Are and What They Were* (New York, 1848); Thomas L. Wilson, *Aristocracy of Boston* (Boston, 1848), a unique listing in that it offered no estimates of wealth; A. Forbes and J. W. Green, *The Rich Men of Massachusetts* (Boston, 1852); and *"Our First Men": A Calendar of Wealth, Fashion and Gentility* (Boston, 1846). The latter publication, like the one for Brooklyn, offers wealth estimates that appear to be based on the published assessors' data or the estimates that appear in the assessors' notebooks.

Tax Assessments

The Assessor's Office of the City of Boston published annual *List[s] of [the assessed worth of] Persons, Copartnerships, and Corporations who were Taxed Twenty-five Dollars and Upwards in the City of Boston, for the Year[s] 1833–1849* (Boston, 1834–50). New York City and Brooklyn published no such lists, while the the Philadelphia publication did not distinguish between owners and users of real property. My lists of the New York City rich were created from the annual tax assessors' notebooks, located in the Municipal Archives and Records Center of New York City; the Brooklyn lists were constructed from the tax assessors' notebooks for 1810 and 1841, located in the Long Island Historical Society. Contemporary evaluations of the strengths and weaknesses of the assessment data are discussed in Edward Pessen, "The Wealthiest New Yorkers of the Jacksonian Era: A New List," *New-York Historical Society Quarterly, LIV* (April 1970), pp. 148–52; Pessen, "The Egalitarian Myth and the American Social Reality: Wealth, Mobility, and Equality in the 'Era of the Common Man,' " *Amer. Hist. Rev., 76* (Oct. 1971), pp. 995, 998; and Peter R. Knights, *The Plain People of Boston, 1830–1860: A Study in City Growth* (New York, 1971), p. 71.

Directories

Directories, whether general or specialized, are invaluable contemporary sources on the addresses and occupations of the rich, as well as on a variety of other matters, including lists of officers of political and other bodies. For the early part of the period New York City directories were published by Longworth; later Doggett succeeded him. The city's professional and business directories were put out by Driggs, Twitt, and Francis F. Ripley. In 1837 J. Disturnell published *Classified Mercantile Directories for the Cities of New-York and Brooklyn.* Alden Spooner published Brooklyn directories in the 1820s, Lewis Nichols published them in the 1830s, while in the 1840s Brooklyn directories were published by Thomas and John W. Leslie, and by the partnership of William J. Hearne and Edwin Van Nostrand. Philadelphia directories during the period were published by McElroy and by Robert Desilver. Publishers of Boston directories included Charles Stimpson, James French, and George Adams. Sidney Goldstein discusses the value of directories in "City Directories as Sources of Migration Data," *American Journal of Sociology, LX* (Sept. 1954), pp. 169–76, as does Peter R. Knights, "City Directories as Aids to Ante-Bellum Urban Studies: A Research Note," *Historical Methods Newsletter, II* (Sept. 1969), pp. 1–10.

Modern Wealth Studies of Other Times, Other Places

In recent years the distribution of wealth in colonial America has been intensively examined. Valuable studies that focus on this or related themes are Alice Hanson Jones, "Wealth Estimates for the American Middle Colonies, 1774," *Economic Development and Cultural Change, 18* (July 1970), pp. 1–172; Jackson Turner Main, *The Social Structure of Revolutionary America* (Princeton, 1965); Donald Warner Koch, "Income Distribution and Political Structure in Seventeenth-Century Salem," Essex Institute *Historical Collections, CV* (Jan. 1969), pp. 50–71; William

I. Davisson, "Essex County Wealth Trends: Wealth and Economic Growth in Seventeenth-Century Massachusetts," *ibid., CIII* (Oct. 1967), pp. 291–342; James T. Lemon and Gary B. Nash, "The Distribution of Wealth in Eighteenth-Century America: A Century of Changes in Chester County, Pennsylvania, 1693–1802," *Journal of Social History, 2* (Fall 1968), pp. 1–24; James Henretta, "Economic Development and Social Structure in Colonial Boston," *William and Mary Quarterly, XXII* (Jan. 1965), pp. 79–92; Allan Kulikoff, "The Progress of Inequality in Revolutionary Boston," *ibid., XXVIII* (July 1971), pp. 375–412; Charles S. Grant, *Democracy in the Connecticut Frontier Town of Kent* (New York, 1961); Robert M. Zemsky, "Power, Influence and Status: Leadership Patterns in the Massachusetts Assembly, 1740–1755," *Wm. and Mary Quar.*, XXVI (Oct. 1969), pp. 502–20; and Michael Zuckerman, "The Social Context of Democracy in Massachusetts, *ibid., XXV* (Oct. 1968), pp. 523–44.

Good recent examinations of later periods include Robert E. Gallman, "Trends in the Size Distribution of Wealth in the Nineteenth Century: Some Speculations," in Lee Soltow, ed., *Six Papers on the Size Distribution of Wealth and Income* (New York, 1969); Gavin Wright, " 'Economic Democracy' and the Concentration of Agricultural Wealth in the Cotton South, 1850–1860," *Agricultural History, XLIV* (Jan. 1970), pp. 63–94; and George Blackburn and Sherman L. Richards, Jr., "A Demographic History of the West: Manistee County, Michigan, 1860," *Journal of American History, LVII* (Dec. 1970), pp. 600–18. Also valuable are two unpublished papers presented at the annual meeting of the Organization of American Historians, April 16, 1971, in New Orleans: Michael B. Katz, "Patterns of Inequality, Wealth and Power in a Nineteenth-Century City [Hamilton, Ontario]"; and Robert Doherty, "Property Distribution in Jacksonian America [in New England]."

Class and Mobility

The Rags-to-Riches Myth

Two interesting modern studies are John G. Cawalti, *Apostles of the Self-Made Man* (Chicago, 1965); and Irvin G. Wyllie, *The Self-Made Man in America: The Myth of Rags to Riches* (New York, 1966). Contemporary authors who contributed to the vogue of the self-made man are discussed in chapter 5.

Geographical Mobility

Geographical or physical mobility and its connection with social mobility are discussed in Sidney Goldstein, "Migration: Dynamic of the American City," *American Quarterly, VI* (Winter 1954), pp. 337–48;

Lowell E. Gallaway and Richard K. Vedder, "Mobility of Native Americans," *Journal of Economic History, XXXVI* (Sept. 1971), pp. 613–49; Peter R. Knights, "Population Turnover, Persistence, and Residential Mobility in Boston, 1830–1860," in Thernstrom and Sennett, *Nineteenth-Century Cities;* Thernstrom and Knights, "Men in Motion: Some Data and Speculations about Urban Population Mobility in Nineteenth-Century America," *Journal of Interdisciplinary History, I* (Autumn 1970), pp. 7–35; Knights, *The Plain People of Boston;* Goldstein, "Repeated Migration as a Factor in High Mobility Rates," *American Sociological Review, 19* (Oct. 1954), pp. 536–41; Goldstein, *Patterns of Mobility, 1910–1950: The Norristown Study* (Philadelphia, 1958); Stuart Blumin, "The Restless Citizen: Vertical Mobility, Migration, and Social Participation in Mid-Nineteenth Century America [Kingston, New York]" (unpublished paper presented at the Conference on Social Science Concepts in American Political History, October, 1969, at Brockport, New York); and Richard Scudder and C. Arnold Anderson, "Migration and Vertical Occupational Mobility," *Amer. Soc. Rev., 19* (June 1954), pp. 329–34.

Sociological Discussion of Class and Social Mobility

There is a vast sociological literature on the related themes of class and social mobility. Although the reader who is neither a mathematician nor a statistician will find much of the modern discussion hard to follow, these studies are indispensable to the student who wishes to keep abreast of sociological thinking on these concepts. Particularly valuable are the following: Reinhard Bendix and Seymour Martin Lipset, eds., *Class, Status, and Power: Social Stratification in Comparative Perspective,* 2nd ed. (New York, 1966), a repository of valuable essays on mobility in the United States and elsewhere; Bernard Barber, *Social Stratification: A Comparative Analysis of Structure and Process* (New York, 1957), in a sense the "pioneer" text on the recent reexamination of class and vertical mobility; Raymond W. Mack, Linton Freeman, and Seymour Yellin, *Social Mobility: Thirty Years of Research and Theory* (Syracuse, 1957); D. V. Glass, ed., *Social Mobility in Britain* (London, 1967), which contains theoretical essays concerned with broader themes than are indicated in the book's title; Ralf Dahrendorf, *Class and Class Conflict in Industrial Society* (Stanford, 1959); Charles F. Westoff, Marvin Bressler, and Philip C. Sagi, "The Concept of Social Mobility: An Empirical Inquiry," *Amer. Soc. Rev., 25* (June 1960), pp. 375–85, very good on the diverse meanings and definitions of social mobility given by scholars; Lipset and Bendix, *Social Mobility in Industrial Society* (Berkeley, 1963); Ely Chinoy, "Social Mobility Trends in the United States," *Amer. Soc. Rev., 20* (April 1955), pp. 180–86; Gerhard E. Lenski, "Trends in Inter-Generational Occupation Mobility in the United States," *ibid., 23* (Oct. 1958), pp. 514–23; Lenski, *Power and Privilege: A Theory of Social Stratification* (New York, 1966); Paul K. Hatt, "Occupation and Social Stratification," *Amer. Jour. Soc., LV* (May 1950), pp. 533–43; Joseph J. Sprengler, "Changes in Income Distribution and Social Stratification: A Note," *ibid., LIX* (1953–1954), pp. 247–59; Elton F. Jackson and Harry Crockett, Jr., "Occupational Mobility in the United States: A Point Estimate and Trend Comparison," *Amer. Soc. Rev., 29* (Feb. 1964), pp. 5–15; Otis Dudley Duncan, "The Trend of Occupational Mobility in the United States," *ibid., 30* (Aug. 1965), pp. 491–98; Neil J. Smelser and Lipset, eds., *Social Structure and Mobility in Economic Development* (Chicago, 1966); J. A. Jackson, ed., *Social Stratification* (Cambridge, England, 1968); W. Lloyd Warner and Paul S. Lunt, *The Social Life of a Modern Community* (New Haven, 1941); Warner, with Marchia Meeker and Kenneth Eels, *Social Class in America: A Manual for the Measurement of Social Status* (New York, 1960); J. O. Hertzler, "Some Tendencies Toward a Closed Class System in the United States," *Social Forces, 30* (March 1952), pp. 313–23; Joseph A. Kahl, *The American Class Structure* (New York, 1957); Lipset and Hans L. Zetterberg, "A Theory of Social Mobility," *Transactions* of the 3rd World Congress of Sociology, *II* (1956), pp. 155–77; John Porter, "The Future of Upward Mobility," *Amer. Soc. Rev., 33* (Feb. 1968), pp. 5–19; Melvin Tumin, *Social Stratification: The Forms and Functions of Inequality* (Engelwood Cliffs, 1967); Kurt B. Mayer, "Class and Status in the United States," *Quarterly Review, 303* (Oct. 1965), pp. 450–59; Natalie Rogoff, *Recent Trends in Occupational Mobility* (Glencoe, 1953), which represented a methodological breakthrough at the time of its publication; Saburo Yosuda, "A Methodological Inquiry into Social Mobility," *Amer. Soc. Rev., 29* (Feb. 1964), pp. 16–23; Gosta Carlsson, *Social Mobility and Class Structure* (Lund, 1958); Leo A. Goodman, "On the Measurement of Social Mobility: An Index of Status Persistence," *Amer. Soc. Rev., 34* (Dec. 1969), pp. 831–50; and Lipset, "Social Mobility and Equal Opportunity," *The Public Interest, 29* (Fall 1972), pp. 90–108, written for a lay reader.

Historical Studies of Social Mobility

There is a small but growing number of historical studies of social mobility. Interesting recent examples are Kenneth A. Lockridge, *A New England Town The First Hundred Years: Dedham, Massachusetts, 1636–1736* (New York, 1970); Main, *Social Structure of Revolutionary America;* Philip J. Greven, Jr., *Four Generations: Population, Land, and Family in Colonial Andover, Massachusetts* (Ithaca, 1970); Stephan Thernstrom, *Poverty and Progress: Social Mobility in a Nineteenth Century City* (Cambridge, 1964); Clyde Griffen, "Making It in America: Social Mobility in Mid-Nineteenth Century Poughkeepsie," *New York History, LI* (Oct. 1970), pp. 479–500; Paul B. Worthman, "Working

Class Mobility in Birmingham, Alabama, 1880–1914," in Tamara K. Hareven, ed., *Anonymous Americans: Explorations in Nineteenth-Century Social History* (Engelwood Cliffs, 1971), pp. 172–213; Gary B. Nash, "The Philadelphia Bench and Bar, 1800–1861," *Comparative Studies in Society and History, VII* (Jan. 1965), pp. 203–220; P. M. G. Harris, "The Social Origins of American Leaders: the Demographic Foundations," *Perspectives in American History, III* (1969), pp. 159–344, ingenious, fascinating, fantastic, and fanciful; William Miller, ed., *Men in Business: Essays on the Historical Role of the Entrepreneur* (New York, 1962); Daniel Scott Smith, "Cyclical, Secular, and Structural Changes in American Elite Composition," *Persp. in Amer. Hist., IV* (1970), pp. 351–74, which, among other things, criticizes P. M. G. Harris's study; and the invaluable Thernstrom and Sennett, *Nineteenth-Century Cities,* particularly Herbert G. Gutman, "The Reality of the Rags-to-Riches 'Myth': The Case of the Paterson, New Jersey, Locomotive, Iron, and Machinery Manufacturers, 1830–1880;" and Stuart Blumin, "Mobility and Change in Ante-Bellum Philadelphia."

Older but still useful studies are Frank W. Taussig and C. S. Joslyn, *American Business Leaders: A Study in Social Origins and Social Stratification* (New York, 1932); W. Lloyd Warner and James C. Abegglen, *Occupational Mobility in American Business and Industry 1928–1952* (Minneapolis, 1955); and C. Wright Mills, "The American Business Elite: A Collective Portrait," *Journal of Economic History, V* [Supplement: "The Tasks of Economic History"] (1945), pp. 20–44, which makes sweeping conclusions on the basis of thin evidence drawn from the *DAB.* Very good unpublished studies are Blumin, "Mobility in a Nineteenth-Century American City: Philadelphia, 1820–1860" (University of Pennsylvania Doctoral Dissertation, 1968); Edmund P. Willis, "Social Origins of Political Leadership in New York City From the Revolution to 1815" (Ph.D. diss., University of California, Berkeley, 1967); and Gordon H. Kirk, Jr., "The Promise of American Life: Social Mobility in a Nineteenth Century Immigrant Community, Holland, Michigan, 1847–1894" (Ph.D. diss., Michigan State University, 1970).

Useful comments on some of the problems associated with the historical study of social mobility are Blumin, "The Historical Study of Vertical Mobility," *Historical Methods Newsletter, I* (Sept. 1968), pp. 1–13; and Thernstrom, "Notes on the Historical Study of Social Mobility," in Don Karl Rowney and James Q. Graham, Jr., eds., *Quantitative History* (Homewood, 1969).

Elite Marriages

The theoretical significance of marriage as an indicator of status is considered in most modern sociology texts. Particularly good are Harold M. Hodges, Jr., *Social Stratification: Class in America* (Cambridge, 1964); Jerzy Berent, "Social Mobility and Marriage," in Glass, *Social Mobility in Britain;* Zick Rubin, "Do American Women Marry Up?" *Amer. Soc. Rev., 33* (Oct. 1968), pp. 750–60; and William J. Goode, "Family and Mobility," in Bendix and Lipset, *Class, Status, and Power.* Data on the marital behavior of the rich and elite were drawn from church records, newspaper accounts, and above all from the varied genealogical and manuscript sources on families.

Elite Residential Patterns

My treatment of the residential patterns of the rich and eminent was based on data drawn chiefly from directories and primary sources that indicated addresses and changes in residence over time.

On the Theoretical Significance of Residence. The landmark theoretical discussion of urban residential patterns and their relationship to transportation developments is Robert Park, Ernest W. Burgess, and Roderick D. McKenzie, eds., *The City* (Chicago, 1925). Also valuable are Burgess "Residential Segregation in American Cities," *Annals* of American Academy of Political and Social Science, *CXL* (1928); Walter Firey, *Land Use in Central Boston* (Cambridge, 1947), which offers interesting summaries of earlier work and criticisms of the leading theories of urban ecology; Homer Hoyt, *Structure and Growth of Residential Neighborhoods in the United States* (Washington, 1939); Hoyt, *Principles of Urban Real Estate* (New York, 1939); Norman J. Johnston, "The Caste and Class of the Urban Form of Historic Philadelphia," *Journal of the American Institute of Planners, XXXII* (Nov. 1966), pp. 334–49; Leo F. Schnore, "The Timing of Metropolitan Decentralization: A Contribution to the Debate," *ibid., XXV* (Nov. 1959), pp. 200–206; Charles J. Kennedy, "Commuter Services in the Boston Area, 1835–1860," *Business History Review, XXXVI* (Summer 1962), pp. 153–70; George R. Taylor, "The Beginnings of Mass Transportation in Urban America," *Smithsonian Journal of History, I (Summer and Autumn, 1966)*, pp. 35–50, 31–54; David Ward, "The Emergence of Central Immigrant Ghettoes in American Cities: 1840–1920," *Annals of the Association of American Geographers, LVIII* (June 1968), pp. 343–59; Ward, "The Industrial Revolution and the Emergence of Boston's Central Business District," *Economic Geography, 42* (April 1966), pp. 152–71; Sam Bass Warner, Jr., *Streetcar Suburbs: The Process of Growth in Boston, 1870–1900* (Cambridge, 1962); and Leo F. Schnore and Peter R. Knights, "Residence and Social Structure: Boston in the Ante-Bellum Period," in Thernstrom and Sennett, *Nineteenth-Century Cities.*

Elite Residences in New York City and Brooklyn

The histories of New York City by Phelps Stokes, Lossing, Wilson, and Lamb and Harrison provide rewarding if occasional nuggets on upper-class streets and neighborhoods. Hone's diary is a treasure trove on the housing sites and choices of New York City's upper crust. The reminiscences of Dodge and Francis are also valuable, as is Charles Lockwood, "The Bond Street Area," *New-York Hist. Soc. Quar., LVI* (Oct. 1972), pp. 309–20, an interesting discussion of the rise and fall of Bond Street as an elite enclave in the nineteenth century.

Good on the lofty status of Brooklyn Heights are J. T. Bailey, *An Historical Sketch of the City of Brooklyn* (New York, 1840); *Old Brooklyn Heights* (New York, 1927); Stiles, *Civil Political, Professional and Ecclesiastical History of Brooklyn, I,* p. 364; and Weld, *Brooklyn Village.* For other Brooklyn neighborhoods inhabited by the eminent—even if few of them—Vanderbilt, *Social History of Flatbush;* Charles A. Ditmas, *Historic Homesteads of Kings County* (New York, 1881); Bergen, *Early Settlers of Kings County;* Thomas M. Strong, *History of the Town of Flatbush* (New York, 1842); and Judd, "A City's Streets," are useful.

Elite Residences in Boston and Philadelphia

Winsor's *Memorial History* contains material of value on Boston neighborhoods, as do other of the city's local histories. Worthwhile data and/or discussions appear in Walter Muir Whitehill, *Boston: A Topographical History* (Cambridge, 1959); Thomas W. Tucker, *Bannister's Lane, 1708–1899* (Boston, 1899); Walter H. Kilham, *Boston After Bulfinch: An Account of Its Architecture 1800–1900* (Cambridge, 1946); Nathaniel B. Shurtleff, *A Topographical and Historical Description of Boston* (Boston, 1871); Annie Haven Thwing, *The Crooked and Narrow Streets of the Town of Boston 1630–1822* (Boston, 1920); Alexander S. Porter, "Changes of Values in Real Estate in Boston: The Past One Hundred Years," *Collections of the Bostonian Society, I* (1888), pp. 57–74; Robert Means Lawrence, *Old Park Street and Its Vicinity* (Boston, 1922); and Wendell D. Garett, *Apthorp House, 1760–1960* (Cambridge, 1967).

For Philadelphia all of the writings of Westcott are valuable. Particularly good for this purpose are Westcott's *The Historic Mansions and Buildings of Philadelphia with Some Notice of Their Owners and Occupants* (Philadelphia, 1877); Carroll Frey, *The Independent Square Neighborhood* (Philadelphia, 1926); Theodore B. White, ed., *Philadelphia Architecture in the Nineteenth Century* (Philadelphia, 1953); William S. Hastings, "Philadelphia Microcosm," *Pa. Magazine, XCI* (April 1967), pp. 164–80; Joseph Jackson, *America's Most Historic Highway: Market Street, Philadelphia* (Philadelphia, 1926); and Charles J. Cohen, *Rittenhouse Square* (Philadelphia, 1922).

Clubs and Voluntary Associations

The Sociological Literature on Their Significance

Most comprehensive modern sociology texts examine the significance of club memberships as clues to lifestyle and status. Valuable recent discussions of the characteristics of twentieth-century joiners are David L. Sills, *The Volunteers: Means and Ends in a National Organization* (Glencoe, 1957); and Murray Hausknecht, *The Joiners* (New York, 1962). Hodges, *Social Stratification,* provides a useful summary of the periodical literature of the past quarter century on this theme.

Social Clubs

In my discussion of upper-class memberships, I have distinguished between "purely social clubs" and "socially purposive organizations." The former were joined out of a search for pleasurable use of leisure and what Baltzell has called the "ascription of status." Useful data on the social clubs appear in contemporary diaries and correspondence, in many of the miscellaneous historical and genealogical sources already discussed, and in publications of the clubs themselves, such as the *Constitution, By-Laws and Standing Rules of the Union Club, & a List of the Members* (New York, 1853). Valuable secondary sources on particular clubs are John Durand, *Prehistoric Notes of the Century Club* (New York, 1882); *The Philadelphia Club, 1834–1934, Being a Brief History of the Club for the First Hundred Years of Its Existence* (Philadelphia, 1934); Hugh Whitney and Walter Muir Whitehill, "The Somerset Club," in *The Somerset Club, 1851–1951* (Boston, 1951); John H. Gourlie, *The Origin and History of "The Century"* (New York, 1856); Francis Gerry Fairfield, *The Clubs of New York* (New York, 1873); Reginald T. Townsend, *Mother of Clubs Being the History of the First Hundred Years of the Union Club of the City of New York* (New York, 1936); Anne Marie Dolan, "The Literary Salon in New York, 1830–1860" (Ph.D. diss., Columbia University, 1957); Allan Nevins, "The Century 1847–1866," in *The Century 1847–1946* (New York, 1947); and Alexander W. Williams, *A Social History of the Greater Boston Clubs* (Barre, Mass., 1970).

Socially Purposive Associations

The urban elite joined hundreds of these ephemeral groups in the early nineteenth century. Information on these affiliations is afforded by personal papers, a variety of secondary accounts, and above all by the contemporary records published by these associations. They published thousands of pamphlets that typically contain accounts of their origins and formation; charters or constitutions and purposes; qualifications for membership; lists of officers and directors and—more rarely—members; committee reports; and annual summaries of activities. In view of the unprepossessing nature of these publications, not to mention their sameness and their quantity, there is no point in listing them. They are, however, indispensable to any study of the topic.

Secondary accounts of particular local voluntary associations are much fewer in number. The good nineteenth-century local histories have useful information on this as on other subjects. Additional worthwhile older studies include Austin Baxter Keep, *History of the New York Society Library* (New York, 1908); Herman Leroy Fairchild, *A History of the New York Academy of Sciences* (New York, 1887); William Oland Bourne, *History of the Public School Society of New York* (New York, 1870); Henry J. Cammann and Hugh N. Camp, *The Charities of New York, Brooklyn, and Staten Island* (New York, 1868); Josiah Quincy, *The History of the Boston Athenaeum* (Cambridge, 1851); N. I. Bowditch, *A History of the Massachusetts General Hospital* (Cambridge, 1872); and several studies done two scholarly generations ago: Rebecca Hooper Eastman, *The Story of the Brooklyn Institute of Arts and Sciences, 1824–1924* (Brooklyn, 1924); Asa Earl Martin, "The Temperance Movement in Pennsylvania Prior to the Civil War," *Pa. Magazine, XLIX* (1925), pp. 195–230; Warren F. Hewitt, "Samuel Breck and the Pennsylvania School Law of 1834," *Pennsylvania History, I* (April 1934), pp. 63–75; Joseph J. McCadden, "Roberts Vaux and His Associates in the Pennsylvania Society for the Promotion of Public Schools," *ibid., III* (Jan. 1936), pp. 1–17; and Mark Anthony DeWolfe Howe, *The Humane Society of the Commonwealth of Massachusetts: An Historical Review, 1785–1916* (Cambridge, 1918).

A number of modern studies are distinguished by their excellence and the greater breadth of the treatment they give the issues. Among these are Benjamin J. Klebaner, "The Home Relief Controversy in Philadelphia, 1782–1861," *Pa. Magazine, LXXVIII* (Oct. 1954), pp. 413–23; Gerald N. Grob, *The State and the Mentally Ill: A History of Worcester State Hospital in Massachusetts, 1830–1920* (Chapel Hill, 1966). Also valuable are Roy Lubove, "The New York Association for Improving the Condition of the Poor: the Formative Years," *New-York Hist. Soc. Quar., XLIII* (July 1959), pp. 307–27, which is concerned with the status of social activists, as are Robert S. Pickett, *House of Refuge: Origins of Juvenile Reform in New York State, 1815–1857* (Syracuse, 1969); Raymond A. Mohl, *Poverty in New York, 1783–1825* (New York, 1971), concerned with the motives as well as the status of those who worked to alleviate poverty; M. J. Heale, "The New York Society for the Prevention of Pauperism, 1817–1823," *New-York Hist. Soc. Quar.*, LV (April 1971), pp. 153–76, which disagrees with Mohl's interpretation of the motives of elite do-gooders; William W. Cutler, III "Status, Values, and the Education of the Poor: The Trustees of the New York Public School Society, 1805–1853," *American Quarterly, XXIV* (March 1972), pp. 69–85; and Walter S. Glazer, "Participation and Power: Voluntary Associations and the Functional Organization of Cincinnati in 1840," *Historical Methods Newsletter, 5* (Sept. 1972), pp. 151–68.

More descriptive if no less valuable—and perhaps more interesting for their avoidance of abstract correlations—are R. W. G. Vail, *Knickerbocker Birthday: A SesquiCentennial History of the New-York Historical*

Society, 1805–1954 (New York, 1954); Eliot Clark, *History of the National Academy of Design, 1825–1953* (New York, 1954); Mary Bartlett Cowdrey, *The American Academy of Fine Arts and American Art-Union* [with a *History of the American Academy* by Theodore Sizer] (New York, 1953); William Cullen Bryant, II "Poetry and Painting: A Love Affair of Long Ago," *Amer. Quar., XXII* (Winter 1970), pp. 859–82; O. A. Pendleton, "Poor Relief in Philadelphia, 1790–1840," *Pa. Magazine, LXX* (April 1946), pp. 161–72; Harold Schwartz, *Samuel Gridley Howe: Social Reformer, 1801–1876* (Cambridge, 1956); and Lance Edwin Davis and Peter Lester Payne, "From Benevolence to Business: The Story of Two Savings Banks," *Business History Review, XXXII* (Winter 1958), pp. 386–406.

Excluded is the literature on the famous national reform and antislavery societies, since it is discussed at length in a number of modern studies. Also omitted are titles on the national Protestant societies that composed what Clifford S. Griffin describes as the "benevolent empire"; Griffin, *Their Brothers' Keepers: Moral Stewardship in the United States, 1800–1865* (New Brunswick, 1960). This literature is also discussed at length by Griffin and other recent authors.

Urban Politics

Modern studies of antebellum urban politics are in short supply. My discussion is based on primary materials on the political actors, minutes of the common councils, proceedings of boards of aldermen, volumes of laws and ordinances, council reports, and published evaluations of early nineteenth century municipal politics. A number of modern theoretical studies have also influenced my thinking.

Analytical Studies

Political scientists and sociologists have created a substantial body of analytical work on the theory and practice of local government and the role played in it by the rich and socially prestigious. Useful "political science" contributions are Robert A. Dahl, *Who Governs? Democracy and Power in an American City* (New Haven, 1961); Floyd Hunter, *Community Power Structure: The Study of Decision Makers* (Chapel Hill, 1953); Dahl, "A Critique of the Ruling Elite Model," *American Political Science Review, LII* (1958), pp. 463–69; Nelson W. Polsby, *Community Power and Political Theory* (New Haven, 1963); Norton E. Long, "Political Science and the City," in Schnore, *Social Science and the City;* Arnold M. Rose, *The Power Structure: Political Process in American Society* (New York, 1967); Edward C. Banfield, *Political Influence* (New York, 1961); and Lenski, *Power and Privilege.*

New York City and Brooklyn Politics

Comprehensive modern studies are lacking for the politics of Boston, Philadelphia, Brooklyn, and New York City during the second quarter of the nineteenth century. Useful, if less than comprehensive studies of the metropolis, are Arthur W. MacMahon, *The Statutory Sources of New York City Government* (New York, 1923); Robert Ludlow Fowler, "Constitutional and Legal History of New York," in Wilson, *Memorial History of the City of New York*, vol. III; Frederick Shaw, *History of the New York City Legislature* (New York, 1954); Sidney I. Pomerantz, *New York, An American City, 1783–1803: A Study of Urban Life* (New York, 1938); and James F. Richardson, "The Struggle to Establish a London-Style Police Force for New York City," *New-York Hist. Soc. Quar., XLIX* (April 1965), pp. 175–98. Relevant unpublished studies of aspects of antebellum New York City politics are Gabriel A. Almond, "Plutocracy and Politics in New York City" (Ph.D. diss., University of Chicago, 1938), which is not quite as lively as its title; Norman Dain, "The Social Composition of the Leadership of Tammany Hall in New York City: 1855–1865" (Columbia University Master's Essay, 1957); and two very useful doctoral dissertations done at New York University: Leo Hershkowitz, "New York City, 1834 to 1840, A Study in Local Politics" (1960); and Ira M. Leonard, "New York City Politics 1841–1844: Nativism and Reform" (1965).

For Brooklyn, in addition to Stiles' excellent histories, Weld, *Brooklyn Village*, and Jacob Judd, "The History of Brooklyn, 1834–1855, Political And Administrative Aspects" (Ph.D. diss., New York University, 1959), are helpful.

Philadelphia Politics

There are useful discussions in the local histories by Westcott, Young, and Oberholtzer. Also valuable are Eli K. Price, *The History of the Consolidation of the City of Philadelphia* (Philadelphia, 1873); Edward P. Allinson and Boies Penrose, *Philadelphia, 1681–1887, A History of Municipal Development* (Philadelphia, 1887); Philip S. Klein, *Pennsylvania Politics, 1817–1832: A Game Without Rules* (Philadelphia, 1940); and Warner, *The Private City: Philadelphia in Three Periods of Its Growth.*

Boston Politics

Among the valuable studies of politics in early-nineteenth century Boston are Josiah Quincy, *A Municipal History of the Town and City of Boston* (Boston, 1852); William Minot, Jr., *Taxation in Massachusetts* (Boston, 1877); James McKellar Bugbee, "Boston Under the Mayors, 1822–1880," in Winsor, *Memorial History of Boston*, III, pp. 217–92;

C. W. Ernst, *Constitutional History of Boston* (Boston, 1894); Charles Huse, *Financial History of Boston* (Boston, 1916); John Koren, *Boston 1822 to 1922, The Story of Its Government* (Boston, 1923); and an excellent study, albeit of one aspect of Boston political history: Roger Lane, *Policing the City: Boston, 1822–1885* (Cambridge, 1967).

I shall not repeat here the many excellent political studies of the northeastern cities in the colonial era or of other cities during the Jacksonian era and later, that are cited in the footnotes.

Index *

* The indexer has not included every name cited in the text. Contemporaries mentioned only in passing or as part of a larger group, rather than in a substantive individual reference, are omitted. Also excluded are individuals referred to only once, the names of whose prominent families or relatives *do* appear in the index. Particular organizations are also typically omitted, references to them appearing under the general activities they were concerned with.

1 2 3 4 5 6 7 8 9 10